Going Coed

Women's Experiences
in Formerly Men's
Colleges and Universities,
1950–2000

Going Coed

Women's Experiences
in Formerly Men's
Colleges and Universities,
1950–2000

*Edited by Leslie Miller-Bernal
and Susan L. Poulson*

Vanderbilt University Press / Nashville

This book is printed on acid-free paper.
Manufactured in the United States of America

Library of Congress Cataloging-in-Publication Data

Miller-Bernal, Leslie, 1946–
Going coed : women's experiences in formerly men's
   colleges and universities, 1950–2000 / Leslie Miller-
   Bernal and Susan L. Poulson, Eds.—1st ed.
      p.   cm.
Includes bibliographical references and index.
ISBN 0-8265-1448-0 (cloth : alk. paper)
ISBN 0-8265-1449-9 (pbk. : alk. paper)
      1. Coeducation–United States–History–20th century.
2. Women college students–United States–History–20th
century.
I. Poulson, Susan L., 1959–   II. Title.
LB3066.M55 2004
378.1'982'0973-dc22

                                        2004009659

To our loving and supportive partners,
Martin and Bill

Contents

Preface

More than a quarter-century ago, the last great wave of coeducation swept through American higher education. Although the numbers of students and institutions involved were comparatively small, the transition redefined educational norms and expanded women's access to men's colleges and universities. Since many of the institutions were among the nation's elite, their adoption of coeducation ended the association of male-only status with academic prestige. The courts determined that state universities could no longer retain all-male colleges, and in Catholic higher education, where gender segregation had been a distinctive characteristic, male-only colleges disappeared altogether. Yet coeducation did not necessarily bring educational equity for men and women. Physical access to an institution did not mean that the women were represented in positions of power, that policies were changed to reflect a more diverse constituency, or even that they were nominally accepted as equals.

The aim of this book is to explore this most recent wave of coeducation and some of the consequences for women. It will review why various institutions admitted women, how they prepared for coeducation, and some of women's experiences in the newly coeducational institutions. It builds on earlier scholarship in several commendable academic studies of the history of coeducation.[1]

Education is much more than the absorption and synthesis of knowledge; it is a formative part of an individual's socialization. The college experience often takes place as a student is forming a political and social identity that sometimes departs from the family culture in which he or she has been raised. In higher education, where many students reside on campus, the college becomes an archetype of the larger world. In and out of the classroom, students absorb, adapt, and shape the messages about the meaning and organization of life. Much of this social organization is subconscious. In campus buildings, rooms, and meeting areas, students acquire a cultural knowledge of who belongs there and what constitute legitimate activities. When women first arrived on formerly male campuses, they faced a culture that had no established place for them, which had no process of acculturation for women, and few mentors and role models. Women in formerly male colleges faced the challenge of redefining those subtle, quiet norms, in the minds of others as well as in their own.

In a sense, women struggled with otherness. The representative student in these institutions was male, with a supportive history and culture. Women were the outsiders seeking a comfortable place within. Otherness is reflected in the very word "coeducation." "Co-" is defined as "with, together, joint, or jointly," which theoretically implies that either men or women could be "coeds." Yet "coed" is defined as "a young woman being educated at the same institution with young men." She is the "co-" to the education of men. Ironically, a woman student at a formerly women's college would be a coed at that institution as well.

Coed is also unique for perpetuating the concept of relational otherness. The American system of higher education has in the past been segregated by race and to some extent by religion as well. Yet the words for these segments are descriptive, such as black, Native American, or Catholic, and not relational as the word "coed" implies. The etymology of coed reflects the varying status of women as students. When the word first appeared around the time of the Civil War it had derogatory connotations. In later years coed was often used with sexual connotations.

There are six sections to this book. In Section I we provide a brief history of coeducation so that the recent trend can be placed in historical context. A chapter on historically black and Catholic higher education reveals two traditions that are nearly opposite in gender organization. Most historically black colleges and universities have been coeducational from their beginnings, in part due to their greater willingness to mix men and women. Also, with few resources and daunting racial oppression, black educators were often more concerned with "race uplift" than with the intricacies of sex segregation. American Catholics, in contrast, developed a network of colleges and universities with a strict and enduring practice of sexual segregation. Partly because of ideology and partly because the religious communities that established most Catholic institutions were themselves all male or female, Catholic higher education was single-sex until the early twentieth century. Coeducation then gradually expanded, in the face of frequent ecclesiastic opposition.

In Section II the contributors provide case studies of two universities that adopted coeducation before the great wave of coeducation in the 1960s and 1970s. These chapters highlight the extent to which the mere presence of women may—or may not—transform the nature of higher education in a pre-feminist era. At the University of Rochester, which had veered between single sex and coeducation in the late nineteenth and early twentieth centuries, the admission of women in the 1950s brought women on campus without a transformation in student culture or academics that encouraged gender equity. Historically black Lincoln University resisted admitting women even after many men who would have applied began to attend predominantly white universities that were opening up to minorities. Lincoln finally admitted women students when other attempts to maintain enrollment failed, and in recent years, women have come to dominate the university, in numbers, academics, and as leaders of many campus organizations.

The case study of Yale and Princeton in Section III analyzes perhaps the two most influential instances of all-male institutions adopting coeducation. After an unsuccessful exploration of a merger with Vassar, Yale, like Princeton, admitted women in 1969. With their high educational status now linked to coeducation, these two universities broke the long-standing association between elite status and single-sex education. Since higher education often acts as a peer group, with the prominent institutions setting trends and patterns, the adoption of coeducation by Yale and Princeton meant that less-prestigious single-sex institutions seeking to maintain or enhance their status would be more inclined to admit women.

Admitting women to a college or university is academically a simple process. Culturally, however, coeducation, especially in a time of feminist ferment, meant that women students often experienced alienation or outright discrimination. As the case studies of Dartmouth, Lehigh, the University of Virginia, and Boston College attest in Section IV, this was particularly true in the earliest years of coeducation at institutions with a traditional masculine culture.

Colleges and universities vary in their structure, of course. As the chapters in Section V indicate, structural arrangements could facilitate or delay coeducation. Georgetown, for example, as a singular institution already partly coeducational and unencumbered by a formal relationship with other institutions, made the decision to admit women with little turmoil. Hamilton College's coordinate relationship with Kirkland College facilitated the change to coeducation and made the resulting single institution more gender equitable than it otherwise would have been. Rutgers University, however, vacillated for years before adopting coeducation. Educators at Douglass College, a women's college within Rutgers University, believed that the admission of women to the all-male College of Arts and Sciences would not only hurt their own institution but also provide an inferior education for women students. They successfully delayed coeducation at Rutgers for several years.

The case studies in Section VI address institutions of higher education that are often ignored in the study of higher education. The study of women's entry into West Point and the Virginia Military Institute compares how these highly traditional institutions adapted over time, and in varying degrees, to the presence of women and how the experiences of women there have changed as a result. For-profit technical colleges have developed successful strategies to recruit and retain older, poor, and women students, regardless of these colleges' curriculum, which has traditionally appealed to young men. In contrast, community colleges have not been as successful in supporting and retaining these nontraditional students.

In the conclusion, we synthesize some of the trends common to many of the case studies. We highlight the challenges that women have faced and the strategies that they have used to overcome them. Our conclusion provides a broad assessment of how women have fared at these institutions and what remains to be done.

The contributing authors bring historical as well as sociological insights to their studies. Both approaches are useful because the history of coeducation includes not just institutional change but an investigation of how people react to their physical and social environments. Colleges and universities are hierarchical organizations, with students divided by year, by major, by residential location, and by social activities. In addition, there are strata of faculty, staff, administration, and boards of trustees, with relationships of power within and between them. American higher education has also retained strong ties to tradition. Songs, rituals, and symbols at many of these institutions go back for decades, if not centuries. The insights and methodologies of history and sociology are thus useful to understanding how women adapted to and altered these tradition-bound, hierarchical organizations.

The editors reflect this dual perspective. Leslie Miller-Bernal is a sociologist teaching at a small, private women's college, Wells, which has stimulated her interest in comparisons of women's experiences in single-sex and coeducational institutions. She was an undergraduate at a time when prestigious colleges like Williams, Dartmouth, and Yale were still all male. Although she herself studied at Middlebury, which described itself as coeducational, the separation between women and men students and the differing regulations for each made it clear that it was still a men's college with "coeds." Susan Poulson is a historian teaching at a Catholic institution, the University of Scranton; in her Ph.D. dissertation she studied the transition to coeducation of formerly all-male, Catholic Georgetown. Her own higher education occurred at a time when virtually all formerly men's colleges had become coeducational, so women's right to study at this institution was no longer discussed.

We are excited about this project for several reasons. First, this is the first comprehensive look at women's experiences at a variety of formerly male institutions that adopted coeducation in the mid- to late twentieth century. All the case studies are written expressly for this book. Second, the issue of coeducation is still ongoing. Several small institutions recently adopted coeducation, and the courts forced two influential academies, the Citadel and the Virginia Military Institute, to admit women over fierce opposition. Academics continue to debate whether women perform better in single-sex or coeducational institutions. Third, this period of tremendous increase in the access of women to higher education is part of a larger social trend of women's integration into the workforce and increased social respect. In short, this is part of a larger, important story of social equity to which we are happy to contribute.

The genesis of this project was a conference on coeducation held at Trinity College in Hartford, Connecticut, in October 2000. We would like to express our gratitude to Jack Dougherty for initiating the conference and for suggesting that there was a need for a book such as this.

Note

1. See Geraldine Joncich Clifford, ed., *Lone Voyagers: Academic Women in Coeducational Institutions, 1870–1937* (New York: Feminist Press, 1989); Florence Howe, *Myths of Coeducation* (Bloomington: Indiana University Press, 1984); Carol Lasser, ed., *Educating Men and Women Together: Coeducation in a Changing World* (Urbana: University of Illinois Press, 1987); Leslie Miller-Bernal, , *Separate by Degree: Women's Students' Experiences in Single-Sex and Coeducational Colleges* (New York: Peter Lang, 2000); Rosalind Rosenberg, *Beyond Separate Spheres: The Intellectual Roots of Modern Feminism* (New Haven: Yale University Press, 1982); and Barbara Miller Solomon, *In the Company of Educated Women: A History of Women and Higher Education in America* (New Haven: Yale University Press, 1985).

The History of Coeducation

The two chapters in this introductory section provide a context for the case studies that follow. In Chapter 1, Miller-Bernal traces major developments in higher education for women in the United States from pre–Civil War times until the beginning of the twenty-first century. As this volume focuses on women's experiences since the mid-twentieth century, however, she devotes considerable attention to the developments in women's access to higher education after World War II. Many formerly men's colleges opened up to women during the tumultuous late 1960s, due to demographic trends, financial factors, and cultural changes. Chapter 1 also discusses the limitations of coeducation or the ways in which coeducation does not necessarily mean gender equality.

In Chapter 2, Poulson and Miller-Bernal focus on the history of coeducation in Catholic colleges and historically black colleges and universities (HBCUs). As the authors show, both types of institutions have played important roles in enabling women to have access to higher education. Catholic institutions have mainly been single-sex until recently, however, whereas most black institutions were founded as and remained coeducational. Concerns about religious morality encouraged the separation of women from men at Catholic institutions; at HBCUs, cultural support for coeducation, as well as financial restrictions, resulted in coeducational institutions. Regardless of their historical roots, Catholic colleges and HBCUs found that they were affected by some of the same trends in higher education that made many men's colleges become coeducational around 1970. Their different histories, however, meant that they faced some unique challenges as well.

1

Introduction

Coeducation: An Uneven Progression

Leslie Miller-Bernal

> Coeducation must now take up the task of exploring the innovations
> necessary . . . to fulfill the promise of true educational equity for men
> and women.
>
> —Carol Lasser

Coeducation in the United States today is almost universal. Less than forty years ago, however, some of the most prestigious colleges and universities, including Princeton, Yale, Amherst, and Williams, were for men only. Then, in a rather short period of time, the push of women for access to all colleges, begun in the nineteenth century, succeeded in virtually every instance.[1] This chapter provides a brief overview of the history of coeducation in the United States, focusing particularly on the recent period of men's institutions' transition to coeducation.[2] The case studies of formerly men's colleges presented in this book describe how different institutions became coeducational during the latter part of the twentieth century and explore the experiences of women during and after the transition. This chapter discusses the broader cultural context within which such major institutional changes occurred.

Coeducation's Beginnings

The distinction of the first coeducational college belongs to Oberlin, which opened its doors to women and black Americans in 1833.[3] At the time women's opportunities for higher education were extremely limited, and blacks of either sex had virtually no opportunity for higher education.[4] The great age of colleges for women had not yet begun, as almost all originated after the Civil War, the opening of Vassar College in 1865 being the most noteworthy.[5] Some scholars

stress the inequitable treatment of women at Oberlin in terms of college regulations, the course of study that most women followed, the religiously mandated
subservience to the men students, and the gendered division of required manual
labor; nonetheless, a college that admitted both women and men, blacks and
whites, was revolutionary.[6]

A few colleges in the Midwest followed Oberlin's coeducational example,
with Antioch perhaps being the most notable for having women on its faculty.[7]
Most colleges that opened right after the Civil War were single-sex, however.
Before 1870, only one out of every six women pursuing higher education studied at a coeducational college, excluding normal schools that trained teachers.[8]
Many people believed that women were mentally and physically unfit for higher
education; at the very least, they thought that the form and content of college
education needed to be adapted to women's physiology, something that was
easier to accomplish in women's colleges. Retired Harvard doctor and professor
Edward H. Clarke was one of the most famous and forceful proponents of such
views. His book, *Sex in Education; or a Fair Chance for the Girls* (1873), was
reprinted many times and had a widespread influence, leading even an ambitious woman like M. Carey Thomas, future president of Bryn Mawr College,
to worry that she would harm herself if she pursued collegiate work.[9]

Despite such ideological opposition, women continued to make inroads
into higher education. Their success was due in part to social, economic, and
political developments. During the Civil War, some men's colleges, such as
the University of Wisconsin, turned to women to fill empty spaces in their
classrooms.[10] More women than men were graduating from the burgeoning
public school system, which prepared women for collegiate work and made
them available to train to become schoolteachers. Women were acceptable,
even desirable, as teachers because teaching was seen as a natural extension of
women's maternal nature, and women could be paid considerably lower salaries
than men.[11] Ideological opposition to women's higher education lessened, too,
as various studies demonstrated that college-educated women were as healthy
as other women.[12]

The nineteenth-century women's movement made education one of its
major planks. The first women's rights convention held in Seneca Falls, New
York, in 1848, for example, called for women's "thorough education" so that
they could take their rightful place in teaching, not only youth but also students
of "theology, medicine, or law."[13] Almost all women's rights advocates favored
coeducation over single-sex education because they believed that women's colleges provided inferior education.[14] Groups of women petitioned many men's
colleges and universities for entry, or sometimes for lesser privileges such as
the opportunity to take their exams, as women did at Harvard, Columbia, and
Hobart.[15] At least some of these campaigns were successful, especially when
accompanied by large monetary gifts.

The federal government's passage of the Morrill Acts in 1862 and 1890 also encouraged coeducation.[16] The first act, named after the Vermont congressman who initiated the legislation, mandated the sale of public lands to establish state institutions for "branches of learning . . . related to agriculture and the mechanic arts."[17] This practical thrust eventually extended to teaching, and since the legislation did not specifically exclude women, most land grant institutions, outside of the South, were ultimately persuaded to admit women. The 1890 legislation was important because it appropriated annual funds for the so-called land grant colleges, allowing some previously precarious state universities to survive. The 1890 act also set a precedent through the federal government's stipulation that states would not receive money for the land grant institutions if they denied education to students on the basis of their race.[18]

Historian Barbara Solomon considers the opening of the University of Chicago in 1892 a "landmark in the history of coeducation."[19] Sponsored and funded by Baptists and John D. Rockefeller, Chicago began as a coeducational university. Moreover, its young president, William R. Harper, actively recruited women undergraduates, graduate students, and faculty. By then, many other institutions were coeducational, including such universities as Cornell, Syracuse, Boston, Stanford, Michigan, and Wisconsin, and colleges like Swarthmore, Middlebury, Grinnell, Antioch, Oberlin, and Lewis and Clark. The proportion of coeducational institutions was higher in the Midwest and West, where financial pressures were greater, than in the Northeast and South.[20] The Northeast resisted the tide of coeducation due to its single-sex tradition and greater economic resources. Even though the South was impoverished after the Civil War, its conservative social traditions meant that there was more public support for separate education for women and men. Coeducation in the South first appeared in the state institutions in Texas, Arkansas, and Mississippi and in the black colleges; it came later to such states in the Old South as Virginia.[21]

Women's enrollment in coeducational institutions increased dramatically at the end of the nineteenth century. Whereas only about two in five women who were enrolled in institutions of higher education in 1870 attended coeducational colleges and universities, just ten years later, about three in five did so.[22] The usefulness of higher education for women or men was not widely accepted, however; only about 2 percent of young people, ages 18 to 24, attended college.[23] As higher education became a vehicle for social mobility, women experienced increasing discrimination, in admissions as well as in their college experiences.

A Backlash against Coeducation

Reactions against women students at coeducational institutions often began when their enrollments rose faster than men's, sometimes surpassing men's.

Resentment was exacerbated by women students' academic success; in college after college, women took a disproportionate share of academic prizes.[24] Men students and their trustee allies, who were often alumni, did not accept this situation passively, and they frequently took steps to limit the numbers of women students, if not to bar them completely from their institutions. Such actions against women students may have been most common in colleges and universities that originated as men's institutions. Middlebury College, for example, had been all male from 1800 to 1883, at which time it succumbed to pressure from townspeople and admitted six women as an "experiment"—really to prevent the college from closing due to very low enrollments. By 1902 women at Middlebury made up about 40 percent of the student body and in the previous year's entering classes, women actually outnumbered men. Senior men formed a society to oppose coeducation, and the trustees responded sympathetically by attempting to limit the number of women students and by petitioning the state of Vermont to establish a coordinate college for women, which became a partial reality only thirty years later.[25] The University of Rochester was successful in reverting back to its previously all-male status. It had admitted women only reluctantly in 1900, after women, including Susan B. Anthony, struggled to raise the funds that the university demanded. Yet in 1912 the university became all male again by establishing a coordinate institution for women that lasted until the 1950s.[26] Similarly, Wesleyan in Middletown, Connecticut, originally a college for men, admitted women in 1872, only to bar them completely in 1913; Wesleyan did not become coeducational again until 1970.

The fear that colleges and universities were being "feminized" was part of a larger cultural pattern at the end of the nineteenth and beginning of the twentieth century in which white men felt threatened by women and immigrants.[27] Some institutions, such as Stanford, responded to this fear by placing quotas on women's admission. Restricting the number of women students had the ironic consequence of making them academically stronger than the more easily admitted men students, reinforcing the tendency of women students to take college prizes. Men's colleges tried to avoid coeducation even when they felt pressure, financial or otherwise, to educate women. Hobart College in Geneva, New York, for example, incorporated women in 1908 in order to receive the funds of a benefactor and expand its curriculum. It admitted women not by becoming coeducational, however, but rather by creating a dependent annex named after the benefactor, William Smith.[28] Establishing coordinate women's institutions, with varying degrees of separateness, was a common way men's colleges tried to avoid being tainted by coeducation. In some cases, like at coeducational Cornell or Middlebury, the women's colleges were never fully institutionalized or recognized outside the campus. Although it can be argued that such separation actually benefited women students in many ways, men's colleges were not concerned with devising the best form of education for women but rather with preserving or enhancing their prestige.[29]

Within coeducational institutions, women were usually marginalized and separated as much as possible from men students.[30] Classes, particularly large introductory ones; chapel; campus organizations; and even commencement exercises were frequently segregated by gender. By the end of the nineteenth century, men's sports, particularly football, were a major part of campus life; women students were expected to be spectators.[31] In many colleges and universities, fraternity members held most of the campus leadership positions; even when sororities existed, they were much less important to campus life. Thus while coeducation meant that women could attend the same institutions as men, their academic and extracurricular experiences were not equivalent to those of men students. The superiority of men presumed in the larger culture was not challenged within institutions of higher education.

Coeducation in the Twentieth Century

Coeducation was the normative form of higher education in the United States by the end of the nineteenth century. This trend continued throughout the twentieth century, although the rate of change was slow until the late 1960s. In 1945, slightly more than 70 percent of all institutions were coeducational; this percentage increased to about 75 percent in 1955 and then remained virtually stable until 1965.[32]

Although only a minority of institutions were men's or women's colleges by the mid-twentieth century, this minority included some of the most prestigious colleges and universities, virtually all in the eastern states. Harvard, Princeton, Yale, Columbia, Williams, Amherst, and Dartmouth were some of the elite men's colleges, whereas the most select women's colleges, the "seven sisters" as they were known colloquially, were Barnard, Bryn Mawr, Mount Holyoke, Radcliffe, Smith, Vassar, and Wellesley. Not all the colleges for men and women were prestigious, however; many lesser known ones, particularly Catholic institutions, existed as well. There were actually more women's colleges in the early 1960s than at any previous time.[33]

In coeducational institutions women enjoyed the college life that developed in the 1920s as more middle-class youth attended college. Although students were not monolithic in their orientation to college, an increasing number saw college as a time for fun, not only study. Campus clubs, informal social life in the dorms, dances, sporting events (particularly football), and the "Greeks" (fraternities and sororities) were all part of the expectations of what college life should be.[34] Women students did not generally hold campus-wide leadership positions, however, and were barred from the most prestigious organizations like fraternities. Even though sexuality became freer in the 1920s, with women flaunting their freedom by smoking, dancing, and bobbing their hair, colleges were concerned with preserving women's "reputations." Acting in loco parentis, they insisted on regulating women students' social lives through such practices as chaperonage, parietal hours, and dress codes.[35] Men students were generally given more freedom.[36] The strictness of regulations varied, of course, with black colleges and religious colleges generally being the most restrictive.

As increasing numbers of young people attended college and higher education became a major vehicle for social mobility, stratification among institutions became more rigid.[37] One way that colleges attempted to preserve or enhance their status was through limiting the numbers of students who were not white, Anglo-Saxon Protestants. Quotas on Jews existed at most liberal arts colleges and some of the elite institutions, including Yale, Harvard, and Princeton, particularly during the "Red scare" years after World War I.[38] Institutions also set quotas on Catholics and blacks, with some colleges, like Princeton, barring blacks completely. Discrimination extended to women, too, with many colleges and universities ensuring that men students remained in the majority. Cornell, one of the earliest coeducational universities, limited women's enrollment to 25 percent.[39] The proportion of Catholics at secular institutions generally increased during the twentieth century, and so did the number of blacks at northern, predominantly white institutions, but before World War II, these numbers remained low, especially for black college students, over 90 percent of whom continued to attend traditional black colleges.[40]

The national depression that began in 1929 and the two world wars were difficult times for men's and coeducational institutions. Enrollments fell drastically, which in turn created serious financial problems, particularly for small liberal arts colleges that were tuition dependent. The situation would have been worse had not the federal government come to the assistance of higher education. In the course of the depression, the federal government spent over $93 million on the education of over 600,000 students through the National Youth Administration.[41] During the wars, the fall in men's enrollment was made up for in part by the federal government establishing training camps on campuses, with enlisted men taking specially designed courses. During World War II, for example, 131 colleges and universities were chosen to train 120,000 navy men.[42] On coeducational campuses the war had the additional effect of putting women students in charge of many campus activities that had previously been controlled by men. Even though women dominated coeducational campuses during the wars, they were seen as exceptional times, with men expected to resume control once the wars ended.

World War II was a "decisive breaking point" in the history of colleges and universities in the United States.[43] The G.I. Bill, the popular name for the Servicemen's Readjustment Act of 1944, enabled many men to attend college by paying tuition and a monthly stipend to each veteran attending college. College enrollments soared, with more working-class and lower-middle-class men able to receive higher education, which in turn meant that colleges and universities were able to reestablish quotas for women students. For the first time, the number of women who received college degrees, relative to the number of men, fell.[44] Fighting the Nazis also raised awareness of discrimination against Jews; particularly at the higher status institutions, Jewish student enrollment increased and more Jewish professors were hired, marking the beginning of the ethnic transformation of American universities.[45]

Expansion at institutions of higher education continued during the 1950s. In 1950 the federal government allotted $300 million for long-term loans to private and public colleges for building dormitories to accommodate the large increases in enrollment after the war.[46] Foundations and the federal government provided increased money for natural and social scientific research, particularly after the Soviets' success with Sputnik in 1957.[47]

The decade of the 1960s began during this unprecedented period of growth in higher education. About 700 new institutions were established between 1960 and 1969; three-quarters of them were public institutions, and some of them were experimental, for example, Old Westbury, Federal City College, and Livingston.[48] Many existing colleges and universities considered how they could expand. Given cultural changes, one way that came to seem natural was for single-sex institutions to become coeducational, which more than 40 percent of them did during the next two decades.[49] The old idea of coordinate colleges began to resurface as a way of avoiding full coeducation while taking advantage of an untapped source of enrollment. Hamilton College, for example, an old and traditional men's college, set about emulating the Claremont cluster college idea, beginning its cluster with a small, experimental college for women (see Chapter 10). In the mid-1960s, a women's college, Wells, considered building a coordinate college for men.[50] At about the same time, officials at Yale and Vassar College discussed a coordinate arrangement, but instead, both institutions became coeducational a few years later.[51]

And yet, even as late as 1968, almost as many elite colleges were men's colleges as were coeducational, whereas very few of the colleges that educational researchers Astin and Lee defined as "invisible" (small, nonselective institutions) were men's colleges, and most of these were Roman Catholic.[52] Men's colleges that had previously admitted women had been concerned about lowering their status, even though it was generally acknowledged that women students raised academic standards. The questions asked in a study of men students' attitudes at a private university in New York City—presumably NYU—that admitted women in 1960 to its engineering and arts and sciences colleges reveal these concerns. The researcher's questions included, for example, whether the men thought that the reputation of their college had been lowered, whether they thought that entrance standards had become higher, and whether classes had become less interesting.[53] Cultural changes that occurred during the 1960s, particularly at the end of the decade, made these concerns seem irrelevant at best to a majority of young people.

Figure 1.1 shows the dramatic decline in the number of single-sex colleges after the early 1960s. Depending on the references used and the definitions employed (whether a researcher includes, for example, coordinate colleges as single-sex), the precise numbers of men's or women's colleges vary. Nonetheless, the trends are clear: by 1994, the number of women's colleges was less than one-third of what it had been in the early 1960s, and men's colleges all but disappeared during this same time interval. The rate of decrease was greatest between 1962 and 1972; after 1982 the decline was more moderate.

Forces Favoring the Resurgence of Coeducation

Cultural and Political Factors

The decade of the 1960s is most famous as a period of political and social unrest that included the civil rights movement, the anti–Vietnam War movement, the environmental movement, a sexual "revolution," the women's movement, and the gay liberation movement.[54] The beginning of college student activism is usually dated to the Port Huron statement of Students for a Democratic Society (SDS) in 1962 and the Free Speech Movement in Berkeley in 1964. College students also became involved with various protests associated with the civil rights movement: sit-in demonstrations, voter registration drives, and marches. As the United States became increasingly embroiled in Vietnam, antiwar protest became the major focus of student concerns, with the first "teach-ins" on the war occurring in 1965. Protests against the war reached their greatest fervor

Figure 1.1. Numbers of Men's and Women's Colleges Over Time

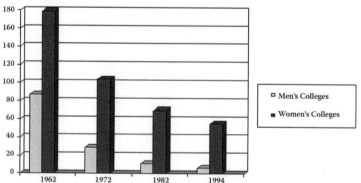

Sources: Gene R. Hawes, The New American Guide to Colleges, 2d ed. (New York: Columbia University Press, 1962); James Cass and Max Birnbaum, Comparative Guide to American Colleges, 5th ed. (New York: Harper and Row, 1972) and 16th ed. (New York: Harper and Row, 1994); Barron's Profiles of American Colleges, 13th ed. (Woodbury, N.Y.: Barron's Educational Series, 1982).

after national guardsmen and police killed some student protestors at Kent State and Jackson State in 1970. While large universities, such as Columbia, Cornell, Berkeley, Wisconsin, and Michigan, became associated with radicalism, it has been estimated that by 1969 over half of campuses nationwide had experienced some form of demonstration.[55]

The 1960s also involved the development of a counterculture, in which many young people demonstrated their disdain for conventional life. Use of illegal drugs like marijuana and hallucinogens (LSD and mescaline) was one aspect of this counterculture, as were clothing and hairstyle changes (women going braless, men growing their hair long, for instance), rock music festivals, and communal living experiments. A sexual revolution, feasible due to the availability of birth control pills, made it more acceptable for women and men to live together before marriage. By the end of the 1960s gay students were beginning to voice their concerns and form their own organizations. At about the same time, the second wave of the women's movement became more visible and active; the term "sexism" was coined in 1969, and women began to call attention to gender inequities in employment and education, as well as to violence against women.[56]

On campuses the ramifications of these cultural changes included a decline in fraternity and sorority membership or even disbanding what seemed to be discriminatory and old-fashioned organizations. Students put pressure on their institutions to admit minority students, hire minority faculty, and establish black studies programs. In response to students' demands to be treated as adults, most college regulations associated with in loco parentis were changed. Many dormitories became coeducational, sign-in policies and limited visiting hours were ended, and the main form of restrictions became those dictated by state and federal laws concerning drinking and drugs. Students were often given a role in college governance by having representatives on faculty and board of trustee committees.

The cultural mood of the times called for closer ties between men and women, as well as between blacks and whites. Integration of all sorts seemed natural; single-sex institutions and organizations seemed old-fashioned or backward. At coordinate colleges, students clamored for complete coeducation. A student editorial at coordinate Hobart and William Smith Colleges, expressed it this way: "Hobart and William Smith are one college . . . we're friends no longer; we've been lovers for years, it's time we got married."[57] Administrators at men's and women's colleges began to worry that they would lose students to more popular coeducational institutions. In 1969, for example, the new president of Wells commented that "if the present preoccupation with co-education continues for very long, it may well close off the possibility of sustaining a first-class, single-sex undergraduate college."[58] Various trial coeducation programs were initiated; small groups of students from such men's colleges as Colgate,

Trinity, and Yale studied at women's colleges (Vassar and Wells, for example) while women students went to these men's colleges.[59] Especially at men's colleges, coeducation was seen as a way to ensure enrollments and to maintain or even increase academic standards, since many very well qualified women would want to attend prestigious, formerly all-male colleges. In Yale's first coeducational class in 1969, for instance, 2,850 women applied for 240 places.[60]

Beginning in the late 1960s, many of the most prestigious men's colleges and a few prestigious women's colleges became coeducational: Princeton, Yale, Williams, Amherst, Dartmouth, and Wesleyan were some of the elite men's colleges that admitted women; Vassar was the most famous women's college that admitted men, but it was joined by Skidmore, Connecticut College (for Women), and Elmira. High-status colleges' transition to coeducation then became a factor influencing other colleges to change.[61] At Trinity College in Hartford, Connecticut, for example, the news that other men's colleges were considering coeducation or had decided to admit women helped convince college constituencies that Trinity, too, should adopt coeducation. Particularly influential was the Princeton University trustee report, released in September 1968, that concluded that Princeton had to become coeducational in order to "change with the times."[62] By the mid-1980s very few men's colleges remained. Women's colleges had declined in number, too, but the women's movement and studies of sexism in the academy had given them new justification for their existence, as will be described below.

Economic Factors

Part of the reason many colleges decided to become coeducational was financial. In 1968–69, the "number one concern of virtually all college presidents" was funding.[63] The incredible growth of enrollment during the 1950s and 1960s, from around 3 million students in the early 1950s to almost 7 million by 1968, required institutions to build and maintain many new facilities.[64] Competition over funding became more intense, a situation many administrators, who had come to their jobs during the previous "golden age," were unprepared for.[65] Also, high inflation during the 1970s depreciated the value of available resources.[66] One researcher who studied 41 institutions across the country found that the majority had financial problems, leading him to call the beginning of the 1970s a "new depression" period in higher education.[67]

Not all men and women's colleges that were experiencing economic problems decided to become coeducational, of course, and not all those that did make this transition had financial difficulties (especially the most elite men's colleges like Yale and Princeton). Yet some researchers reported that, in general, it was the most financially troubled single-sex institutions that became coeducational. A 1971 study of all 631 U.S. liberal arts colleges found that 169 were single-sex. When the researchers restudied these colleges in 1986, they found that 68 of these single-sex colleges had become coeducational. It was generally the single-sex colleges that had had higher debts and lower endowments that made this transition.[68]

Demographic Factors

Postsecondary enrollments continued to rise after the 1960s, but not as rapidly as they did in the 1950s and 1960s. By the early 1970s, the "baby boom" generation (those born during the high-birth-rate years at the end of World War II) had finished college. Enrollments kept rising, however, partly because a greater proportion of each cohort of high school women attended college. Men's proportions began to rise a bit later, in 1979.[69] Even though enrollments did not fall as some people had predicted, the characteristics of students who attended college and the types of institutions they attended made becoming coeducational advantageous to men's colleges.

Many men's colleges were contemplating coeducation just at the time that the proportion of women students was rising. In 1950 women made up only 24 percent of college graduates, but by 1960 they accounted for 35 percent of graduates.[70] Men's colleges that became coeducational in the late 1960s and early 1970s were able to take advantage of the increasing percentage of women enrolling in college. Moreover, due to the influence of the women's movement, more women were majoring in fields formerly dominated by men and planning to go into professions that previously had been male domains.[71] Thus men's colleges could see women not only as students who would revive major fields like modern languages, the arts, and humanities, which were traditionally elected by women, but also as students who would help maintain enrollments in mathematics and the sciences.

Most men's colleges were small, private liberal arts colleges, an increasingly vulnerable type of postsecondary institution. Over the course of this century, the proportion of students who attend public institutions has grown tremendously. Whereas in the earlier part of the century, about half of college students attended public institutions, this proportion rose to 76 percent by the 1970s.[72] This means that private colleges have faced increasing competition for students. By admitting women, men's colleges were able to expand their admissions pool.

Arguments in favor of men's colleges becoming coeducational were often linked to equal access and increasing student diversity. The 1972 Education Amendment that established need-based Pell grants supported the tendency of colleges and universities to be more inclusive of lower-income students.[73] These grants helped bring the median family income of college students closer to the national median family income level by the 1970s, whereas in the 1960s students had come from much wealthier families.[74] The Reagan-Bush administrations, however, changed the predominant form of student aid to guaranteed student loans, which has been described as having a "chilling effect on the participation rates for needy students."[75] Likewise, the proportion of minorities attending colleges has not continued to increase much since 1980, and a high proportion of black students attend community colleges.[76]

Private men's colleges that became coeducational in the late 1960s benefited in terms of increased enrollment and campus climate. Richard Anderson's study of 40 private institutions, some of which changed from being religious to secular and others of which changed from being single-sex to coeducational, found that men's change colleges did well on virtually every measure—increased enrollment, improvements in students' scholarship, better student morale, and increases in colleges' equity value over a ten-year interval. Women's colleges that admitted men, however, did not fare nearly so well, except in terms of increased enrollment.[77]

Coeducation Today

For about the past two decades, women students in the United States have predominated at all levels of higher education except the doctoral level. Since 1979 women have made up the majority of all undergraduates (but the majority of full-time undergraduates since 1985), and in 1999 they constituted 56 percent of all undergraduates. At the graduate level women have predominated since 1984 (including both part-time and full-time graduate students). In 1999 women earned 58 percent of the masters degrees awarded that year. In 2002 for the first time more U.S. women than men earned their doctorates.[78]

Today women have access to virtually all institutions of higher education. In 1975 Congress passed legislation that made federal military institutions co-educational. State military academies have more recently become coeducational (see Chapter 11 for a comparison of coeducation at West Point and Virginia Military Institute). Only a few private colleges remain all men, most notably Wabash in Indiana, Morehouse in Georgia, Hampden-Sydney in Virginia, and two-year Deep Springs in California.

Coeducation cannot be assumed to be the same as equal education, however. Research spawned by the second wave of the women's movement demonstrated that women still faced disadvantages in institutions of higher education. Today, as the case studies of this book demonstrate, women remain underrepresented at the highest levels of faculty, trustees, and administration, although their representation has generally increased since the 1960s. Women students at most coeducational institutions are less likely than men students to hold such key leadership positions as president of the student body or editor of student publications. Moreover, studies conducted during the 1980s found that classroom climates in coeducational institutions were "chilly," with women students being less likely to be called on to answer provocative questions, more likely to be interrupted, and in other ways, being treated as less important than men students.[79] Duke University's recent study of the "climate for women" found "disparities" between men and women undergraduates' experiences, including separate leadership tracks, less mentoring of women students, and pressure on women to fit an ideal of "effortless perfection."[80] Women students continue to be much more likely than men students to be sexually harassed or raped. Such findings have given women's colleges a continuing raison d'être, since they have a high proportion of women on their faculty and administration, and no men students are present to dominate curricular and co-curricular activities. Moreover, some (but not all) research has found that graduates of women's colleges are more likely than women graduates of coeducational institutions to succeed in later life.[81]

Government has been one source of pressure on coeducational colleges and universities to treat women more equally. Federal antidiscriminatory legislation has been used to sue institutions that have not hired qualified women faculty and staff or paid them salaries equal to men. As early as 1970, 43 colleges and universities were charged with discriminatory employment practices against women, using executive orders that had previously been applied only for racial discrimination and whose ultimate sanction was canceling all federal contracts held by the institution. The institutions were charged with having discriminatory admission quotas for undergraduate and graduate students, as well as hiring practices and salary differentials that favored men.[82]

Women's sports at all educational levels have been greatly expanded due to Title IX of the Educational Amendments Act of 1972, which prohibits sex discrimination at institutions that receive federal funds, especially since Congress passed a law in 1987 that strengthened its enforcement. By the mid-1990s women accounted for slightly more than one-third of all college athletes but received slightly less than one-third of all athletic scholarships.[83] Since 1987 the number of women's basketball and track teams has risen by about 26 percent, but this is much lower than the 200 to 300 percent rise in women's soccer, rowing, golf, and lacrosse teams. Thus the fastest rising women's sports are those in which minority women are underrepresented.[84] Moreover, women's college sports still receive only about one-fifth of athletic budgets, and female coaches have had to sue to try to get pay that is in any way equal to that of male coaches.

Coeducational institutions have responded to their women students and faculty by establishing women's studies programs, women's resource centers, and sexual harassment policies, and by appointing more women faculty and administrators. By the early 1990s, there were about 620 women's studies departments in institutions of higher education across the United States and about 30 centers for research and scholarship on women.[85] Research on sexual harassment, first introduced as a legal concept in 1979 by Catherine MacKinnon, proliferated during the late 1980s and 1990s. Studies have found that peer harassment is more common than faculty-student harassment, although the latter may have more severe consequences, particularly for graduate students who have very close contacts with faculty and who depend more on them for their careers. On the positive side, one study found that the incidence of faculty-student harassment decreased after an institution established a sexual harassment policy and grievance procedure.[86] Women as a proportion of all faculty now stands at over 30 percent, but the percent is lower in prestigious institutions and in the upper ranks.[87] Women have moved slowly into the upper reaches of college administration. In 2001, about 20 percent of all college presidents were women, up from about 10 percent in the early 1990s.[88]

Case studies show that to make coeducational institutions more gender equal requires actions on many fronts. Looking at a private liberal arts college in New England and two universities (one southern public and one premier private research university oriented toward the sciences), all of which had successful affirmative action plans that substantially increased the percentage of women faculty, indicated that the following factors were important: a reasonable proportion of women students (more than 10 or 20 percent), federal mandates, administrative leadership, and women faculty's united actions. The role and importance of each of these factors for producing successful affirmative action varied with the particular institution, however.[89] Another case study described how the long-time coeducational Lewis and Clark College became motivated to deal with its gender inequities: the college received a National Endowment for the Humanities (NEH) grant in 1981 for faculty development; Gerda Lerner, a famous feminist scholar, visited the campus; and college feminists received encouragement from two women administrators. In a short period of time, Lewis and Clark faculty voted to make the integration of women's studies into the curriculum a "top institutional priority," developed a task force on sexual harassment and affirmative action, and created a highly successful annual women's studies symposium.[90] Although Lewis and Clark did not create a women's studies program, it did develop a gender studies concentration.

The case studies of *Going Coed* contribute to understanding variations among coeducational institutions but within a particular subset: those that since the 1950s have made a transition from being men's colleges or universities to becoming coeducational. The chapters that follow focus on factors that led to this transition and on the experiences of women students at these schools. Before presenting the case studies, we present brief historical overviews of two types of institutions of higher education whose experiences with coeducation are different from most: Catholic colleges, which tended to be single-sex long after most institutions became coeducational, and historically black colleges, almost all of which were coeducational from their nineteenth-century beginnings.

Notes

The epigraph comes from Carol Lasser, "Introduction" in *Educating Men and Women Together,* ed. Carol Lasser (Urbana: University of Illinois Press, 1957), 6.

1. A handful of men's colleges remain, the best known being Wabash, Morehouse (in coordination with the women's college Spelman), Hampden-Sydney, and the two-year Deep Springs.
2. For histories of earlier periods, see Lasser and also Barbara Miller Solomon, *In the Company of Educated Women* (New Haven: Yale University Press, 1985).
3. At the time, however, the term "coeducational" was apparently not used. It was not until the 1850s that "coed" came into use, with derogatory connotations. See Virginia Kemp Fish, "The Struggle over Women's Education in the Nineteenth Century: A Social Movement and Countermovement," in *Women and Social Protest,* ed. Guida West and Rhoda Lois Blumberg (New York: Oxford University Press, 1990), 266.
4. Some college histories report isolated cases of a black man being admitted, how purposefully it is not always possible to tell. See, for example, David Stameshkin, *The Town's College: Middlebury College, 1800–1915* (Middlebury, Vt.: Middlebury College Press, 1985), 108–9, who briefly mentions a black student at Middlebury who graduated in 1823.
5. Vassar is considered by many scholars to be the most important early women's college because it was the first to have a substantial endowment and a curriculum that was about the same as men's colleges of the time.
6. Ronald W. Hogeland, "Coeducation of the Sexes at Oberlin College: A Study of Social Ideas in Mid-nineteenth Century America," *Journal of Social History* 6 (1972–73): 160–76, takes a more critical view of Oberlin's purported gender equity, while such scholars as Solomon; Susan Poulson, "A Quiet Revolution: The Transition to Coeducation at Georgetown and Rutgers Colleges, 1960–1975" (Ph.D. diss., Georgetown University, 1989); and Lori Ginzberg, "The 'Joint Education of the Sexes': Oberlin's Original Vision," in Lasser, *Educating Men and Women,* 67–80, stress the revolutionary nature of Oberlin.
7. John Rury and Glenn Harper, "The Trouble with Coeducation: Mann and Women at Antioch, 1853–1860," *History of Education Quarterly* 26 (1986): 481–502.
8. Mabel Newcomer, *A Century of Higher Education for Women* (New York: Harper and Row, 1959), 19.
9. M. Carey Thomas, "Present Tendencies in Women's College and University Education," *Education Review* 35 (1908): 64–85.
10. Poulson, 12.
11. Barbara Sicherman, "Colleges and Careers: Historical Perspectives on the Lives and Work Patterns of Women College Graduates," in *Women and Higher Education in American History,* ed. John Mack Faragher and Florence Howe (New York: Norton, 1988), 13–164.
12. Leslie Miller-Bernal, *Separate by Degree: Women Students' Experiences in Single-Sex and Coeducational Colleges* (New York: Peter Lang, 2000), 14.
13. Miriam Schneir, ed., *Feminism: The Essential Historical Writings* (New York: Vintage, 1972).

14. Miller-Bernal, 203–5.
15. See, for example, the discussion of the beginnings of Radcliffe and Barnard in Helen Lefkowitz Horowitz, *Alma Mater* (Boston: Beacon, 1984), and Miller-Bernal's discussion of women's attempts to enter Middlebury in the 1870s and Hobart in the 1890s.
16. A good discussion of the implications of the Morrill Acts for the education of women can be found in John S. Brubacher and Willis Rudy, *Higher Education in Transition*, 4th ed. (New Brunswick, N.J.: Transaction Publishers, 1997), 62–64, and especially 67. See also Poulson and Solomon.
17. Cited by Christopher J. Lucas, *American Higher Education: A History* (New York: St. Martin's Griffin, 1994), 148.
18. For the implications of the 1890 legislation for institutional survival, see Lucas, 149; Brubacher and Rudy, 229, discuss the legislation's acceptance of racially "separate but equal" education.
19. Solomon, 57.
20. Rosalind Rosenberg, "The Limits of Access: The History of Coeducation in America," in *Women and Higher Education in American History*, ed. John Mack Faragher and Florence Howe (New York: Norton, 1988).
21. Ibid., 111.
22. Newcomer, 49.
23. David O. Levine, *The American College and the Culture of Aspiration, 1915–1960* (Ithaca, N.Y.: Cornell University Press, 1986), 13.
24. Patricia A. Palmieri, "From Republican Motherhood to Race Suicide: Arguments on the Higher Education of Women in the United States, 1820–1920," in Lasser, *Educating Men and Women.*
25. Miller-Bernal, 45–52.
26. Arthur J. May, *A History of the University of Rochester, 1850–1962* (Rochester, N.Y.: University of Rochester, 1977). See Chapter 4 for a discussion of the University of Rochester's transition from a coordinate institution to a fully coeducational one.
27. Roger Daniels, *Not Like Us: Immigrants and Minorities in America, 1890–1924* (Chicago: Ivan R. Dee, 1997).
28. Miller-Bernal, 73–76. Not until 1943 did William Smith achieve legal parity with Hobart College, 120–21.
29. Leslie Miller-Bernal, "Conservative Intent, Liberating Outcomes: The History of Coordinate Colleges for Women" in *Doing Gender in Policy and Practices: Perspectives on Single-Sex and Coeducational Schooling*, ed. Amanda Datnow and Lea Hubbard (New York: RoutledgeFalmer, 2002).
30. Lynn D. Gordon, *Gender and Higher Education in the Progressive Era* (New Haven: Yale University Press, 1990).
31. See Laurence R. Veysey, *The Emergence of the American University* (Chicago: University of Chicago Press, 1965), and Helen Lefkowitz Horowitz, *Campus Life* (Chicago: University of Chicago Press, 1987), for excellent discussions of the development of campus life from the nineteenth to the twentieth century.
32. Barbara Heyns and Joyce Adair Bird, "Recent Trends in the Higher Education of Women," in *The Undergraduate Woman*, ed. Pamela Perun (Lexington, Mass.: D. C. Heath, 1982), 66.

33. Erich Studer-Ellis, "Diverse Institutional Forces and Fundamental Organizational Change: Women's Colleges and the 'Coed or Dead' Question" (delivered at the Annual Meetings of the American Sociological Association, Washington, D.C., August 22, 1995), 17.

34. Horowitz, *Campus Life.*

35. See ibid., Dorothy M. Brown, *Setting a Course: American Women in the 1920s* (Boston: Twayne, 1987), and Paula S. Fass, *The Damned and the Beautiful—American Youth in the 1920s* (New York: Oxford University Press, 1977), for discussions of changes in campus life during the 1920s.

36. Even as late as the mid-1960s, when I was a student at Middlebury College in Vermont, only women students had to be in their dorms by ten or eleven every weekday night; women students could not wear pants to classes or the library; and while men students could drink alcohol openly outside their dorms, women students could be suspended if caught drinking.

37. Levine, 17.

38. Marcia Graham Synnott, *The Half-Opened Door: Discrimination and Admissions at Harvard, Yale, and Princeton, 1900–1970* (Westport, Conn.: Greenwood, 1979).

39. Harvey Strum, "Discrimination at Syracuse University," *History of Higher Education* 4 (1984): 102–3.

40. Barbara Astone and Elsa Nuñez-Wormack, *Pursuing Diversity* (Washington, D.C.: Clearinghouse on Higher Education, George Washington University Publications, 1990), 7.

41. Brubacher and Rudy, 230.

42. Stameshkin, 79.

43. Veysey, 13.

44. Jerry A. Jacobs, "Gender Inequality and Higher Education," *Annual Review of Sociology* 22 (1996): 155–56.

45. Veysey, 14.

46. Brubacher and Rudy, 232.

47. Benson Snyder, "Change Despite Turmoil at M.I.T.," in *Academic Transformation,* ed. David Riesman and Verne A. Stadtman (New York: McGraw-Hill, 1973), 162.

48. Verne A. Stadtman, *Academic Adaptations: Higher Education Prepares for the 1980s and 1990s* (San Francisco: Jossey-Bass, 1980), 4.

49. Edward J. Zajac and Matthew S. Kraatz, "A Diametric Forces Model of Strategic Change: Assessing the Antecedents and Consequences of Restructuring in the Higher Education Industry," *Strategic Management Journal* 14 (1993): 95.

50. Miller-Bernal, *Separate by Degree,* 170.

51. Janet Lever and Pepper Schwartz, *Women at Yale* (Indianapolis: Bobbs-Merrill, 1971).

52. Alexander W. Astin and Calvin B. T. Lee, *The Invisible College: A Profile of Small, Private Colleges with Limited Resources* (New York: McGraw-Hill, 1972), 31.

53. Marilyn J. Sermul, "The Effects of Coeducation on Attitudes of Male College Students," *Journal of Educational Sociology* 35 (1961): 11–17.

54. Much has been written on the student protests of the 1960s. I have found Flacks's two books particularly helpful, as well as the collection of case studies edited by Reisman

and Stadtman. See Richard Flacks, *Youth and Social Change* (Chicago: Markham Publishing, 1971) and *Making History: The Radical Tradition in American Life* (New York: Columbia University Press, 1988), and Riesman and Stadtman.

55. Horowitz, *Campus Life*, 221.
56. David Tyack and Elisabeth Hansot, *Learning Together* (New Haven: Yale University Press; New York: Russell Sage Foundation, 1990).
57. Miller-Bernal, *Separate by Degree*, 179.
58. Ibid., 171.
59. Lever and Schwartz, 31; Peter J. Knapp in collaboration with Anne H. Knapp, *Trinity College in the Twentieth Century* (Hartford, Conn.: Trinity College, 2000), 375.
60. Lever and Schwartz, 44.
61. Studer-Ellis, 11.
62. Knapp and Knapp, 365–66.
63. Stadtman, 3.
64. Brubacher and Willis, 424.
65. Martine F. Hammond, "Survival of Small Private Colleges: Three Case Studies," *Journal of Higher Education* 55 (1984): 360–88.
66. Stadtman, 6.
67. Earl F. Cheit, *The New Depression in Higher Education* (New York: McGraw-Hill, for the Carnegie Commission on Higher Education and the Ford Foundation, 1971).
68. Zajac and Kraatz, 95–96.
69. Margaret Gordon, "The Economy and Higher Education," in *Higher Learning in America, 1980–2000,* ed. Arthur Levine (Baltimore: Johns Hopkins University Press, 1993), 31–33.
70. In terms of women's participation in higher education, the 1950s and 1960s were actually an aberration. Just before World War II, women constituted about 40 percent of college graduates. See Jacobs, 156.
71. Ibid., 168–69.
72. Brubacher and Rudy, 389.
73. David W. Breneman, "Liberal Arts Colleges: What Price Survival?" in Levine, *Higher Learning,* 90.
74. Eric L. Dey and Sylvia Hurtado, "College Students in Changing Contexts," in *Higher Education in American Society,* 3d ed., ed. Philip G. Altbach, Robert O. Berdahl, and Patricia J. Glimport (Amherst, N.Y.: Promotheus Books, 1994), 252.
75. Flora Mancuso Edwards, "Behind the Open Door: Disadvantaged Students," in Levine, *Higher Learning,* 320.
76. Philip G. Altbach, Kofi Lomotey, and Shariba Rivers Kyle, "Race in Higher Education," in *American Higher Education in the Twenty-first Century,* ed. Philip G. Altbach, Robert O. Berdahl, and Patricia J. Gumport (Baltimore: Johns Hopkins University Press, 1999), 451, discuss trends in minority student enrollments. Kevin J. Dougherty, "The Community College: The Impact, Origin, and Future of a Contradictory Institution," in *Schools & Society,* ed. Jeanne H. Ballantine and Joan Z. Spade (Belmont, Calif.: Wadsworth, 2001), 373, notes that community colleges enroll a large share of "disadvantaged" students and that 44 percent of all minority college students attend community colleges.

77. Richard E. Anderson, "A Financial and Environmental Analysis of Strategic Policy Changes at Small Private Colleges," *Journal of Higher Education* 49 (1978): 30–46.

78. See *http://nces.ed.gov//pubs2002/digest2001*, Tables 172, 188, 189, and 247. The more recent doctorate figures can be found at *http://www.norc.org/issues/docdata.htm*

79. Bernice Resnick Sandler, "The Classroom Climate: Still a Chilly One for Women," in Lasser, *Educating Men and Women*, 113–23.

80. Women's Initiative, "The Steering Committee's Report," Duke University, 2003.

81. M. Elizabeth Tidball's "baccalaureate origin" studies are the best-known research on the long-term benefits of women's colleges, although some scholars have disputed her findings. For an overview of this work, see Miller-Bernal, *Separate by Degree*, 212–16.

82. Nancy Gruchow, "Discrimination: Women Charge Universities, Colleges with Bias," *Science* 168 (1970): 559–61.

83. Dorothy McBride Stetson, *Women's Rights in the USA*, 2d ed. (New York: Garland, 1997), 153.

84. Welch Suggs, "Left Behind," *Chronicle of Higher Education*, November 30, 2001, A35–A37.

85. Brubacher and Rudy, 413.

86. Jacobs, 172–73.

87. Ibid., 171.

88. Julianne Basinger, "Most Female College Presidents Earn Less, Face More Challenges Than Male Peers, Report Says," *Chronicle of Higher Education*, October 29, 2001, *http://chronicle.com/daily/2001/10/2001/02902n.htm.*

89. Patricia B. Hyer, "Affirmative Action for Women Faculty: Case Studies of Three Successful Institutions," *Journal of Higher Education* 56 (1985): 282–99.

90. Susan Kirschner, Jane Monnig Atkinson, and Elizabeth Arch, "Reassessing Coeducation," in *Women's Place in the Academy*, ed. Marilyn R. Schuster and Susan R. Van Dyne (Totowa, N.J.: Rowman and Allanheld, 1985), 30–47.

2

Two Unique Histories of Coeducation
Catholic and Historically Black Institutions

Susan L. Poulson and Leslie Miller-Bernal

In the nineteenth century many white Protestant men in the United States pursued higher education as a means of upward mobility. In contrast, black Americans were barred from most colleges; besides, given the devastating impact of slavery, their first concern was primary and secondary education. Catholic enrollment in institutions of higher education was limited for several reasons: many colleges and universities put quotas on their admission and, as recent immigrants, Catholics often could not afford college tuition.[1] Beginning in the 1850s, but primarily after the Civil War, black and white educators established historically black colleges and universities (HBCUs) for the important task of "race uplift." Catholics, too, created an extensive network of colleges and universities in order to preserve the faith and morals of young Catholics as they sought higher education. While the aims of blacks and Catholics were somewhat similar, the two traditions created opposite forms of gender organization. From their beginnings, almost all HBCUs were coeducational, whereas Catholic institutions were almost entirely single-sex and remained so longer than most of their peer institutions. In this chapter we discuss the history of both types of colleges, beginning with Catholic colleges and universities since they appeared on the American educational landscape earlier than HBCUs did.

Catholic Higher Education

In the past 220 years Catholics have developed an extensive system of higher education in America. Like many other private educational networks, the history of Catholic higher education is filled with struggles to establish institutions under difficult circumstances, with little money, and scarce students and faculty, but strong determination and leadership. The result is a network of approximately 230 institutions that educates 670,000 students, or about 12 percent of all Catholic college students.[2]

In addition to institution-building, Catholics have had the task of perpetuating and defending the faith while adapting to American culture and modern life. Catholic colleges and universities have played an important part in this mission. In response to forces internal and external to the Church, the content of the curriculum and the nature of piety at Catholic colleges and universities have evolved over time. Gender was a central issue in both institution building and acculturation. Because single-sex religious communities established most Catholic colleges and universities as single-sex institutions, the separate education of men and women was a pervasive feature of Catholic higher education. Historically, coeducation not only contradicted traditional Church teachings about gender roles but was also seen as highly disruptive to the institutional network established by the early twentieth century. However, coeducation did come to Catholic higher education, slowly at first, encountering opposition from conservative critics and ecclesiastic authority. After World War II the pace of change increased. In the 1960s and early 1970s, the virtual collapse of sexual segregation in formerly men's colleges undermined the gender ideals of traditional Catholicism. This change made Catholic higher education more like other American colleges and universities, reflecting a larger trend toward the acculturation of American Catholicism within the broader society.

The Early Period of Catholic Higher Education

Although Catholics were some of the earliest settlers in the colonies, they were relatively late in establishing their first college. This can be explained, in part, because the Church's primary task in early America was missionary service. With an entire continent of non-Christians, the possibilities for propagation of the faith were compelling and received highest priority. In 1789 John Carroll, a prosperous planter from southern Maryland, established Georgetown Academy, now Georgetown University, the first Catholic institution of higher education in America. Carroll had been educated at Catholic schools in France, had briefly entered the novitiate of the Society of Jesus, and became the first bishop in the American Catholic church. The most propitious location was Maryland, a refuge for Catholics since its colonial beginnings and the state that had the largest Catholic population.[3] In 1791, St. Mary's Seminary, the first American Catholic seminary, also opened its doors to male students in a converted tavern in Baltimore.[4]

Georgetown was not only America's first Catholic college but also its first Jesuit college. St. Ignatius Loyola founded the Society of Jesus in the sixteenth century.[5] Dedicated to the reinvigoration and defense of the faith, Jesuits have become the largest vowed religious order in the Church. They administer an extensive network of secondary and higher Catholic educational institutions around the world. Today there are 28 Jesuit colleges and universities in the United States, most of them large urban institutions formed to educate the more than 80 percent of Catholics who lived in cities in the nineteenth and early twentieth centuries.[6]

In the half-century following the establishment of Georgetown, six additional Catholic colleges for men were founded. Then came an extraordinary period of expansion. In the last half of the nineteenth century 152 Catholic colleges for men were established, two-thirds by religious communities, one-fifth by bishops, 12 by priests, and two by laymen. In the first half of the twentieth century, Catholics added 73 colleges for men. Religious communities founded more than half of these; bishops established 19.[7]

The early Catholic educational institutions were established at a time when anti-Catholic sentiment was embedded in American culture. People feared "popery" and believed that foreign despotism was intent on undermining the American republic. The vehemence of anti-Catholicism varied by location. Probably the most contentious area was in New England, the heart of radical Protestantism, and along the eastern seaboard, where Catholics immigrated in large numbers. Catholic education became a focal point of hostility. "Romanism . . . has her colleges," worried Protestants warned. "She knows the best educated, and the best trained minds will always be the leaders."[8] The Jesuits became a particular target, described as "synonymous with all of ambition, craft, and treachery, duplicity and talent, to be conceived by the human mind."[9] Some universities would not admit Catholics; others would, but the social climate for Catholics was often so hostile that they were discouraged from attending. Thus, some of the historic insularity of American Catholicism has been a response to a hostile environment.

Historically, the leadership of Catholic colleges has come from the presidency, which, along with other key administrative positions, was held by clerics.[10] Most presidents were appointed by religious superiors on the basis of sound ecclesiastical and moral standing and were generally cooperative in their relationships with the local bishops and other ecclesiastic authority. All incorporated colleges had a board of trustees, entirely clerical in the early years, and usually appointed from the president's faculty and administrative subordinates. The president and administrators also had responsibility for developing the religious and moral sensibilities of their students and the religious community affiliated with the institution. Few presidents in the nineteenth century had college experience as a teacher or student. Most had been educated in seminaries and were appointed on the basis of past clerical responsibilities. Since they had neither the time nor inclination to develop academic qualification or extensive scholarly interests, college presidents' training and background, according to Catholic college historian Edward J. Power, "confirmed their allegiance to customary educational policies."[11]

Religious practices have significant impact on student life at faith-based institutions. At Catholic institutions in the nineteenth century, much of the daily rigor and routine was influenced by prevailing norms of piety. Serving a largely immigrant population with its long-held traditions and conservative habits, the nature of Catholic worship was what historian Jay Dolan has called "devotional Catholicism," which has four major characteristics: a strong emphasis on clerical authority and lay obedience, a pervasive belief in the sinful nature of humanity and the necessity for strict behavioral norms to restrain it, a regular engagement in various rituals as a means of reaching the sacred, and a belief in the power of miracles. Devotional Catholicism gave the immigrant population a distinctive identity in a diverse religious marketplace. Its emphasis on authority and infallibility provided them with emotional and psychological comfort in a tumultuous world.[12]

In the nineteenth century, Catholic colleges and universities were traditional and conservative educational institutions for two reasons: prejudice made Catholics defensive, concerned with preserving and defending the faith and insulating their students from heresy, and conservative devotional Catholicism was the predominant form of piety. In the late nineteenth century, American Catholic higher education engaged in a contentious debate over how to respond to challenges of the modern world, a debate that periodically reemerges to this day. As historian Philip Gleason notes in his comprehensive study *Contending with Modernity*, adapting to the modern world has been a persistent and sometimes divisive issue for American Catholics. The controversy in the late nineteenth century, known as Americanism, centered on the newly established Catholic University, which for many Catholics exhibited the rising stature of Catholic higher education and its ambitions to equal other research-oriented universities. The "conservatives" held a deep mistrust of the modern world and believed that Catholics should adhere to traditional teachings, exhibit papal loyalty, and be ready to respond to all challenges to the faith. The "liberals" recognized that the modern world challenged tradition in many ways but also brought new opportunities, especially in the areas of human freedom and understanding society and nature. It was necessary, they believed, to filter out what was bad and incorporate the good to be found in modern civilization. The papal letter Testum Benevolentiae of 1899 put a rest to the controversy when Pope Leo XIII delivered a "stiff reprimand" to this accommodationist philosophy.[13]

American Catholic Higher Education for Women

Higher education for American Catholic women developed more than a century after the first institution for Catholic men was established. Yet during the next century, women's colleges were established with remarkable frequency. With many of its institutions founded by individual orders of women religious who held varying ideals of women's education, Catholic higher education for women developed into a mosaic that ranged from ambitious liberal arts colleges to academically marginal institutions with a strong vocational emphasis.

Women's Catholic higher education began in the midst of a debate among Catholics about the propriety of higher education for women. Some critics were concerned that college education would encourage women to develop professional careers, and that this, ultimately, would threaten church and society. Opponents proclaimed ugly stereotypes. "Smartness is not becoming to women," one remarked. "The college graduate, the bluestocking, the lecturing woman, is frequently the most unwomanly creature." In the late nineteenth century when women were expected to marry and have many children, educated women were often feared because they were more likely to remain single or have fewer children. Many families who had little money to spare financed their sons' but not their daughters' education in the belief that what could further the economic prospects of their sons was useless for their daughters. Supporters of higher education for women, including the renowned Bishop John Lancaster Spalding of Peoria and Boston College president, Thomas I. Gasson, S.J., became vocal in their defense. Women were fully capable of multiple accomplishments, Spalding argued, but had been restricted by men to the domestic sphere. A woman should be able to be "wherever she can live globally and do useful work. The career open to ability applies to her not less than to man."[14]

Several practical conditions and concerns prompted reluctant Catholics to support higher education for women. Church leaders at the Third Plenary Council of 1884 called for the development of a massive parochial school system and for the education of women to staff them. In 1880, there were about 2,246 schools that educated more than 400,000 students. Thirty years later there were nearly 5,000 schools and more than a million students.[15] Because women could not attend male Catholic institutions, they left the Catholic system to obtain their college degrees. Concerns about the piety and morals of Catholic women who might attend Protestant or secular institutions created an additional incentive for the establishment of Catholic women's colleges. For example, after Catholic University rejected women who applied for admission between 1895 and 1900, more than 20 of them attended secular colleges. Also, most Catholic women students wanted to attend a college close to home and to settle near their families. Many bishops who had to develop the parochial school system in their area and needed local colleges for women consequently began to support the idea of a Catholic woman's college.[16]

The first Catholic college for women was the College of Notre Dame of Maryland, founded by the School Sisters of Notre Dame in 1895 when they added college courses to their academy for girls. Four years later, six graduates became the first women to graduate from a Catholic college. In 1900 women's higher education took a further step when the Sisters of Notre Dame de Namur opened Trinity College, the first women's Catholic college to be established as a college. A diverse, powerful group within the hierarchy who advocated women's higher education supported its establishment. Located in Washington, D.C., near the nascent Catholic University, Trinity College was intended to be a first-rate institution, "equal if not superior to those of our best non-Catholic colleges," the prospectus proclaimed. Sister Julia McGroarty, founder of the college, visited several women's colleges along the East Coast to study their curricula and living arrangements. The Sisters of Notre Dame, who constituted the majority of faculty, studied at Oxford and London Universities in preparation, and additional faculty were Catholic University professors willing to teach on an adjunct basis.[17]

Following the establishment of the College of Notre Dame and Trinity College, women religious opened dozens of new colleges, often in response to states' minimum education requirements or certification for teaching at public and private schools. Women religious who wanted to teach at the elementary and secondary level had to attend college. By 1955, there were 116 four-year colleges and 24 junior colleges in women's Catholic higher education. The majority of these colleges developed from convent academies, which also offered secondary education to girls. By 1970, there were 137 four-year Catholic colleges for women.[18]

According to historian, Mary J. Oates, C.S.J., many of these Catholic women's colleges suffered from financial problems and weak academic programs. They also continued to "reinforce conservative attitudes on women's place." Traditionalists warned that educating women for careers was "fool's gold" and that a student should study fields "which gratify her natural inclinations and which contribute directly to her preparation for motherhood." One consequence of this pedagogy was a frequent emphasis on vocational training in traditional, low-paying occupations, such as nursing, library science, and domestic science. Another notable aspect of women's Catholic colleges was the relatively high percentage of women religious students, who as recently as the mid-twentieth-century accounted for 20 percent of all students.[19]

Like any institution, the success and quality of a Catholic women's college seemed to depend greatly on strong leadership. At St. Mary's College, for example, Mother Pauline O'Neill, C.S.C., president during the first three decades of the twentieth century, built a distinctive college environment by building a physical environment for the college separate from the high school, emphasizing the strong liberal arts background, and bringing famous and influential speakers on campus. Several leaders of the better-quality Catholic women's colleges recognized that the entire system of Catholic higher education for women suffered from the poor reputation of the lesser quality colleges. Some made various proposals to overcome this handicap, including encouraging women religious to resist Episcopal appeals to open more colleges and to consolidate existing colleges into larger, better-financed institutions.[20]

Developments in Catholic Higher Education at the Turn of the Twentieth Century

In the late 1800s and early 1900s Catholic higher education continued its explosive expansion. From 1880 to 1920 Catholic colleges opened their doors at an average of more than one per year. Most of these colleges were located along the eastern seaboard, but colleges were also founded further west in growing numbers. Graduate and professional education in Catholic institutions increased as well. Around the time of the Civil War, a few colleges sporadically awarded master's degrees. In 1877, Georgetown established the first formal program of graduate study that required particular courses and a scholarly essay to be archived at the college. Other Catholic colleges quickly followed in its wake, with the Catholic University of America being the first to award an earned doctorate in 1895. These early graduate programs were of variable quality, and the primary emphasis continued to be on undergraduate education until after World War II. Like many other universities during this period, Catholic institutions struggled to staff and finance the necessary courses. Yet over time several developed respectable graduate programs.[21]

Another major development was ideological and curricular. Neo-scholastic philosophy became prevalent in Catholic institutions and provided a broad coherence to Catholic higher education in the first half of the twentieth century. This philosophy, perfected by St. Thomas, gave clarity and articulation to Catholic thought and practice. It overcame the belief that "modern science and scholarship had completely discredited orthodox teaching and reduced traditional Christian faith to the same level as primitive superstition." The integrative, seamless nature of neo-scholasticism gave Catholics a confidence in their beliefs that contributed to their intense devotion and to the assumption that there was a Catholic viewpoint on all aspects of life.[22]

Coeducation also emerged for the first time in Catholic higher education during the early twentieth century. While in 1900, coeducation did not exist in any Catholic institution, by 1930 almost half of the Catholic men's colleges had admitted women to some part of their institution. Also, almost half of all women enrolled in Catholic colleges and universities received their education in coeducational institutions by mid-century. Compared to secular colleges and universities, this was late. Catholic higher education resisted coeducation because it contradicted long-held beliefs about proper gender roles. Many feared it would undermine the unique nature of the sexes: "A girl," one clerical critic wrote in 1906, "is bound to lose something of this bloom [femininity] by close contact with Masculine youth." A second critic proclaimed that "If our Catholic women are to retain their sweetness and refinement, they must be educated by women in schools for women and along the lines demanded by women's nature."[23]

The first Catholic colleges and universities to adopt coeducation did so quietly, using "subterfuge" to shield themselves from critical ecclesiastic scrutiny.[24] Marquette University in Milwaukee became the first coeducational Catholic institution when it admitted women religious into its summer program in 1909. Leaders at other institutions followed suit. Yet there continued to be significant resistance to the expansion of coeducation, particularly in the hierarchy. In a 1929 papal encyclical, Pope Pius XI declared that "False also and harmful to Christian education is the so-called method of 'co-education,' founded upon confusion of ideas that mistakes a leveling promiscuity and equality for the legitimate association of the sexes."[25] Wlodimir Ledochowski, S.J., Jesuit superior general from 1915 to 1942, stated that coeducation at undergraduate schools was undesirable and should be a temporary measure until Catholic women's education could be provided. Ledochowski denied permission to several universities to become coeducational, including the University of San Francisco and Gonzaga University. In 1938 he ordered that Spring Hill College be closed rather than admit women to stave off bankruptcy.[26] Like earlier critics of coeducation at Protestant and secular universities, some Catholics worried about the potential for promiscuity in coeducational institutions. Coeducation, one critic wrote, "is equivalent to bringing high explosives closely together and expecting them to fuse. While economic considerations have permitted it to exist in this country, traditionally education has always been conducted on a basis of segregation, except for the elementary years and the graduate and professional schools."[27]

Xavier University in New Orleans was an interesting exception to this ecclesiastic opposition to coeducation. Mary Katherine Drexel, scion of the famed banking family, devoted her life and considerable fortune to the Church. As Drexel's particular interest was the struggles of blacks and Native Americans, she founded a new community of women religious, called the Sisters of Blessed Sacrament for Indian and Colored People, dedicated to their welfare.[28] In 1915 Drexel established Xavier, a coeducational preparatory school for black students, which ten years later received a charter as an undergraduate collegiate program.[29] She received special permission from the apostolic delegate to retain coeducation to educate black Catholics at a time when the Church hierarchy was clearly opposed to it.[30] Xavier has continued to flourish; in the late twentieth century it developed an excellent reputation for its pharmacy and premedical programs and was considered one of the "fastest growing and most successful of the historically black private colleges."[31]

Catholic colleges and universities faced tremendous difficulties during the depression. Largely funded by tuition revenue, colleges scrambled as students left or postponed college because of financial crisis. At Georgetown, for example, nearly half of the student body dropped out between 1929 and 1933. While the number of Catholic women's colleges stayed the same, some Catholic men's colleges turned to coeducation to fend off the problems of fewer students and declining revenues. In 1931, for example, the provincial of the Missouri Province wrote that Marquette University was near bankruptcy and could not afford to bar women from enrollment. Jesuit supporters of coeducation hoped that the General Congregation of 1938 would provide an opportunity to defend coeducation against its opponents. Supporters argued that since women lacked the opportunity for graduate education at Catholic institutions, they would have to pursue their education outside those institutions. In addition, the Executive Committee of the Jesuit Educational Association (JEA), the umbrella organizations of Jesuit institutions, favored coeducation on the grounds that Jesuit education should extend to women, as they "are taking their place alongside of men in important positions of responsibility."[32] The committee also emphasized a more restricted interpretation of the 1929 papal encyclical, recalling that "due regard" was expected to be made "for time and place."

In 1939 the JEA appointed a special commission on coeducation to address the controversial issue. Its report was generally favorable. It cited a joint pastoral letter by American bishops after World War I, which the commission believed spoke favorably about women entering professional fields. The report indicated unanimous approval of coeducation by administrators of Jesuit schools that the committee interviewed. It underscored the concern that educating women in a Catholic school was important for the preservation of piety. At non-Catholic schools, the report stated, women are "exposed to proximate danger of loss of both faith and morals through daily and intimate contact with naturalistic, communistic, atheistic, and generally pagan philosophies which in turn they will pass on to great numbers who come under their sphere of influence."[33]

The commission gave practical guidelines to those institutions considering adapting coeducation, including the appointment of a "competent and thoroughly Catholic woman" as dean of women and the assignment of each female student to a "wise and prudent priest" for spiritual guidance. Opposition to coeducation continued, however. Zachary Maher, the assistant to the Jesuit superior general for United States, criticized the JEA report, arguing that "We Jesuits are not qualified educators of women. It is not our profession, nor are we trained for it. The education of men, which is our real work, is hampered by the presence of women."[34] In 1942, Ledochowski restated his policy that coeducation at undergraduate schools was undesirable and should be temporary until other arrangements could be made.

Postwar Developments in Catholic Higher Education

At the end of World War II, the student population at Catholic colleges and universities increased markedly. Propelled by the same forces that significantly expanded American higher education, such as the G.I. Bill, an expanding economy, and a growing middle class, students flocked to Catholic colleges and universities. As Catholics worked their way up the social ladder, many needed a college degree, which in turn led to the establishment of new Catholic institutions. Between 1945 and 1955, Catholics established twenty-five new colleges and universities.[35]

Catholic higher education was also profoundly affected by fundamental changes in the broad scope of American Catholicism. In what David J. O'Brien labels a "Trinitarian Change," there were three areas of historic transformation in the postwar period: the gradual collapse of the American Catholic subculture, Catholic renewal, and the enormous cultural changes taking place in American society as a whole. For decades Catholics had been an immigrant flock with a somewhat isolated subculture. In the postwar era, Catholics sought to advance into the middle class, which meant living in religiously diverse suburbs. Consequently, they began to lose much of the geographic and cultural isolation that underlay traditional Catholic culture.[36]

The postwar period was also a time of Catholic renewal, in which Church leaders sought to reorient and reinvigorate the means of fulfilling their mission. It was a period of liberalization, and as in most liberal eras, there was tremendous optimism. Catholicism reached new heights of acceptance in the United States, perhaps best symbolized by the election of John F. Kennedy to the presidency in 1960. In Rome, Pope John XXIII convened what is commonly known as Vatican II, which made far-reaching changes to the Church. The council called for greater tolerance toward other religions, declared in favor of human rights, altered the liturgy, and allowed greater autonomy to local churches in the divergent cultures of the world. While most Catholics in America welcomed these changes, many others felt disoriented. Declining attendance in Catholic schools and large numbers of priests and women religious who renounced their vows made some wonder if the Church could sustain its fundamental institutions. From a broader perspective, according to Dolan, the old devotional Catholicism was withering away as the older generation passed, and a new form of "being Catholic" was emerging.[37]

The Church faced further challenges as a new wave of Catholic immigrants, this time from Latin America and East Asia, immigrated to the United States. From 1947 to 1987, the percentage of Americans who identified themselves as Roman Catholic rose from 20 to 28 percent. Projections of current population trends place Catholics at parity with Protestants by the middle of the twenty-first century.[38] This trend also means, however, that the church mission is complicated by ministering to a segment of native-born Catholics, who are on average slightly better educated and more prosperous than Protestants, and to a large, poor immigrant population that still practices devotional Catholicism.

Finally, these changes in American Catholicism were concurrent with and influenced by the tumultuous cultural changes of the 1960s. Catholics were caught up in and divided by the sharp political divisions of that period. With the rise of women's liberation and a new consciousness about gender subordination, many Catholics became unhappy with the exclusion of women from the priesthood and the proscription of artificial birth control. Catholics divided over the Vietnam War. Even when the hierarchy determined in 1971 that the war was unjustifiable, many Catholics, like other Americans, continued to support it. The most contentious issue, still to this day, occurred in 1973 when the U.S. Supreme Court legalized abortion in the *Roe v. Wade* decision. While clerical authority was united in its opposition to abortion and the National Conference of Catholic Bishops made opposition to abortion a high priority, the laity was divided.[39]

What emerged in the wake of these changes was a vastly different Church, with greater diversity in how Catholics practice their faith. Many elderly and millions of immigrants from Catholic countries remain traditional. However, many acculturated middle-class American Catholics have come to practice what is called "cafeteria" Catholicism, in which the faithful select which parts of Church teaching they will follow and which parts they will ignore. In the area of sexuality, for example, most Catholics ignore church teachings that prohibit artificial birth control.[40]

These changes in American Catholicism deeply affected Catholic college life. First, the presence of religion became less pervasive. There were fewer priests and women religious on campus; most colleges reduced the required number of theology courses; and there were numerous other changes made at individual campuses that reflected a more fluid religious devotion. For example, at the University of Scranton, few professors followed the tradition of beginning class with the Lord's Prayer. Mandatory daily mass at Georgetown became voluntary. Students seemed less pious than their predecessors, a trend rued by a 1972 report entitled, "The End of American Catholicism?" Neo-scholasticism, which had for decades provided Catholics with a certainty of faith and reason, fell out of favor.

Coeducation at Catholic Institutions in the Postwar Period

Concurrent with these changes, coeducation in institutions of higher education dramatically expanded. Between 1955 and 1965, the number of Catholic coeducational colleges rose nearly sevenfold, from 38 to 263; nearly half of all students in Catholic colleges were then attending coeducational institutions. The numbers, however, varied according to region. In the Northwest, for example, half of all Catholic colleges were coeducational as early as 1954, but in the more conservative East, opposition to coeducation was much stronger. Nevertheless, the advance of coeducation seriously undermined the traditional gender segregation endemic to Catholic higher education.

There was vocal opposition to coeducation from those most likely to suffer from its spread: Catholic women's colleges. A poll of presidents of Catholic colleges and universities taken in the mid-1960s indicated that there were distinct differences in the attitudes toward coeducation held by leaders of male and female institutions. While the men questioned preferred coeducation by a two-to-one margin, women presidents preferred coordinate and separate education by a two-to-one margin. Leaders of Catholic women's colleges professed concern about the type of education women would receive at a men's school. At a "Workshop on Higher Education" held at the Catholic University in the summer 1950, Sister Honora stated that "men will have to be educated as men; women as women. This means that men's institutions which have been operating as coeducational will either stop accepting women students or treat them justly, that is, will provide them type of education that Catholic educators know women ought to have."[41] This resistance was, of course, a response to the devastating effect that coeducation at men's colleges had on women's colleges. As one women's college president wrote: "The problem seems basically to devolve upon the old question—what becomes of the women's college? In most cases of mergers, the women's colleges becomes submersed [sic] by the stronger men's institution. Our college is presently at a crisis. A nearby man's college plans to become coeducational. This means either we 'join or perish' and yet in the liberal arts department we are much superior."[42]

As in the rest of higher education, there was a rush toward coeducation in the late 1960s and early 1970s. Numerous Catholic institutions, including Boston College, Georgetown, and Notre Dame, opened their doors to women. There were several reasons for the sudden change. First, many institutions were in financial crisis and needed to expand their student bodies in order to sustain their expanding physical plants and rising academic ambitions. The admission of women would allow this while maintaining and in many cases improving the quality of the student body. Second, in an era of rising awareness of racial and gender inequity in society, the exclusion of women seemed outdated. Third, some faculty who were increasingly restive over university governance issues wanted their daughters to be able to attend their institutions. Fourth, administrators were aware of a growing student preference for a coeducational environment. Finally, ecclesiastic opposition to the spread of coeducation disappeared. Jesuit universities were in the process of disincorporation, whereby the university was legally separated from control of the Jesuit community, and new lay-dominated boards were instituted. In the postconciliar spirit, there is no evidence of Jesuit opposition to coeducation.[43]

The admission of women to formerly-male Catholic colleges has brought profound changes to campus life. Prior to coeducation, gender segregation had been a pervasive part of Catholic education. Girded by physical separation, a highly gendered ideology, and an in loco parentis system intended in part to restrict contact with the other sex, women and men students previously lived in an environment that reminded them daily of their prescribed gender roles. Coeducation, together with the destruction of the in loco parentis system, undermined the traditional environment. Like many changes in history, the new student culture that allowed greater student freedom and more open and active sexuality was an unanticipated result. When educators pressed for coeducation in the mid-1960s, none foresaw the dramatic transformation of campus culture.

From a broader perspective, coeducation was part of a larger process of acculturation of American Catholicism. The adoption of coeducation by the vast majority of Catholic colleges and universities has meant that it has lost one of its most distinctive features: gender segregation. Catholic students today reside in a campus environment not very different from state, Protestant, and private secular universities. Indeed, students today are often surprised at how different their campus culture is from just 40 years ago. These profound changes in gender relations, combined with other factors, have prompted many Catholics to ponder what it is that makes their efforts distinctly Catholic. Over the past several decades, there has been a decline in the number of priests and women religious on Catholic campuses, institutions have reduced the traditionally heavy requirements in theology and religious studies, mandatory mass has been eliminated, many of the faculty are non-Catholic, and more of the students are non-Catholic. While in the past decade enrollment in Catholic higher education has expanded by nearly 20 percent, some ask what distinguishes the Catholic college or university?

Development of Black Colleges and Universities

The history of black colleges and universities is somewhat similar to the history of Catholic colleges. Discrimination faced by both blacks and Catholics was an important factor in the development of their own institutions of higher education. An additional motivation for Catholics, particularly at first, was to protect the religious faith of their students. In contrast, an additional motivation for blacks was "race uplift." Black Americans realized that without education, they could not hope to overcome the degradations of slavery.

Few black Americans had educational opportunities of any sort before the Civil War. Many southern states made it illegal to teach slaves to read and write because literacy was believed to cause insurrections.[44] When opportunities arose, however, blacks showed great determination to learn as the belief was strong that only through education could they advance. Some blacks who lived in the free states did attend school, while others, at great risks to themselves, operated illegal schools in southern states before and during the Civil War.[45]

Only a very small number of blacks managed to be admitted to institutions of higher education prior to the Civil War, mostly to Oberlin but also in isolated cases to such colleges as Bowdoin and Middlebury. Before 1840, it is estimated that only 15 blacks (all men) had received any higher education.[46] The first two African-American women who received bachelor's degrees, both from Oberlin, were Mary Jane Patterson in 1862 and Fanny Jackson in 1865.[47] Most black colleges were founded after the Civil War, with notable exceptions being two colleges north of the Mason and Dixon line: Lincoln University in Chester County, Pennsylvania, which was founded by Presbyterians in 1854 as Ashmun Institute for the training of male missionaries to Africa (see Chapter 4), and Wilberforce University in Ohio, which was founded by the Methodists in 1856.[48]

Beginning in 1860, northern benevolent societies; denominational bodies, including the prominent American Missionary Association (AMA) of the Congregational Church; black churches; and the Freedmen's Bureau worked to establish black colleges for the education of liberated slaves.[49] Women from northern states were particularly likely to respond with missionary zeal to the need for teachers for former slaves. It has been estimated that about four-fifths of the more than 7,000 teachers in freedmen's schools between 1861 and 1875 were women.[50]

Given former slaves' needs for basic education, many of the "colleges" represented their founders' hopes for the future more than actual institutions of higher education.[51] Typically, the colleges devoted most of their resources to secondary and even primary education. Even as late as 1900, for example, about 40 percent of total enrollment in black institutions was precollegiate, compared to about 25 percent of all students in American colleges.[52]

Black Americans were determined to obtain an education despite formidable obstacles, as they saw education as an important part of the movement for "self-help."[53] Southern communities were hostile to the idea of former slaves being educated and threatened black schools and their students.[54] Not only did blacks face waves of violence, some initiated by the newly organized Ku Klux Klan, but students also found it very difficult to raise the money for schooling.

Nonetheless, institutions such as Fisk enjoyed high enrollments immediately on opening, due to blacks' "extraordinary thirst for knowledge."[55] And yet the schools' facilities were, on the whole, extremely primitive. Freedmen were educated in abandoned barracks, barns, and hastily constructed shelters. They had few books, and teachers had to act as social workers as well as instructors.[56]

Federal legislation, in particular the two Morrill land grant acts, benefited black higher education. The first act in 1862 said nothing about education of blacks, but three states—Virginia, South Carolina, and Mississippi—used some of the money they received to support institutions for blacks' agricultural and mechanical education. Virginia allocated about one-third of its grant to Hampton Institute.[57] The Morrill Act of 1890 gave specific federal encouragement to black colleges by its stipulation that states would not receive funds for their tax-supported "land grant" institutions unless they provided equivalent education for Blacks. Rather than establishing racially integrated colleges, many southern states created separate institutions for blacks, not surprisingly as this was around the time of the *Plessy v. Ferguson* Supreme Court ruling that validated the "separate but equal" doctrine. Black land grant colleges were not equal, however, but suffered from inadequate funding and the pressure to provide only industrial training. Yet they fared much better, financially, than the AMA-supported black institutions. In 1890, for instance, 14 land grant colleges received almost $250,000, compared to $175,000 for 20 of the AMA's largest schools.[58]

Almost all the early black colleges were coeducational, in contrast to southern white educational institutions, which opposed coeducation "vociferously."[59] Blacks favored coeducation in part because, like white institutions in the Midwest, limited financial support made single-sex institutions an unaffordable luxury. As historian Glenda Gilmore vividly expressed it in *Gender and Jim Crow,* "At a time when mother, father, and toddlers learned in the same classroom, the southern white norm of single-sex institutions was out of the question."[60] Another important reason that the black community supported coeducation was that it fit into their "evangelically driven ethos of 'usefulness,' " which meant that women were to be educated for serious public roles, in contrast to the "ornamental" education of most southern white women of the time.[61] As early as the 1830s when slavery had been abolished in northern states, articles in the black press encouraged women to become educated to help improve the race.[62] This "race uplift" theme continued to be viewed as more of women's responsibility than men's. Education and marriage were not viewed as incompatible, and women's need to earn an income was widely recognized. Only during the brief period of Reconstruction after the Civil War did some prominent black leaders endorse the idea of separate spheres, saying that black women, like white women, should be educated for motherhood.[63]

Industrial Education vs. the Liberal Arts

As Reconstruction ended and the Freedmen's Bureau closed, the situation for black higher education became dire. Some black leaders, most famously Booker T. Washington, acceded to the pressures to lessen antagonism with southern communities by focusing not on integration or liberal arts education but rather by promoting segregation and education that prepared blacks for manual labor and service jobs.[64] Washington implemented his educational views as the principal of Tuskegee Institute, which opened in 1881 and, along with Hampton, became famous for its vocational curriculum. Within institutes of industrial education (not only at Hampton and Tuskegee, but after 1880, at Central Tennessee College, Clark University, Claflin University, and other institutions), men and women learned different trades. Women, for example, could study nursing or sewing, whereas men might learn farming or carpentry.[65] Industrial education led to disadvantages for women because it took money away from teacher training programs where women predominated. In North Carolina, for example, whites closed four black state normal schools and established industrial programs for men at the remaining three schools.[66]

Not all blacks agreed with Booker T. Washington that industrial education, supported by many rich and powerful whites, was the only realistic form of education for blacks. W. E. B. Du Bois was the most outspoken critic of Washington's views. Du Bois, who had received a Ph.D. from Harvard, believed that progress depended on blacks being led by a "talented tenth" that had rigorous, classical education. Du Bois was not opposed to vocational education, however, for those students who wanted it or who were unable to pursue academic programs.[67] Although Du Bois did not have as extensive a political network as Washington, he made his views heard through his prolific writings and as editor of the journal *Crisis,* the official journal of the National Association for the Advancement of Colored People (NAACP), from 1910 to 1934.[68]

The years between 1895 and 1917 were a time of "starvation" for black liberal arts colleges.[69] Industrial philanthropists favored vocational education for blacks, as they believed such programs were "the fundamental solution to the race problem."[70] A key survey of black higher education, conducted in 1916 by the Phelps-Stokes Fund and published a year later by the U.S. Bureau of Education, concluded that "inadequacy and poverty are the outstanding characteristics of every type and grade of education for Negroes in the United States."[71] The survey found black institutions to be poorly equipped, ineffectively organized, and needing to devote many of their resources to secondary education since less than 3 percent of their students were of true college grade. The report favored industrial education because it was considered to be "best adapted to the great majority of the colored people at the present time."[72] A significant result of the report was increased support for black colleges from such important philanthropies as the General Education Board and the Julius

Rosenwald Fund, as well as more state support.[73] Not surprisingly, given the bias of the Phelps-Stoke report and northern industrialists toward industrial education, in 1926–27 the endowment of the two major industrial education institutes, Tuskegee and Hampton, was over $14 million, whereas that of remaining 77 black schools was only about $6.5 million.[74]

Black Women's Involvement in Higher Education

From the beginning, black women were involved in black colleges as students and as faculty. Wilberforce had women teachers from its opening in 1856; one of its most famous women faculty members was the writer and activist, Mary Church Terrell, who taught there for a few years after her graduation from Oberlin in 1884. Another Oberlin graduate, Helen Morgan, joined the Fisk University faculty in 1869 and remained for 38 years as a professor of Latin, refusing to take Vassar's offer of a higher salary. She is credited as being one of the first women in the country to attain the rank of full professor at a coeducational institution.[75] Fisk also had at least three black women teachers, all alumnae of Fisk, between 1870 and 1900.[76] Similarly, Livingstone College in Salisbury, North Carolina, controlled and financed by the African Methodist Episcopal Zion Church, had women and men on its faculty. When it opened in 1880 its first student was a woman. Moreover, two women were among the ten students to receive the first bachelor's degrees awarded by the college in 1888, making black women the first women in North Carolina to earn bachelor's degrees.[77]

The white and black communities both considered higher education of black women to be critical, although their reasons were different. White Americans believed black women were promiscuous and therefore needed education to make them fit to be the moral leaders of their families; black Americans wanted women to be educated in order for them to be able to take jobs, particularly as teachers, that would contribute to family income and would put them beyond the sexual predations of white men.[78] Nonetheless, until the twentieth century, fewer black women than black men graduated from college; through 1890, only 30 black women in the century had earned baccalaureate degrees, compared to more than 300 black men.[79] But this changed rapidly, so that fairly early on in the twentieth century, the number of black women with college degrees equaled and then exceeded the number of black men.[80] By 1935, women constituted 57 percent of the total enrollment of close to 30,000 in private and public black institutions; their majority was greater in public institutions (about 61 percent of about 12,600) than in private institutions (53.5 percent of about 16,600).[81]

Within HBCUs, women received stern, paternalistic messages, holding them to high moral standards and encouraging them to consider the needs of their communities for "racial uplift."[82] For women to obtain and succeed in professions like teaching, it was believed that they would have to be "extremely circumspect and never give even the slightest hint of impropriety."[83] To be respectable, women were expected to be skillful and hard working at domestic tasks, too. In other words, women were to succeed in both the private and public spheres, all the time mindful of how they would be viewed by and useful to the larger community. The stress on controlling women's social lives at black colleges, including extensive chaperonage and dress regulations, meant that they had less freedom than women students at white colleges.[84] Even as late as 1933, when the dean of women at Howard, Lucy Slowe, conducted a study of black colleges, fewer than 50 percent gave women opportunity for self-government.[85]

Demands of the "New Negro"

In the early decades of the twentieth century, but particularly after World War I when blacks returned from "the war to make the world safe for democracy," black students began to protest the lack of black control over their collegiate institutions and programs of study. Their militancy was an important part of a larger black movement for equality and racial justice that was motivated, in part, by veterans being less willing to accept the racism in the United States after they had received more equal treatment in Europe during the war.[86] As racial repression increased and southerners attempted to prevent blacks from migrating to the North where there were labor shortages, major race riots occurred, including those during the "Red Summer" of 1919. The Marcus Garvey black nationalist movement, the more liberal black press, and the Harlem Renaissance, were other signs of the "new Negro" who rejected compromise and instead sought self-determination.[87]

Although the student protests did not always result immediately in the appointment of blacks to the administration, trustees, or faculty, they did ultimately encourage that development. At Fisk, for example, the trustees approved having alumni representation in 1926, one year after a famous student strike, and the first black dean was appointed in 1927.[88] Not until 1946, however, did a black become president of Fisk—the internationally known scholar, Professor Charles Johnson.[89]

One ironic consequence of the segregation of the Jim Crow era was that in black state colleges founded around World War I, there were only black faculty and administrators. White southerners would not take positions in these institutions, and there was opposition to having northerners teach. Some states even made it illegal for white people to teach in publicly supported black institutions; Florida maintained such a law until 1941.[90]

Consolidation and the Reinforcement of Coeducation

From their beginnings, black colleges have been underfunded, but at certain times and places institutions' financial problems have become so severe that their demise seemed inevitable. Some of the characteristics of HBCUs can be understood as a consequence of colleges' attempts to survive. The temptation to develop a vocational curriculum, for example, was great given the willingness of northern philanthropists and southern states to support such programs, as discussed above. In fact, some institutions may have claimed to be "agricultural and mechanical schools," when their curriculum was actually more academic, in an attempt to obtain needed monetary support.[91] Financial problems, during the Great Depression especially, also led to the consolidation of colleges and sometimes as part of that process, the change from single-sex to coeducation.

Reducing the total number of black colleges and strengthening the remainder seemed sensible as a means of achieving accreditation, which as early as the 1890s had begun to be important in higher education. Black colleges were not taken seriously by accrediting agencies until 1928 when the southern association rated them separately.[92] Consolidation was also favored by philanthropic organizations, which concentrated their donations on a few select institutions and urged the development of "university centers" in several southern cities. The first plan was drawn up in Atlanta in 1929 for a "university college" consisting of Spelman, Morehouse, and Atlanta University. Other consolidations included those in New Orleans and Nashville.[93]

Before 1900 only whites had founded single-sex institutions of higher education for blacks. Two white women founded Spelman College in Atlanta in 1881, for example, for the education of black women. But by 1900 influential black men were establishing institutions just for men, and in response some black women established educational institutions for women. Mary McLeod Bethune, for instance, established a school for black girls in 1904 in Daytona, Florida. As part of the consolidation movement, it merged with Cookman College (for men) in 1923, becoming a four-year liberal arts institution.[94] In 1928 the U.S. Bureau of Education reported that there were only seven black institutions that were not coeducational: four for men (Morehouse, Johnson C. Smith University, Lincoln University in Pennsylvania, and the Agricultural and Technical College in Greensboro, North Carolina) and three for women (Spelman, Barber, and Bennett).[95] The consolidation movement also affected the oldest institution for the education of black women, Barber-Scotia College in Concord, North Carolina, which had originally been a seminary for black girls. In 1932 it became affiliated with Johnson C. Smith University in Charlotte.[96]

Education Trends for Black Americans after World War II

Three major changes in higher education for black Americans occurred after World War II. The most dramatic development was the large increase in the numbers of black students who attended predominantly white institutions (PWIs), the majority in northern states. Other trends included more black administrators in predominantly black institutions (PBIs), and more black professors in white colleges.[97] These trends fit with large cultural changes, including the growth of the black middle class, northern migration of blacks that peaked in the 1950s, greater cultural recognition of black achievements in literature and other fields, and greater sensitivity of the U.S. government of its need, as a world power, to demonstrate its fairness to all its citizens.

The increase in the number of black students attending predominantly white institutions was given particular impetus by the 1954 Supreme Court ruling *Brown v. Board of Education,* which outlawed segregated schools.[98] In the 1930s, 85 percent of black students were enrolled in PBIs, mostly in the South; by 1970, 75 percent were attending PWIs, including once legally segregated schools in the South.[99]

These enrollment trends created difficulties for HBCUs. Despite increases in financial support for southern black institutions from such philanthropic organizations as the Ford Foundation, and despite the improvement in academic programs at privately supported black colleges, a 1976 Carnegie Commission report noted that these institutions had lost some of their best students to predominantly white national colleges and universities.[100] They had also lost their most able faculty and scholars. These developments led the report to conclude that southern black colleges were "likely to remain at the bottom of the educational ladder, providing compensatory education for the disadvantaged."[101]

A different view of the role of black colleges was suggested by their increases in enrollment between 1966 and 1973, from about 138,000 to 163,500.[102] Even more telling is that in 1972, 52.2 percent of bachelor's degrees earned by black Americans were at HBCUs, even though only 35 percent of black college students were enrolled in them. Many black students in PWIs were in 2-year colleges. So from this perspective, HBCUs were still the " 'backbone' of the black academic community."[103]

Moving into Twenty-First Century

By the end of the twentieth century, there were more than 2.5 million living black Americans with college degrees. Black women continued to predominate in higher education, so that in terms of enrollment, nearly 63 percent of all African Americans enrolled in colleges and universities were women; black women earned 58 percent of all master's degrees and 54 percent of all professional degrees.[104] Explanations for these trends point to the conditions of inner cities—their chaotic schools, drug abuse, crime, violence, and lack of role models—which have greater effects on men than on women. Some argue that racial discrimination in employment is also more intense against black men, as corporate management tends to see black men as "more threatening" than black women. Such discrimination lowers black men's self-esteem and their educational aspirations.[105]

Black colleges still struggle with underfunding. Major federal agencies gave more than $1.5 billion in federal research grants to five universities in 1990, for example, but less than $330 million to historically black colleges.[106] Black colleges are overrepresented among colleges that accrediting agencies place on probation for financial problems.[107] The need to become "more aggressive in seeking federal funds for research and development from Congress" is the declared aim of Frederick Humphries, who in January 2002 became the president of the National Association for Equal Opportunity in Higher Education, which represents 117 historically black and predominantly black colleges and universities.[108]

Desegregation remains an issue at southern state educational institutions. The most famous lawsuit, the Ayers case, originated in 1975 with a father seeking equal educational opportunity for his son at historically black Jackson State University in Mississippi. In recent years, however, black institutions have been under pressure to integrate their student bodies. A 1992 Supreme Court ruling on the Ayers case, *United States v. Kirk Fordice* (Fordice was a Mississippi governor), required 11 states to remove policies and practices that keep public colleges racially identifiable. Most attempts to get white students to enroll in historically black institutions have not been very successful. In some states, such as Alabama, attempts to attract whites to black institutions have included lowering the required grade point average for white students to receive scholarships. Such policies to achieve diversity have made officials at black colleges worried that they will lose their distinctive mission. Black enrollments at historically white state universities have increased; in fall 2000, for example, blacks at Mississippi's flagship institution, the University of Mississippi's main campus, constituted more than 12 percent of the student body, and the percentages were higher at the state's less prestigious PWIs. White enrollment at the historically black universities in Mississippi has remained very low, however, less than 5 percent.[109]

Discrimination and prejudice continue to affect black students on and off campus. In the early 1990s, a spate of "ugly racial incidents" occurred on a number of college campuses across the United States. At the same time, researchers found declining support among whites for race-targeted social policies. Times of retrenchment and financial constraints, which typified the early 1990s, tend to result in "a dilution of higher education's commitment to Blacks and other minorities."[110]

Justifications for Black Colleges and Universities Today

While many people might believe that predominantly black colleges and universities are unnecessary given legally mandated integration, the persistence of racism means that black institutions still have a "special mission." Black students on white campuses report experiencing isolation, alienation, and a lack of support. On historically black campuses, on the other hand, black students feel a sense of "empowerment/ownership—a sense that 'this is our campus.' " Various researchers report finding that despite the lower social class family backgrounds and poorer academic records of black students who attend PBIs in comparison to those who attend PWIs, the former do better in terms of persistence rates, academic performance, involvement in campus activities, and occupational aspirations. Like everyone else, in other words, black students do better in environments where they feel "protected, accepted, and socially connected."[111]

Black colleges' "special mission" is also manifest in their willingness to enroll students who otherwise might not be able to attend college because of social, financial, or academic weaknesses.[112] Unlike white institutions where such factors tend to reinforce a "presumption of inferiority," one of the "most persistent barriers to minority achievement," black institutions are more likely to see these student characteristics as amenable to correction.[113]

The importance of black institutions continues beyond undergraduate work. For example, Meharry, one of the country's four black medical schools, *each year* graduates 15 percent of all blacks who earn degrees in medicine, dentistry, and biomedical sciences. A 1998 study showed that 40 percent of all black physicians and dentists in practice in the United States had graduated from Meharry. Enrollment at Meharry in 2000–2001 was predominantly female; in medicine and dentistry, 51 percent of the students were women; 71 percent of the Ph.D. students were women, as well as 60 percent of those in the M.A. program and 80 percent of students in the school of allied health.[114]

Some research indicates that attending a black institution may be even more important for black men than for black women. A study of 870 black men and women who attended three PBIs and four PWIs in Atlanta found that black women in PWIs do better than black men in PWIs in terms of intellectual adjustment and perceived changes in themselves and freedom from traditional sex-role constraints. Yet attending white colleges was not easy for either sex. Both women and men in black schools showed better intellectual adjustment than their counterparts in white schools. Black women on either type of campus, however, were "anxious about their own competence." The black women set lower goals for themselves than the men did, even though their academic performance was better. Overall, the study found that passivity was black women's major problem, but it was easier for them to be assertive on white campuses where there were fewer black men around.[115]

A more recent study concluded that historically black women's colleges produce the largest proportion of successful women, up to six times greater than the mean for historically black coeducational institutions and up to ten times greater than mean for predominantly white women's colleges. Lowest of all in terms of producing successful black women are predominantly white coeducational institutions.[116] Such findings demonstrate the continuing need for "special focus colleges." They do more for their students even though they receive substantially less support than more prestigious institutions.[117]

At least one analyst believes that women's "plight" on black coeducational campuses is "dismal." This researcher has written that most black women academics find the "attitudes of black male colleagues in black institutions" to be "sexist." It may well be significant that at least until the early 1990s, only 5 of 116 black colleges in the country had women's studies programs or women's centers.[118]

Catholic and Black Institutions Compared

Black colleges and Catholic colleges both have played important roles for their constituencies. They enabled black and Catholic Americans to obtain higher education when many institutions refused them admission. Even when colleges and universities began to accept Catholics and, much later, blacks, both groups saw reasons to continue their own system of higher education. Catholics wanted to retain separate institutions in order to preserve a particular religious, often conservative, value system. Blacks wanted their own institutions because they knew that members of their community experienced deleterious effects of racism at PWIs. Black institutions have also been willing to admit and give special support to students who would not be accepted at mainstream institutions.

In terms of their histories of coeducation, however, black and Catholic colleges are very different. The black community has been eager to educate both men and women as part of a desire for race uplift. Women's work, particularly as teachers, was accepted and not seen as conflicting with their maternal role. Due to this ideology and the need to use meager financial resources as efficiently as possible, almost all black colleges were coeducational from their beginnings. Catholics, in contrast, had a traditional view of women's roles that stressed the importance of women's staying in the home to raise children. Early Catholic institutions were for men only. Catholic women's education received a much lower priority; even when Catholic women's colleges were established at the end of the nineteenth century, the curriculum was often practical rather than rigorously academic. Not until the mid-twentieth century did many Catholic institutions become coeducational.

By examining two groups of higher educational institutions that have somewhat different histories from predominantly white, secular colleges and universities, it is possible to see how the larger culture affects all educational institutions but to a greater or lesser extent and at different periods of time. Black colleges became coeducational earlier than many white institutions because of the beliefs and needs of the black community. In the late 1960s, when many other formerly men's institutions were just becoming coeducational, black colleges faced a different threat: the loss of some of their most academically able students to PWIs. One of the only remaining black men's colleges, Lincoln University in Pennsylvania, discussed in Chapter 4 of this volume, became coeducational at that time as an attempt to maintain or even increase enrollments of academically able students. Catholic colleges, in contrast, resisted coeducation for a long time, preferring to establish women's colleges in addition to men's colleges. In the late 1960s, however, Catholic institutions were challenged by the loss of a large, traditional, conservative Catholic subculture; the increase in secularism; and cultural preferences for coeducation. Survival did not seem possible for many all-male Catholic colleges; admitting women boosted enrollments, finances, and usually academic standing.

The case studies that follow show how formerly men's colleges of varying types became coeducational and how women have fared in the process. We begin with University of Rochester, which has a complicated history with respect to coeducation, having been a men's institution, a coeducational university, a coordinate men's and women's institution, and finally a coeducational institution again at the relatively early year of 1952.

Notes

1. For examples of how quotas affected the enrollments of Catholics, as well as Jews, blacks, and women, at several institutions, see Marcia Graham Synnott, *The Half-Opened Door: Discrimination and Admissions at Harvard, Yale and Princeton, 1900–1970* (Westport, Conn.: Greenwood Press, 1979), and Harvey Strum, "Discrimination at Syracuse University," *History of Higher Education* 4 (1984): 102–3.

2. Michael J. James, Associate Executive Director, Association of Catholic Colleges and Universities, e-mail communication to Susan L. Poulson, June 9, 2003; source: Higher Education Research Institute, UCLA.

3. Robert Emmett Curran, S.J., *From Academy to University, 1789–1889*, vol. 1 of *The Bicentennial History of Georgetown University* (Washington, D.C.: Georgetown University Press, 1993), 1–56.

4. Jay P. Dolan, *The American Catholic Experience: A History from Colonial Times to the Present* (Garden City, N.Y.: Doubleday, 1985), 107.

5. David Mitchell, *The Jesuits: A History* (New York: Franklin Watts, 1981).

6. James W. Sauve, S.J., "Jesuit Higher Education Worldwide," in *Jesuit Higher Education: Essays on the American Tradition of Excellence*, ed. Rolando E. Bonachea (Pittsburgh:

Duquesne University Press, 1989), 161–63, cited by James Tunstead Burtchaell, *The Dying of the Light: The Disengagement of Colleges and Universities from their Christian Churches* (Grand Rapids, Mich.: William B. Eerdmans, 1998), 566.

7. Edward J. Power, *Catholic Higher Education in America: A History* (New York: Appleton-Century-Crofts, 1972), 42–43.

8. Daniel Rice, "A Plea for Higher Education and for Macalester and Albert Lea Colleges" (pamphlet), 1882, 5; C. Harve Geiger, *The Program of Higher Education of the Presbyterian Church in the United States of America: An Historical Analysis of Its Growth in the United States* (Cedar Rapids, Iowa: Laurance Press, 1940), 59, cited in Burtchaell, 572.

9. "Notices of the Papal Church in the United States," *Quarterly Review* 2, no. 7 (February 1830): 189–99, cited in Burtchaell, 572.

10. A historic moment took place at Georgetown University in 2001, when the first non-cleric assumed the presidency of a Jesuit institution.

11. Power, 85.

12. Dolan, 221–39.

13. Philip Gleason, *Contending with Modernity: Catholic Higher Education in the Twentieth Century* (New York: Oxford University Press, 1995), 11.

14. J. L. Spalding, "Woman and the Higher Education," in *Opportunity and Other Essays* (1900; reprint, Freeport, N.Y.: Essay Index Reprint Series, Books for Libraries Press, 1968), 58, cited by Mary J. Oates, C.S.J., "The Development of Catholic Colleges for Women, 1895–1960," in *U.S. Catholic Historian* 7, no. 4 (1988): 414.

15. Martin E. Marty, *A Short History of American Catholicism* (Allen, Texas: Thomas More, 1995), 134.

16. Power, 302–17; Oates, 414–16.

17. Kathleen A. Mahoney, "American Colleges for Women: Historical Origins," in Schier, Tracy and Cynthia Russett, eds. *Catholic Women's Colleges in America* (Baltimore and London: Johns Hopkins University Press, 2002), 26. Oates, 414–16. Quote is from "Prospectus: Trinity College (for the Higher Education of Women)" Washington, D.C., 1899, Trinity College Archives.

18. Power, 304.

19. Oates, 416–19.

20. Ibid., 422–23.

21. Power, 340–50.

22. Philip Gleason, *Keeping the Faith: American Catholicism Past and Present* (Notre Dame, Ind.: University of Notre Dame Press, 1987), 167.

23. Thomas Ewing Sherman, Rev., "Higher Education of Catholic Women," in "Report of the Proceedings and Addresses of the Third Annual Meeting: Catholic Educational Association," The Association's Secretary's Office, Columbus, Ohio, 1906, 94-95, cited by Donald H. Winandy, "Catholic Educational Leaders on Coeducation in Institutions of Higher Education Affiliated with the Roman Catholic Church in the United States of America," (Ph.D. diss., Florida State University, 1968), 32.

24. William Leahy, "Jesuits, Catholics and Higher Education in Twentieth Century America" (Ph.D. diss., Stanford University, 1986), 82–83.

25. Pius XI, "Christian Education of Youth," in *Five Great Encyclicals* (New York: Paulist Press, 1939), cited in Winandy, 56–57.

26. "Letters of Fr. Ledochowski," box 15, Jesuit Education Association Collection, Boston College Archives (hereafter referred to as JEA); cited in Leahy, 144.

27. William F. Cunningham, *Pivotal Problems of Education* (New York: Macmillan, 1940), 185, cited in Winandy, 11.

28. Historically, there have been comparatively few black Catholics. Today, while nearly one-third percent of all Americans are Catholic, only 3 percent of Catholics are black. The religious affiliations of most blacks were established during slavery, when slaves tended to adopt the prevailing religion in their community. Catholicism became a powerful force in America after this period of religious formation and was influential only where Catholic immigrants settled, mostly along the Eastern seaboard and in the Midwest, where there was a small black population until after World War I. See George Gallup Jr. and Jim Castelli, *The American Catholic People: Their Beliefs, Practices, and Values* (Garden City, N.Y.: Doubleday, 1987), 121–23.

29. Henry N. Drewry and Humphrey Doermann, *Stand and Prosper: Private Black Colleges and Their Students* (Princeton: Princeton University Press, 2001), 174.

30. James J. Kenneally, *History of American Catholic Women* (New York: Crossroads, 1990), 56.

31. Drewry and Doermann, 173.

32. "Concerning the Admission of Women to Our Colleges and Universities," supplement to the minutes of the JEA Executive Committee meeting, December 12–13, 1937, Loyola University, Chicago, "Education #6," drawer 74, Archives of the California Province of the Society of Jesus, Los Gatos, Calif., cited in Leahy, 153.

33. Jesuit Education Association, "Report of the Commission on Coeducation," February 12, 1940, section D2b, JEA; quoted in Leahy, 35.

34. Ibid., quoted in Loretta P. Higgins, "The Development of Coeducation at Boston College" (Ph.D. diss., Boston College, 1986), 35.

35. For a comprehensive list of Catholic institutions of higher education in the United States, see Burtchaell, 557–61.

36. See David J. O'Brien, *From the Heart of the American Church: Catholic Higher Education and American Culture* (Maryknoll, N.Y.: Orbis Books, 1994), 21–34.

37. See "A New Catholicism" in Dolan, 421–54.

38. George Gallup and Jim Castelli, *The American Catholic People: Their Beliefs, Practices and Values* (Garden City: Doubleday, 1987), 2.

39. Ibid., 90–100.

40. Ibid., 6.

41. Sister M. Honora, "Integration of Catholic Education for Men and Women," in *Integration in Catholic Colleges and Universities,* ed. Roy J. Deferrari (Washington, D.C.: Catholic University of America Press, 1950), 322, quoted in Winandy, "Catholic Educational Leaders," 11.

42. Winandy, "Catholic Educational Leaders," 130. Winandy does not cite the source for this quote.

43. See Chapter 9 in this volume, "A Religious and a Public University: The Transitions to Coeducation at Georgetown and Rutgers Universities."

44. Jeanne L. Noble, *The Negro Woman's College Education* (New York: Teachers College, Columbia University, 1956), 17.

45. Drewry and Doermann, 39.

46. Noble, 17.

47. Linda M. Perkins, "The Education of Black Women in the Nineteenth Century," in *Women and Higher Education in American History*, ed. John Mack and Florence Howe (New York: Norton, 1988), 70.

48. John Brubacher and Willis Rudy, *Higher Education in Transition*, 3d ed. (New Brunswick, NJ: Transaction, 1997), 74. In 1863 Wilberforce was taken over by the African Methodist Episcopalian church, making it the earliest black-controlled institution of higher education. See James D. Anderson, *The Education of Blacks in the South, 1860–1935* (Chapel Hill: University of North Carolina Press, 1988), 240.

49. The Freedmen's Bureau was technically called the Bureau of Refugees, Freedmen and Abandoned Lands. President Johnson established it in 1865, but it was not until 1867 that Congress was able to override Johnson's veto and appropriate about a half million dollars to the bureau for educational purposes. See Dwight Oliver Wendell Holmes, *The Evolution of the Negro College* (New York: Arno, 1969), 35–38.

50. Ronald E. Butchart, "The Real Heroes of their Age: The Freedmen's Teachers," Presidential Address, History of Education Society, Yale University, October 20, 2001.

51. Thomas Jesse Jones, *Negro Education: A Study of the Private and Higher Schools for Colored People in the United States* (1916; reprint, New York: Arno Press, 1969), 11.

52. Anderson, 249.

53. Perkins, 66.

54. Such hostility was not limited to southern communities. Riots occurred in Connecticut and New Jersey over attempts to start schools for blacks; in New Hampshire, a black schoolhouse was hauled off into a swamp. See Ruth Danenhower Wilson, "Negro Colleges of Liberal Arts," *American Scholar* 19 (1950): 461–70.

55. Joe M. Richardson, *A History of Fisk University, 1865–1946* (Tuscaloosa: University of Alabama Press, 1980), 8.

56. Holmes, 93.

57. See ibid., 151, and George S. Dickerman, "History of Negro Education," in *Negro Education: A Study of the Private and Higher Schools for Colored People in the United States* (1916; reprint, New York: Arno, 1969), 259.

58. Dickerman, 260.

59. Glenda Elizabeth Gilmore, *Gender and Jim Crow: Women and the Politics of White Supremacy in North Carolina, 1896–1920* (Chapel Hill: University of North Carolina Press, 1996), 37.

60. Ibid., 36.

61. Ibid., 36–37.

62. Perkins, 69.

63. Ibid., 76.

64. Brubacher and Rudy, 76.

65. Holmes, 112.

66. Gilmore, 141.

67. Drewry and Doermann, 65.

68. Ibid. Of special note is Du Bois's essay in *The Souls of Black Folk* (1903), "Of Mr. Booker T. Washington and Others."

69. Wilson, 464.
70. Anderson, 272.
71. Jones, 9.
72. Ibid., 260.
73. Holmes, 14.
74. Ibid., 185.
75. Richardson, 21.
76. Ibid., 51.
77. Gilmore, 39–40.
78. See Elizabeth L. Ihle, "Black Women's Education in the South: The Dual Burdens of Sex and Race," in *Changing Education,* ed. Joyce Antler and Sari Knopp Biklen (Albany: State University of New York Press, 1990), and Stephanie J. Shaw, *What a Woman Ought To Be and To Do: Black Professional Workers During the Jim Crow Era* (Chicago: University of Chicago Press, 1996), 14.
79. Perkins, 76–78.
80. Jeanne Noble, "The Higher Education of Black Women in the Twentieth Century," in *Women and Higher Education in American History,* ed. John Mack Faragher and Florence Howe (New York: Norton, 1988).
81. Anderson, 275.
82. Ihle, 73; Noble, "Higher Education," 92.
83. Shaw, 14.
84. Ibid., 87.
85. Noble, "Higher Education," 93, 160–161.
86. Anderson, 263.
87. Ibid.; Raymond Wolters, *The New Negro on Campus: Black College Rebellions of the 1920s* (Princeton: Princeton University Press, 1975).
88. Richardson, 103.
89. Ibid., 135.
90. Wilson, 465.
91. Drewry and Doermann, 64.
92. Anderson, 250.
93. Amy Thompson McCandless, *The Past in the Present: Women's Higher Education in the Twentieth-Century American South* (Tuscaloosa: University of Alabama Press, 1999), 179–80.
94. Ibid., 41; Perkins, 81.
95. Arthur J. Klein, "Survey of Negro Colleges and Universities," Department of the Interior, Bureau of Education, 1928, 53.
96. Holmes, 134; McCandless, 180.
97. John Hope Franklin, *From Slavery to Freedom,* 4th ed. (New York: Knopf, 1974), 418.
98. Before the 1954 ruling, in the 1930s, blacks had brought lawsuits in their attempts to get into professional schools. The Supreme Court ruled in 1938 that provision had to be made within the state for legal education for blacks (ibid., 419). In the late 1940s, due to the Supreme Court ruling that equal public education must be offered to black and white students, Southern legislators were examining the programs at their black state

colleges and "exaggerate[d], rather than minimize[d], the academic opportunities in the state institutions, to avoid admitting Negroes to the main state universities" (Wilson, 467). Black students admitted to graduate schools of state universities sometimes had to stay behind a screen (470).

99. Richard B. Freeman, *Black Elite. A Report Prepared for the Carnegie Commission on Higher Education* (New York: McGraw-Hill, 1976), 47.

100. Black colleges had also been able to drop high school grades since there were many more public high schools for blacks (Wilson, 467).

101. Freeman, 52.

102. Fran Brown and Madelon D. Stent, *Minorities in U.S. Institutions of Higher Education* (New York: Praeger, 1977), 30.

103. Ibid., 63.

104. "In Higher Education Black Women Are Far Outpacing Black Men," *Journal of Blacks in Higher Education* 17 (1997): 84–86.

105. Ibid. Research also shows, however, that black men earn somewhat more than black women; in 1997, the median usual weekly earning of full-time black men workers was 468 dollars, compared to 400 dollars for black women. See *Monthly Labor Review*, January 27, 1999: *www.bls.gov/opub/ted/1999/Jan*. On the other hand, women's unemployment rate, for both blacks and whites, is lower than men's. Moreover, an African-American man living in a region with high unemployment can expect pay 25 percent lower than the same man would get in a region with a jobless rate that is 1 percent lower. Black women's pay rate is slightly less affected by the level of unemployment—their pay would be 22 percent lower. See Heather Boushev, "Unemployment, Pay, and Race," *Left Business Observer,* July 1998, *www.leftbusinessobserver.com/race_curve*. Also, a telephone survey in January 2003 found that black men were much more likely than black women to say that they had been stopped by police "just because of your race" (65 percent of black men compared to 22 percent of black women), and black men were less likely to rate race relations in the nation positively—36 percent of black men did, versus 50 percent of black women. See *www.abcnews.go.com/sections/us/dailynews/poll_race030123.html*.

106. *Jet,* February 8, 1993, 26.

107. See Beth McMurtie, "Accreditor Imposes Range of Sanctions on 21 Southern Colleges," *Chronicle of Higher Education,* December 19, 2001, in which it is reported that three of the seven colleges placed on probation were historically black colleges. The reasons given for placing them on probation included financial problems in every case.

108. Sara Hebel, "Black-College Group Chooses Florida A&M President as its new Leader," *Chronicle of Higher Education,* December 5, 2001: *http://chronicle.com/daily/2001/12/2001.*

109. Many articles on the Ayers case have appeared in *The Chronicle of Higher Education.* See, for example, Jay Heubert, "For the Supreme Court, a Stark Choice on Civil Rights," November 6, 1991, and Sara Hebel, "A Pivotal Moment for Desegregation," October 27, 2000.

110. Walter R. Allen, "The Color of Success: African-American College Student Outcomes at Predominantly White and Historically Black Public Colleges and Universities," *Harvard Educational Review* 62 (1992): 26–44.

111. Ibid., 40.

112. Ibid., 28.

113. Margaret B. Wilkerson, "How Equal is Equal Education: Race, Class, and Gender," in *Educating Men and Women Together*, ed. Carol Lasser, Carol (Urbana: University of Illinois Press, 1987), 137.

114. David Hefner, "Breathing New Life into Meharry," *Black Issues in Higher Education*, July 19, 2001, 28–33.

115. Jacqueline Fleming, *Blacks in College: A Comparative Study of Students' Success in Black and in White Institutions* (San Francisco: Jossey-Bass, 1984), 144–46.

116. Lisa E. Wolf-Wendel, "Models of Excellence: The Baccalaureate Origins of Successful European American Women, African American Women, and Latinas," *Journal of Higher Education* 69 (1998): 141–46.

117. Tribal colleges are another type of special focus institution. The American Indian Higher Education Consortium (AIHEC) began with six institutions, all coeducational, in 1972 but increased to 31 by 1994. A majority of the institutions in AIHEC grant associate degrees; six offer bachelor's degrees, and three offer master's. Almost all of the 31 institutions are located west of the Mississippi. AIHEC institutions share some characteristics with HBCUs, including a good representation of women in official capacities and a preponderance of women students. In 1996, 32 percent of presidents of AIHEC colleges were women; 49 percent of faculty members were women; and almost two-thirds of the students were women See AIHEC newsletter, October 1998.

118. "At a Black College, Race Often Takes Precedence over Gender," *Chronicle of Higher Education*, July 14, 1993.

Coeducation before the Late 1960s

While many former men's colleges became coeducational between 1968 and 1972, some admitted women in the 1950s. The two institutions discussed in this section, University of Rochester and Lincoln University, are good examples of the transition to coeducation before the twentieth-century women's movement was influential. When the University of Rochester became coeducational in 1954, it was actually for the second time. Because the university had been involved with women's higher education, both through coeducation in 1900 and then through an affiliated women's college, coeducation in 1955 was not an abrupt break with the past. Lundt, Poulson, and Miller-Bernal argue that the lack of commitment to gender equity meant that women's interests or needs did not get addressed until the women's movement of the 1970s.

One might expect that Lincoln University, a historically black institution, would have favored coeducation since almost all other black colleges were co-educational. Lincoln saw itself as the "black Princeton," however, and like that institution did not want to lower its prestige by admitting women. But Lincoln faced severe financial constraints that Princeton did not, and it also experienced a decline in its enrollment of academically elite students as predominantly white institutions opened to minorities. Miller-Bernal and Pevar argue that admitting women became a way of overcoming these problems. Similar to the University of Rochester, Lincoln University did not at first commit itself to gender equity. Even today, concerns about racism complicate feminist issues.

3

To Coeducation and Back Again

Gender and Organization at the University of Rochester

Christine Lundt, Susan L. Poulson, and Leslie Miller-Bernal

The history of women at the University of Rochester is noteworthy for the dramatic changes in the ways women have been incorporated. Women's rights activists, including the famous Susan B. Anthony, and their wealthy allies successfully pressured the university to admit women in 1900. After only a dozen years, however, the university's president and board of trustees reversed this decision and created a coordinate college for the women students, which lasted until 1955. The decision in 1955 to become coeducational a second time, like the earlier decisions, was not done for reasons of sexual equality, although administrators and trustees often used concerns about gender to justify their policy shifts. Instead, the major concern was what was best for the institution; in the 1950s this translated into policies that the president believed would enhance the university's reputation in science and research.

The placement and organization of the sexes at the University of Rochester reveals a great deal about what shapes an institution of higher education. Internal and external interest groups, concerns about academic prestige, corporate ideals of management, presidential leadership, and prevailing gender norms all influence university policy. The effects of policies are not always intended, however. Coeducation implies a certain level of equality, since all classes and most extracurricular activities are open to women students. Educating women separately from men, through a coordinate arrangement, reduced University of Rochester women students' access to academic opportunities. At the same time, coordination enabled them to exercise leadership and gave them role models at a time when few women in society had such advantages. In this chapter we discuss reasons that the University of Rochester implemented first coeducation, then coordination, then coeducation again, as well as the implications of these different arrangements for the position of women at the university.

Early Beginnings: From Single-Sex to Coeducation

From the late nineteenth century to the mid-twentieth century, the University of Rochester vacillated between single-sex, coordinate, and coeducation. Rochester was established in 1850 as an all-male institution, like most colleges of its time. The first attempts to integrate women into the university were unsuccessful. In 1851, Azariah Boody, a devout Episcopalian who made his fortune in the railroad industry, and Lewis H. Morgan, a lawyer and one of the founders of modern anthropology, helped establish the Barleywood Female University, Rochester's first institution of higher education for women. After Barleywood failed in 1853, however, Boody donated the Barleywood land to the University of Rochester.[1] In the 1890s, Morgan joined Edward Mott Moore, a wealthy Rochester physician, in a second attempt to open a women's college. Moore was a well-known founder of Rochester's public parks and a "lifelong advocate for the higher education of women."[2] Despite their prominence and dedication to their cause, however, Morgan and Moore found insufficient support from the local community and abandoned their efforts.

Undaunted by these failures, supporters of coeducation at Rochester continued their efforts and had a breakthrough when a new president, David J. Hill, assumed office in the 1890s. Hill was the former president of Bucknell and had overseen its transition to coeducation.[3] Rochester native Susan B. Anthony and her famous cohort, Elizabeth Cady Stanton, asked Hill about the possibility of admitting women to the University of Rochester. He replied that his wife had just given birth to twins and "that if the Creator could risk placing sexes in such near relations, they might with safety walk on the same campus and pursue the same curriculum together."[4] With an administration friendly to the idea of coeducation, local Rochester women campaigned to get women admitted to the university. In 1893, Susan B. Anthony paid for Helen Wilkinson to become the first woman to enter the University of Rochester. President Hill admitted nineteen-year-old Wilkinson as a nonmatriculating full-time student. Wilkinson endured being ignored by the faculty during her first two weeks of classes, as well as being jeered by a good number of the men, especially the football players. She withdrew after two years for reasons of poor health.[5]

Women's rights advocates remained determined to bring coeducation to the University of Rochester. In 1898, the board of trustees voted ten to three in favor of coeducation, but put the financial burden of raising necessary funds on local women. "Women should be admitted . . . upon the same terms and under the same conditions as men . . . ," the trustees declared, "when the women of Rochester shall raise the necessary funds for the use of the University." The price tag for coeducation was estimated to be $100,000, a substantial sum for that time, in order to construct the necessary buildings for an increased enrollment. The trustees avoided committing themselves completely to coeducation by also stipulating that it would only occur "under such conditions as may be decided upon by the Executive Committee of this Board."[6] Undaunted, coeducation's supporters set out to raise the required money but found the prospects insufficient. After exhausting local philanthropy, the women appealed to the board, and the board accepted $50,000 instead. However, the day before the money was due, Anthony learned that the "Co-ed Fund" was still shy $8,000. Despite her age of eighty and the hot, humid weather, she traveled around town in her carriage, gathering additional pledges, including her own $2,000 life insurance policy.[7]

Nineteen hundred was a fateful year for coeducation at the University of Rochester. Coeducation officially began as 32 female undergraduates (15 first-year, 5 transfers, and 12 special or part-time) and 199 male undergraduates (50 first-year, 114 upperclassmen, and 35 special or part-time) arrived on campus.[8] Ironically, however, 1900 was also the year in which a new president, Rush Rhees, began his lengthy tenure during which he undermined coeducation and replaced it with coordinate education. Rhees, an ordained Baptist minister whose view of gender stemmed from biblical ideals, had spent the previous decade at the prestigious Newton Theological Institution, where he was a well-regarded professor of New Testament studies.

As expected, coeducation enabled the University of Rochester to expand its student body rapidly. By 1910, women's full-time enrollment increased more than sevenfold, from 21 to 150, while the men's increased by just under one-quarter, from 210 to 261. This meant that total enrollment had nearly doubled in ten years. By 1914, women constituted 40 percent of the student body, which was consistent with the national enrollment statistics for women at coeducational institutions.[9] However, the retention rates for men and women students differed significantly. While 70 percent of women graduated, only 40 percent of entering men graduated, apparently lured away by relatively well-paying jobs available in the rapidly industrializing economy. Also, as a group the men were more marginal in academic achievement, and some were unable to maintain college-level work.[10]

Coeducation prompted a noticeable shift in majors. Between 1905 and 1909 the number of men who obtained a bachelor's degree in arts or philosophy dropped from 82 to 45 percent, while the percentage of men who graduated with a Bachelor of Science degree rose from 18 to 55 percent. Traditionally, most female students pursued a classical education that was the hallmark of the well-bred women who did not seek employment after graduation. Between 1905 and 1909, the percentage of women at the university who graduated with a Bachelor of Arts degree dropped from 67 to 47 percent; the rest graduated with a Bachelor of Philosophy degree. Women's entry into the sciences came later.[11]

Without a strong feminist spirit on campus, and with a president opposed to coeducation, women at the University of Rochester had little chance of equitable treatment. Soon after his arrival, President Rhees made clear his preference for coordinate education and began to undermine coeducation. The trustees' decision to admit women, he wrote, "requires that the . . . [women] receive equal attention, *equivalent* instruction [emphasis added], and the same standards of admission and graduation" as the men. Rhees wanted separate instruction and separate space for women. Separate instruction, he believed, allowed for the "full and frank discussion" of such subjects as literature and hygiene that was prohibited in the current "mixed" recitation sections. Separate space would bring about "the cultivation of feelings of social unity among women that may develop here some of the social advantages of the separate colleges for women." "Ultimately," he stated, it would be "necessary for us to have a woman's building with which there would naturally be a woman's gym."[12]

Rhees put this philosophy of separation into action. He initiated and taught a required course in "college ethics" that had separate sections for male and female students. In 1902, Rhees and Professor Joseph H. Gilmore began separate Bible classes for men and women; Rhees instructed the men, while Professor Gilmore taught the women in his home.[13] The university also sexually segregated debate classes, each sex tending to debate subjects in their "sphere": men focused primarily on politics and sports, while the women focused on the family and education. When students attended compulsory chapel service, they sat in sexually segregated pews.[14] Thus two formative subjects—religion, which instructs the biblical ideal of gender behavior, and debate, which gives one the tools to verbally challenge and evaluate—were taught under the guidelines of sexual segregation. In turn, this arrangement helped "normalize" the separation of men and women.

In addition to introducing segregated class instruction, Rhees initiated other policies that undermined the academic support and recognition of women. In his first year as president, the trustees approved Rhees's motion that, "out of consideration of equity," women were ineligible for the existing 100 scholarships, as the donors had designated them for the students when the university was all male. However, there was no indication that any attempt was made to contact the donors to clarify their intent after the university became coeducational. Four years later, there were 13 scholarships available for 64 women and 104 scholarships available for 166 men.[15] Also, while in the early years of coeducation women earned a highly disproportionate number of Phi Beta Kappa awards, complaints by male students and faculty led administrators to change the membership criteria from solely a grade point average, to being "primarily the best" in their class.[16] The number and percentage of male students getting into Phi Beta Kappa increased thereafter. President Rhees suppressed the recognition of women even at graduation, vowing that except to receive their diplomas, women "have never appeared in the commencement and so long as I have my way they never will."[17]

President Rhees also sought to extend sexual segregation beyond the classroom. In the fall of 1901, for example, after the freshmen class elected a coeducational slate of officers, Rhees successfully prevailed upon the two elected women to resign their offices and to form a separate Women Students' Association. While a full complement of activities and organizations were available to the male students, only a few clubs were open to women. All the men graduating in the class of 1904 belonged to at least one student group or club; in comparison, only three in four women had extracurricular involvement.[18] Insufficient space was a problem for women. For the first five years, women were restricted to the "Girls' Room" for their meals, studying, socializing, and meetings. A large, dark classroom at the end of a hallway in an academic building, the Girls' Room was the only one provided for the women students' use. It contained a piano, a few chairs, a table, a large picture of Susan B. Anthony, and later a coatroom and small kitchen.[19]

Similarly, although Rhees was a member of one of the six national fraternities on campus, he forbade the establishment of any national sororities at the University of Rochester. He did allow local sororities. One alumna said that she believed that Rhees feared that "sororities furnished a united front and gave courage to the minority group of women."[20]

The campus media reflected the growing separation of men and women students. Women and men worked together on the university yearbook, the *Interpres*, until the fall of 1908 when the men of the junior class of 1909 summarily excluded women from the yearbook. When the next year's junior class began to plan their annual, the male students debated the question of including women. Rhees intervened and suggested to the women that they withdraw and start their own annual.[21] The women agreed and subsequently published the *Croceus*, which they dedicated to Susan B. Anthony. Rhees applauded this "gradual separation and . . . natural development of student independence" and stated that the existence of *Croceus* "demonstrates equality . . . of women in college."[22] One woman student, however, expressed her disagreement through a poem in the *Croceus*:

> There was a space when I kept pace
> With styles throughout the land . . .
> But now, alack, I'm told 'Stand back!
> Room for the truly great!'
> My sails curtailed, my taste assailed,
> I share the co-ed's fate . . . [23]

Extracurricular activities differed for women and men. While almost all the active women were involved in conventional social activities, such as the religious and local Greek organizations, men's activities were more diverse. This was partly because men had many more options, but it also reflected a double standard for student conduct. At many colleges and universities across the country, the men's "antisocial or unconventional behavior was tolerated . . . the 'coeds' were subjected to intense scrutiny and quick condemnation."[24] For example, although several alumni published their criticism of university policies on coeducation and of the women's high number of Phi Beta Kappa keys in the *Campus* and local newspapers, the women were bitterly criticized for complaining to a local news reporter about their treatment by male students and were denied an opportunity to publish their thoughts in the *Campus.*

Women students encountered a variety of reactions from university constituencies. Some women felt that relations between men and women students were amiable; others felt hostility. Years later, several alumnae recalled how some men, particularly upperclassmen and alumni, treated women students poorly. One alumna remembered President Rhees being "insulting" to women at a student assembly. In a speech to the Women's Students Association in 1903, a first-year student expressed her hope that "the misogynists at the University of Rochester would be buried beneath the ground."[25] The men generally described their conduct as "gentlemanly" or, if a bit too rowdy, as just involving "harmless pranks."[26] A few chastised their fellow male students for their rude treatment of women or tried to change the male-only traditions. But these were few and far between. Men who attempted to change the revered student traditions by including women were publicly criticized, as were those who reported dissension among the men. Several fraternities had a policy of expelling members who dated "coeds."[27] Some male students claimed that coeducation did not affect them much, since they studied in male-dominated areas and dated women who were not University of Rochester students. President Rhees generally characterized the campus climate as "calm," due in large measure to the "dignity and wisdom of the students" but also, in part, to changes he had made in recognition of "the distinctiveness of the natures and interests" of the two groups of students.[28]

The conditions necessary for gender equity were almost completely absent. In addition to an unsupportive administration and broad cultural prejudices, there was only one woman on the faculty, a part-time art instructor. Women students had little of the suffragists' spirit that had earlier inspired women's social and political advancement. In 1909, women students established a chapter of the New York State branch of the College Equal Suffrage League, but records show only three members. In 1912, the organization's name was changed to the "Pro and Con Suffrage Club," indicating a shift in focus from advocacy to ambivalence. The change reflected the fact that "a majority of the girls were undecided as to what stand they should take." By 1913, there was no further mention of the club's existence at the University of Rochester.[29]

Financial incentives enabled President Rhees to fulfill his desire for a separate college for women. Ironically, the University of Rochester used money from supporters of women's education to resegregate women students. To honor

Susan B. Anthony, who had sometimes shared tea with the women students, several women raised money for a women's building. President Rhees put his stamp on the project and insisted that the money not be raised locally, that the women's building be located off-campus, that university officials have the power to determine the type of building to be built, and that donors be informed that the university will not be under any obligation to "advocate the political theories of Miss Anthony."[30] While the women raised only a third of the initial goal of $75,000 dollars, additional money became available in 1909 from a bequest from long-time supporter of women's education, Lewis Henry Morgan.[31]

In anticipation of a separate college for women, Rhees hired the first dean of women, Annette Munro, in 1909, to be a "friend and counselor" to women students. Munro supported Rhees's philosophy that women needed a course of study different from men and admonished them to "not ape the men, sweet girls; such conduct is the worst." Munro dismissed women students' complaints about their inequitable treatment as a product of either their ignorance or ill breeding. "Your name," she advised, "should never be published till you are married or dead."[32]

In 1912 Rhees used an offer of the presidency of Amherst to wrangle a concession from the University of Rochester's trustees. Rhees informed the trustees that he would turn down the offered presidency only if they agreed to create a coordinate college for women and conduct a million dollar endowment campaign to partly fund it. The trustees agreed, stating that it would be "in the interest of the most satisfactory college life and successful college training for our women to create a separate college for them."[33] With the subsequent donation of land adjacent to the University of Rochester campus and another donation from a wealthy local family, the physical structure for the College for Women was underway.

Other institutions mirrored Rochester's drift toward coordinate education. At the turn of the twentieth century, there were several colleges and universities that changed from coeducation to coordinate education; one excluded women altogether. An early reaction was at Stanford University in 1899. The university's benefactress, Mrs. Leland Stanford, insisted that the number of women admitted be capped at 500 to prevent the perception that Stanford was a predominantly women's institution. At Tufts and Chicago, trustees endorsed measures designed to segregate instruction by sex. While some at the University of Wisconsin tried to adopt a similar plan, they were ultimately unsuccessful. At Wesleyan, where the reaction against coeducation was most extreme, women students were barred from undergraduate education altogether.

The reaction against coeducation was in part a response to specific concerns within the institutions. Because a large number of colleges and universities were still all male and local educational opportunities for women were often limited, women frequently constituted what was believed to be a disproportionate share of the student body at coeducational schools. Given the lower intellectual prestige traditionally associated with women, their concentration in liberal arts also threatened to lower its status within male academia.[34]

Coeducation was also feared because it had begun to challenge cultural boundaries that had kept men and women apart and, ultimately, women subordinate to men. By the turn of the century, assertions of women's mental and physical inferiority, once widely believed, were less frequent and effective. Experience with coeducation had shown that women were not only fully capable but, in relative numbers, actually outperformed their male counterparts in academic honors. The debate over coeducation evolved from a controversy over the mental and physical capacity of women to a question of the appropriate form of education for the duties and responsibilities of each sex. At the root of the debate lay a fear of the loss of gender distinctions: the "feminization" of men and the acquisition by women of characteristics traditionally associated with masculinity. The growth and development of domestic science partially appeased that fear, but coeducation along with parallel developments in larger society continued to challenge cultural assumptions that sustained separate spheres for the lives of men and women.

With curricular revisions introduced at the University of Rochester in the spring of 1913, the separate education of women was nearly complete. Division of women and men in academic study at the lower levels and in most extracurricular activities, a separate administration for the women's college, and an educational philosophy that supported coordination were all in place to bring about the resegregation of women beginning in the fall of 1914. President Rhees had succeeded in his decade-and-a-half-long effort to separate men and women.

Coordinate Education, 1914–1955

The goal for the new College for Women, which opened in 1914, was to provide education for women that was equal to men's education but suited to women's roles. Coordinate education proponents hoped that it would create "social unity among women," reduce men's hostility toward women's academic success, boost male enrollment, and increase women's access to courses that they would otherwise avoid due to predominant male enrollments. The 41 years of coordinate education had a mixed legacy for the education of women. In terms of physical plant, extracurricular activities, and curriculum, the education of women suffered. Yet it also provided the benefits typical of a single-sex women's institution: greater opportunity for leadership and more professional role models for women students.

With the opening of two buildings for women's education in 1914, the coordinate College for Women furthered the separation of men and women students. In the 1920s, in order to alleviate overcrowding and to accommodate the expected addition of professional programs in education, engineering, and business, Rhees announced that the College for Men would move three miles to a new location. This meant that the faculty and most of the undergraduate library collection would also be relocated.

The University of Rochester's developing research orientation came somewhat at the expense of undergraduate education. In 1919 the university officially changed its charter to that of a research university and within six years added numerous graduate programs, including the School of Medicine and Dental Dispensary, and the Eastman School of Music. Although such expansions were typical signs of healthy growth in a research university, they came at a cost to the education of undergraduates, especially women. As higher education became more specialized, gender-related segregation in the academic disciplines increased. In preparation for the establishment of separate campuses, the faculty revised the curriculum by lowering the number of required general education courses and increasing the credit requirements in the student's chosen area of concentration.[35] Since upper-level courses were coeducational, women students who wanted to take upper-level classes had to travel to the men's campus, which the Dean of Women Janet Clark described as "a time-consuming, exhausting and aggravating business."[36]

Increasing academic specialization exacerbated the division between men and women's education. For years, administrators at the Women's College wanted to create a social sciences institute, which would provide alumnae employed in the field of social work with an opportunity for graduate study and provide the Women's College with a distinct intellectual focus. University administrators, however, did not support the idea, yet they continued to develop new scientific and graduate programs that served traditionally male interests.[37] Dean Clark noted the poor science facilities and instruction available to women at their own campus, but her pleas to the various science departments to redress theses inequities went unheeded.[38]

Some faculty and departments limited women's educational opportunities by undermining the policy of coeducational classes at the upper-level. In the early 1930s, for example, the math department complained about the high number of women enrolled in advanced and elective courses at the Men's College. The department found that coed classes "resulted in inconvenience to both the members of the department and to the students" and deemed it "desirable to separate men and women in advanced courses."[39] To achieve this end, they intentionally limited the number of elective course offerings. Similarly, the English department restricted women's access to upper-level courses. As English professor John Slater noted in a letter to President Rhees,

It has not infrequently occurred that our own English-concentrating women students have been unable because of a conflict to get a desired elective in their junior year when it was given on their own campus, and have requested permission to take it with the men the following year. All such requests are submitted to a vote of the department, and but few have been granted, because most of us believe that separate classes are desirable, especially in some subjects.[40]

Some of the anticipated benefits of coordinate education for women did not materialize. The percentage of women on the faculty remained the same even as the student body expanded. Between 1925 and 1955, women made up only 10 to 16 percent of faculty, while 33 to 48 percent of students were women. Furthermore, most women faculty members taught in "female subjects" and clustered in the lower levels of the academic hierarchy.[41]

Housing options for women continued to be troublesome. Approximately 20 percent of the university's male and female students lived on campus in 1935.[42] While men could live in fraternity houses and dormitories, women were required to live with a relative or at an approved boarding house or with a family in exchange for domestic labor. In the early 1930s the Women's College opened its first co-op dorms, where women students reduced their room and board costs by performing domestic chores.[43]

Several factors discouraged women from participating in extracurricular activities. Fraternities exercised almost total control over the key extracurricular clubs.[44] The Board of Control, which decided how student activity fees should be apportioned to clubs, was entirely comprised of fraternity members, who often excluded women and minorities from membership in the most powerful student organizations. A faculty adviser and alumnus ruled that the Men's College newspaper, the *Campus,* stop reporting news about women. In response, women began their own newspaper, the *Cloister Window,* later *Tower Times,* which existed until coordinate education ended in 1955. Thus, while women did gain leadership experience, it was often by default rather than by design. Some activities and clubs, such as dramatics and some department clubs, remained coeducational, but the hour-long commute to the men's campus, where most of these were housed, made it difficult for women students to participate. Internal dynamics between resident and commuter students at the Women's College also hampered extracurricular participation. Commuters were not as influenced by peer culture and generally had less available time to join activities.[45] In 1948 a third of respondents at the Women's College said that they felt put off by the fact that dorm students often controlled extracurricular activities.[46]

A Return to Coeducation

After 41 years of coordinate education, the University of Rochester abruptly returned to coeducation in the mid-1950s. This was largely due to the new president, Cornelius de Kiewiet, who viewed separate education as an inefficient use of resources and made the resumption of coeducation a top priority. Educated at European universities and widely traveled, de Kiewiet was an accomplished scholar of European history who had held a variety of administrative posts, including acting president at Cornell. Like Rochester's earlier presidents, de Kiewiet sought to enhance the prestige of the university and attract new revenue for increasing academic specialization, but he believed it was first necessary to unify the separate units. "The magnitude and power of the assembled and coherent institution," he wrote, "[would] . . . best command and attract support."[47] De Kiewiet predicted that "with men and women together, the educational pace would be faster, the intellectual challenge sharper, to the enormous benefit of the university itself."[48]

De Kiewiet also saw coeducation as a better form of education for both men and women. "I've never myself been partial to education by sexual division," he later recalled. "There's an enrichment that takes place when a variety of people are brought together in the same environment."[49]

The return to coeducation did not occur, however, without "a great deal of opposition," as one faculty member recalled.[50] While such resistance is commonly encountered when an institution makes a dramatic change, a contributing factor in this case stemmed from the leadership style of de Kiewiet. His brisk and unilateral managerial style offended some members of the university. Even a close friend observed that "he seemed impatient with slow movement of persuasion, and so relied upon force to accomplish what he saw as needing to be done. . . . Thus the sincere convictions and natural self-esteem of honorable men and women were ignored by a man who must have seemed fiendishly intelligent, but devoid of patience or sympathy with other human beings."[51]

The university became coeducational in 1955 with little fanfare and almost no preparation. Female enrollment continued to be restricted by an admissions quota, so for many years the percentage of women in the student body remained stagnant. While total undergraduate enrollment increased 32 percent from 1955 to 1961, the percentage of women students remained between 33 and 36 percent, which was a little under the national average of 38 percent. This restriction resulted in a pool of women who were on average more academically talented than the men; while only about one-third of the seniors were women, they usually made up about half of the graduates in the honor studies program and at least half of the seniors elected to Phi Beta Kappa.[52]

The financial and instructional benefits from the merger seemed to be somewhat less than anticipated, but the effect of the merger on female faculty members was predictably devastating. From 1956 to 1961 the women's already meager representation on the faculty shrank further, from 11 to 8 percent, even as the overall size of the faculty increased. The loss of so many female faculty members, described as "independent, intelligent women" who were "great role models," reinforced the status of the University of Rochester as an institution dedicated to research and helped to undermine the precarious position of professional women in society.[53]

A further decline in women's power stemmed from the loss of administrative clout. The first dean of women appointed by President Rhees in 1909, Annette Munro, had been more of a social role model, a woman with few academic qualifications. Subsequent deans, however, were models of academic achievement. Not surprisingly, Janet Clark, the sitting dean of women, resigned after she learned of de Kiewiet's intention to adopt coeducation. In 1961 the University of Rochester eliminated the Office of the Dean of Women as well as the dean of men. For about seven years, Margaret Habein, previously the last dean of the College for Women, was the dean of the new Office of Instructional and Student Services, which was second in rank in the College of Arts and Science.[54] After her departure, however, the title of the office was changed to dean of students and the function was enlarged to cover all students on the main campus. From 1957 until 1965, the deans of students were men.[55] Helen Nowlis was then appointed dean of students, but her tenure lasted for only for about a year.[56]

The return of coeducation had an immediate impact on campus social life. Administrators took this opportunity of campus-wide reorganization to introduce stricter rules governing student behavior, which made some students resentful. Past problems with rowdy behavior and abuse of alcohol prompted administrators to cancel two annual campus-wide festivities. In addition, the fraternities preempted administrative regulation by imposing a stricter set of rules and penalties on themselves.[57] For the women's residence halls the administration also imposed more rigid regulations than those for men. Women complained about curfew and sign-out regulations that the men did not have, and the Middle States Association report of 1960 on the University of Rochester criticized the "seemingly unnecessary differences in regulations for men and women students."[58] The regulations, however, stayed in place until challenged by students in the late 1960s.

The merger brought positive and negative developments for women in extracurricular activities. The number of coeducational activities increased. Indeed, by 1957 there were more than 100 mostly coeducational clubs and activities on campus. A number of student organizations from the former Women's College did not survive the merger, however. Also, the men retained almost all of the decision-making power in the coeducational clubs, with the exception of the first year after the merger, when women won top positions at the campus newspaper, the radio station, and the new student governing body, called the College Congress. One explanation for the women's coup was given by an alumnus and fraternity member: "The first year of the coeducational system, women were elected to [head] most student body organizations rather than men since they voted in one block and only put up one candidate for each position."[59]

After the first year of coeducation, male students, particularly fraternity members, regained leadership and held on to it for the next decade. Reflecting the contemporary culture, the 1960 Middle States Association report applauded the new place of women on campus, seeing it as appropriate for their social roles: "The male members of the faculty and the student body have accepted the presence of women in all coeducational areas of the University, and the women enjoy a proper place in the life and interests of the institution. Women are involved in student activities, holding a fair share of officer positions and committee memberships in both appointive and elective posts."[60]

The locus of women's leadership shifted to the dormitories. While women sometimes served as vice presidents and secretaries in the coeducational clubs and held a minority of positions in the College Cabinet (formerly the College Congress), women held all the leadership positions in the only dormitory for women, named the Women's Center. It became the primary source of whatever social unity there was among women students through an extensive number of committees that nourished residential life. The Women's Center became a female subculture on campus, with a legislative body, an Honor Board, a Girls' Organization for women commuters, and various other committees. Women students' support for these organizations is indicated by an 80 percent turnout rate for dormitory elections, compared to a 37 percent rate in student government elections.[61]

The return to coeducation brought no noticeable ideological development in gender equity. Men and women generally endorsed existing gender roles that encouraged women to remain in the domestic realm. In a 1959 student editorial printed in the *Campus Times,* Patsy Runk argued against feminist ideals. "Modern woman in getting out of the home and into the world," she wrote, "has too often become confused in the process. Independence, at first exhilarating, has become an intoxicant, hindering her effective performance as a wife and mother." She also noted the recent observations of a professor that "many coeds keep their brains in a bushel basket. Not only have they lost interest in the demand for political equality, but in intellectual matters they tend, if they know anything, to conceal what they know."[62] A 1970s survey of graduates from 1959 revealed how women accepted prevailing norms. I "rode off with a white knight to the land of white picket fences, fulfilling the traditional '50s role of making biscuits and babies," one alumna commented. "Twenty-five years ago, I trusted in the inevitability of marrying, having children and, in some magical way, becoming a writer," another recalled.[63]

Although both alumni and alumnae commented that socializing between the sexes increased after the fall of 1955, men generally were much less certain whether coeducation improved relations between men and women. One alumnus recalled: "I don't think there was a change at the time, but [coeducation] set the stage for today's attitudes of more openness which are better than those of the '50s."[64] Alumnae tended to say that interaction between the sexes was more relaxed and frequent. One pointed out the advantage of diversity: "It was really hard to have a decent social life [at the Women's College]. A few guys would come over but it was a very small group. . . . Over at the Men's Campus, we got to know lots of people and it was natural. You went to class together, you hung out at Todd Union, etc."[65]

The transition back to coeducation at the University of Rochester was remarkable for how little it affected gender relations. Women lost some of the benefits of coordination, such as their own student government and publications, but gained access to educational opportunities and more social contact with men. Greater changes awaited the social movements of the later 1960s.

The Coeducation Years, 1960–2001

Changes in Student Culture

Traditional forms of gender relations continued during the early 1960s, at the University of Rochester and in the country more generally. Campus culture celebrated distinctly different gender roles; men students were encouraged to be involved in sports and to be the leaders of clubs, while women students were expected to be concerned with their physical appearance and dating. The 1960–61 University of Rochester catalog, for example, mentioned that men's "prize scholarships" were based on several criteria, including the usual "literary and scholastic ability and attainments," but also "qualities of manhood."[66] The 1963–64 *Student Handbook* reassured women students that dormitory services in their residence hall would have a representative to supply them with cosmetics. A section on "women's athletics" began with the question, "Say, girls [*sic*] are last fall's skirts a bit snugger than usual?"[67] One hint that changes were afoot, however, was in the *Handbook's* description of a new dormitory complex that housed men and women, although they did live on separate floors and several faculty members lived there, too.

In the early 1970s, along with student protests at the university over civil rights and the Vietnam War, women's issues began to be recognized. In November 1970, for example, Jill Johnston, a controversial writer for the *Village Voice*, spoke at the university on homosexuality and women's liberation.[68] Women students formed an activist organization, the Women's Coalition, in the fall of 1972, as a response to a "Women's Weekend" the previous semester. The coalition still exists, although over the years it has had its "ups and downs."[69] At about the same time it began, faculty and staff formed a Women's Committee to get to know each other and talk about issues connected to being a woman at the university.[70] Although the academic field of women's studies was still a ways off, the university did begin to sponsor some events directed at women students' needs, for instance, a panel discussion of science careers for women.[71]

Campus Life and Academics for Women Students
While nationally, women have formed the majority of undergraduate students since 1979, at the University of Rochester, women are still slightly in the minority, although their proportion is higher than it was in the 1960s. In 1961, women made up 37 percent of the slightly more than 2,000 undergraduates in the College of Arts and Science.[72] The proportion of women had reached 45 percent by 1990, where it remained during the next decade; undergraduate enrollment likewise remained at about 4,300.[73] In 2000 the university's minority students (excluding foreign students) comprised almost one-quarter of those undergraduates whose racial/ethnic group was known. There were more men than women students in all groups except African Americans and American Indian/Eskimos, but both of these groups were a very small proportion of all students, together only about 5 percent.[74]

In the 45 years since the university became coeducational for the second time, women's academic performance relative to men's has been uneven, at least as indicated by their election to Phi Beta Kappa. In 1970, when women were 39 percent of the graduating class, they were also 39 percent of the honors studies graduates and 37 percent of the seniors elected to Phi Beta Kappa. In 1980, women were only 29 percent of those seniors elected to Phi Beta Kappa, while they represented 37 percent of seniors. In 1990, women's academic performance improved, as they made up 38 percent of the Phi Beta Kappa seniors, slightly less than their percentage among their class. In 2000, women were 51 percent of the seniors elected to Phi Beta Kappa, slightly more than their proportion (49 percent) in the class as a whole.[75]

Women students have been the leaders of many campus organizations in the years since the University became coeducational. Women were the editors-in-chief of the student newspaper in four of ten years examined (1960, 1965, 1970, 1975, 1980, 1985, 1990, 1995, 2000, and 2002). Some committees appear to have been consciously planned to have a woman and man as co-chairs.[76] A key leadership position that appears to have favored men, however, is the president of the student government. In the 1995 election, for example, four out of the five candidates were men; when votes were counted, a man won a "landslide," and the woman came in fourth.[77] In ten years examined (1963, 1965, 1980, 1985, 1992, 1994, 1995, 1996, 1999, and 2000) only once, in 1999, was a woman, who was also African-American, elected to this important office.[78]

Following national patterns and stimulated or at least reinforced by Title IX equity requirements, women's sports have increased remarkably since the 1960s. Women at the university have 11 varsity sports teams, including the crew and alpine ski teams, which are coeducational. In contrast to the past, photographs of the women's teams appear in the yearbook and student newspaper. Participation in athletics may not be as extensive among women as among men students, however. In 1990 a Middle States report noted that only about 15–20 percent of 5,000 intramural participants were women.[79] The report indicated that women students wanted an "individual perspective" that stresses fitness, nutrition, and weight control.

Examining the representation of women in photographs and articles in the student newspaper suggests that women students' integration into the coeducational university was greater at first and then declined before increasing again. In the newspaper's five issues during the month of September 1960, women appeared in 31 percent of the photos that contained people. Five years later, in the newspaper's eight issues in October 1965, women were represented in only 15 percent of the photos. Few articles during that month dealt with women as subjects. If women were mentioned at all, it was almost always as "coeds," from men students' perspective. For example, "coed hours" in the dorms were discussed rather than rules to permit men in women's dorms and women in men's.[80] Photos containing women increased somewhat during the 1970s, and by the early 1980s women were routinely found in over 30 percent.

Photos of women's sports, however, reveal a different pattern. Women's sports were not covered at all until the mid-1970s, but by the early 1980s, the student newspaper always carried some articles about women's sports teams, frequently accompanied by photos. By the mid-1980s, it was not unusual to find that half of the sports photos in the student newspaper were of women's teams. In February 1985, the women's basketball team won the New York Division III state championship; in that month, there were more photos of women's sports teams in the newspaper than there were of men's.[81]

Fraternities and sororities often play an important role in student life, both by creating solidarity among their members and, especially in the case of fraternities, providing links to campus leadership positions and ties to trustees. At the University of Rochester fraternities for men students originated at the time of the university's opening in 1850. Presidents encouraged the building of fraternity houses in the 1890s to assist in making the university a residential institution.[82] The first sororities were founded during the early years of the first coeducational period, although they were locals only—that is, not affiliated with any national organization.

Fraternity membership has varied over time. During the social protests of the 1960s, fraternities were viewed as discriminatory and elitist. Consequently, membership declined from a high of 59 percent in 1954 to a low of 14 percent in the late 1960s. Sororities disbanded in 1970 and were not reinstated until 1978, but then they became affiliated with nationals.[83] In the early 1980s, only about 15 percent of undergraduates belonged to Greek societies. Problems with fraternities have surfaced at various times. In the 1980s the university had to pressure them to renovate their houses or face demolition. On occasion, fraternity members have been involved in violent incidents, including an alleged rape of a young woman that led to the banning of a fraternity for ten years.[84]

By the early 1980s, black Greek letter organizations (BGLOs) had formed, providing an important focus of identity for minority men and women in this predominantly white institution. The initial issue of the student publication, *The Messenger*, which is devoted to a discussion of "race-ethnicity-class," contained an article that described the benefits of these organizations. Black folklore and oral traditions are promoted, for example, through competitive but friendly "stepping," the writer noted. Each BGLO is judged by the precision of their steps, who is wearing the "phattest" outfits, and who can come up with the wittiest "disses."[85] A couple of years later, however, the same magazine published an article about how harmful pledging is in historically black fraternities. The male author argued that the "psychologically and physically intense" process that aims to make pledges "men" could be even more harmful than what is done in white fraternities.[86] In 2000, the university appointed a black woman, Monica Miranda, as the director for Greek affairs. Miranda does not believe that there is a danger of self-segregation with "the emergence of so many minority fraternities and sororities" because of the leadership roles that many members have taken in the wider university community.[87]

Women's Studies

As an academic program, women's studies at the University of Rochester is about 20 years old. Women's studies courses and a newsletter on women's issues have existed slightly longer, however, since at least 1981. An active, feminist community at the university has addressed such issues as the status of women faculty and administrators, safety of women on campus, childcare, and maternity leave. The newsletter announces events of interest to women, for example, Take Back the Night marches and the Rally for Women's Lives in Washington, D.C. It also notifies the community when famous women speak on campus, including Carol Gilligan, Elaine Showalter, Sonia Johnson, Cynthia Fuchs Epstein, Geraldine Ferraro, Maya Angelou, and Dr. Susan B. Anthony, an author and the namesake and great niece of the nineteenth-century women's rights activist.[88]

Women's studies is a strong academic program, involving 109 "associates" (faculty members who are sufficiently interested to be invited to the institute's meetings and who receive a newsletter) from across the university. More than 300 students enroll in women's studies courses each semester. Although there are no faculty members who have sole or joint appointments in women's studies, many are involved in teaching women's studies courses. Between 1998 and 2002, 50 faculty associates offered more than 100 such courses.[89] Unlike programs at other universities, involved faculty do not come just from the humanities and social sciences, but from parts of the university such as the nursing program, engineering school, and the Eastman School of Music. Besides offering a minor and a major in women's studies, which generally has about six graduates per year, the program gives certificates for graduate work, offers faculty research seminars, and benefits from visiting scholars. Since 1986, women's studies has had an endowed Susan B. Anthony chair, which has been occupied by outstanding feminist scholars.

In the mid-1990s the women's studies program split between an academic, research-oriented side called the Susan B. Anthony Institute and an activist or more political part called the Susan B. Anthony Center for Women's Leadership. While this division resulted from conflict and created some bitterness, according to Susan Gustafson, a professor of German and acting director of the institute in 2002–2003, this is all "past history now." The institute and center co-sponsor some events, and the director of the Anthony Center teaches a course annually, "Women in Politics," for the program. The split enables the institute to operate like other, comparable academic programs at the university (for example, Visual Studies and the Frederick Douglass Institute). It also means that the center can engage in political advocacy work that might get neglected if both of these structures did not exist.[90]

The activist Anthony Center sponsors annual events: a celebration of Susan B. Anthony's birthday, where awards and scholarships are announced; a Susan B. Anthony and Elizabeth Cady Stanton "conversation," where nationally known speakers give a talk on a particular topic of interest to women; and a legacy five-kilometer race that ends up at the Susan B. Anthony house, which is a museum and National Historic Landmark in the city of Rochester. The center does not just sponsor events, however; it also offers help to students when incidents that are offensive or harmful to women occur on campus, and it encourages relations with the outside community by, for example, canvassing politicians at the local level to determine the percentage of women and to assess their needs for training. According to Nora Bredes, the director of the Anthony Center, the university is good at providing students with internship opportunities in the community, such as at battered women's shelters.[91] The acting director of the institute also noted the popularity of women's studies internships; she said that usually they sponsor 12 to 15 interns per year. [92]

Women's Visibility at the University

In order for women students to feel that an educational institution belongs to them as much as to men, they need to have their presence acknowledged. This acknowledgement encompasses a symbolic domain of iconography and representation of their history in official documents, as well as a physical domain of women's presence in the official hierarchy of the university. Overall, the University of Rochester does better in the symbolic realm, partly because of the great fame of the first woman connected to its history, Susan B. Anthony, than it does in the physical domain.

As previously discussed, the university pays homage to the legacy of Susan B. Anthony by naming various programs and prizes after her and by having paintings of her on campus. It is hard to imagine that any student could be unaware that Susan B. Anthony was connected to the university's history. Likewise, those catalogs that have presented the university's history, as well as the current Web site, mention Susan B. Anthony's role in getting women students admitted in 1900; interestingly, though, they do not always discuss the more than 40 years in which women were segregated in a coordinate institution.[93] Beyond Susan B. Anthony, however, there is not much iconography devoted to women. Among paintings in the main library (Rush Rhees), there are six paintings, all of men, in the reading room and another six paintings of men in the main hallway. The main hallway does have stone statues of women, but the women are representatives of virtues, not real women, and depicted in classical Greek garb. The only part of the library where there are paintings of women is in the hall that leads to the Special Collections; three of these ten paintings are of women, all deans in the former College for Women. Another indicator of the symbolic representation of women is in the number of buildings named after women: 6 of 56 or 11 percent. The issue of buildings' names is called to students' attention in the student handbook, which has a section entitled, "The People for Whom the Buildings Are Named." Besides the six buildings named after women, another one is named after Lewis Henry Morgan, who is described not only as an anthropologist but also as a financial backer of the higher education of women.[94]

In the early 1980s, women faculty members were concerned about the university's inability to attract and retain women in faculty and administrative line positions. Twenty-five of them met with several top administrators to discuss what they perceived to be a "climate of tolerance for sexist behavior at the University." In the two-hour meeting, the women asked for "aggressive leadership" from the administration to "construct and implement solutions."[95] A few months later, some women faculty members of the College of Arts and Science noted the high rate at which women rejected job offers at the university. They wondered how much market factors contributed to the low proportion of women on the faculty and how much it was due to the university having "a public image as not being a good place for women."[96]

The University of Rochester continues to have a low representation of women among faculty, administrators, and trustees (see Table 3.1). The greatest improvement in the years since the university became coeducational for a second time has been in the percentage of women faculty, which has increased from about 5 percent to 23 percent. It is important to recognize, however, that these figures include all full-time faculty—tenured, tenure-track but not yet tenured, and non-tenure-track. Comparing faculty in these separate categories for 1990 and 2000, we find that there has been an improvement in the percentage of tenured faculty who are women, from 11 to 17 percent. But in the category of tenure-track but not yet tenured, women's percentage actually decreased

Table 3.1. Women among Faculty, Administration, and Trustees, 1960–2000

	Full-Time Faculty		Administrators		Trustees	
	Women (%)	Total	Women (%)	Total	Women (%)	Total
1960	5	152	0	7[a]	11.0	28
1970	5	312	8	13	10.0	30
1980	9	312	0	17	12.5	40
1990	19	374	0	9	16.0	50[b]
2000	23	326	14	7	15.0	53[b]

Sources: University of Rochester, *Official Bulletins*, 1960–2001; official reports prepared for the Equal Employment Opportunity Commission, Rush Rhees Library, University of Rochester.

a. Includes president, provost, all vice presidents, dean of students, and dean of the College of Arts and Science.
b. Includes both trustees and "senior" trustees.

between 1990 and 2000, from 35 to 28 percent. Women's percentage in the last category, non-tenure-track, increased from 21 to 29 percent, but the benefits of this could be described as mixed—good for women students to have more women role models, but not very good for the women in these positions.

The proportion of top administrators who are women has increased a little between 1960 and 2000, but since the actual number (as opposed to percent) in 2000 was only one, the improvement may not be stable. The proportion of trustees who are women has improved very slightly, from 11 to 15 percent, surprisingly low for a university that has had women students for more than 100 years.

Conclusion

The University of Rochester's transitions from being a university for men, a coeducational university, a university with coordinate men's and women's colleges, and finally a coeducational university reveal the relative advantages for women of one type of arrangement over another. Moreover, since most formerly men's colleges became coeducational later, at about the same time as the 1970s women's movement, women's experiences at the University of Rochester show that coeducation alone does not bring benefits to women.

While Susan B. Anthony's victory in gaining admission for women in 1900 seemed short-lived, given President Rush Rhees's determination to leave women students on an inferior campus and devote most academic resources to men, coordination did benefit women in some ways. As Linda Gordon, a historian of education who teaches at the University of Rochester, has noted, coordination meant that the women students had their own dean and physician, were spared harassment by male students, and had the opportunity to run their own student government and yearbook.[97] Thus coordination may have been chosen with men's interests in mind, but its consequences were not entirely negative for women. Similarly, although coeducation seemed progressive because it provided women with the same formal academic opportunities as men, it was not implemented to further gender equality but primarily for prestige and financial reasons. Like coordination, coeducation had mixed benefits for women. The number of women on the faculty declined and women students lost leadership positions, but coeducation meant that women had equitable access to classes and academic resources.

In contrast to the experience of many institutions that adopted coeducation later, in the 1960s and 1970s, changes in gender boundaries and gender norms did not accompany women's integration into the University of Rochester's main campus. It is tempting to think that the inclusion of a formerly excluded group would automatically transform its marginal status, but as the University of Rochester's experience shows, there must be an accompanying ideological and social change for such a transformation to take place. In fact, it may take longer for an institution that was already coeducational to achieve the same degree of gender equality as those formerly all-male institutions that became coeducational at the same moment in time as the women's movement. The University of Rochester has responded to the women's movement in various ways, including having a strong women's studies program, events that celebrate women's accomplishments, and a student women's group, but it still has low representation of women in the faculty, administration, and board of trustees. The university has not conducted a major study of gender relations or classroom climate. At least implicitly, administrators and trustees seem to accept the status quo for women at the university.

Notes

1. This rural property on Prince Street became the site of the University of Rochester's first campus and, in the 1930s, the campus of the College for Women. The record is not clear why Barleywood failed, but it was probably for financial reasons.

2. Arthur May, "The History of the University of Rochester" folder 9, p. 27, Manuscript Collection, Department of Rare Books and Special Collections, Rush Rhees Library, University of Rochester (hereafter abbreviated RRL); Jesse Rosenberger, *Rochester, the Making of a University,* (Rochester, N.Y.: University of Rochester Press, 1927), 240. All archival sources are located in RRL unless otherwise noted.

3. Arthur May, *The History of the University of Rochester, 1850–1962* (Rochester, N.Y.: University of Rochester, 1977), 95.

4. Elizabeth Cady Stanton, *Eighty Years and More: Reminiscences, 1815–1897* (Boston: Northeastern University Press, 1993), 434.

5. "A Fair Applicant," *Rochester Post-Express*, September 20, 1893, in the scrapbook of Helen Wilkinson; May, *History*, 118.

6. University of Rochester (UR) Board of Trustees, "Record of Meetings," vol. 3: 25.

7. May, *History*, 121.

8. UR, *Annual Catalogue*, 1900–1901.

9. UR, *Annual Catalogue*, 1904–05, 151–64; 1913–14, 155–69.

10. Blake McKelvey, *Rochester: The Quest for Quality, 1890–1925* (Cambridge: Harvard University Press, 1956), 234; Rosenberger, 293.

11. UR, *Annual Catalogue* 1904–05, 138–139; 1908–09, 151–52. A few underclasswomen in 1909 were studying sciences: 1 of the 30 juniors, 3 of the 24 sophomore women, and 4 of the 40 first-year women. These patterns are easy to discern because during these years of coeducation, the male students of each class were listed first in the catalogues, followed by the women, without any heading indicating that this was the organization.

12. UR Board of Trustees, "Record of Annual Meeting," vol. 3: 85–89.

13. By 1905, Professor Gilmore's class comprised an equal number of male and female students, while Rhees had created separate sections for men and women of his class; *Campus*, December 13, 1905, 8.

14. Ibid.; UR Board of Trustees, "Record of Annual Meeting," vol. 3: 85; UR, *Annual Catalogue*, 1904–5, 27–31.

15. UR Board of Trustees, "Record of Annual Meeting," vol. 3: 85; UR, *Annual Catalogue*, 1904–05, 27–31.

16. Record of the Iota Chapter of New York, Phi Beta Kappa Society, 282, Center for Academic Support, UR.

17. May, *History*, 150.

18. *Interpres*, 1904.

19. May, *History*, 121.

20. *Interpres*, 1905, 58–60 and 93–95; May, *History*, 153.

21. *Croceus*, 1910, 63.

22. Ibid., 33.

23. Ibid., 169.

24. Geraldine Clifford, *Lone Voyagers: Academic Women in Coeducational Institutions, 1870–1930* (New York: Feminist Press, 1989), 14.

25. V. Twitchell '04 to Helen Cross, M. Seligman '03 to Cross, "Correspondence to Helen R. Cross," box 3; F. Henderson '09, "Class Day for Women," 1909, box 1. Both in College for Women Memorabilia and Photographs, RRL.

26. *Campus*, February 11, 1902, 5; January 19, 1901, 6.

27. Dr. Avalyn E. Woodward, '05, interview by H. Bergeson, January 10, 1975, Friends' Oral History Materials (1970s), 15.

28. Dr. Leland Wood '08, interview by H. Bergeson, February 27, 1976, Friends' Oral History Materials (1970s), 2; Rhees, *Annual Reports of the President and Treasurer*, 1901–02, 11.

29. *Croceus*, 1912, 124; 1913, 128.

30. May, *History*, 135.

31. David McDonald, "Organizing Womanhood: Women's Culture and the Politics of Woman Suffrage in New York States, 1865–1917," (Ph.D. diss., State University of New York at Stony Brook, 1987), 172; May, *History*, 135. "A Bequest for Founding of Female College," newspaper clipping, n.d.; Executive Committee, vol. 5: 287.

32. F.H.P., "Freshman Meditation on Monroe Doctrine" in *Croceus*, 1915, 99; Rhees and Munro, *Annual Reports of the President and the Treasurer*, 1909–10, 9–12.

33. Executive Committee, vol. 4: 83 and 86.

34. Leslie Miller-Bernal, *Separate by Degree: Women Students' Experiences in Single-Sex and Coeducational Colleges* (New York: Peter Lang, 2000), 109–10.

35. UR, "Faculty Meeting Minutes Record," special meeting of November 22, 1927, vol. 9:40.

36. Janet Clark, "The College for Women, 1900–1950," in *The University of Rochester: The First Hundred Years*, (New York: University of Rochester, 1950), 60.

37. Alice Wood Wynd, interview by H. Bergeson, June 18, 1975, Friends' Oral History Materials (1970s).

38. "Minutes of the Advisor Committee for November, 1939," College for Women Subject Files, 1930–55, box 1.

39. Charles Watkeys, "Report of Progress of Reporting Committee on the Ten Year Plan," Charles Watkeys Papers, box 3, files 6 and 8.

40. John Slater to Rush Rhees, May 10, 1932, Charles Watkeys Papers, box 3, file 6.

41. Patricia Hammer, *The Decade of Elusive Promise: Professional Women in the United States, 1920–1930* (Ann Arbor: UMI Research Press, 1979), 134.

42. "Questions Asked by President Valentine Previous to His Election as President of UR," Rush Rhees correspondence, July 1934–June 1935.

43. UR Board of Trustees, "Executive Committee Meeting Minutes," vol. 8: 72; Munro to Dean Morriss of Pembroke College, February 4, 1930, and to President Ellen Pendleton of Wellesley College, February 4, 1930, College for Women 1930–1955, box 5, folder 8.

44. Susan Ware, *Holding Their Own: American Women in the 1930s* (Boston: Twayne, 1982), 61.

45. Paula Fass, *The Damned and the Beautiful: American Youth in the 1920s* (New York: Oxford University Press, 1977) 135–36.

46. *Tower Times*, May 14, 1948, 1.

47. Cornelius de Kiewiet, *Annual Report of the President, 1957*, 12–13.

48. Bernard Schilling, "C.W. de Kiewiet, 1986," personal possession of Christine Lundt.

49. Cornelius de Kiewiet, interview by Jack End, September 3, 1971, Oral History Tapes Transcriptions from Mary Jean Corless, DeKiewiet papers.

50. Professor B., interview by Christine Lundt, February 9, 1999.

51. Schilling.

52. Office of the Registrar, "M/F Enrollment Summary," October 1955 and October 1961; Record of the Iota Chapter, 149–63; "One Hundred Eleventh Commencement Program," University Ephemera 1900–1961.

53. Professor J. W. Johnson, interview by Christine Lundt, February 22, 1999.

54. "The 1959 Report Prepared for the Middle State Association, Part A: The University as a Whole," 62.

55. UR, *Annual Catalogue*, 1957–61.

56. From 1968 to 1979, there was no position called dean of students. There was a male provost, however. In 1980, a man served as the dean of student life; in 1982 another man became what was once again called the dean of students. Since 2000, two different women have been associate vice presidents and deans of students. UR, *Annual Catalogue*, 1965–2002.

57. *Campus Times*, November 11, 1955, 1.

58. "Middle States Association Report," April 23, 1960, Dean of Students 1930–62, box 3.

59. Alum 15 to Christine Lundt, signed document, December 21, 1996. As part of Lundt's doctoral research study, 33 alumni and alumnae from the years of transition from coordinate to coeducation were surveyed about the effects of the change.

60. Dean of Students [Joseph Cole], "[Review of the] Middle States Association's Report, Part I," June 29, 1960, Dean of Students 1930–62, box 3.

61. *Campus Times*, December 12, 1958; February 6, 1959, 1.

62. Patsy Runk, "A Woman's Place," *Campus Times*, February 27, 1959, 4.

63. "Twenty-fifth Reunion Profile: Class of 1959–Biographical Updates, Spring 1984," University Ephemera 1900–1961.

64. Alum 5 to Christine Lundt, December 18, 1996.

65. Alum 9 interview by Christine Lundt, March 24, 1999.

66. UR, *Official Bulletin*, 1960–61, Undergraduate Studies, 43.

67. UR, *Student Handbook*, 1963–64, 27.

68. *Campus Times*, November 6, 1970.

69. In 2002 the president of the Women's Caucus, Elyse Gilbert, described its major concerns as being both local and global, including petitioning to have emergency contraception become available over-the-counter, sexual assault and abuse awareness, the availability of birth control on campus, female genital mutilation awareness, and increasing people's knowledge about women's rights in Afghanistan. The Women's Caucus also put on "The Vagina Monologues." Elyse Gilbert to Leslie Miller-Bernal, e-mail, December 3, 2002.

70. *Women Studies Newsletter*, April 1984, 4.

71. *Campus Times*, December 4, 1975, 1.

72. Office of University Registrar, enrollment information, November 5, 1965, UR.

73. UR, self-study for the Middle States Association, 1991, vol. 1.

74. Office of the University Registrar, IPEDS-EF1, information on declared ethnic origin, Fall 2000, 3–11, UR.

75. UR commencement programs, 1970, 1980, 1990, 2000, RRL; Office of the University Registrar, IPEDS-EF1, Fall 2000.

76. Examples of committees co-chaired by a woman and man student are a 1965 Convocation Committee, and a 1965 Social and Traditions committee. *Campus Times* October 12 and 19, 1965.

77. *Campus Times*, April 13 and 20, 1995. The April 27, 1995, issue contained an interview with the winner of the election, Kaleb Michaud, a physics major had who suffered from rheumatoid arthritis since he was three years old.

78. The minority students did not seem entirely happy with this woman's leadership. An article in the *UR Messenger*, the student publication devoted to minority issues, asked

what it would have taken for "Ms. Morey to fully support the minority population that she claims to represent." See *UR Messenger*, February 1999, 9.

79. Middle States Association, 1990 report, Appendix 8G, 2.
80. See *Campus Times*, October 22, 1965, 2. A telling detail was the discussion of whether men's ties on the door as an indication that they had a woman in their room, a practice that had been used the previous year, "provided too much privacy."
81. *Campus Times*, December 5, 1975; January 21, 24, and 29, 1980; February 4, 25, 1985.
82. Betsy Brayer, "Greek Revival," *Rochester Review*, winter 1983, 15.
83. Ibid., 17.
84. *Campus Times*, summer 2002, 7.
85. *UR Messenger*, May 1996, 12.
86. *UR Messenger*, April 1998, 8.
87. *UR Messenger*, February 2000, 13.
88. *Women's Studies Newsletter* (title varies over time), 1981–95.
89. Ibid.
90. Susan Gustafson, acting director of the Susan B. Anthony Institute, interview by Leslie Miller-Bernal, November 8, 2002.
91. Nora Bredes, director of the Susan B. Anthony Center for Women's Leadership, interview by Leslie Miller-Bernal, November 7, 2002.
92. Gustafson.
93. The 2002 website for the university, in a section entitled "History and Distinctions," mentions the admission of women in 1900 and the expansion of the university under President Rush Rhees, and then simply says: "In 1955, the Colleges for Men and Women were merged into what is now the College." In other words, it does not make explicit that the university was coeducational for 12 years before the two coordinate institutions were established. See www.rochester.edu/news/facts/history.html (accessed December 3, 2002).
94. UR, *Student Handbook*, 2002–3, 73–76, available at *www.rochester.edu*.
95. *Women's Studies Newsletter*, April 1981.
96. *Women's Studies Newsletter*, November 1982, 3.
97. *Women's Studies Newsletter*, April 1984, 2.

4

A Historically Black Men's College Admits Women

The Case of Lincoln University

Leslie Miller-Bernal and Susan Gunn Pevar

Most historically black colleges and universities (HBCUs) originated as co-educational institutions. The black community's support of women's work and education, its lack of endorsement of the concept of "true womanhood," and its financial constraints made coeducation more appealing than separate colleges. A few black colleges that had been single-sex became coeducational in the 1920s when philanthropists favored large, consolidated institutions. Lincoln University in Chester County, Pennsylvania, is therefore unusual in having been established in 1854 as a college for black men and in having remained all male for about 100 years. As an all-male university, Lincoln was small but prestigious. Known as the "black Princeton," partly because of its ties to that all-male university, Lincoln achieved recognition for its famous graduates, including the renowned poet Langston Hughes; the first black U.S. Supreme Court justice, Thurgood Marshall; the first president of Ghana, Kwame Nkrumah; and the first leader of Nigeria, Nnamdi Azikiwe.

This chapter focuses on the gradual incorporation of women into the student body at Lincoln University, beginning in the 1950s. We are interested in not only the reasons women gained admission but also the effects of coeducation on this historically black institution and the experiences of female students themselves. To start, we present a brief overview of Lincoln University's founding and first one hundred years.

Lincoln University's Founding

John Miller Dickey (1806–1878), a white Presbyterian minister from Oxford, Pennsylvania (about 40 miles west of Philadelphia), was the man who had the vision and wherewithal to establish a college in 1854 for the education of free black men. Dickey's motivation was political as well as religious. As a supporter of the American Colonization Society, he believed that the solution to the "problem" of free blacks was to have them emigrate and settle in the colony of Liberia. By educating free black men, yet another goal could be accomplished: having them serve as missionaries to convert Africans to Christianity since Dickey believed that black missionaries were more physically suited to the African climate than were whites.[1]

Lincoln was originally called Ashmun Institute, named for Jehudi Ashmun (1794–1828), a white Congregational minister who was an agent for the American Colonization Society and who died after six years of service in Liberia.[2] The name was a signal that the college's founder was committed to gradualism rather than to the "radical" goal of the immediate end of slavery advocated by such abolitionists as William Lloyd Garrison and Arthur Tappan. This compromise position, delicate though it was, helped the fledgling educational institution survive in a county very close to the borders of such slave states as Delaware and Maryland. Chester County, where the college was located, contained a mixture of gradualist Scotch-Irish Presbyterians, almost all of whom were committed to preserving the Union and abolishing slavery slowly, and Quakers, most of whom were gradualists, although some favored immediate emancipation.[3] The site chosen for the college was a small settlement of free blacks named Hinsonville, after one its residents who had emigrated to Canada.[4] Not surprisingly, given the presence of free blacks and radical abolitionists, several homes were stops on the Underground Railroad. It has been estimated that more than 50,000 slaves were helped in their escape through Chester County between 1825 and 1861.[5]

In 1854, after a serious struggle, the Pennsylvania State Legislature granted a charter for Ashmun Institute—for the "scientific, classical and theological education of colored youth of the male sex." Without Dickey's powerful friends, many involved in the colonization movement, the bill would never have passed the Pennsylvania Senate.[6] Fund-raising took more time, even though Dickey himself purchased the 30-acre farm where the college was built.[7] Ashmun Institute finally opened in January 1857 with four students, two in a preparatory course and two in the theology department.[8]

Ashmun Institute's early years were very difficult and became even more so during the Civil War, when enrollment dropped. After the war, the African colonization scheme seemed less appropriate. Recognizing the need for trained blacks to serve as community leaders, Ashmun Institute's trustees applied to the state for a modified charter. In 1866 the institution's name was changed to Lincoln University, and it was empowered to confer all literary degrees usually conferred by "University Corporations."[9]

Lincoln University as a Men's Institution

Religious, conservative, financially strapped, and academically rigorous are characteristics that describe Lincoln University for most of its history. The Presbyterian Church may not have given Lincoln much financial support,[10] but until 1932 all presidents, and even all the faculty except those in science, were Presbyterian ministers.[11] The first lay president, Walter Wright, was not appointed until 1936.[12] A large majority of students in the nineteenth century, about 70 percent, attended Lincoln in order to prepare for the ministry; it was not until the turn of the twentieth century that graduates began to enter secular occupations such as medicine, a trend that accelerated after World War I.[13] The goal at Lincoln was to educate men for the ministry; therefore, its presidents refused to develop industrial education even when northern philanthropists were giving considerable sums to institutions like Hampton and Tuskegee that provided blacks with vocational training. It was clearly difficult to resist the pressure to become a vocational institution.[14] The great promoter of industrial education for blacks, Booker T. Washington, was given an honorary degree at Lincoln in 1894 and was the commencement speaker in 1909. A year after he spoke, a scientific agricultural course was announced in Lincoln's catalog but never appeared thereafter.[15]

With the exception of a brief period after the Civil War, Lincoln's trustees were conservative white men who believed and were comfortable saying that Lincoln represented "God's work *of* white men *for* Negroes."[16] As early as the 1870s and continuing through the mid-1890s, alumni pushed for the appointment of some blacks to the faculty and for alumni representation on the board of trustees.[17] Radical, sophisticated alumni controlled the alumni magazine; their contacts around the country enabled them to publicize their demands and to enlist the support of such famous activists as Frederick Douglass.[18] The trustees did not budge, however, even when alumni attached promised monetary gifts to their demands or created negative publicity.[19] After the alumni generation of the 1870s and 1880s, no others openly challenged the president and board's authority. For the next thirty years, students came primarily from the South and trained for the ministry. The first alumnus president of Lincoln, historian Dr. Horace Mann Bond, later wrote, "Southern prospects were likely to be less recalcitrant, as students and as alumni, than the products of a North tainted by the touch of 'radical abolitionism' and 'immediatism.' " Bond noted that after the period in which some alumni challenged the administration, Lincoln had a "policy of favoring candidates from the South and West over against those from the Northeast." The result was that Lincoln had many southern students who were "more docile as students and more tractable as alumni than the sophisticated Northerners."[20]

Changes in the racial composition of Lincoln's faculty and trustees finally occurred about a decade after the end of World War I, late in the era of the "New Negro" and the Harlem Renaissance.[21] While students on many other campuses of HBCUs engaged in strikes and riots in attempts to get administrations and trustees to hire more blacks and develop a curriculum that reflected African Americans' concerns, Lincoln's students were generally more conservative and preoccupied with such pastimes as freshmen hazing, fraternities, and sports.[22] Alumni became more active again, however, in opposition to trustees' attempts to choose a new president without their input. The already-published poet Langston Hughes was a student at Lincoln at that time. With two other students Hughes conducted a survey for a sociology course in 1929 on various aspects of student life, including students' feelings about having an entirely white faculty. The damning finding that received publicity in the black press was that the majority, 64 percent, of the 129 juniors and seniors interviewed were *against* having mixed race faculty. Their reasons included that having black faculty would introduce favoritism, that Lincoln was doing fine as it was, that students would not cooperate with black faculty, and that Lincoln was financially supported by whites (an argument administrators and trustees made). Seven students even expressed the view that white faculty provided greater advantages for students. Hughes argued that such responses indicated students believed "in their own inferiority" and that Lincoln had "failed in instilling in these students the very qualities of self-reliance and self-respect which any capable American leader should have."[23]

Obtaining sufficient financial support to survive has always been difficult for Lincoln. Every national crisis, such as wars and depressions, hit Lincoln particularly hard. A proposal to change its charter to become a normal school, which would have required admitting women, was one way the institution attempted to achieve state financial support in the mid-nineteenth century.[24] During the panic of 1873 Lincoln was on the verge of bankruptcy but saved itself by publicizing its first large group of students from Liberia, ten boys, aged 9 to 16. Administrators took "before" and "after" photos of the young men to demonstrate the benefits of a Christian education for Africans. The university sent thousand of letters with the photos to churches and prospective donors.[25] This strategy was typical of the time, as prior to the last decade of the nineteenth century when Lincoln received some major gifts, the university primarily depended on small gifts from churches, Sunday schools, and individuals.[26]

Lincoln compared favorably to other educational institutions in 1900 in terms of educational expenditures per student. Yet its deficit grew as it received fewer donations in a period when northern philanthropists favored industrial education.[27] The national depression that began in 1929 was particularly difficult for Lincoln; enrollments fell and again it was on the edge of bankruptcy. This time it was saved by attaining the status of a "state-aided" institution, which gave it a boost of $50,000 in 1939.[28] In 1943 Lincoln joined with other HBCUs in forming the United Negro College Fund and conducting a joint fund-raising campaign, from which Lincoln's share came to about $23,000.[29]

Given the precarious finances of Lincoln, institutional survival in and of itself has been an achievement. Insufficient money has meant that facilities have been inadequate, even primitive. For the first two decades of the twentieth century, there were no additions to the physical plant.[30] In 1929 Langston Hughes wrote about the "antiquated, overcrowded, and uncomfortable" dorms, which had no hot water. For 320 students, there were only six showers in the bathhouse. Conditions in the refectory appalled Hughes—dirty tablecloths and plates, not very nutritious food, and too much noise from too many students for the size of the hall. "Three meals a day in such a place can easily neutralize whatever 'culture' three hours or more a day spent in the classrooms seek to instill," Hughes wrote.[31] Thirty years later, a self-study at Lincoln noted that the physical plant was still "badly in need of attention."[32]

Despite severe financial constraints and poor facilities, students at Lincoln received a fine, if traditional, liberal arts education. Lincoln had close ties with and modeled itself after Princeton, another all-male, Presbyterian institution. During Lincoln's first century, four of its presidents, serving a combined total of 80 years, were Princeton Seminary graduates. From its early days, Lincoln stressed oratory and debates and had two literary societies that competed for members. In the early part of the twentieth century Lincoln distinguished itself by establishing an honors course. It also benefited from having older and more mature students, and a significant number of African students who tended to be particularly serious about their studies.[33] In addition to the outstanding, famous alumni mentioned above, Lincoln educated a disproportionate share of black ministers, physicians, and lawyers.[34]

Signs of Change in the Mid-twentieth Century

At the conclusion of World War II, Lincoln appointed its first black president, Dr. Horace Mann Bond, a historian and alumnus from the class of 1923. During his tenure, from 1945 to 1957, the question of coeducation surfaced.[35] In 1953 the charter was changed, eliminating the phrase that Lincoln was for the education of "colored youth of the male sex." This change legalized what had already occurred on a tiny scale—the attendance of a few women—and enabled Ruth Fales, the widow of a faculty member, to graduate.[36] Lincoln did not become a truly coeducational institution for more than a decade, however. Status concerns, preoccupation with making Lincoln multiracial, insufficient resources, and alumni and board opposition were some of the reasons that allowing women to attend did not have much of an impact at first on the gender composition of the student body.

Even before World War II, administrators began to be concerned that Lincoln was losing its best students to other institutions.[37] After the war, when many northern colleges and universities admitted some blacks, Jews, and other minorities, Lincoln found that it was competing with many more institutions for the students it had once easily enrolled. One response was to point out that Lincoln always had been open to men of all races and that it needed to revive its multiracial commitment. Such was the message of President Bond's "New Program," announced in the centennial year 1954: Lincoln would become an international and intercultural campus. Rather than admitting women in significant numbers, as the 1953 charter change permitted, trustees and administrators apparently favored solving enrollment and financial difficulties by seeking to increase the number of non-African-American male students, which meant, primarily, white students and African students.[38] Like other men's colleges of the time, Lincoln was at first unwilling to forfeit the prestige of its all-male status.

President Bond supported coeducation, in contrast to many trustees. Their differences surfaced at a meeting of the board in April 1953, after the charter change was legally complete. Several statements of trustees at the meeting made it clear that trustees were anxious not to have the change in charter and the awarding of a degree to Ruth Fales interpreted as an endorsement of coeducation. The minutes of the April meeting record that "the Board had made no commitment in favor of co-education."[39] Instead, the trustees recommended studying further "whether the new University should be coeducational."[40] Shortly after the April meeting, the immediate past president of the Alumni Association and an alumnus representative to the board of trustees, Dr. Harold Scott, wrote to Bond saying that at the meeting, he had gotten the "impression" that Bond was "defending the co-educational system." Bond's lengthy reply made clear that while he would follow trustees' decisions, he favored making Lincoln coeducational. In fact, President Bond compared the attitudes of the alumni who were "bitterly opposed to the coeducation of the sexes" to the attitudes of whites who favored segregation.[41]

Bond's public statement about coeducation, approved by the board, declared that despite the recent change in the charter, Lincoln remained "an institution for men" until the board had time for further study.[42] Bond stated further that only under "extraordinary circumstances" would women be admitted.[43] Lincoln remained an almost entirely male institution for more than another ten years. Fewer than ten women students at a time were enrolled before 1958, and even though the numbers then increased, they remained less than 25, or under 5 percent of the student body, until 1964.[44]

The trustees' unanimous vote in April 1958 to take "immediate measures" to make Lincoln a coeducational institution led to discussions that reveal the complicated ways race and gender are related.[45] A chapter of a report written at about that time, "Lincoln University Today," focused on racial integration as well as coeducation. The appeal of Lincoln to whites, the authors claimed, was twofold: its low cost and its willingness to provide a sound liberal arts education to those who might not otherwise be able to "achieve" higher education. The deplorable condition of the campus's buildings was believed to make the recruitment of white students more difficult, however. The authors surmised that the enrollment of women would present a "slight hazard" to racial integration since the "first" women students were expected to be black. Not just any woman would be appropriate as a Lincoln student, the authors contended. Rather, Lincoln should enroll "a high type of woman student both as to family background and academic standing."[46] Presumably the report's authors had in mind a student like Deborah Redd, the fourth woman to graduate from Lincoln. An article on Redd in the student newspaper in May 1958 mentioned that she was the niece of a popular Lincoln University professor, Dr. Harold Farrell, had always been on the dean's list, was active in dramatics and the school newspaper, and planned to teach French after graduation. The photo accompanying the article shows a demurely dressed young woman, with eyes cast modestly down and hands clasped in her lap—altogether respectable.[47]

Even though the "immediate measures" to turn Lincoln into a coeducational institution did not materialize, trustees and administrators continued to discuss issues connected to coeducation. An interesting report on the subject of coeducation was prepared in October 1959 by Eleanor Wolf, the first woman elected to the board of trustees, who was also white and Jewish. Wolf's report described conditions necessary to make coeducation "well-balanced" and "a deeply satisfying educational experience." She advocated having a highly qualified dean of women hired a year in advance to sit on major educational policy committees in order to ensure "the co-equal status of the oncoming women's program." Wolf also argued that the university should hire more women faculty and should appoint a "Negro woman" to the board of trustees. Yet Wolf was not at all radical but rather argued that coeducation should be "very conservative, socially and academically" because she feared that students would "force a natural liberality." She was particularly concerned about the possibility of white women becoming boarding students. Making it appear that she was not alone in her concerns, she wrote that "it has been suggested" that white women who would want to become boarders might be "bohemian" or "over-emotional." Given the "serious difficulties" such women students would create, Wolf recommended that "at least initially" white women should be admitted only as day students and that "a very careful selection process" be implemented.[48]

College constituencies had mixed, but mostly favorable, views of coeducation. As early as 1954, alumni had been surveyed about their opinions, but fewer than 10 percent responded. Dividing the alumni into age groups revealed that only among the oldest alumni was a slight majority opposed to coeducation (five of nine men who had graduated between 1901 and 1910). For two younger age groups a majority favored coeducation.[49] Students and faculty generally viewed coeducation in terms of how it would affect men students.[50] Articles in the student newspaper written during the 1950s and early 1960s reasoned that "coeds" were being brought in to make men students more polite, more attentive to their physical appearance, more academically competitive, and more religious. Admitting women could help with the perennial problem of college apathy, some people argued, by reinvigorating campus organizations and debates. Sometimes these advantages were contrasted with vague disadvantages, such as the "very great sacrifices" that becoming coeducational would entail.[51] One student wrote in 1959 that the subject had been "much discussed" on campus and that it invoked "much stress." Yet the writer favored coeducation, believing that Lincoln men would change from being "bedraggled, dirty, uncouth" students to "dapper" men deserving to be put on the cover of *Esquire.* Faculty and administrators tended to stress the academic advantages of coeducation. In 1960 President Armistead Grubb noted that some alumni "bridle at the prospect of high heels punching holes in our sacred soil," but his attitudes had changed when he had to reject a woman applicant who had "straight A's in solid subjects and an I.Q. of 127."[52]

Over time Lincoln's transition to a coeducational institution became less and less contested. The low number of women students was primarily due to insufficient resources to build a women's dormitory needed because of the university's rural location. In 1965, a report, "Resident Coeducation at Lincoln University," continued the discussion of the advantages and disadvantages of "substantial coeducation" but made the arguments in favor seem almost indisputable.[53] For example, a concern of the prior decade, that the admission of women might negatively affect the university's goal of racial integration, was presented, followed by the statement: "Many do not accept this assumption."[54] The report also discussed the curricular implications of becoming a coeducational institution; it assumed that female students would be more interested in the humanities than men students were and that pressure would develop to add courses in music, art, and elementary education.

One new issue that surfaced in this report was a concern with black men. The report's authors noted that the experiences of both predominantly white and predominantly black coeducational colleges indicated that the average academic level of entering women would be higher than that of men. While coeds might be good for raising Lincoln's academic standards, the 1965 report contained this warning: "There are many who have studied the problems of Negro education who argue that the need to produce more educated men is much greater than the need for educated women. If this is true, Lincoln would not be providing its maximum service to society if women students were to place a restriction not otherwise necessary on the admission of men."[55]

Experiences of Early Women Residential Students

Residential coeducation was declared to have come to Lincoln in the fall of 1965, but only 20 women could be accommodated in a small building that had previously been used as an alumni guest house. Including day students, the total number of women students on campus that year was 45 out of 589.[56] Given the trends in overall enrollment, it is clear that at least at first, coeducation did not affect men students' admission. Lincoln's enrollments increased by about 25 percent, from 589 in 1965 to 738 in 1966, similar to the increases at many other colleges and universities.[57] Women's enrollments remained low, however, until 1967 when a women's dormitory that accommodated 135 students finally opened.

Many women students felt somewhat uncomfortable in the initial years of coeducation, as articles about them in college publications revealed. Photos in an alumni magazine article on these students mostly portrayed them in stereotypically feminine ways—on the telephone, for instance, at a formal tea, or socializing with men. The accompanying article was more serious, however. The young women interviewed made some perceptive and fairly critical remarks about their reception. One woman said, "The majority of fellows still do not want to accept the female as part of the student body nor treat her equally in that respect." Another commented that while she did not experience "animosity," she did not feel "welcome" either, attributing some of this reaction to women's "shattering" Lincoln's "all-male tradition." Men students who implied that she and other women were only at Lincoln "to find husbands" were particularly irritating to this student. Even though the women who were interviewed talked about how the "boy-girl ratio" may have made Lincoln "ideal" socially, they felt it was not ideal academically. With so few women students, some of the women did not believe that the situation was ideal socially, either. "We are under constant critical scrutiny," one woman commented, which she felt tended to "undermine a girl's self-confidence," although she also claimed that such scrutiny might help build self-confidence by forcing the women students to "assert" themselves both academically and socially in order "to survive."[58]

A woman who teaches at Lincoln today has almost entirely positive recollections of the years that she attended the university, from 1967 to 1971. She recalls enjoying the intensive "social whirl," particularly sorority functions and being chosen as a "sweetheart" of a fraternity. She also benefited from such academic experiences as traveling to Mexico and attending theatrical performances in Philadelphia as part of her English major. Although this alumna faculty member had a few negative experiences, for instance, having to accept a "C" in a course because she was unwilling to go to a male professor's parties where she knew she would experience some harassment, she was clearly pleased that she had attended Lincoln rather than any of the other colleges that had accepted her.[59]

Student Activism: Civil Rights, Student Rights, and the Women's Movement

The early years of residential coeducation coincided with growing student activism, at Lincoln as well as at most other colleges and universities. On issues of race, Lincoln students had become politically active even before the 1960s. Lincoln's chapter of the National Association for the Advancement of Colored People (NAACP) fought segregation of public facilities in the nearby town of Oxford after four students were arrested in 1950 for sitting in the white section of the movie theatre.[60] During the same years Lincoln students knew that a famous alumnus, Thurgood Marshall '30, was leading the fight against segregation in public schools, culminating in the *Brown v. Board of Education* decision in 1954, which outlawed separate but "equal" schools.[61]

Ironically, integration of educational institutions led to enrollment difficulties for HBCUs, as increasing numbers of black students chose to attend predominantly white institutions. Administrators at Lincoln were emphatic about the continuing importance of historically black institutions, yet at the same time they attempted to integrate their own student body by increasing the number of white students in attendance.[62] Some Lincoln students worried that their institution might enroll too many white students, especially since they believed that most white students did not get involved in campus activities. In 1960 the student president of the Lincoln NAACP chapter made a "stirring" assembly speech in which he suggested that if the behavior of the white students then on campus was how they would act under "total integration," Lincoln should "stop" integration. Five years later, an article in the student newspaper discussed "myths of Lincoln," including that it was a "happily integrated college." Students were said to fear that Lincoln would be "taken over by whites," which the article reported had happened at Virginia State College and Lincoln University in Missouri.[63] What Lincoln should instead strive for, the article's author argued, was to be a "truly multi-racial institution" in which integration was planned and in which white students would "not only work for grades but for Lincoln."[64]

Understandably, a white woman student at Lincoln, the editor-in-chief of the student newspaper in 1965, held different views. Noting that white students then constituted about 20 percent of the student body, the editor bemoaned the actions of some students to discourage white students from participating in campus activities and to "openly bar non-Negro students from attending." Her goal for Lincoln was to assume "its position of leadership in the field of meaningful integration" so that students could continue to learn about students whose backgrounds were "very different" from their own.[65]

Like students on other campuses in the mid-1960s, Lincoln students protested college policies. They argued that they should be treated as adults who were free to make their own decisions. Thus they objected to compulsory assemblies, and in fact, walked out of one in protest in the spring of 1965.[66] Men students met with the dean to discuss sex on campus and the "monastery-like atmosphere" then prevailing. The dean, who had the memorable name of Kinsey, said he understood "normal wants and desires" of the men students but was "unalterably opposed to allowing University buildings to provide the privacy some individuals would like, presumably to engage in just those activities."[67]

Student activism at Lincoln was complicated by gender and race. Some men students had been opposed to coeducation because they saw that it would inevitably bring about greater social regulations, which it did. Moreover, women were more strictly regulated than men students, which some of them protested. The associate dean, Mamie Walker, defended regulating women more closely than men because of women's "relative defenselessness," and she added that in the family "there's a special concern for safety of women." Women students chafed at these regulations, with one saying, "We should be given a little more freedom and a little less supervision." During a student panel in early 1968, a woman student called for birth control to be more readily available "as it was worse than useless to legislate morality." A member of the audience connected this issue to race by denouncing the attempt to force white middle-class morality on the student body. His statement was given an enthusiastic ovation.[68]

Even though women students were actively involved in campus life by the late 1960s, as evidenced by their participation in protests and by the articles they wrote for the student newspaper, their presence was still not completely accepted. In 1967, when women's enrollment had increased to just under 25 percent of registered students, a man student wrote in the student newspaper that one of the "pet topics on the subject of changes" at the university was coeducation. He argued that while coeducation had both advantages and disadvantages, the latter "by far" outweighed the former because they led to frustrations for men students, a decrease in their being able to concentrate, and a decline in school spirit. A woman student also wrote about being aware of men students' "resentment" that women had destroyed something "sacred," the old Lincoln at which there were few restrictions and essentially no curfew.[69]

Toward the end of the 1960s, students occasionally debated the proper role of women and the value of the women's movement. Some men students involved in the black power movement argued that women's equality was a white person's concept. In December, 1968, for example, a student identified as "Mfuasi" wrote in the student newspaper that a "Sister" had to realize that she "becomes Black only through the criteria set down by the brothers," which meant being "submissive" and fulfilling three functions: being an inspiration to her man, educating her children, and working in community development. This view did not go unchallenged, however. In the next issue, a woman wrote a response in which she called for "unity" of the sexes and for women to be educated so that they could properly educate their children. Moreover, she said that women were "inherently submissive" so that "brothers" should not become "emotionally involved with reducing Black sisters to a state of submission." Interestingly, the same issue also contained a rebuttal to Mfuasi from "Spartacus," self-identified as white, who attributed the oppression of black women to the long history of racism, which resulted in black men identifying with an oppressor-slave mentality. Spartacus argued that there "can be no sound liberation movement, black or otherwise, which does not struggle at the same time for women."[70]

More articles on women's roles, the women's movement, and feminism appeared in the student newspaper during the 1970s. Some were summaries of talks given at Lincoln by guests who were successful professional or businesswomen. Others were articles that had originally appeared elsewhere, on such feminist topics as International Women's Year, COYOTE (an organization for the decriminalization of prostitution), and female genital mutilation. Still others were contentious exchanges among students, debating whether gender equality was appropriate for black people.[71]

Clearly it was not easy for Lincoln's women students to embrace feminist issues. Racism has often seemed more critical than sexism, and some black men (and women) have seen women's liberation as a white women's issue that benefited whites at the expense of blacks. One guest speaker on Lincoln's campus in 1977 tried to put both issues in perspective. C. Delores Tucker, the first woman and first black to hold the office of the secretary of the Commonwealth of Pennsylvania, spoke on "ERA's Relevance for Black Women." She pointed out that black women were at the bottom of the employment ladder, victims of sexism as well as racism, and noted that in Pennsylvania eight times as many black men as women made over $11,000. Yet, her point was that "the Black man is not our oppressor, any more than we are his," and that black women should "stand by" black men's side. She noted that women's liberation should not be confused with male subjugation. Quoting Sissy Farenthold, first president of the National Women's Political Caucus and, at the time, president of Wells College, Tucker said, "Sisterhood does not mean the end of brotherhood, but the beginning of humanhood."[72]

Achieving State-Related Status

The 1970s was a difficult decade for Lincoln University, as it was for many predominantly black colleges.[73] Federal legislation, particularly the Higher Education Act of 1965, resulted in black students being given more financial aid so that they were able to attend a greater range of colleges and universities. No longer could black universities be assured that the most academically qualified students would attend their institutions. Earlier hopes that Lincoln could regain its past status by raising its standards—"in order not to be a sanctuary for those Negro students who are turned away from integrated schools because they are found scholastically unfit," as acting president Donald Yelton said in 1960—seemed unrealistic.[74] Lincoln enrolled an increasing number of students who needed special assistance to achieve academic success. To counter the effect that this would have on the university's intellectual life, Lincoln considered ways of attracting students who were talented in science so that they could serve as "pace setters" or a "leavening influence" for the rest of the students.[75] At the same time, the university trained faculty to teach students who had academic deficiencies and provided special programs for underprepared students, including workshops and academic counseling.[76] While many community members were concerned about the university's decline in standards, a woman editor-in-chief of the student newspaper wrote a perceptive editorial in 1977 about the "new responsibility" of black colleges: "to educate those who are academically lacking, to give them a chance." While she recognized the need to have programs to help academically deficient students, she noted that the students themselves had to be motivated: "It's the student's responsibility to themselves and to their race to make it," she said, evoking the race uplift ideal of the nineteenth century.[77]

In early 1969 the president of Lincoln, Marvin Wachman, announced that the university was being recommended for the designation as a "state-related institution." The advantages, Wachman noted, were that financial support would enable the university to "hold tuition and fees at a reasonable level"; at the same time, staff salaries could increase to "competitive standards" and the university could expand "modestly."[78] Although the governor of Pennsylvania would appoint one-third of Lincoln's trustees, there would be "no change in independence," he argued. Despite Wachman's reassurances, students were fearful of what this designation would mean; in particular, they were reluctant to trade lowered tuition for losing their identity as a predominantly black institution.[79]

Lincoln did not become a state-related institution until three years later, in 1972. A statement prepared to convince legislators that it should be so designated argued that Lincoln was the only institution whose "total commitment" was to prepare students, "the majority of whom come from backgrounds of poverty and deprivation," to return to their communities to work on solving poverty and urban problems. Noting that it is not easy to "deal with quality education and compensatory education at the same time," the statement concluded by pointing out the advantages to granting Lincoln the status of a state-related institution. The Commonwealth of Pennsylvania would benefit from having an institution with many years of experience in training people to deal with pressing social problems, and Lincoln would benefit from being able to expand and intensify its academic mission.[80] When the governor signed the bill that made Lincoln a state-related institution, Herman R. Branson, who by then was president of the university, called it "unquestionably the most signifi-cant event in Lincoln's history."[81] Within the decade, the appropriations from the commonwealth amounted to more than one-third of the revenues Lincoln received for educational and general operations.[82]

Lincoln at the End of the Twentieth Century and Beginning of the Twenty-First

Lincoln University today can be described as a diverse institution, if not di-verse in the ways envisioned by its trustees in the 1950s. Rather than Lincoln students' varying much by race and ethnicity, they vary more by gender, social background, and in some relatively invisible ways, by their religion and politi-cal attitudes in particular. Campus debates reveal the complex intersections of race and gender, the difficulties of being attentive to women's needs while not ignoring the impact of racism on black men's and women's lives.

Since 1982 women have formed the majority of Lincoln's undergraduate students.[83] Their percentage has increased gradually from 51 percent to slightly more than 60 percent in the early years of the twenty-first century.[84] Interest-ingly, many students and even some faculty believe that the percentage of women is much higher. One man student said three times during an interview that the gender ratio was 16 women to 1 man, which would make women over 90 percent of the students! Although this student may not have recognized the implications of what he said, even faculty gave figures as high as seven to one. A common belief was that the class that entered in September 2001 had 500 women but only 100 men. A person in the admissions office said he was aware of this rumor but that the real figure was 350 women and 250 men, which means that women were 58 percent of the entering class.[85] Because men tend to be weaker students, however, their attrition is higher, so the gender ratio may be somewhat more imbalanced than official statistics indicate.

Misperceptions about Lincoln's gender ratio probably arise because women students dominate in other ways than their numbers. Women are the heads of a high percentage of campus clubs, and women students excel academically, forming a disproportionate number of those on the dean's list and in honor societies.[86] Yet women students do not dominate Lincoln in all ways. Up through 2002, very few presidents of the student governing association (SGA) have been women, and men's sports teams are taken much more seriously than women's.[87] The Greek scene has been relatively quiet on campus, since various fraternities and sororities were suspended in the 1990s due to hazing incidents, but com-munity members say that when they were active, fraternities were viewed as more important than sororities, as is typically the case at coeducational institu-tions. Since 1969, when the first woman was elected class president, there have been years when all or almost all class officers have been men.[88] More recently, however, class presidents and the student newspaper editor-in-chief have often been women. In 2001–2002, the presidents of three of the four classes were women; the editor-in-chief was a man.

Given that Lincoln was a men's college for about 100 years, it is not surprising that there are still residues of men's traditions. One tradition, perhaps unique to Lincoln, was that of the Rabble, informal but powerful cliques that passed judgments on others and exercised social control through ridicule.[89] Even after women were admitted to Lincoln, the student newspaper carried a column on the Rabble. In 1974, an editorial criticized the Rabble for being "only interested in the malicious or derogatory." The examples given focused on sexual relations—who is pregnant by whom, who broke up with whom, who is homosexual.[90] Another male-oriented tradition that received a great deal of attention in the student newspaper was choosing and crowning a Homecoming Queen. Although the name changed to "Miss Lincoln" (or Ms. Lincoln) after women were admitted, the stress on women's physical characteristics and social graces continued.[91] Interestingly, since 1989, there has also been a Mr. Lincoln crowned during homecoming weekends, presumably an attempt to make this tradition more gender equal.

Some clubs that have originated since Lincoln became coeducational have maintained and even reinforced traditional gender patterns. Cheerleaders, for example, are all women and although it is undeniable that they engage in physically demanding routines, it is also true that they take the traditional female role of supporting men's sports teams and are evaluated partly, at least, on their physical attractiveness.[92] Ziana Fashion Club is one of the most popular clubs on campus. Men are involved, but women dominate this club, which stresses clothing styles and dance routines. The woman who was president of this fashion club in 2001–2002 noted that many men try out for it, and although quite a few are accepted, many drop out when they realize how much work and discipline are required.[93]

Women leaders at Lincoln report feeling supported by the university and comfortable with their high achievements. It was striking that when asked if they felt that men students dominated in classes or in extracurricular activities, they sometimes misinterpreted the question as asking how men students felt given the dominance of women. None of the women leaders seemed concerned that Lincoln did not have a women's studies program; in fact, few had any idea about this area of scholarship. Yet, students occasionally make comments that reveal some awareness that women's perspectives are not always acknowledged. One female student said that in a black psychology class she took, she questioned why the class dealt with the psychology of black *men* but not women. It is interesting that this woman noticed this lack and also that she was comfortable enough to question her professor about it.[94]

Although Lincoln does not have a women's studies program and only established a Women's Center in the 2002–2003 academic year, since the late 1970s the university has held conferences and talks specifically oriented toward women's issues.[95] Some examples are a rape workshop in 1979 that had two outside speakers from a Rape Crisis Council; two "WomanSense" conferences focusing on skills women need in the work world in order to be successful and problems they would likely encounter, including sexual harassment; and in 1996, the "First Annual Women's Conference," which focused on relations among young women on campus and led to the establishment of a campus chapter of the National Coalition of 100 Black Women.[96] Lincoln also has a chapter of the National Council of Negro Women, originally established in 1935 by Mary McLeod Bethune to "forge black women's organizations into a powerful coalition."[97]

The relative lack of focus on feminist issues at Lincoln derives from several factors. Historically black colleges like Lincoln have generally been conservative institutions in which traditional, religious values prevail. Moreover, the black community is very concerned about the plight of its men. While Lincoln and other HBCUs relaxed parietal regulations during the 1960s, their students are still more strictly regulated than students in many northern, predominantly white institutions. As the dean of students at Lincoln explained, the black community expects colleges to act as an "extension" of the family, "nurturing" but also "disciplining" their students. An example of Lincoln University's traditionalism is its relatively strict "intervisitation" policy (rules about the hours during which members of the opposite sex may visit the dorms, which are almost all single-sex).[98]

While it is difficult to assess how many students at Lincoln or at any college are religious, it is clear that religion plays an important role in campus life. Some faculty estimated that about half the students that they knew well were very religious. During the 1970s, the campus had a student organization called "Militants for Christ," whose stated purpose was to create an "atmosphere of deep spiritual concern." In 1991 the student newspaper mentioned that the campus was having a "prayer break" twice a week, and in 1993 religious revival services were held in chapel over four days. In recent years, the student newspaper has had a "spirituality editor" and has frequently devoted a page to spirituality. In the 1990s, the "religious corner" of the paper included Islam as well as Christianity.[99]

Many people at Lincoln believe that men students need extra support and encouragement. Dean Judith Thomas, who has been a faculty member at Lincoln since 1974, talked about how black families, "Raise our daughters, love our sons." She reported feeling particularly pleased when men students try hard, whereas she expects such behavior from women students.[100] Women students generally accept their traditional role of sacrificing themselves to support their "brothers." When the Million Man March took place in 1995, women students staged a rally for the Lincoln men who participated, both before they left and when they returned to campus. A woman faculty member who raised money for a bus to take the men to Washington was quoted approvingly in the student newspaper for her views that "sistas" should act as "real women" by encouraging men to be "real" men. Yet she admonished Lincoln women to "not let them [men] abuse or use us. We must help them straighten their backs and stand tall. We should help them get themselves together by getting into their studies."[101]

Sexual relations among students are complicated by some of these same factors. On the one hand, while there appears to be a general acceptance of sexuality, the deeply religious nature of many students makes for serious discussions about what types of sexual relations are permissible.[102] In April 1995, for example, an article on the religion page of the student newspaper, *The Lincolnian,* explained why God included a "no-sex-before-marriage clause"—not to make people "miserable" but to be sure people "would have time to get to know Him." In September 2000 *The Lincolnian's* spirituality page had an article by a Christian student who stated, "Premarital sex is a sin and is wrong."[103] Not only are students, particularly women students, cautioned about being too promiscuous, not "respecting" themselves or others, but also homosexuality is seldom discussed. While the student newspaper has occasionally had articles favoring acceptance of homosexuality, there is no club for gay or bisexual students on campus.[104] This may be changing, however. During the 2001–2002 academic year, an antigay letter in the paper prompted vigorous protest, and students reported that many gay students, particularly lesbians in the freshman class, were "out."[105] It is also notable that Lincoln does have an organization for students with AIDS, which has been active in distributing condoms.

Another factor complicating heterosexual relations is the imbalance between women and men students. Various members of the academic community have expressed the view that women compete among themselves for the attention of men and appear to be more willing to tolerate behavior from men that others might consider abusive.[106] The dean of students said in 2002 that he believed this gender imbalance was one of the factors responsible for physical fights among women and between women and men. He was concerned that students, many from inner cities, learn to establish "healthy" relationships with each other.[107]

An incident that occurred in 2000–2001 reveals once again the complex relations between gender and race. A woman president of the SGA accused one of the SGA vice-presidents of sexual harassment but later said she had lied and offered an apology. Naturally, this caused an uproar on campus, with some people simply concluding that women were unfit for certain types of leadership positions. A perceptive article by "a Lincoln man" in the student newspaper discussed the broader significance of this incident, asking the SGA president how she could believe that her apology was "sufficient" when "all of the world is eager to see the Black male locked away in jails like some animal, in some cases for what [she] . . . had falsely accused" the male student of doing. This writer also said he was "sickened" on behalf of all the women who had genuine complaints about sexual harassment but "no one believes them because women like you thought it was a joke and used it as a pawn in your quest for absolute power." The article concluded with a moving statement that "As an African-American male I find that it is difficult to live in this world with all of the negative stereotypes that surround me. I have been labeled a thief, gangster, rapist, and . . . disappointment to my people."[108]

Conclusion

Lincoln University has experienced many changes since the 1960s that make it a very different institution from what it was during its first hundred years. Not only has it become a coeducational university in which women predominate, but it has also become part of the Pennsylvania state university system. The change from private to public is a symptom of the change in the student body, which no longer includes the economic and academic black elite but instead has more students from financially stressed families, many of whom are single-parent families in inner cities.

Areas of male dominance still exist at Lincoln, of course, reflecting sexism in society at large as well as the university's long history as a men's institution. The importance placed on men's rather than women's sports, the tendency for men students to be elected president of the student governing association, and the greater male iconography on campus are some indicators of this dominance.[109] Yet what may be more surprising is the extent to which women are acknowledged and the areas in which they dominate: a few dorms are named after women; the chapel, which was built long before the college admitted women, has a woman's name; women excel academically, are the heads of a majority of clubs, and frequently are the editors-in-chief of the student newspaper.[110] In short, it seems that Lincoln as a coeducational institution is more comfortable for and supportive of its women students than many other coeducational institutions of higher education.

There are reasons not to conclude too readily that Lincoln is a woman-friendly institution, however. Concerns about black men students mean that all segments of the community—administrators, faculty, staff, and students, including women students—want to encourage men students to such an extent that at times, women students' interests may be compromised. Also problematic is the status of women faculty, administrators, and members of the board of trustees.[111] Men dominate the higher ranks of faculty and administration, and even recent searches for new members of the president's "cabinet" have not interviewed women candidates. Although Lincoln had a woman president, Dr. Niara Sudarkasa, from 1987 to 1998, her administration ended in a scandal, which has made some administrators doubtful that trustees would approach another woman in the foreseeable future.[112]

Given the threats to the survival of black institutions, and the severe financial difficulties they have faced, it is understandable why issues of gender equality have often not been seen as critical. The needs for functioning buildings and money for scholarships inevitably take precedence over issues of equality, especially since women students achieve so highly at Lincoln. Moreover, the university reflects the larger black community's traditional, religious values and its great concern about the welfare of its men. The "stigma" of race that Glenn Loury and others discuss affects black men more than women, as witnessed by their high rates of imprisonment.[113] Black women face a difficult path in expressing their race loyalty and love of their "brothers" while not accepting subordination for themselves. As long ago as 1977 black feminists in the Combahee River Collective succinctly described this challenge: "Our situation as Black people necessitates that we have solidarity around the fact of race. . . . We struggle together with Black men against racism, while we also struggle with Black men about sexism."[114]

Women students at Lincoln generally believe that these struggles are worth it. Many expressed the view that being at a black institution has provided them with a special environment in which they have been enabled to flourish. A senior chemistry major talked about the benefits of being able to "learn without any prejudices. . . . Everyone looks the same. . . . You get to work and work hard . . . [and can develop] self-pride. . . . I would never go anywhere else."[115]

Notes

1. Horace Mann Bond, *Education for Freedom: A History of Lincoln University, Pennsylvania* (Princeton: Princeton University Press and Lincoln University, 1976), 209, presents recollections of Dickey in which he said that he believed blacks were "possibly better fitted for the deadly climate by their bodily constitution." Andrew Murray, "The Founding of Lincoln University," *Journal of Presbyterian History* (winter 1973): 398, describes how the early experiences of Presbyterian missionaries in Liberia demonstrated that "American Negroes had no innate immunity to tropical diseases."
2. Bond, 151–60.
3. Dickey himself married a woman raised as a Quaker, Sarah Emlen Cresson (1806–1878). However, her older brother, the philanthropist Elliott Cresson, was active in the American Colonization Society, even serving as its secretary. See Bond, 37, 115.
4. Emory Hinson emigrated to upper Canada in 1851 to escape possible kidnapping from slave raiders who did not care whether or not a black person was legally free. See Bond, 225.
5. Ibid., 196.

6. Ibid., 230.
7. Ibid., 226.
8. Murray, 408.
9. Bond, 262–63.
10. Bond notes that Lincoln never received "substantial assistance" from the Presbyterian Church (ibid., 367).
11. "History and New Design," no author but presumed to be Horace Mann Bond, undated, 11, Special Collections, Langston Hughes Memorial Library, Lincoln University, Pennsylvania (hereafter abbreviated SC).
12. Bond, 398.
13. "History and New Design," 10.
14. Several sources mention the "not entirely apocryphal" story that in 1891 Lincoln's president, Dr. Isaac Rendall, refused the offer of a philanthropist of $200,000 to endow a department of manual arts. See "History and New Design," 9, as well as Ruth Danenhower Wilson, "Negro Colleges of Liberal Arts," *American Scholar* 19 (1950): 465, who adds that it was a Philadelphia merchant who later became a great patron of Hampton.
15. Bond, 406.
16. Ibid., 431.
17. Bond says that in the 1880s, the radical alumni also wanted Lincoln to alter its curriculum to include training in the manual arts. This is not so strange as it may at first seem, as progressive educational institutions connected with radical abolitionists, such as Oberlin and the Oneida Institute, combined manual labor with academic work. The Lincoln alumni commented on the introduction of an industrial education course at Howard in 1884 (ibid., 343).
18. See Douglass's letter in the fifth issue of the first volume of the *Alumni Magazine,* 124, SC, in which he wrote, "I am . . . entirely with you in your effort to counteract the tendency in colored institutions . . . to repress and discourage the colored man's ambition to do and to be something more than a subordinate when he is qualified to occupy superior positions." The alumni's campaign with the larger public led a Baltimore Catholic newspaper to remind its readers that the Jesuit institution, Georgetown University, had had a black priest, Father Patrick Healy, as president between 1874 and 1882 (Bond, 348). See Chapter 9 in this volume for a discussion of coeducation at Georgetown.
19. Key alumni in this campaign were Dr. Nathan Mossell, class of 1879, who was the first black graduate of the University of Pennsylvania Medical School, and Francis Grimké, the nephew of the famous abolitionist and feminist sisters Angelina Grimké Weld and Sarah Grimké. Francis Grimké and his two brothers were the sons of Henry Grimké by the slave woman, Nancy Weston. Their aunts did not learn of their existence until 1868 when they happened to see their nephews' names mentioned in the *Anti-Slavery Standard.* All three Grimké brothers attended Lincoln; Francis and his brother Archibald, graduated in 1870, and had outstanding careers in the ministry and law, respectively. See Bond, 316–20. Dr. Mossell tried in vain in 1886 to get Francis Grimké appointed to the faculty by offering Lincoln $700 toward the endowment of a professorial chair if it would be given to a "colored man" (ibid., 339–49).

20. Ibid., 356–57.

21. Lincoln was similar to other historically black institutions controlled by northern religious denominations in being late in appointing blacks to the faculty, administration, and trustees. See Henry N. Drewry and Humphrey Doermann, *Stand and Prosper: Private Black Colleges and Their Students* (Princeton: Princeton University Press, 2001), 55–56.

22. Raymond Wolters, *The New Negro on Campus* (Princeton: Princeton University Press, 1975), 280–81. See also Langston Hughes's account in his autobiography, *The Big Sea* (New York: Hill and Wang, 1940), 280–84.

23. Langston Hughes, "Three Students Look at Lincoln: A Survey of the College of Lincoln University by Three Members of Professor Labaree's Class in Sociology," March 1929, SC.

24. See "Sermons, Addresses, Correspondence and Catalogs of Lincoln University, 1853–1874," SC.

25. Bond, 491–92.

26. Ibid., 461, 482.

27. Ibid., 480.

28. Ibid., 399–400. Credit also needs to be given to the liberal university president Dr. William Hallock Johnson, a former faculty member who during his tenure of thirteen years, 1926 to 1939, raised over a million dollars. See ibid., 395.

29. Ibid., 401, 484.

30. Ibid., 462.

31. Hughes, "Three Students," 26.

32. "Lincoln University Today," 1959, 26, SC. Problems with the physical plant are still evident today, as noted by various administrators interviewed by Leslie Miller-Bernal.

33. "History and New Design," 9, mentions that the class of 1900 entered in 1896 with an average age of 21. Lincoln students themselves recognized the superior academic performance of students from Africa. See *The Lincolnian*, June 1952. This point was also mentioned in "Lincoln University Today," 27.

34. "History and New Design," 12.

35. About a decade earlier, during World War II, Lincoln University faculty, administrators, and students also discussed the possibility of becoming a coeducational institution to counter falling enrollments. Campus opinion divided sharply on the desirability of coeducation, and many people argued that careful planning was necessary, as well as extensive renovations of campus buildings. See articles in the student newspaper, *The Lincolnian*, March 24, 1942, and April 10, 1942.

36. In the early 1950s, three women were "special" (i.e., non-matriculating) students with local addresses, according to the *Lincoln University Bulletin*, 1950–51, 95.

37. "Lincoln University Today," 1959, 134. In 1934, Lincoln conducted a coeducational summer school, which may have resulted from a desire to see what having women students would be like and been an attempt to raise money during the depression. Only 23 students attended, however, 13 of whom were women, and 10 faculty members taught, so it would not seem to have been a success. See the *Catalogue of Lincoln University*, 1934–35, 59, SC.

38. Herman J. Branson, president of Lincoln in the 1970s, presents figures in Bond, xvii, on total enrollment that show Lincoln's decline from 483 students in 1950 to 313 in

1953. Enrollment fell even lower in 1955, to 274 students, but from then on increased. In its centennial year (1953–54), Lincoln also had a budget deficit of almost $60,000, despite an appropriation from the Commonwealth of Pennsylvania of $190,000 for that year.

39. Lincoln University Board of Trustees minutes, 1945–59, 488, SC.

40. Ibid., 489. The committee's members were board president Lewis Stevens, Julius Rosenwald, and Ralph Bunche.

41. Moreover, Dr. Bond noted that Lincoln's trustees had voted more than 75 years earlier, in 1874, to admit women, for two reasons: in response to the Grimké sisters' pressure and in an attempt to have Lincoln qualify for the state of Pennsylvania's normal school appropriations. He also mentioned how the Grimké sisters had given Lincoln a scholarship for women students, should they be admitted. See Harold R. Scott to Bond, April 29, 1953, and Bond to Scott, undated reply, Horace Mann Bond Archive, SC. Bond's attitudes toward coeducation appear to be a good example of why biographer Williams describes him as a "forward-looking man." See Roger M. Williams, *The Bonds: An American Family* (New York: Atheneum, 1971), 163. Other actions of Bond would also earn him this description, in particular, his support of students who held a sit-in to protest racial segregation in the nearby town of Oxford, and his invitation to alumnus Nkrumah to receive an honorary law degree in 1951, just after Nkrumah had been released from prison. Williams notes that this invitation "startled the academic world," and when the degree was given, there was an "outpouring of Pan-African sentiment" (ibid., 154).

42. Although it was stated at the time that the faculty approved Bond's public statement about coeducation, there is no record of their formal vote. Moreover, the faculty did pass a resolution in October 1954 recommending to the board of trustees that "measures be taken to implement the receiving of resident women students by September, 1955." The board did not agree, however, believing that more efforts should be taken to increase the male student body and improve college facilities. It accepted the faculty report and referred it to a committee for further study (Lincoln University Board of Trustees minutes, 1945–59, 525).

43. "A Statement on the Admission of Women," Horace Mann Bond Archive, Charter, 1952–54, drawer 4-A. The "extraordinary circumstances" meant that women who were members of faculty families, employees of Lincoln, or lived with their families in nearby communities were permitted to attend so that Lincoln would not have to assume any responsibility for their housing or supervision.

44. Memo to the Registrar's Office, Dean of Students, and Director of Student Union, November 21, 1963, SC.

45. "Lincoln University Today," 35. See also *The Lincolnian*, May 15, 1958, which also noted that the seminary of Lincoln University was being closed in June 1959.

46. "Lincoln University Today," 136.

47. *The Lincolnian*, May 15, 1958. Interestingly, one of the questions the unnamed reporter posed to this woman student was "if she ever regretted coming to an *all-male school*" (emphasis added).

48. "Co-Education at Lincoln," memo from Eleanor K. Wolf to Walter M. Phillips, October 6, 1959, SC.

49. "Self-Study: Alumni Information 1954" file, Horace Mann Bond Archive.

50. "Lincoln University Today," 113.

51. See, for example, Kalu Ezera, "Rights and Duties," *The Lincolnian*, February 26, 1953. The sacrifices alluded to might have been the greater social regulations that a coeducational institution would require. Lincoln had been known for its lack of supervision of students, an aspect that Langston Hughes for one was ambivalent about. Other articles about coeducation in the student newspaper include those on May 16, 1953; April 15, 1958; March 16, 1959; and May 16, 1960.

52. "From the President's Desk," *Lincoln University Bulletin*, spring 1960, 3, SC.

53. This report is undated, but information presented within it makes it clear that it had to have been written in spring 1965. See "Resident Coeducation at Lincoln University," n.d., SC.

54. Ibid., 5.

55. Ibid., 22.

56. "Tradition Topples," *Lincoln University Bulletin*, fall 1965, 4, 16.

57. Herman R. Branson in Bond, xvii.

58. "Tradition Topples." This article in the alumni magazine also had photos of the new "counselor" for the students, a white woman, Mary Miner, who had been a dean of women at the University of Basutoland in southern Africa. An article in the student newspaper in the fall of 1965 was based on the same interviews of the new resident women students. It comes across as a more serious article, however, in that it presents the exact questions the women were asked, and they are identified by name. Moreover, it has no photos to "lighten up" the story. See Carol Black, "What Do Coeds Feel About Lincoln Univ.?," *The Lincolnian*, November 1, 1965.

59. Jean Butler White, interview by Leslie Miller-Bernal, Lincoln University, January 22, 2002. It may be relevant to note that Ms. Butler-White was actually not a residential student, except for her first couple of months as an undergraduate.

60. The case against the owner of the Oxford Theater and two policemen was not settled until late 1953. See articles in *The Lincolnian*, March 17, 1951; June 5, 1951; November 14, 1951; and October 17, 1953. Williams, 156, mentions that it was ex-GIs who would not tolerate segregation and that President Bond joined the demonstrations. A decade later, about 100 Lincoln students and 12 faculty members picketed the still segregated hotel in Oxford, but this time the issue was settled in two days and did not involve a court case. See *The Lincolnian*, December 15, 1961.

61. Thurgood Marshall was the leading attorney for the NAACP for this landmark case and was assisted by another Lincoln alumnus, Robert Carter '46. Marshall was appointed to the Supreme Court by President Lyndon Johnson in 1967.

62. Articles in *The Lincolnian* discuss this trend, such as those on March 15, 1958, and October 15, 1960.

63. According to the *College Board College Handbook 2002*, Lincoln University, Missouri, had a student population in 2002 that was only 29 percent African American (although it is still listed as a HBCU); the percentage of whites is much higher among graduate students, however, than among undergraduates. At Virginia State, however, black students made up 96 percent of the student body in 2002.

64. "Lincoln's Future Offers Challenge," *The Lincolnian*, October 15, 1960, 1, and "The Shaft," *The Lincolnian*, March 15, 1966, 5. Another article in *The Lincolnian* on Feb-

ruary 15, 1965, 3, also discussed fears that "reverse integration" would make Lincoln become predominantly white.

65. Florence V. Collins, "Editorial: A Lincoln Tradition," *The Lincolnian*, November 1, 1965, 2.

66. *The Lincolnian*, May 1, 1965. Just four years before, a social psychology class survey of 50 students on campus found that a slight majority, 52 percent, favored assembly attendance being required. See *The Lincolnian*, May 15, 1961.

67. *The Lincolnian*, November 1, 1966.

68. See articles in the following issues in *The Lincolnian:* December 1, 1966, 1, for the interview with Associate Dean Walker; March 15, 1967, 5, for women students' views of the associate dean; January 15, 1968, 1, for the student panel on concerns about Lincoln. While Lincoln students wanted more freedom during the 1960s, black faculty, more than white faculty, supported restrictions, according to the recollections of Susan Gunn Pevar's mother, who at the time had a position at the university working with students.

69. The article by the male student appeared in the May 1, 1967, issue of *The Lincolnian;* the letter to the editor by the female student can be found in the December 15, 1967 issue.

70. See Mfuasi, "Black Student's Cultural Views," *The Lincolnian*, December 20, 1968; Bernadine Tinner, "Another Student's Cultural Views," *The Lincolnian*, February 15, 1969, 8 and Spartacus, "New Image for Black Women," *The Lincolnian*, February 15, 1969, 8.

71. See articles in *The Lincolnian*, February 15, 1977, and March 1, 1977.

72. "ERA's Relevance for Black Women," *The Lincolnian*, September 15, 1977, 1, 3.

73. Drewry and Doermann, 8–10.

74. See the report of Yelton's remarks in *The Lincolnian*, October 15, 1960, 1.

75. Thomas M. Jones, "Changeover—Summary Report of the Curriculum Self Study Project, 1965–68, Lincoln University," SC.

76. See the self-study report prepared for the Commission on Higher Education, Middle States Association of Colleges and Schools, fall 1980, 6–7, SC, for a discussion of enrichment programs for the increasing number of students with "developmental academic and social needs" and the need to train faculty to work effectively with such students. Dean Judith Thomas recalled that when she first came to Lincoln in 1974, faculty development workshops were held every Saturday to enable faculty to work better with the type of students then enrolling at Lincoln. Judith Thomas, interview by Leslie Miller-Bernal, telephone,March 6, 2002.The first reading lab to assist students who were found to be deficient in reading ability was actually established in the autumn of 1957. See *The Lincolnian*, November 15, 1957. As recently as fall 2001, the numbers of students in developmental courses was reported to be rising; while 70 students took Basic Writing Skills in 2000, 120 did so in 2001 (*The Lincolnian*, November 26, 2001).

77. Donnellda Rice in *The Lincolnian*, January 31, 1977. A similar article was written a few years later about a Black College Day demonstration in Washington, D.C., in which the point was made that "Black institutions accept some of the same young people that White institutions would write off as illiterate" and that with hard work these people receive degrees. See *The Lincolnian*, October 17, 1980, 1.

78. Memo from Marvin Wachman to the faculty and student body, January 13, 1969, SC.
79. *The Lincolnian*, February 15, 1969, contains an article summarizing President Wachman's statements about state-related institutions, as well as an editorial against the change.
80. "A Brief Statement Concerning Lincoln University and House Bill No. 796," February 1972, SC.
81. Memo from Herman R. Branson to all members of the Lincoln University Faculty and Staff, July 6, 1972, SC. The other institutions that are state-related are Temple University, Pennsylvania State University, and University of Pittsburgh. Becoming state-related meant that Lincoln could not be a member of the United Negro College Fund since the UNCF raises money only for private colleges. This did not matter, however, as the university had already withdrawn from the fund (in 1960) as part of its attempt to become a racially integrated institution. See Bond, 401.
82. Self-study report, fall 1980.
83. Lincoln University has offered graduate programs in selected fields since 1977. For a while, in the early 1980s, it also attempted to offer associate or two-year degrees.
84. Enrollment figures provided by the Institutional Research Department, Lincoln University.
85. Darrell Edwards, Assistant Director of Admissions, interview by Leslie Miller-Bernal, Lincoln University, January 23, 2002.
86. The high academic achievements of women students were commented on frequently by both students and faculty and can be easily corroborated by women students' preponderance on the dean's list and in honor societies. See, for example, *The Lincolnian*, April 20, 1979, in which at least 59 percent of those listed as on the dean's list were women, at a time when women constituted about 49 percent of the student body. A photo of students on the dean's list in *The Lincolnian*, February 12, 1982, showed 10 women out of 14; an article about the Alpha Chi National Honor Society on March 25, 1983, mentioned that its president was a woman and the majority of members were women. With respect to women in campus leadership positions, a list of campus organizations for the 2001–2 academic year showed that of those 44 with a president indicated, 64 percent had a woman president. This does not show as much dominance by women students as community members described, but perhaps some of the clubs listed were not very active or visible.
87. The first woman elected president of the SGA was Karen DeVaughn in 1974. By 1981, only three women had been elected SGA president. See *The Lincolnian*, October 1, 1974, for information on Karen DeVaughn. An article in October 2, 1981, 3, describes the third SGA president, Pamela Keys, as a woman who "senses . . . sexual oppression" and plans to do something to change it. She was mistakenly called the second president, but this mistake was corrected in a later issue. The greater attention to men's sports was corroborated by female students interviewed by Leslie Miller-Bernal, as well as the generally greater newspaper coverage they receive and the greater attendance at men's games, particularly basketball.
88. In 1979, for example, presidents of three of the four classes, including the senior class, were men, and all the officers of the class of 1982 were men. See *The Lincolnian*, October 12, 1979, 4.

89. "Lincoln University Today," 98–101.

90. *The Lincolnian*, December 2, 1974, 2.

91. Women students interviewed in the spring of 2002 did not attach any importance to calling the honored woman Ms. Lincoln rather than Miss Lincoln. One student thought the distinction was a matter of age, with the title Ms. being more appropriate for mature women; another student thought that Ms. might be used in the newspaper to save on the number of letters required. Women students also believed that the criteria for choosing Miss Lincoln did not include beauty. Rather, they mentioned that women so chosen needed to be talented, really strong women, good public speakers, have an appealing platform, and in general, serve as good representatives of Lincoln. Dionna Staley, Dana Gaskill, Cortina McCurry, Kimberly Bassett, and Evita Poole, interviews by Leslie Miller-Bernal, January 24, 2002, and March 19, 2002. Reading the student newspaper gives the impression that beauty is a criterion in who is chosen as Miss Lincoln, however. The women may not be the most beautiful women on campus, but they are certainly very attractive. An article about the "new Miss Lincoln" in 1984 mentioned that she was "definitely qualified" given her "intelligence, pose, and beauty" (*The Lincolnian*, November 9, 1984). The 1992 queen was planning to represent Lincoln in the Miss Collegiate African-American Pageant the following summer. See *The Lincolnian*, October–November 1992.

92. An article in *The Lincolnian*, March 28, 1980, 8, illustrated these contradictory aspects of cheerleading. The article began by calling cheerleaders "lovely young ladies . . . those beautiful cheerleaders" but also noted how hard they worked, how responsible they were, and how many injuries they sustained. When traveling, the cheerleaders were required to "adhere to a certain dress code and conduct themselves as ladies."

93. Poole, interview.

94. Gaskill, interview.

95. The new Women's Center is designed for students, faculty, staff, and local community groups. Its mission is described as follows: "[It] will promote and assist students in making healthy, positive lifestyle choices in six dimensions of human development: intellectual, social, emotional, spiritual, physical, and cultural. The Women's Center will provide programs and activities that result in self-improvement and self-empowerment." Since it is a new campus organization, its programs are still developing, but examples include self-improvement workshops in such areas as self-esteem and conflict resolution, support groups for weight management and relationships, and academic workshops ("The Women's Center," brochure, Lincoln University, 2003).

96. See reports of these women-focused events in the following issues of *The Lincolnian*: October 12, 1979, 1; October 22, 1993; and March 1996.

97. Joe William Trotter Jr., *The African American Experience* (Boston: Houghton Mifflin, 2001), 458.

98. Jerryl Briggs, Dean of Students, interview by Leslie Miller-Bernal, Lincoln University, March 21, 2002.

99. See *The Lincolnian*, February 16, 1970, 2, and September 15, 1978, 3, for descriptions of "Militants for Christ." The "prayer break" is mentioned in *The Lincolnian*, October 15–November 15, 1991, and the religious revival services in *The Lincolnian*, October 22, 1993, 5.

100. Judith Thomas, Dean of Social Sciences, interview by Leslie Miller-Bernal, Lincoln University, January 24, 2002.

101. *The Lincolnian*, December 1995, 1, quoting Dr. Brenda Savage.

102. An interesting article on sexuality, entitled "Are We Our Own Worst Enemy?" appeared in 1980 in the student newspaper. The author, Tonya Tolson, mentioned the "ongoing sexual revolution" and how "we black women" seemed to have entered it "rather casually." She mentioned that men "respect" women who are not "the subjects of their whispered lies" and counseled women to do whatever they chose to do "discreetly." See *The Lincolnian*, February 23, 1980, 6. In April 1995 a page in *The Lincolnian* called the "Sexuality Special" had one article that linked sexual behavior to our "patriarchal society" in which "boys" learn from songs that it's "okay to do IT whenever and with whoever will give IT to them."

103. *The Lincolnian*, April 1995 and September 2000.

104. For some articles and letters to the editor favorable to or accepting of homosexuality, see the following issues of *The Lincolnian*: March 1, 1977 (where discrimination on the basis of sexual preference is mentioned); Renee Johnson, "Do Gays Have the Right to Teach Our Children?" March 9, 1979, 5; James Davis, "Homosexuality and the Family: A Guide to a Better Understanding," April 20, 1979, 5; "Is Love at Lincoln?" February 20, 1981, 5.

105. Letters to the editor, *The Lincolnian*, November 26, 2001, and January 24, 2002. During interviews in the spring of 2002, several students talked about the increasing number of "out" lesbians on campus. Some students said that gay men were not socially accepted, whereas others said that they were. One student, who was very religious, said that she believed homosexuality to be wrong. In general, faculty and administrators who were interviewed were unaware of "out" homosexuals, with the exception of the dean of students. Interviews by Leslie Miller-Bernal, Lincoln University, January 2002 and March 2002.

106. An example of the kind of behavior that women students have put up with was discussed in an editorial of Vannetta Lafe Baile in 1983. In response to women being asked what "sisters" want from their "brothers," she said that the answer was "maturity." She told men students that they should "respect" themselves and "learn how to respect Black women." She complained about men students' verbal abuse of women, their referring to women as "bitches, whores, and dykes," and also advised Lincoln women that they should not allow themselves "to be used and abused physically, mentally and sexually." The editorial was written in response to an incident in which men threw some women down a hill in the snow, injuring one of them in the back. See *The Lincolnian*, February 11, 1983. When social activist and comedian Dick Gregory visited the campus, he discussed this incident, talking about the "ignorance" it displayed and noting that at a white university, the men would not have done this to white women students. Gregory also was upset that the administration had done nothing about the incident. See *The Lincolnian*, March 5, 1984. Similarly, in 1992, female resident advisers and SGA officers held a forum at which they encouraged women students to have self-respect and not allow men to "beat" on them. "If he's beating on you . . . he has no respect for you. If you really respected yourself then you would not let him beat on you" (*The Lincolnian*, October–November 1992).

107. Briggs, interview. Some students have also noted the effects of the gender imbalance on men and women's relationships on campus. An article in the *The Lincolnian*, on the "Sexuality Special" page, April 1995, argued that Lincoln's "low men to women ratios" led men not to be faithful to just one woman since they had "plenty of access to IT."

108. A Lincoln Man, "SGA President Cries Wolf," *The Lincolnian*, December 2000, 2.

109. The most noticeable statue on campus, erected in 1989, portrays Frederick Douglass; in the student dining hall, a wall of photographs of outstanding alumni features only men. The online bulletin's historical sketch of Lincoln does not mention anything about the history of women at the university.

110. One of the dorms is actually named after a lesbian playwright, Lorraine Hansberry, although her sexual identification was not widely known until after her death and after this dorm was built. The Mary Dod Brown Chapel, erected in 1900, was named after the daughter of one of Lincoln's most substantial donors. Susan Dod Brown had once hired Isaac Norton Rendall, later to be the president of Lincoln, as a tutor for her son during the time Rendall was a student at Princeton. Brown's daughter, Mary, died at the age of nine following a tragic shooting accident. See Bond, 301–2.

111. In 1997–98, women made up 39 percent of full-time faculty. The percentage of women in faculty ranks was as follows: 21.7 percent of full professors, 30.8 percent of associate professors, 55.2 percent of assistant professors, 41.7 percent of instructors, and 44.4 percent of lecturers. These percentages had changed little since 1992. The board of trustees remained 11–24 percent femalebetween 1987 and 1995. More than 80 percent of honorary degree recipients were men for the years 1986–96. See Lincoln University's "Self Study Report for the Commission on Higher Education," Middle States Association of Colleges and Schools, 1997–98, SC. In 2002, the university president and all vice presidents were men; two of the three academic deans (newly created positions) were women. While the board of trustees' chair was a woman in 2002, 78 percent of the trustees were men.

112. Information about the administrative problems of President Sudarkasa are discussed in two issues of *Black Issues in Higher Education,* August 6, 1998, and October 1, 1998. An article in *Essence,* May 1989, 106, discusses some of her achievements. Some administrators interviewed by Leslie Miller-Bernal in spring, 2002 ventured the opinion that despite Dr. Sudarkasa's notable achievements, including strengthening the international curriculum and increasing Lincoln's visibility, the scandals at the end of her administration would probably make the trustees reluctant to appoint another woman.

113. Glenn C. Loury, *The Anatomy of Racial Inequality* (Cambridge: Harvard University Press, 2002). See especially Chapter 3, "Racial Stigma," 55–107.

114. This manifesto has been reprinted in several books, including Gloria T. Hull, Patricia Bell Scott, and Barbara Smith, eds., *But Some of Us Are Brave* (Old Westbury, N.Y.: The Feminist Press, 1982), and Beverly Guy-Sheftall, ed., *Words of Fire* (New York: New Press, 1995).

115. Bassett, interview.

Conversion to Coeducation
in the Ivy League

The academic world has long paid close attention to what the most prestigious institutions do. Thus when Princeton and Yale decided to investigate and then implement coeducation in the late 1960s, many other men's colleges also began to think about admitting women. In Chapter 5 Synnott explains how Princeton and Yale became coeducational, after they both considered and then rejected the idea of establishing women's coordinate institutions. She explores the role that competition between these two universities played in the process of admitting women and then in adapting to their needs. Given the great financial and academic resources of these institutions, their ability to implement coeducation thoroughly might be taken as a yardstick by which to measure other efforts. As Chapter 5 also demonstrates, however, it took pressure from women—students, faculty, and administrators—to make Princeton and Yale move toward being gender-equitable institutions. This is not to say that today these two prestigious institutions are models of gender equity in every respect; particularly in the area of having sufficient women as senior administrators and tenured faculty, Yale and Princeton are still not gender-equal coeducational universities.

5

A Friendly Rivalry

Yale and Princeton Universities Pursue Parallel Paths to Coeducation

Marcia Synnott

> Can this University, being a national institution, continue to justify denying educational opportunities to any person because of race, creed, or sex? We think not.
>
> —Gardner Patterson, special report on
> "The Education of Women at Princeton," July 12, 1968.

By the 1960s, among the eight Ivy League colleges only Dartmouth, Princeton, and Yale were still male-only, and they felt increasing pressure to include the education of undergraduate women in their institutional missions. The other five Ivy League colleges educated women, mostly through some type of coordinate relationship with a woman's college. Their gender ratios preserved male dominance: Brown-Pembroke (64:36); Columbia-Barnard (64:36); Cornell (75:25); Harvard-Radcliffe (80:20); and the University of Pennsylvania (70:30). Given the opportunity to attend these five colleges, or other prestigious co-educational universities like Stanford, why did women want to attend Yale and Princeton? After all, Yale and Princeton were known to have thoroughly masculine campus environments, fiercely devoted alumni, competitive athletic rivalries, and mostly all-white student bodies who were selected as much on secondary school affiliations and alumni connections as on high grade point averages and test scores. A *New Yorker* cartoon captured one of the reasons: "Princeton, did you say?" one woman asked another at a cocktail party, "How interesting. I'm a Yale man myself." The struggle to define oneself as either a "Princeton woman" or a "Yale woman" would take much longer—until undergraduate women were sufficiently numerous to contribute to each others' education and establish an unmistakable visual presence on campus.[1]

From 1967 to 2001, Yale and Princeton followed parallel paths in their decisions to admit women, to increase their numbers, to assimilate them into their academic and social cultures, and to recruit female faculty members and administrators. Both institutions also worked to maintain alumni loyalty as they implemented these far-reaching changes. At some stages in the process, Yale was the leader, and Princeton had to catch up. At other times, their roles were reversed. Without the example of the other, perhaps neither would have made the progress it did in recruiting and integrating women into the student body and faculty.

This essay focuses principally on the enrollment of women undergraduates, although a complete assessment of women's progress should mention their enrollments in the graduate and professional schools and the hiring of female faculty members. Charting the progress of women at Yale is more complicated than at Princeton because in addition to Yale College (founded in 1701), Yale University (1887) consists of a Graduate School of Arts and Sciences (1847) and ten professional schools. In contrast, Princeton consists primarily of an undergraduate college (1746), which awards Bachelor of Arts and Bachelor of Science in Engineering degrees, and the Graduate School of Arts and Sciences (1900), which awards Master of Arts and Ph.D. degrees.[2]

Yale and Princeton Women before Coeducation

Women have attended Yale since the nineteenth century, principally as graduate students in the School of Fine Arts. In 1886, Alice Rufie Blake Jordan was the first woman to receive a Yale degree—in law. However, the Law School then shut the door on women until 1919. The Yale Graduate School of Arts and Sciences increased the number of women from one student in 1892, to around 25 percent by the 1960s. In the majority of the professional schools, women tended to average about 10 percent or slightly higher, which suggested an informal gender quota. Yale first raised the issue of coeducation at the undergraduate level when, in 1953, admissions dean Arthur Howe suggested to the faculty that admitting women might benefit the university, given that a majority of its applicants were from public, rather than from all-male private schools. Then, in 1962, Yale College faculty agreed with the report of the President's Committee on the Freshman Year, chaired by psychology professor Leonard W. Doob, that the university "had a national duty to provide the rigorous training for women that we supply for men." However, alumni were cool to the suggestion that Yale admit women, an issue that President Alfred Whitney Griswold's death bequeathed to his successor, Kingman Brewster Jr.[3]

Princeton had no women graduate students until much later than Yale. In 1961, Mary Bunting, then dean of Douglass College, convinced both the Princeton Graduate School dean and President Robert Goheen to admit Sabra

Follett Meservey, wife of a Princeton professor, as its first female degree candidate in the doctoral program in Oriental Studies. Meservey received an M.A. from Princeton in 1964 and a Ph.D. in 1966, but it took the university three years to translate the Latin on her diploma into the feminine. Quietly admitting other women to graduate study, Princeton awarded its first graduate degrees to a woman to T'sai-ying Cheng, who earned a master's in 1963 and a doctorate in 1964 in biochemical science. By the late 1960s, 102 of approximately 1,500 graduate students were women. Princeton was also slower than Yale to consider admitting women to undergraduate study. The university became receptive to the idea of admitting women as regular, as opposed to special students, when public school applicants began to exceed those from private schools. During World War II women had enrolled as special students in a government-sponsored course in photogrammetry. Then, beginning in 1963, women came as junior transfer students in the Carnegie Foundation–sponsored "Critical Languages Program," when they resided either in a dormitory at the institutionally separate Princeton Theological Seminary or in a private home.[4]

Coordinate Education or Coeducation?

By the mid-1960s, administrators at Yale and Princeton recognized that, given the national trend toward coeducation, the admission of women undergraduates was inevitable and would even benefit male undergraduates educationally. To avoid being seen as behind the times, and to ensure that the most highly qualified men students would continue to apply, both universities began to consider how best to incorporate women. Initially, Yale and Princeton thought about admitting women undergraduates through a coordinate relationship—Yale with Vassar College and Princeton with Sarah Lawrence College, but both rejected that model because of its limitations.

Although Princeton students had occasionally called for coeducation, for example in 1942 with a pamphlet, "The Equalizer," Yale took the first serious steps toward admitting women. In 1966 the Yale Corporation adopted "coeducation 'in principle,' " as long as it did not reduce the number of male freshmen and could be achieved through coordination with a women's college. Yale's initiative received acknowledgment in the *Daily Princetonian* a few years later, in an article that called 1966 "the year of the Eli." In March 1966 the Yale undergraduate newspaper, the *Yale Daily News*, published a 19-part series that endorsed the idea of Yale's developing a coordinate relationship with a women's college. Later that same year, Yale president Kingman Brewster Jr. and Vassar president Alan Simpson endorsed a Vassar-Yale study to examine the feasibility of that Seven Sister college's relocation to New Haven. But in November 1967, Vassar declined Yale's proposal in favor of admitting its own male students.[5]

Despite Vassar's rebuff, both Brewster and the Yale Corporation continued to favor coordination, perhaps because Yale was geographically close to two coordinate models, Harvard-Radcliffe in Cambridge, Massachusetts, and Columbia-Barnard in New York City. To assess the various ways of educating women, Brewster appointed a president's ad hoc committee. He also conferred with Radcliffe's president Mary Bunting, who disabused him of the merits of coordination. Bunting emphasized that Harvard and Radcliffe undergraduates were demanding coresidency, which would be adopted as an experiment in the spring of 1970. Brewster thus became persuaded of the merits of Yale's becoming coeducational, and on May 13, 1968, he issued his proposal for "Women at Yale."[6]

Sarah Lawrence also rejected Princeton's relocation offer in May 1967, preferring to admit men to its own Bronxville, New York, campus. Because qualified seniors were choosing coeducational colleges, Princeton's president Goheen recognized that coeducation was "inevitable" but that its "strategy, priority and timing" had yet to be determined. He quickly responded to the board of trustees' charge, in June 1967, to explore both sides of "the advisability and feasibility of Princeton's entering significantly into the education of women at the undergraduate level." Goheen appointed a ten-member Faculty-Administration Committee, chaired by Professor Gardner Patterson, a Harvard-educated Ph.D. and former director of the Woodrow Wilson School of Public and International Affairs. The committee sampled the opinions of Princeton alumni, faculty, and students, as well as the views of high school seniors.[7]

In September 1968 the committee chaired by Patterson released its "special report" on "The Education of Women at Princeton." The report contained careful planning and detailed capital cost projections for new housing, dining rooms, a student center (estimated at $24.3 to $25.7 million) and additional operating expenses. The report noted that the Vassar-Yale study had determined that women at Radcliffe, Pembroke, and Douglass preferred coeducational classes. Therefore, the authors argued, Princeton should "be coeducational from the start, with a single Board of Trustees, a single administration, a single faculty, a single budget and a single curriculum." The report advocated that the number of women students should rise as quickly as possible to 1,000, with male students remaining at about 3,200.[8]

Making and Implementing the Decision to Become Coeducational

Princeton's 1968 Patterson report quickly achieved the status of a "classic," due to its unequivocal commitment to the principle of equal education for women and its detailed analysis of the many factors involved, including the institutional resources required.[9] The Patterson committee voted almost unanimously in favor of coeducation. The exception was "Jerry" Horton '42, the director of development, who wrote that he believed that admitting women would change Princeton's unique "charisma" by weakening "class cohesion" and, as a result, alumni giving. He also questioned the educational worth of women's contributions to classroom discussion. Instead of improving Princeton's "social atmosphere," their presence would "cut down on time now devoted to studies and other pursuits." However, the *Daily Princetonian* rejected Horton's premise: "Princeton's uniqueness is the uniqueness of the locker room, the New York YMCA, and the Alaskan Army barracks. Today's student is not looking for that sort of charismatic experience."[10]

Both the Undergraduate Assembly (UGA) and the faculty overwhelmingly approved the Patterson report's recommendation of coeducation. In its first editorial in fourteen years, the November 26, 1968, *Princeton Alumni Weekly* endorsed coeducation as a "self-evident conclusion," but many alumni were opposed. For example, the Alumni Committee to Involve Ourselves Now (ACTION), Philadelphia alumni, and certain alumni wives, who realized that the new women at Princeton would have different aspirations than they had, all favored retaining Princeton's male-only status. The Special Trustees' Committee on the Education of Women at Princeton, under chairman Harold H. Helm '20, held special coeducation discussions in 25 cities. Though Helm did not initially favor coeducation, committee vice-chairman Laurance S. Rockefeller '32 supported it. On January 10, 1969, the full board of trustees voted 24 to 8, with four members absent, to accept the recommendation of the Helm committee that it commit Princeton "in principle" to implementing undergraduate coeducation, "the largest single decision that has faced Princeton in this century."[11]

Nevertheless, an ad hoc eight-member faculty-administration Implementation Committee, chaired by President Goheen, still had to persuade the trustees to give their final approval. This committee included Provost William Bowen, Neil Rudenstine, the new dean of students who favored "coeducation as a needed step toward 'opening up the Princeton environment,' " and two undergraduates. After meeting in February 1969 with a group of leading educators, the committee concluded that, of five existing models, the most appropriate was the educationally and cost effective Stanford University model, a "single institution with an established ratio of women to men students." That was also the advice of a few academic women outside of Princeton. Though pointing out that co-ordination had functioned positively to protect women when they entered the larger university world, Dr. Suzanne Rudolph, a professor at the University of Chicago, doubted "that most young women today want such protection, even if some of them could still use it." Painfully cognizant of the limitations that a separate corporate and residential structure placed on Radcliffe's quest for equality within Harvard, President Bunting advised, by telephone, "Don't settle for building the kind of thing we are trying to escape from." The committee concluded that coeducation was "the right decision to make in 1969."[12]

In his February 1969 report to the Special Trustee Committee on Coeducation, Goheen urged the admission of women in the fall to give the university "some experience of our own with women students." Though additional endowment for student aid for women would be necessary, Goheen estimated that $7.8 million was needed for new and renovated facilities for the first 650 women, well below the more than $25 million estimated by the Patterson committee for 1,000 female undergraduates. The lower cost estimate was also a result of Princeton's having constructed new buildings in the liberal arts, social and natural sciences, and engineering during the late 1950s and early 1960s. Gifts from donors enabled Princeton to purchase and renovate buildings to house female students. President Goheen estimated that the university would be able to offer college housing to 375 additional students by the fall of 1970 and to another 220 students in 1973; further construction would enable women's enrollment to increase even more. His goal was to raise the number of women " 'as promptly as possible' to at least 1,000 undergraduates," a one-to-three ratio with men. Even that, President Goheen said, was "probably too low for the long run."[13]

The effect of coeducation on alumni contributions concerned both Yale and Princeton, as indicated by correspondence between Yale provost Charles Taylor and Provost Bowen. Yale alumni initially increased their giving, despite the corporation's acceptance of coeducation as a principle and despite campus protests against the Vietnam War. At Princeton, demonstrations by students against the Vietnam War and demands by Students for a Democratic Society (SDS) and black students that universities fight racism at home and in South Africa had some negative impact on alumni giving. The percentage of Princeton alumni fund contributors dropped from 70 percent in 1960 to 56 percent in 1968–70, but it rose again, to 60 percent, by 1972. In 1969–70 the Yale Alumni Fund exceeded a previous record by raising $5,109,074 from 33,883 alumni, but by 1971 the university was in a serious financial crisis due to rising expenses, which led to efforts to reassure alumni that their sons would receive "a special sympathetic and understanding hearing." Legacies' chances of being admitted to Yale subsequently increased fivefold.[14]

Yale undergraduates became increasingly dissatisfied with their university's lack of action about admitting women after the publication of Princeton's "elaborate blueprint for coeducation." In "The Coeducation White Paper: Everything You Need to Know," the *Yale Daily News* reported, on November 7, 1968, that Yale undergraduates wanted coeducation immediately, while Brewster, who was "a very good university president," wanted "the money first." He preferred no locked-in plan, the article said, that would impede his playing to donors' "individual idiosyncrasies." An eager group of Yale undergraduates proposed to bring "girls" to Yale and house them in geodesic domes on the Cross Campus under the tutelage of Rachel Welch and Radcliffe president Bunting. Indeed, by the fall of 1968 Yale found itself in a public relations predicament. Pointing to "a feeling that Yale is being left behind," the editors of the *Yale Alumni Magazine* informed their readers that "the question of women at Yale has not been 'if,' but 'how and how soon.' " Yale had broken "new ground when it undertook to study the possibility of a coordinate link with Vassar," but now, in the light of the Princeton report's recommendation of coeducation, "Yale's position seems vague and equivocal by comparison."[15]

Impressed by the Patterson report's "argumentation for and against varying degrees of co- as against coordinate education," President Brewster and the Yale Corporation acknowledged that in analyzing costs and probable alumni reactions to coeducation, Princeton had been "far more thorough than anything developed at Yale." In his September 23, 1968, memorandum on "Higher Education for Women at Yale," President Brewster analyzed the available options, but he still thought that it might be easier to find a donor, and maintain alumni support, for a coordinate relationship, which would "minimize the dilution or dissipation of the corporate tradition of Yale College." The corporation disagreed. Convinced "that coeducation would improve the quality of Yale College and Yale's ability to attract the students it most wants," it announced in November 1968 that the university would admit 500 women for the fall of 1969, with an eventual goal of enrolling 1,500 women, a ten-to-four ratio. It also directed Brewster to develop a coeducational proposal for new residential facilities and financial aid for women. Drawing on the Patterson's report's cost estimates, Brewster projected the costs of coeducation—buildings, endowment for financial aid, and additional faculty—from $30 million to as much as $55 million. Though he had previously wanted a complete multimillion dollar infrastructure for the education of women, in mid-November 1968 Brewster asked and received faculty approval (200 to 1) for an experimental plan to admit, for the fall of 1969, 250 first year women and about 250 women transfer students. He anticipated that in "proceeding by the route of experience and experimentation rather than of further abstract study," Yale might "evolve a pattern for learning and for living which is more in tune with the needs of tomorrow's students than any which currently exists among our major institutional rivals." However, many women concluded that Yale opted for coeducation not to help women but because it needed women to help the university's image.[16]

To show that "Girls need Yale and Yale needs girls," the Yale Student Advisory Board's Committee on Student Life sponsored, with broad-based support from various student organizations, a Coeducation Week, November 4–10, 1968, for 750 women from twenty-two different colleges. After holding a coeducation rally at the president's house, 1,700 Yale students requested that women and men be admitted under an equal access policy. In response, Henry Chauncey '57, President Brewster's special assistant, emphasized Yale's commitment to graduate a thousand male leaders per class. Yale, like Princeton, initially insisted on admitting the same number of male freshmen in 1969 as in previous classes. "American society had gone head over heels in coeducation," Chauncey said. "Yale and Princeton were way the hell behind times."[17]

Thus by November 1968, Yale had seized the initiative from Princeton in committing itself to admit women in the fall of 1969. President Goheen, not yet certain that Princeton could admit women by then, linked the Yale and Princeton decisions: "Yale certainly helped bring the issue to a boil here . . . just as the Patterson report got things stirring again at Yale." To encourage women to apply for the fall of 1969, Princeton juniors followed Yale's lead by organizing Princeton Coed Week, February 9–14, 1969. Students contributed $600 to bring in some 800 undergraduate women, chosen by a quota system from about 2,500 applicants from 30 colleges in the New England and Middle Atlantic states. The guests encountered a lovely snow-covered campus, and they were treated to flowered toilet paper and fruit baskets. Coed Week proved, said the *Daily Princetonian,* that Princeton's task was "Implementing the Inevitable." President Goheen agreed by announcing on February 12 that Princeton would accept female applicants—it already had 800 on file. But they did not have to pay a fee or be interviewed since the admission office could not admit them until after the board of trustees voted 28 to 3, on April 19, 1969, in favor of becoming coeducational that fall, with a quota on women.[18]

Female Students Enter Princeton and Yale

Both Yale and Princeton prepared for the incoming female students by altering their physical facilities. Princeton renovated Pyne Hall, spending $70,000 in new furniture, matching bedspreads and curtains, and $10,000 in plumbing modifications, although some urinals remained. Electric locks were installed on all the doors to women's entries, which the women soon asked to be disabled. Another $55,000 was spent to improve lighting on campus. A resident couple and six female graduate students agreed to live in Pyne Hall.[19]

In terms of personnel, Princeton was less ready for women students. The university faculty of almost 600 had only one tenured woman, sociologist Suzanne Keller, two women assistant professors, and 17 women lecturers and instructors. Three administrative positions were filled by women: President Goheen hired Halcyone Bohen, Ph.D. in clinical psychology, as the first woman assistant dean of students; Provost Bowen appointed Mary E. Procter as his special assistant, and Patricia Graham, ACE Fellow, served as a coeducation adviser. Procter recalled that she, Bohen, and Graham were "Princeton['s] female Three Musketeers," with each one tackling policies that needed changing. Graham targeted "nepotism and residency rules that were an obstacle to hiring women faculty," while Bohen encouraged "gynecological services at the health center, kitchens, and a more civilized tone in the dormitories." She also welcomed by letter the incoming female undergraduates and developed a Residential Advisers Program. Procter advised departments to distribute groups of women in the various classes and planned "for University day care and smaller, more intimate dining halls." These "Three Musketeers" must have had a positive effect, since, in addition to increasing the number of women on the faculty, Princeton planned to allow part-time teaching and to develop pregnancy leave policies to delay the tenure clock. To improve gynecological services, in 1974 Princeton established Sexual Education, Counseling and Health (SECH), which distributed birth control and protective devices.[20]

On September 7, 1969, in what Jane Leifer '73 described as a "blind date" with Princeton's 223-year history, 171 women matriculated as undergraduates. Of that number 100 were freshmen, who joined 820 males, a one-to-eight ratio. Out of 52 alumni daughters who applied, 22 were admitted. Ten black women were admitted out of 23 applicants. In addition, Princeton enrolled as undergraduate women 50 transfer students and 21 Critical Language students. That fall, the Graduate School relaxed its gender quota, admitting 200 women and 1,300 men, in contrast to only 50 women in 1967. Few undergraduate women really saw themselves as "pioneers," though that was how President Robert Goheen and admission officers welcomed them. Gardner Patterson had feared that "only the tough, aggressive women can make it" in Princeton's masculine culture, yet one of the first-year students was June Fletcher, who had won the title of "Miss Bikini U.S.A." Other Princeton women were assertive, for example, Robin Herman '73 who became a *Daily Princetonian* editor and after graduation, one of the first female professional sportswriters. However, undergraduate women soon complained of either too much male attention or being left dateless by Princeton men who feared rejection.[21]

Like their Princeton counterparts, Yale administrators were concerned about whether an all-male campus could quickly provide enough amenities for women. From the Ford Foundation, Yale received close to $500,000 to help pay for the initial expenses of admitting women, including $150,000 to modify and repaint Vanderbilt Hall, the largest Old Campus dormitory and the only one with bathtubs, for housing first-year women. The presence of undergraduate women was also expected, said Brewster, to "bring the graduate professional women into a much more active intellectual and social participation in the community," thereby changing their "beleaguered minority status" of about 25 percent of the postbaccalaureate enrollment. Indeed, graduate women's experience at Yale—in terms of housing, dining facilities, medical services, and social life—was inferior to that enjoyed by men. At the new University Health Center that Yale opened in July 1971, there were, for the first time, gynecologists, whose services included prescribing methods of birth control, that, though legal in Connecticut after 1965, had not been available to the 800 women graduate students.[22]

Hearing about Princeton's "token integration, overcrowding, the women's sense of isolation, and a strained social situation" made those implementing coeducation at Yale deeply concerned "about our own ratio and admissions policy" and its negative impact on women's morale. Just as Princeton had to find women to assist in the transition to coeducation, so did Yale. In 1969 Yale had only 43 women on the faculty, about 5 percent, out of a total of 839, including visiting scholars. Of these, only two were tenured professors, 17 were assistant professors, and 11 were lecturers. President Brewster asked Elga Wasserman, Ph.D. in chemistry and assistant dean of the sciences in the Graduate School, to become special assistant to the president for coeducation, based in the provost's office. Wasserman described Brewster as "a very shrewd administrator" who did not appoint her as a dean in Yale College because of the resentment men would have felt. After chairing the Planning Committee on Coeducation, Wasserman then chaired the University Committee on Coeducation, which had a Coeducation Advisory Committee that included, among others, Radcliffe College trustee Susan Hilles and UCLA vice-chancellor Rosemary Park. The members of both committees agreed, as a progress report on "Coeducation 1969–70" indicated, that women's representation in the faculty, administration, and the student body should be increased as soon as feasible.[23]

Yale's first women applicants were called "the female versions of Nietzsche's *Uebermensch*" by Jonathan Lear, Yale '70, in the April 1969 *New York Times Magazine.* This label intimidated both them and Yale men, according to Lear, later a well-known author and psychologist. From 2,847 applications, 286 women were offered admission to the class of 1973, a 10 percent acceptance rate, which was less than half the acceptance rate for men. To achieve its desired yield of 1,025 men, Yale admitted more than 20 percent—about 1,600—of 7,200 male applicants. A separate selection process admitted some 470 women transfer students out of about 1,500 applicants. Yale sought women who were bright and diverse, and who, like male applicants, showed "sensitivity, flexibility, motivation, creativity, and integrity."[24]

On September 14, 1969, Yale enrolled its first 588 women undergraduates. The class of 1973 matriculated 1,259 first-year students: 230 women, of whom 48 had Yale fathers, and 1,029 men, of whom, as in the past, about 200 had Yale fathers. Of the 34 first-year black women accepted, 26 matriculated. In the classes of 1971 and 1972, 358 women enrolled as transfer students, 155 as sophomores, and 203 as juniors. There were 44 alumni daughters and 16 black women, 6 in the class of 1971 and 10 in the class of 1972. The total of 588 undergraduate women was a considerably larger number than Princeton's 171, but Yale's 230 first-year women were still only 18.3 percent of the freshman class. A woman assistant dean of Yale College functioned as a "dean of women," and two dozen female graduate and professional school students served as assistants or as freshmen counselors. First-year women were housed in designated entryways in Vanderbilt Hall, which made it difficult for the women to develop friendships with each other. After the first year, each college was permitted to determine its own housing plan. The media exaggerated the women students' strong academic abilities and showed posed photographs of either curious or indifferent males eyeing them, to their embarrassment. "Girls felt their individuality was being absorbed by their identification as a 'Yale Coed,'" wrote Janet Lever and Pepper Schwartz, two Yale doctoral students in sociology, in their book about the experiences of the university's first female undergraduates.[25]

Importing women to campus for weekend mixers continued after both Yale and Princeton became coeducational, which hurt the feelings of women undergraduates. However, some practices ended, for example, "spooning" at Princeton, during which men drummed their spoons on a table when attractive women left a room. By the second year on both campuses, students made less effort to appear attractive to the opposite sex; many began to look at each other as either brothers or sisters. Indeed, at both Princeton and Yale men and women drew closer together intellectually and psychologically as they joined civil rights marches and demonstrated in opposition to the Vietnam War, the U.S. incursion into Cambodia, and the Ohio national guardsmen's killings of four Kent State University students.[26]

Yale's first women students remembered their freshman year with mixed emotions. On the one hand, they responded positively to the academic challenges and loved the "dynamic and almost electric people." On the other hand, many felt the need to escape an overwhelming sense of being "drowned in a male ethos" by enrolling in women's studies courses, first offered in 1970–71, which helped end some women's "sense of isolation." Through the Coeducation Office, women undergraduates created *SHE*, a resource book, and set up a Women's Center. The women's liberation movement influenced female students to get a sexist phrase removed from *Eli Book:* "Treat Yale as you would a good woman. Take advantage of her many gifts, nourish yourself with the fruits of her wisdom, curse if you will, and congratulate yourself the possession of her. But treat her with respect."[27]

Compared to their marginalization in the male-dominated campus social environment, women felt they were the academic peers of men in the classroom. The first women to receive Yale bachelor's degrees in 1971 and 1972, transfer students, had a 95 percent survival rate, and more women than men earned general and departmental honors. The first Yale undergraduate alumnae sought, moreover, the same graduate and professional school training as their male classmates and received, for example, similar LSAT scores. Despite their successes, some 20 percent of Yale alumni would have eliminated undergraduate women altogether. To maintain "his credibility" with alumni, President Brewster rejected the recommendation of the University Committee on Coeducation to reduce temporarily the number of male freshmen from 1,025 to 800 so that 400, rather than 230, first-year women could be admitted to the class of 1975. Many faculty and students favored a two-to-one male-female ratio. The committee recognized, however, that increasing the size of future freshman classes was necessarily dependent on new undergraduate housing.[28]

While Yale committed itself to admitting 1,025 first-year men, the number of first-year women fluctuated. In the fall of 1970, Yale admitted 232 women (18.5 percent) and 1,023 men. After the total number of undergraduate applications had declined by about 2,000, Yale launched more proactive recruitment efforts and in the fall of 1971 admitted 1,294 students, approximately 270 women (21 percent) and 1,024 men. In 1972, Yale accepted 2,313 out of 8,738 applicants, among them 321 women (24 percent) and 1,020 men.[29]

Movement to Sex-Blind Admissions Policies

By the early 1970s, Princeton and Yale seemed to have set relatively similar targets for the enrollment of women and racial minorities. At both institutions, women made up about one-quarter of the graduating seniors in 1976 (28 percent at Princeton, 25 percent at Yale), and racial minorities were about 12 percent (13 percent at Princeton, 11 percent at Yale). By 1974, both Yale and Princeton Universities moved to adopt an "equal access" policy, under which men and women were admitted according to individual qualifications. At Yale, the committee headed by political science professor Robert A. Dahl recommended, in its April 1972 report on coeducation, admission of "the best qualified minority group students both locally and nationally" and admission "on basis of qualifications without regard to sex." Since students were also selected for their potential to contribute, through their diverse backgrounds, to the education of others, "intellectual achievement" was not "the sole criterion for admission." The report anticipated a ratio of 60 men to 40 women in a Yale College of 4,800 students. Both the faculty, by a vote, and the student Yale College Council, by a petition of 3,000 undergraduates, endorsed admissions without regard to sex.[30]

In October 1972, President Brewster reported that Yale's first three years of coeducation had been successful, as had the residential distribution of women on campus. Though he agreed that the current number of 800 women undergraduates was "much too small" for them to make friends with other women, he feared that rapidly increasing their admission while maintaining men's enrollment would make "Yale too big." However, the freshman class, then 1,341, could be increased after two new residential colleges provided space for 500 students in 1975. In a class of 1,475 students, "a sex-blind admissions policy, expected to yield a 60–40 proportion of men to women," would result in 885 men and 590 women. Until then, Brewster proposed lowering men's enrollment from 1,025 to 885, and raising women's to 465 to achieve a 65:35 male-female ratio. On December 9, 1972, the Yale Corporation voted to admit between 100 and 130 additional women to the class of 1977, thereby attaining a two-to-one male-female ratio. The corporation had been influenced by an Association of Yale Alumni poll, to which over 85 percent of alumni responded, that indicated alumni were willing to accept a 60:40 ratio and up to a 10 percent reduction in men's admission, phased in over five years.[31]

Princeton developed a similar rationale to increase the number of its women students, whose admission had raised the academic caliber of freshmen. The number of men matriculating in 1968–69, just before coeducation, had been 882 (out of 5,648 applicants). During the first five years of coeducation, the number of male matriculants remained relatively stable while that of female matriculants climbed, from about 15 percent of enrollment in 1969 to 30 percent in 1973. The increase in the enrollment of entering students from just under 1,000, to about 1,200 was made possible by Princeton's post–World War II building program and generous donations for new dormitories.[32]

Princeton's Commission on the Future of the College, chaired by sociology professor Marvin Bressler, recognized in 1973 that attitudes toward quotas had changed since the 1968 Patterson report, in part because of federal and New Jersey laws. Sharing "the view of many that 'a policy of quotas by sex, however justifiably applied up to now, is intrinsically undesirable' " the Bressler commission saw "a free access policy as being intrinsically fairer, affording equality of opportunity on a merit basis to men and women alike." However, the commission also recognized that Princeton should "maintain existing commitments to some special groups in the admission process, including candidates for the bachelor of science in engineering, alumni sons and daughters, minority students, and students with athletic ability." Since preferences to engineering candidates and to competitive athletes favored male rather than female applicants, an equal access policy would reduce only slightly the number of male freshmen. If the university increased the number of undergraduates from the 4,400 projected in September 1974 (about 3,200 men and 1,200 women) to 4,500–4,600, "the Commission would expect an equal access policy to produce entering classes in the range of 765–770 men and 365–370 women." Faculty, undergraduates, and alumni supported the commission's recommendation, as did the board of trustees, which voted 28 to 3, in January 1974, to adopt an "equal access" or sex-blind admissions policy.[33]

Princeton's admissions statistics show a significant increase in the number of women admitted after 1975 under an equal access policy. While the class of 1979 (which entered in 1975) was only about 24 percent women, the class of 1980 was about 34 percent. As President Bowen pointed out, men and women were "essentially indistinguishable" in terms of admissions ratings on both academic and extracurricular activities. The same was true for their academic attainments, with 10 percent of the women and 9 percent of the men being elected to Phi Beta Kappa. For the spring term of 1979, 38 percent of both the men and the women received "A" grades, but 46 percent of the women, compared to 43 percent of the men, received "B" grades.[34]

Although the percentage of women at Princeton generally rose during the 1970s and early 1980s, in 1986 Princeton found itself behind other Ivy League colleges in enrolling women. Yale's entering class in the fall of 1986, for example, was about 45 percent women, while Princeton's was only 37 percent. President Bowen, who had successfully raised $410.5 million during a five-year "Campaign for Princeton," continued to work on attracting more women undergraduates. Indeed, Princeton lost qualified women to Yale, Harvard, Stanford, and the Massachusetts Institute of Technology. With input from the Women's Studies Program and from student government president, Cecelia "Cece" Rey '87, Princeton revised its admissions brochures to feature its strong curriculum in liberal arts, trained undergraduate women to recruit freshmen, and increased the number of alumnae recruiters. The modification of the 1859 alma mater, "Old Nassau," initiated by undergraduates and approved by the alumni council, also contributed to Princeton's more inclusive image. In the final chorus, after "In praise of Old Nassau," the words, "we sing," replaced "my boys," and "our hearts" replaced "her sons."[35] Princeton's improved methods of recruiting women began to pay off by the mid 1990s (see Table 5.1).[36] For the most part, statistics on the admission of women to Princeton paralleled those at Yale (see Table 5.2).

In the 1960s, Yale and Princeton, like many other colleges, had seriously begun to recruit minority students, increasingly with the help of campus African-American student groups. Assisted by the campus Black Student

Table 5.1. Female Undergraduates Enrolled at Princeton, Fall Semester, 1969–2001 (%)

1969	1974	1976	1979	1986	1988	1994	1998	2001
6	30	32	36	37	39	47.5	46	49

Sources: "Admission" and "Women," Donovan Leitch, *A Princeton Companion* (Princeton: Princeton University Press, 1978), online at *http://mondrian.princeton.edu/CampusWWW/ Companion/admission.html* and *Companion/women.html;* "Women Admits Hit Record High," *Princeton Weekly Bulletin,* April 22, 1985, 1; David Newhouse, "New Class Shows Changing Face of Princeton U," *The Times* (Trenton), September 13, 1994, 1, 6; Don Oberdorfer, *Princeton University: The First 250 Years* (Princeton: Princeton University Press, 1995), 191; Ron Southwick, "Second Generation: Women at Princeton Come Full Circle," *Trenton Times,* May 31, 1998, A1, A9. "A Princeton Profile, 2001–02: Seniors and Alumni," at *www. princeton.edu/pr/facts/profile/01/17.htm,* and "A Princeton Profile, 2001–02: Finances," at *www.princeton.edu/pr/facts/ profile/01/08.htm.*

Alliance, Yale had 70 percent more applications from African Americans in 1968 and admitted about 70 to its freshman class of 1,025; the previous year it had admitted only 40. In 1969, 25 African-American women and 71 African-American men enrolled in the class of 1973. From 1970 to 2002, the number of black students admitted to each class fluctuated between about 70 and 100, reaching a high point of 152 (11.5 percent) in 1997, but dropping to 102 (7.8 percent) in 2002. By the late 1980s the number of black women admitted to Yale consistently outnumbered black men; women made up between 54 and 73 percent of about 100 black students admitted to each of the classes of 1991 to 1996.[37]

Princeton also experienced a similar increase in the number of African-American students, as the number of applicants almost quadrupled from 83 in 1967 to 325 in 1969; of the 121 blacks Princeton admitted to the class of 1973, 69 enrolled compared to just 14 two years earlier. While there were only about 10 African-American women admitted to the class of 1973, compared to about 60 African-American men, for the class of 1977 the percentage of African-American female matriculants was more than three times as great as the number of African-American male matriculants (18 percent of the 369 women were African Americans, compared to 5.5 percent of 845 men).[38]

Table 5.2. Female Undergraduates Enrolled at Yale, Fall Semester, 1969–2001 (%)

1969	1975	1976	1979	1986[a]	1988	1991	1995	2001
12.5	21.15	24	44.7	44.7	42.4	45	48	49.34

Source: "Facts on Women," *Yale Alumni Magazine,* October 1969, 23. "Appendix A: Admission of Women Undergraduates for September 1969," in Elga Wasserman, "Report of the Chairman of the Planning Committee on Coeducation, 1968–1969," May 29, 1969, Records of Kingman Brewster Jr., President of Yale University (RU11, series I), box 60, folder 16; and Wasserman, "Coeducation 1969–70," December 17, 1970, box 60, folder 12, pp. 1–5, 11–17, and "Appendix A: Admission Statistics, Charts 1–4," pp. 18–19. Caroline Kim '96, "Through Women's Eyes," in *Different Voices: A Journal Commemorating 25 Years of Coeducation at Yale,* Rachel Donadio, '96, ed. (New Haven: Yale University, 1995), 20. "Trustees Vote to Increase the Number of Women" and "Transfer Admissions Shrink," *Yale Alumni Magazine,* January 1973, 30; 34. "R. Inslee Clark, Jr., Dean of Admissions, Resigns to Become Horace Mann Headmaster," *Yale Alumni Magazine,* February 1970, 16; Jeffrey Gordon, "Inky's Era," *Yale Alumni Magazine,* March 1970, 32–37. "Henry Chauncey and John Muyskens Take Top Admissions Posts," *Yale Alumni Magazine,* June 1970, 19. Yale University Office of Institutional Research, "Factsheet," at *www.yale.edu/oir.*

a. The enrollment of women at Yale in the fall of 1986 was 44.7 percent for the freshman class (Maureen Nevin Duffy, "Princeton Reviews Policies on Women," *New York Times,* March 15, 1987).

By the beginning of the twentieth-first century, Yale and Princeton's commitment to both effective recruitment and to affirmative action in admissions put them unquestionably among the leaders among six elite private universities in enrolling women undergraduates (48 to 49 percent each). However, Harvard had the highest percentage of minority students (34 percent), followed by Yale (28 percent), Princeton (26 percent), and Amherst, Dartmouth, and Williams (25 percent each).[39]

Curricular Changes with Coeducation

Important in creating an intellectual place for women at Yale and Princeton was the introduction of women's studies courses. At Yale, the number of these courses, most of which were taught as residential college seminars, rose from one to ten between 1970 and 1972. Some undergraduates believed that the establishment of a women's studies program was "the next major step" after coeducation itself. In 1977 Catherine MacKinnon taught the first core course on "Feminism and Humanism: Introduction to Women's Studies." In 1979, women's studies became a permanent program; two years later, in 1981, the faculty approved the women's studies major. Under history professor Nancy Cott, who joined the Yale faculty in 1975 and became the only woman to chair an academic program, the women's studies department encouraged coalition-building, which was facilitated by a three-year (1983–86) National Endowment for the Humanities grant of $170,044. Following the denial of tenure to five professors working in feminist scholarship, students in the fall of 1989 formed the Women's Studies Ad Hoc Committee, which requested that the provost support two more joint appointments in women's studies and form joint tenure review committees. Not only would more women be tenured but, in 1998, a woman psychologist would also become the first professor tenured in the renamed women's and gender studies program, and in 1999 Yale appointed its first male professor as acting chair of the program.[40]

Princeton was slower than Yale to recognize that the curriculum had to change to make the university supportive of female students. Although the Patterson report had argued for coeducation on the basis of women's different perspectives, it had not gone much beyond suggesting that the administration augment the creative arts program, reorient certain introductory courses, and enlarge the Office of Teacher Preparation and Placement. President Bowen acknowledged women's studies' increasing importance after its first course was introduced in 1971, but the university's denial of tenure to female faculty hindered its recognition as a legitimate discipline. In February 1980, psychologist Joan S. Girgus, dean of the college (1977–87), appointed an ad hoc committee of nine senior faculty members and seven undergraduates to study a future role for women's studies. However, a faculty-created committee, Women's Studies,

Hiring and Education Network (WHEN), opposed the administration's committee and presented its own proposals. Finally persuaded of women's studies' intellectual legitimacy, Princeton became, in 1981, one of the last two or three Ivy League universities to approve a women's studies program; it followed Cornell (1972), University of Pennsylvania (1973), Columbia (through Barnard College, 1977), Yale (1979; 1981), Brown (1981), and Dartmouth (1980s). Harvard (1986) was the last school in the Ivy League to approve an undergraduate degree program in women's studies.[41]

Women's studies became stronger at Princeton once Kay B. Warren, Ph.D. Princeton '74, an anthropologist specializing in gender and national development in Latin America, returned in 1982 as an associate professor and director of the newly launched program. Rather than creating a new discipline, she shaped women's studies in relationship to the existing departments to generate interdisciplinary perspectives on "gender and the status of women and men in society." Overall, almost 40 faculty members in ten departments participated in research and course development. A nascent certificate in women's studies was available to undergraduates, and a weekly graduate student/faculty research forum published working papers in *Critical Matrix: The Princeton Journal of Women, Gender, and Culture.* In the mid-1980s, Princeton hired two women faculty who were "certainly major figures," according to Margaret Homans, acting director of Yale's women's studies program: Elaine Showalter, English professor and author of *A Literature of Their Own: British Women Novelists from Brontë to Lessing,* and feminist literary critic and poet Sandra Gilbert.[42]

Female Students' Accomplishments

Like women pioneers at other institutions and at other times, the first groups of women to graduate from Yale and Princeton were exceptionally talented. Annalyn Swan, for example, a transfer from Tulane University, was Princeton's only Marshall scholarship winner in the senior class in 1973. S. Georgia Nugent '73, the first in her family to go to college, who supported herself by a full scholarship and three jobs, went on to earn a Ph.D. from Cornell. She became an assistant professor of classics at her alma mater and then went to Brown University where she was awarded tenure in 1992. After returning to Princeton as assistant to President Harold T. Shapiro, Nugent chaired the President's Standing Committee on the Status of Women, which focused on hiring more women on the faculty, and served as associate provost. In October 2001 she was appointed the first dean of the Harold McGraw Jr. Center for Teaching and Learning. Subsequent Princeton classes had equally outstanding women. At the 1975 commencement, both the valedictorian and the salutatorian were women in a class of 291 women and 736 men. The first women Rhodes scholars, selected in regular competition, included a graduate of Princeton and two from Yale.[43]

Women students earned their share, and sometimes more, of campus leadership positions at Princeton and Yale. Women at Princeton attained the editorships of major campus publications—the venerable *Nassau Literary Magazine* in 1978–79, the *Daily Princetonian* in 1979–80, and, in 1981, the Press Club, which reported on Princeton to the public. In 1976, Valerie Bell, who had benefited from "an experimental program" that helped minority students adjust to Princeton, was the first African-American woman in the Ivy League to be elected president of a senior class. By 1980, the only campus office to which Princeton women had not been elected was chairman of the Undergraduate Student Government (USG). While women at Princeton have participated in many different campus organizations, including religious organizations, debating societies, theatrical production and repertory groups, and choral and a cappella singing groups, they also tend to participate in activities that reinforce socially acceptable gender roles. Women, more than men, are active in the more recently established resident advising, peer counseling, and off-campus volunteer social work activities, such as the Sexual Harassment/ Assault Advising, Resources, and Education (SHARE). Men usually hold the positions on the executive council of the USG and have been almost 80 percent of the managers in student agencies.[44]

During the same years, Yale women attained similar campus positions. In 1978, Yale had its first woman president of the Political Union, a debating forum, and in 1995 women served as the Union's president and speaker. In 1981, a woman served as editor-in-chief of the *Yale Daily News.* Not until 1990, however, was the first woman elected president of the Yale College Council. Building on their undergraduate academic and extracurricular successes, women contributed as alumnae "to the larger world," according to President Richard C. Levin. In keeping with "the tradition of leadership that Yale represents," women "are prominent in law, education, medicine, political and religious life, and the arts, and have become inspirational role models for today's undergraduates."[45]

Among Yale's notable alumnae are the award-winning sculptor Maya Lin '81 M.Arch. '86, whose work is seen in the Washington, D.C. Vietnam Veterans' Memorial, in the Montgomery, Alabama civil rights memorial, and on the Yale campus in the Women's Table, which commemorates coeducation. Lin's Women's Table, inaugurated October 1993, together with female images in historical stained glass windows, statuary, and architecture, began to give women a visual presence on the Yale campus. Other exceptional alumnae include Oscar-wining actor Jodie Foster '81; film producer Sarah Pillsbury '74, perhaps best known for the film, "Desperately Seeking Susan"; attorney and professor Kathleen Cleaver '84, a former Black Panther Central Committee member; and authors Naomi Wolf '84 and Gloria Naylor M.A. '83.[46]

Women undergraduates achieved some of their greatest successes at

Princeton and Yale in competitive athletics. In the fall of 1970, Princeton was a better place for female athletes because it had in place a five-year plan for developing women's athletics, from physical education classes to intramurals to intercollegiate athletics. It had also appointed a new director of physical education, Merrily Dean Baker. When Princeton women pushed to change the university's initial five-year plan by organizing their own intercollegiate teams, or even trying out for some men's teams, physical education classes were integrated. A special university contingency fund paid for such innovations as a Women's Tuesday Night Program that offered recreation, competitive play, and instruction to all women. By the spring of 1971, Princeton had women's intercollegiate teams in tennis, field hockey, swimming, basketball, and squash. The tennis team won the Eastern Intercollegiate Women's Tennis Championship six straight years, 1973–78. The women's crew won the 1972 Eastern Intercollegiate Championship. In their first decade at Princeton, women won seven National Intercollegiate Championships in squash, and four out of six Ivy League basketball championships, following the inauguration of Ivy Group competition in women's sports in 1974. By the mid-1990s, Princeton had developed, said the *Daily Princetonian,* "one of the premier women's athletics programs in the country," especially in crew and lacrosse.[47]

Yale opened to women most of Payne Whitney Gymnasium, the world's largest indoor athletic facility, as soon as the university became coeducational. It proceeded cautiously in developing a women's program, however, by having its Governing Board of Athletics report on "which sports are 'safe' " for women. Student requests in 1970 led Yale to hire a part-time coach and instructor in tennis, field hockey, and later squash. Female soccer players paid for their own coach. Women also began to play club sports in basketball, fencing, and gymnastics, supported by funds for "women's activities."[48]

A significant milestone in Yale women's athletics was the 1973 appointment of Joni Evans Barnett as director of recreational and instructional programs in Payne Whitney Gymnasium. Between 1973 and 1979, thirteen women's sports attained "varsity status": tennis, field hockey, squash, basketball, crew, fencing, gymnastics, swimming, lacrosse, volleyball, cross-country, track and field, and softball. On December 4, 1974, the Yale women's basketball team defeated Radcliffe 42–27, its first victory in Ivy League competition. Then in 1976 the "Title IX strip" occurred. Twenty-one women crew members went to the physical education director's office and "bared their breasts," which were inscribed with "Title IX," to protest their lack of equal locker rooms and shower facilities. In September 1982, the Yale Women's Athletic Organization was formed to promote publicity and community events and to handle grievances. By 1986, women's varsity sports were adequately funded for their competition within Division I. Now athletics are an important recruiting tool for both women and men. Since 1989 about two-thirds of both male and female athletes have reported that their recruitment as athletes was a major factor in their matriculating. By 2001–2, Yale women participated in 18 varsity sports, and men in 16; sailing was the one coed sport. The 12 residential colleges supported an intramural sports program that actively encouraged women's participation; there were also 35 club sport teams in, for example, polo, equestrian, ballroom dance, and cycling.[49]

Male undergraduates and alumni accepted women as athletes earlier than they accepted them as social peers. Consequently, women at both Yale and Princeton felt that their respective universities should have done more, sooner, to integrate them into the university. To counterbalance campus organizations that excluded them, women students defined spaces for themselves on campus and formed their own organizations, calling them sororities at Princeton, but fraternities at Yale. The four at Yale, which belonged to the National Pan Hellenic Conference, "welcomed" their pledges with food and gifts, rather than hazing them in "Hell Nights," and emphasized "friendship, moral and intellectual excellence, and a strong commitment to community service." The women received some support from Yale's male fraternities, most notably a $100,000 donation for women's scholarships from St. Anthony's Hall in 1969 and membership offers two years later.[50]

Most of the male fraternities were forced to turn their houses over to Yale for financial reasons, but Yale's secret societies survived. In April 1971 four of them voted to accept women members: Book and Snake, Manuscript, Berzelius, and Elihu; in 1989, Scroll and Key admitted its first women. In recognition that women were 45 percent of undergraduates, the fifteen graduating seniors in Skull and Bones (1832), the oldest Yale secret society, announced in April 1991 that they would tap six women and nine men for membership. However, the alumni board locked the "tomb" and nullified the tap, forcing the "locked-outs" to seek refuge in Manuscript's clubhouse. Subsequent votes by Skull and Bones alumni in 1992 narrowly approved admitting women, but such secrecy surrounds Skull and Bones that little is known about when women were admitted and how many. Indeed, said President George W. Bush '68, who had joined Skull and Bones twenty years after his father, the society was "so secret I can't say anything more. It was a chance to make fourteen new friends." According to the Yale campus tabloid *Rumpus*, at least six women were among the seniors of 2000. The last all-male secret society, Wolf's Head, had admitted women by 2001.[51]

However, the greatest bastion of male resistance to women at Yale was Mory's, the privately owned, one-hundred-year-old men's eating and drinking club, home of the singing group, the Whiffenpoofs. After it added the word "male" to its membership qualifications in September 1969, women undergraduates requested that Yale cease to hold meetings there that used departmental and university funds. President Brewster agreed not to chair meetings at Mory's. The Connecticut Liquor Commission revoked Mory's license, leading to an unsuccessful appeal to the Court of Common Pleas. In 1974, women, who had been admitted as guests since 1950, became members, and in 1981 Mory's put up photographs of all the captains of women's athletic teams. Among them may have been the photograph of women's varsity soccer team captain, Shannon O'Brien '80, a former Massachusetts state treasurer and 2002 Democratic gubernatorial candidate.[52]

At Princeton, women's struggle for social integration, like that of other minority groups, involved gaining admission to the privately owned eating clubs for upperclassmen. Their "Bicker" or selections process had become less popular by the late 1960s. Yet the clubs still reinforced the university's image as a place for well-to-do white males, dubbed "Princeton Charlies." In the spring of 1971, 8 of Princeton's 12 clubs became "open," permitting women to join the bicker process, and 64 women became members. Within a decade, a woman was elected both the president of Tower and also the president of the Inter-Club Council. But four clubs continued to exclude women: Cannon (until 1979); Cottage Club (until 1988); and Tiger Inn and Ivy Club (until 1991). Even within the coeducational clubs women encountered sexism. Men in the coeducational clubs often ignored women during the "weekend syndrome," when they either imported dates from other colleges or searched for female companionship elsewhere. Moreover, the clubs tolerated nonconsensual sex, encouraged by the availability of alcohol, and dismissed sexual harassment as "a 'stupid' issue." Some clubs hired a female stripper for parties and continued to subscribe to Playboy Channel. The most obnoxious men urinated in front of women students, who responded to such sexism by participating in Take Back the Night marches and joining the Women's Center. Consequently, an alumna of the class of 1977, who had belonged to Cap and Gown and whose husband was a member of Ivy, said, in 1989, that the "one thing" she would "change about Princeton" would be to "burn down every single club on Prospect Avenue."[53]

Women's admission into the most recalcitrant eating clubs owes much to one woman's fight for the principle of gender equality at Princeton. Sally Frank '80, a senior in the Woodrow Wilson School and a member of the local American Civil Liberties Union chapter, filed a sex discrimination suit with the New Jersey Civil Rights Division against Cottage Club, Ivy Club, and Tiger Inn that barred her admission, and against Princeton University that tolerated them. At first she received verbal attacks from students and alumni and was also shunned by some women, who feared her suit would affect their social acceptance on campus and alumni connections. After Frank slowly began to win support from undergraduates, Cottage Club, whose members had earlier poured beer on her head and thrown her into a fountain, voted in 1986 (six years after she had graduated) to accept women and agreed to pay Frank $20,000 but still did not want her as a member. When Princeton contributed $27,500 to Frank's legal fees and denied university recognition to the two remaining male-only clubs, Ivy and Tiger Inn, Frank removed Princeton University from the suit. Finally, in the spring of 1990, Ivy and Tiger Inn voted to allow women to join; their graduate boards delayed, however. In September, the New Jersey Supreme Court unanimously awarded Frank $5,000 in damages, a portion of which she donated to a fund in her name at the Women's Center. Ivy and Tiger Inn clubs opened their bicker process to women in the spring of 1991. For Paige MacLean '93, a member of the Women's Center, the admission of women to the clubs was a way of charting how they had "moved from a process of assimilation to acceptance to fundamental integration." For Debbie Lewis '84, "the theme of Sally's struggle was of belonging, of being at home." In 1990, Frank received the Alumni Council's annual Award for Service to Princeton.[54]

Women's Spaces and Women's Issues

Both Yale and Princeton received generous gifts to build additional residential accommodations to meet housing shortages that occurred when women students entered. Even with better campus accommodations, some women still felt the need for a place of their own to make Princeton as well as Yale "a place for women, as opposed to a place that happened, suddenly, to have some women in it." Influenced by second wave feminism, Yale's Women's Center (December 1970), which relocated several times before receiving some university funding, provided a separate space for eighteen groups to gather and interact, since Yale "wasn't quite prepared for us," as the coordinators said. The Women's Center dealt with such issues as sexual harassment, anorexia, and abortion. Among the different groups were a chapter of the National Organization for Women, two groups focusing on sexual orientation, and three on reproductive health. Later additions included such racial and cultural groups as Asian-American Women's Group, Jewish Women's Discussion Group, the Black Women's Caucus, and a Latina Alpha Rho Lambda Sorority.[55]

Sexual assaults and harassment at Yale created problems for women, particularly before the establishment of uniform sexual harassment grievance procedures. Yale adhered, of course, to the prohibitions against sexual, racial, and other forms of harassment of employees and students mandated by the federal government, dating from the 1964 Civil Rights Act and the Connecticut Commission on Human Rights and Opportunities. But violent acts occurred on campus. For example, in February 1978, a female professor was stabbed and an undergraduate woman raped, prompting Yale to offer a rape prevention course. In March 1979, a Yale College Advisory Committee reported on a detailed procedure for handling student complaints of sexual harassment by faculty or administrators. Legal suits were also an option. Five students brought sexual harassment charges against Yale for tolerating sexual harassment by its professors, but four of the charges were dismissed in court in 1980, and on the fifth charge, Yale was held not culpable. Finding camaraderie and strength in "Take Back the Night" marches, in January 1986 Yale students held their first Rape Awareness Week. In May 1993, Yale found Dean Stephen Kellert guilty of acting improperly toward forestry student Kate Joost, who accused him of sexual harassment. Yale was criticized, however, for not notifying students how their complaints had been handled and for not informing professors' future employers of guilty verdicts. As a result, in 1993 Yale adopted a policy that placed on faculty "the burden of overcoming a presumption" that any sexual relationship "was not consensual on the part of the student." However, Yale College's Grievance Board for Student Complaints of Sexual Harassment has been criticized for not acting promptly. In 1996, after an undergraduate felt she had to complain publicly about unwanted sex with a mathematics professor, the Yale College Chapter ACLU called on Dean Richard Broadhead to state clearly "the University's intolerance of faculty harassment."[56]

Seeking a place of their own on campus, Princeton women undergraduates established their Women's Center in 1971 and sustained it until parts of the Princeton community offered some support in 1974. Finally, in 1977 the center received a budget from the university. Often controversial, the Women's Center was labeled "dangerous" by its opponents because it was allegedly taken over by "a bunch of lesbians . . . [who were] plotting the overthrow of Princeton University!" The university's response was to tell the Women's Center to be "politically neutral." Frustrated by the university's lack of commitment to addressing sexism on campus, women held Take Back the Night marches, during which male students yelled obscenities at them. Finally, the administration hired a full-time director for the Women's Center in 1987. With the appointment of Janis Stout, the Women's Center became activist and feminist. It lobbied for the establishment of the Standing Committee on the Status of Women, which deals with both students and faculty. It advocated sexual harassment counseling services and the implementation of a sexual harassment policy, a responsibility assumed, in 1988, by the Sexual Harassment/Assault Advising, Resources, and Education (SHARE) Program. A male student was subsequently expelled for sexual assault, which led to criticism of SHARE rather than the male student. Concerned about administrative indifference to women's concerns, about 100 Princeton student protesters occupied Nassau Hall, the administration building, in February 1989. About a decade later, in the spring of 1998, a survey that the Standing Committee on the Status of Women mailed to all students indicated continuing incidents of sexual assault and harassment.[57]

Yale became a more supportive community for gay and bisexual people earlier than Princeton did. Gay-Lesbian Awareness Days were first celebrated in April 1982, and Yale agreed to the inclusion of "sexual orientation" in the university's equal opportunity clause in April 1986. By 2001, some members of the LGBT (Lesbian, Gay, Bisexual, and Transgender) Co-op urged students not to choose to be "comfortable and mainstream enough to revert back into political invisibility." They were inspired by the LGBT group at Harvard that was both publicly "out" and activist. In contrast, Princeton was seen for many years as less hospitable to persons identified as LGBTs. In October 1989, students held the first Gay Jeans Day and first Gay Awareness Week. Karen Krahulik '91, captain of the 1991 women's swimming team, who had come out as a lesbian her junior year, was harassed by homophobic male athletes. By her senior year she was joined by enough others to form a small community, though some regretted they had come to Princeton. In 1993, Krahulik was hired as the coordinator for Princeton's Lesbian, Gay, and Bisexual Association. By then, the university had an inclusive affirmative action policy, courses, counseling, and a committee on LGBT issues, and housing for same-sex couples.[58]

Retrospective Views of Alumnae

Symposia at Yale and Princeton celebrated the tenth, twentieth, twenty-fifth, and thirtieth anniversaries of coeducation. Talks made during these celebrations and written collections of alumnae's reminiscences suggested that some women still felt that they remained somewhat on the margins of each institution's history and image. *Women Reflect about Princeton* (WRAP) provided an invaluable cross-section of perspectives, based on responses to a questionnaire about the academic and social experiences of "being a woman at Princeton" during the first 20 years of coeducation. Contributors, who could choose to remain anonymous, included alumnae from all classes, as well as transfer, graduate, and special program students. Moreover, the editors, Kirsten Bibbins '87, Anne Chiang '87, and Heather Stephenson '90, represented the racial diversity among Princeton women: African American, Asian American, and Caucasian. A "WRAP-ping It Up" concluded that there was "no one 'Princeton experience,' not even a 'Princeton woman's experience.' " Individual women were in different ways both shaped by and contributed to such contemporary social movements as women's liberation, African-American civil rights, gay liberation, and the anti–Vietnam War protests. Women who pushed for the Women's Center (1977), the women's studies program (1982), and the SHARE program (1988), the editors perceptively noted, "have changed the face of this University." Their portraits were not, however, displayed in Nassau Hall as were portraits of men who had made significant contributions to Princeton.[59]

Alumnae offered a variety of interesting responses to the question, "What would you change about Princeton?" In retrospect, many felt that equality between men and women may have existed in the classroom, "but the culture of the University was dominated by the clubs," which viewed women as "mere decorative objects." Several respondents emphasized that Princeton needed to study the issue of gender within the university. One of the most positive comments came from Beverly Butler '76, who had worked in the dining hall:

"Princeton, back then, was, finally, a 'choice enabler'—it made choices and dreams possible."[60]

In opening the twentieth anniversary symposia in 1989, the new Princeton president, Harold Shapiro, said that he recognized that more work needed to be done to include women: "If this becomes a better place for women, it will become a better place for men as well." Yet both former presidents Robert Goheen and William Bowen looked back on with pride on their role in implementing coeducation at Princeton. For Goheen, "Having a hand in coeducation [at] Princeton was surely being in on the single most gratifying accomplishment of the university during my presidency." Bowen emphasized that the decision to admit female undergraduates tested Princeton's values: "The stakes were enormous—partly because of the importance of women to the educational quality of Princeton, but also because the issue of coeducation became a test of the institution's ability to change."[61]

The collection of Yale women's perspectives, compiled in 1995, paralleled in many ways the concerns raised by Princeton women. For example, Neomi Rao '95 recognized that women "still face a unique set of questions, questions which in the pursuit of equality we often ignore. Maybe men and women are fundamentally different." She wrote that because of Yale's commitment "to a relatively firm meritocracy," equality was well established in the classroom, and women also succeed in extracurricular activities and athletics according to their abilities. However, "many students feel that Yale's general careerism encourages a belief that a Yale education is wasted on women who decide only to raise a family." But the reality of having a family may force women—and men—to confront differences determined by gender, which "can empower," Rao concluded, "they need not only limit."[62]

Under pressure from women faculty and students, Yale included an observance of its thirtieth anniversary of coeducation in its tercentennial celebrations during 2000–2001. The Women Faculty Forum of almost two dozen women hosted an interdisciplinary conference, "Gender Matters: Women and Yale," on September 20–21, 2001. Over 300 women, but fewer than ten men, attended its first panel on "Women and Universities," whose speakers included such distinguished alumnae as the presidents of three colleges: Bryn Mawr president Nancy J. Vickers M.A. '71, Ph.D. '76; Duke University president Nannerl O. Keohane Ph.D. '67; and Bennett College president Johnnetta Cole LHDH '91, who is also president emerita of Spelman College. Pointing out that "symbolism matters," Keohane emphasized that Wellesley College, where she had previously been president, visually honored women throughout the campus but that with a few exceptions Yale did not. President Levin noted that women's progress in many fields was changing the image of Yale but added that Yale should pioneer in providing ways for two-career couples to have families.[63]

Status of Women on the Faculty, Administration, and Trustees

Faculty at Yale and Princeton remain predominantly male and white, even though some progress has occurred in hiring and tenuring women and minorities. However, women tend to produce less of the published research needed to achieve tenure and promotion because they still handle more family responsibilities than most men and seem more willing than men to counsel students and serve on committees. In the fall of 1995, Princeton's 886-member regular full-time and part-time faculty included 238 women, about 26 percent, an increase from about 10 percent in 1989. At Yale, the number of tenured faculty members who were women rose from 59 (8.5 percent of 695) to 87 (11.9 percent of 729) between 1989 and 1995. During the same period, the number of women on term appointments rose from 233 (30.1 percent of 773) to 278 (34.5 percent of 806). In 1999, women at Yale and Princeton were about 15 percent of the tenured faculty members, slightly more than Harvard (13 percent) but less than Amherst (33 percent), Williams (25 percent), and Dartmouth (21 percent). By 2000, women were about 20 percent of Princeton's 670 full-time faculty members but 52 percent of the nonacademic staff. In 2001, Yale's percentage of tenured faculty members who were women had risen to 17 percent, and they were 34 percent of the professoriat, but this was still far less than the percentage of Ph.D. degrees (45 percent) that Yale had awarded to women in 2000.[64]

Both Yale and Princeton have appointed women to their governing boards. In May 1971, Yale named the first two women to its corporation: Marion Wright Edelman, LLB '63, president and founder of Children's Defense Fund, the first black woman trustee; and history professor Hanna H. Gray, the first not to have any Yale degree. By 2000 three women served on the seven-member Yale Corporation. Princeton's 37-member University Board of Trustees had four women by 1976. Two were alumnae trustees and two were women with alumni lineage selected as charter trustees. Juanita James '74, the first African-American woman on the board, noted that though there were relatively few female senior professors and administrators in 1989, eight trustees were women. In 2001–2, ten women served on Princeton's 38-member University Board of Trustees.[65]

Princeton, earlier than Yale, appointed women to major administrative posts. Women filled three deanships in the 1970s: the dean of students; dean of the college; and dean of the graduate school. Although Yale appointed a woman as a dean of one of the residential colleges in April 1970, and another woman as "acting" college master as her husband's successor in 1971, not until April 1991 was psychology department chair, Judith Rodin, selected as the first woman dean of the Yale Graduate School; in 1992 she was appointed university provost. As of 2001–2, three women, all of them white, were prominent among the seven officers of Yale University. The highest ranking was the provost, Alison Fettes

Richard, appointed Yale's chief academic and financial officer in 1994. Linda Koch Lorimer, vice president and university secretary, wished to work with a few other people "to replace Yale's 'old boys' network' with the 'new sisters' connection.' " Women were also appointed to important deanships: dean of the Yale Graduate School of Arts and Sciences in 1998; and dean of the Divinity School in 2001.[66]

However, with the exception of Hanna Gray's year as acting Yale president, it was Princeton that broke the most new ground in appointing women to the highest administrative positions. First, Harold Shapiro, and then Shirley Tilghman were the prime movers in bringing gender equity to Princeton. A pioneering molecular biologist in human-genome research, Tilghman took office as the nineteenth president of Princeton University on June 15, 2001 and was formally installed in September. Though only the second president to have no undergraduate Princeton experience, she had taught there since 1986 and was a single mother of a Princeton senior, her daughter. Recognizing that "Tenure is no friend to women," Tilghman made reforming the tenure system so that it did not continue to discriminate against women an important part of her agenda. During her first year in office, Tilghman brought in eight new senior administrators, among them, a new provost, Amy Gutmann, a former Harvard professor of political theory. With Gutmann's assistance, she recruited three of Harvard's star faculty: international law professor Anne-Marie Slaughter, who became dean of the Woodrow Wilson School of Public and International Affairs, and two outstanding black professors, Cornel West and K. Anthony Appiah. To strengthen the sciences and to attract more women majors, Tilghman appointed a woman as the new dean of the School of Engineering and Applied Science, effective January 2003. From only one female B.S.E. major in the class of 1973, the number majoring in the School of Engineering and Applied Science had risen by the 1990s to one-third of the engineering majors, compared to 15 percent women nationally.[67]

In addition, Tilghman implemented Harold Shapiro's initiative in pledging Princeton to work for gender equity by appointing a President's Task Force on the Status of Women in Natural Sciences and Engineering to develop a long-term recruitment plan. For the lower paid university employees, a majority of whom are women, Tilghman stepped up the ongoing process to raise their wages. "Two women now hold this university's top posts," wrote *Boston Globe* reporter David Abel, "and they are taking the academic sweepstakes to a new level." Because of the new energy, for two years *U.S. News & World Report* has ranked Princeton as "the No. 1 university in the country, compared with Harvard's No. 2."[68]

Conclusion

Given the profound changes at both Princeton and Yale since the inauguration of coeducation in 1969, it was little wonder that, despite some complaints
and reservations, pioneering Yale and Princeton women encouraged their
daughters to follow in their footsteps. In 1998, Natalie Bender entered Yale as
a first-year student, twenty-five years after her mother had been a freshman in
the close-knit first coeducational class of 1973. Her college years were more
predictable, unlike her mother's experiences during the tumultuous days of
the Black Panther trial and Vietnam War protests. Recognizing that she had
"simply nothing comparable to that experience in my generation," Bender came
to Yale not "to make history," but "to get an education and hopefully have some
fun while I'm at it."[69]

A few days before she received her degree from Princeton in 1998, a quarter
of a century after her mother, Barbara, Hidya Green exclaimed: "I feel there's
nothing that I can't do." Barbara Green, an attorney in California, had been a
pioneer on several counts: one of the 100 women in the class of 1973 that spent
four years at Princeton and one of the six black women in that class and one
of twelve black women students on campus. In contrast to her mother, Hidya
Green did not feel that gender was an issue for her. Like her, however, she was
always aware of her African-American identity. Race, not gender, continued
to make her feel like an outsider in most classes, except, of course, in African-
American studies. A competitive athlete in the long and triple jumps, she
captained the women's track and field team. Her postgraduate plans included
studying for a master's degree in physical therapy. Hidya Green's class ring included the years '73 and '98 and the inscription: "B.G. and H.G. shall proceed."
As Barbara Green said: "I thought it was a good tradition to continue."[70]

Notes

The epigraph comes from "The Education of Women at Princeton. A Special Report. A
Report on the Desirability and Feasibility of Princeton Entering Significantly into the
Education of Women at the Undergraduate Level," *Princeton Alumni Weekly,* September
24, 1968, 3–56, 53.

1.   James Cass and Max Birnbaum, *Comparative Guide to American Colleges for Students,
     Parents and Counselors* (New York: Harper and Row, 1965). Marcia Graham Synnott,
     *The Half-Opened Door: Discrimination and Admissions at Harvard, Yale, and Prince-
     ton, 1900–1970* (Westport, Conn.: Greenwood Press, 1979), 3–5. Cartoon by Carl Rose
     in *The New Yorker,* October 4, 1969, 36. Don Oberdorfer, *Princeton University: The
     First 250 Years* (Princeton: Princeton University Press, 1995), 174–91. Gaddis Smith,
     Yale and the External World: The Shaping of the University in the Twentieth Century
     (New Haven: Yale University Press, 2004).

2.   See the Web pages of Yale and Princeton universities.

3.   Susan Kennedy Calhoun, "Women in the Professional Schools: An Advocate of Sexual Equality Examines the Male-Image Professions," *Yale Alumni Magazine*, April 1970, 43–51; "Women Raise the Rate At the Law School," *Yale Alumni Magazine*, August 1972, 31. Caroline Kim '96, "Through Women's Eyes," in *Different Voices: A Journal Commemorating 25 Years of Coeducation at Yale*, Rachel Donadio, '96, ed. (New Haven: Yale University, 1995), 18–21, 18 (The collection was published in conjunction with Yale's celebration "Connections: Celebrating 25 Years of Coeducation at Yale College," March 24–April 1, 1995). "Graduate Education for Women at Yale," report sent by committee chairman E. Wight Bakke to Kingman Brewster Jr., October 8, 1968, Records of Kingman Brewster Jr., President of Yale University (RU11, series I), box 223, folder 1, Women's Education and Yale 1968, Manuscripts and Archives, Yale University Library.

4.   Peter Spencer, "Grad Alumnae Reflect on Early Years," *Princeton Today*, [August 4, 1989], Historical Subject File (HSF) Coeducation clippings, box 125, folder: Coeducation 1988–, University Archives, Department of Rare Books and Special Collections, Princeton University Library. Sabra Meservey Toback, former president of Dutchess Community College in New York, was, in 1989, a lecturer in history at the State University of New York at New Paltz. William K. Selden, *Women of Princeton 1746–1969* (Princeton: Princeton University Office of Printing and Mailing Services, 2000), 3–13, 3. Dorrit Ann Cowan, "Single-Sex to Coeducation at Princeton and Yale: Two Case Studies" (Ed.D. diss., Teachers College, Columbia University, 1982), 74–75, 78–80, 84. "First Women at Princeton" and "The Coming of Coeducation," in *Gender in the Academy: Women and Learning from Plato to Princeton*, an Exhibition Celebrating the 20th Anniversary of Undergraduate Coeducation at Princeton University, organized by Natalie Zemon Davis et al. (Princeton: Princeton University Library, 1990), 39–42. Seventy-five years earlier, Princeton had shared its faculty, course curricula, and libraries for a decade with Evelyn College for Women, chartered in 1889, by a former Princeton professor, Reverend Joshua Hall McIlvaine, class of 1837, and his daughters, Elizabeth and Alice.

5.   Luther Munford, "Coeducation at Princeton: The Struggle of an Idea at a University in Transition," *Daily Princetonian*, October 21, 1969, 5–14, 6, Arthur J. Horton Collection on Coeducation 1967–1980, box 2, folder 8, University Archives, Department of Rare Books and Special Collections, Princeton University Library. This article is the most detailed and best analysis of coeducation at Princeton through the admission of the first women undergraduates in September 1969.

6.   Cowan, 81–84, 88–90. Munford, 6. Bob Whittlesey, "Root of Ivy Coeducation: Yale's Put-Down by Vassar," *Daily Princetonian*, February 1969, 9, 13, 15, clipping, Horton collection, box 2, folder 7. Kingman Brewster Jr., comments, "Women and the University," held at the Biltmore Hotel, New York, March 1, 1969, file 625: Capital Fund Campaign, p. 9, Papers of President Mary I. Bunting, RG 2, series 4, Schlesinger Library, courtesy of the Radcliffe Institute for Advanced Study, Harvard University. "The Coeducation White Paper: Everything You Need to Know," *Yale Daily News*, November 7, 1968, clipping, Brewster records, box 222, folder 18. President Brewster had appointed Edna G. Rostow, Smith College '34, who had a master's in social work from the University of

Connecticut and was married to Law School dean Eugene V. Rostow, to chair the group studying the problems and needs of educating undergraduate women. The members of the Yale President's Ad Hoc Committee were Thaddeus Beal, Yale '39, president of the Harvard Trust bank and a Radcliffe trustee (he then became undersecretary of the army); Rosemary Park, a UCLA vice chancellor; and Janet Murrow, widow of Edward R. Murrow, who had been a Mount Holyoke trustee.

7.   "Sarah Lawrence Discloses Man-Plan," *Daily Princetonian,* February 2, 1968, Horton collection, box 2, folder 8; Whittlesey, 9, 13, 15; Bob Durkee '69, " 'Coeducation Is Inevitable': An Interview with the President," *Princeton Alumni Weekly,* September 26, 1967, 12; and John V. Dippel '68, "The Coeducation Study," *Princeton Alumni Weekly,* December 5, 1967, 6, 11–12, Horton collection, box 2, folder 9. Selden, 3. Cowan, 74–75, 78–79. In June 1967 Goheen argued for coeducation on three grounds: (1) it would make recruitment of male students easier; (2) women undergraduates would "add to the intellectual and cultural life of the university"; and (3) given the greater involvement of women in the contemporary world, Princeton would become "anachronistic" if it remained all male. Patterson left Princeton in late 1969 for a permanent position with the General Agreement on Tariffs and Trade (GATT) in Geneva (Munford, 8).

8.   "The Education of Women at Princeton," 28, 29, 34, 53, 18, 19. (see esp. Table 4-III: "Estimated Capital Costs of Enlarging Princeton by 1000 Women Undergraduates [July 1968 Prices]," 35). To this streamlined version of Patterson's 288-page report were added a letter by James F. Oates Jr. '21, chair of the trustees' executive committee; Robert Goheen's endorsement; and Arthur J. Horton's rebuttal.

9.   "Princeton," and "A General Conclusion," in *The Casebook on Coeducation at Amherst College,* Amherst, Mass., August 24, 1974, II E/33–36 and II E/44–52, Schlesinger Library. See also Howell Chickering Jr., chairman, and John Ward Williams, president ex officio, II C/3–5; and chart: "Institutions Recently Coeducational, Princeton University," II C/10.

10.   "The Education of Women at Princeton," 55–56. Arthur J. Horton's questionnaire, February 11, 1968, Horton collection, box 1, folder 4. "The Next Nine Months" and "Horton's Dissent," *Daily Princetonian,* September 18, 1968, 2. Dorina Yessios, "Overcoming Hurdles: The Decision Process," and "Coeducation 25 Years Ago," *Daily Princetonian* October 7, 1994, 1, 10, 2.

11.   Selden, 3. Marc E. Miller, senior class president, report on the Battle of Philadelphia, October 30, 1968, box 2, folder 4; Geoff Doyle '47 to Bill [Lippincott], handwritten protest on the Newsletter of the Alumni Council of Princeton University, September 13, 1968, Horton collection, box 1, folder 3. On April 10, 1969, fifteen Ohio alumni mailed copies of the alumni ballot to the 33,000 living alumni. In response to the question, "Do you believe that Princeton should continue its all-male tradition?," 18,000 or 51 percent answered affirmatively (Munford, 11–12).

12.   Whittlesey, 9, 13, 15; Robert Wells, "Rudenstine Favors Coeducation," "Bicker 'Objectionable,' " *Daily Princetonian,* February 7, 1968, box 2, folder 8; Department of Public Information release, February 9, 1969, box 2, folder 2; "Summary of Principal Characteristics of Five Models," chart, 14, and "Appraisal," 15–24, 21 and 23–24, in "The Education of Undergraduate Women At Princeton: An Examination of Coordinate Versus Coeducational Patterns," March 1969, box 1, folder 3, Horton collection.

The ad hoc implementation committee rejected both the model exemplified by major state and city universities that imposed no quota on women and the three models with decreasing degrees of coordination: Barnard and Douglass Colleges, which shared some facilities with, respectively, Columbia and Rutgers Universities; Radcliffe College, a separate corporation, which relied on Harvard's faculty; and Middlebury, Pembroke, and Rice, which provided a separate residential college for women. Munford, 12.

13. Robert F. Goheen to the Special Trustee Committee on Coeducation, February 20, 1969, Horton collection, box 2, folder 5; Department of Public Information release on the admission of women and supplementary tables, April 21, 1969, box 2, folder 2.

14. W. G. Bowen to Gardner Patterson, April 16, 1968, and Arthur J. Horton to William G. Bowen, April 18, 1968, Horton collection, box 1, folder 1; and Bruce Beckner, "A Change in Tactics," *Daily Princetonian* [1968], box 2, folder 10. "Princeton," IIE/33–36. "Alumni Fund Tops 1969–70 Record by $252,000" and "Admissions 1971: A Special and Sympathetic Hearing for Alumni Sons," *Yale Alumni Magazine,* October 1971, 30 and 35; "Admissions Edge For Alumni Children," *Yale Alumni Magazine,* December 1971, 24. The Yale faculty voted to terminate academic credit for ROTC courses after the June 1971 commencement. Citing academic freedom, Brewster defended university chaplain William Sloane Coffin, who was arrested in 1968, together with Benjamin Spock '25, for encouraging draft resistance (Julien Dedman, "The Rape of Yale," *Yale Alumni Magazine,* January 1970, 46–48, 48. Carter Wiseman '68, "In the Days of DKE and S.D.S.," *Yale Alumni Magazine,* February 2001, 34–39.

15. "The Coeducation White Paper." "At the University: The Question of Coeducation Is the Fall's Major Issue," *Yale Alumni Magazine,* November 1968, 14–15.

16. Kingman Brewster Jr., "Higher Education for Women at Yale," September 23, 1968, Brewster records, box 172, folder 16; Kingman Brewster Jr., statement to the faculty on coeducation, November 14, 1968, box 61, folder 1; Mary I. Bunting to Kingman Brewster, October 22, 1968, box 222, folder 14. "The Coeducation White Paper." "At the University: The University Dips a Toe into Coeducation: 500 Women to Be Admitted Next Year," *Yale Alumni Magazine,* December 1968, 10–13. Whittlesey, 9, 13, 15.

17. A petition to President Kingman Brewster Jr. on coeducation, received October 15, 1968; Students for a Democratic Society, "Coeducation at Yale," [1969], Brewster records, folder 1, box 61. "At the University: The University Dips a Toe into Coeducation," 10–13; "At the University: The Question of Coeducation," 14–15. Alan Boles '69, "Yes, Virginia, There Is a Yale" (abridged from the 1969 *Yale Banner*), in Donadio, 9, 10, 11. Henry Chauncey, quoted in Munford, 11.

18. Robert Goheen, quoted in Munford, 11, 12–13. "Trustees' Statement on Coeducation," Horton collection, box 2, folder 3. B. J. Phillips, "Coeds at Princeton: Everybody Wins," *Washington Post,* February 16, 1969, H4. "Coeducation: Implementing the Inevitable," *Daily Princetonian,* February 22, 1969, 2. On April 20, 1969, admissions director John T. Osander mailed acceptance letters to the first undergraduate women offered admission; the other forms regretting that they could not be accepted were used as scratch paper. The campus radio station, WPRB, played the Handel's "Hallelujah Chorus."

19. Munford, 13.

20. Kirsten Bibbins, Anne Chiang, and Heather Stephenson, eds., *Women Reflect about Princeton* (Princeton: Princeton University Office of Communications/Publications,

1989), 26, 112–113. Munford, 13. Carlo H. Balestri and Dorina Yessios, "Bridging the Gap through Pressure, Activism," *Daily Princetonian*, October 14, 1994, 1, 8. Bohen, who was later promoted to associate dean, left Princeton in 1977 to practice clinical psychology.

21. "Tigers Purr as 171 Women Enroll at Princeton," *New York Times*, September 8, 1969, 1. Faye Kessin, "A History of Women at Princeton," *Weekly Nassau*, November 9, 1979, 8, HSF Coeducation clippings, box 125, folder: Coeducation 1974–1987, and "O Pioneers," *Princeton Living*, September 1994, folder: Coeducation 1988–. Gardner Patterson, comments, "Women and the University," held at the Biltmore Hotel, New York, March 1, 1969, 4, 5, 14, Bunting papers. Lisa Outar, "On the Vanguard," *Daily Princetonian*, March 10, 1993, 1–3. Bibbins, Chiang, and Stephenson 13–15. Selden, 8. Jane Leifer, *Princeton Alumni Weekly*, May 29, 1973, quoted in Linda Mandeville, "Women and the Ivies, A Report on the Integration of Women into the Mainstream of Ivy League Academic and Extracurricular Life," *Columbia*, October 1982, 12–19, 15 and 14–16.

22. "Coeducation at Yale College: A Brief Chronology," in Donadio, 66–71. Elyssa Folk, "It Was Thirty Years Ago Today: Yale Picks Up Its First Women," *Yale Daily News*, May 19, 2000. Brewster, comments, "Women and the University," 13, 20. Elga Wasserman, "Coeducation 1969–70," progress report by the chairman of the University Committee on Coeducation and Special Assistant to the President on the Education of Women, December 17, 1970, 8–10, Brewster records, box 60, folder 12; "Comments Selected at Random from a Questionnaire Distributed to All Graduate Students Enrolled at Yale, 1967–1968," box 222, folders 12–18; and "Graduate Education for Women at Yale," box 223, folder 1. "Facts on Women," *Yale Alumni Magazine*, October 1969, 23.

23. Minutes of the February 13 [1970] meeting of the University Committee on Coeducation, submitted by Elisabeth McC. Thomas, Brewster records, box 60, folder 14. Mary C. Wright (1917–1970), a scholar of Chinese history, was the first woman tenured in arts and sciences. "Coeducation at Yale College: A Brief Chronology," 68. Rachel Donadio '96, "Interview with Elga Wasserman," in Donadio, 22–24, 23 and 24. "New Directions in the Coeducation Office," *Yale Alumni Magazine*, October 1972, 39. "At the University: The University Dips a Toe into Coeducation," 10–12; "Elga Wasserman to Head Planning for Coeducation," *Yale Alumni Magazine*, December 1968, 12–13. Elga Wasserman to Kingman Brewster, May 11, 1970, Brewster records, box 60, folder 13. "Coeducation 1969–70," 1–5. In this report, also see Elga Wasserman to Georges May, October 28, 1970, and Elga Wasserman to President Kingman Brewster Jr., December 4, 1970, in Appendix G: Correspondence, 1, 15–17; Appendix E: Membership of the Yale College Faculty, October 2, 1969, 28; and Appendix F: Report of three-member subcommittee, by Dr. Robert Arnstein, chair, Professor Edmund S. Morgan, and Katherine Jelly '71, May 19, 1970, 29–30.

24. Jonathan Lear, "How Yale Selected Her First Coeds," *New York Times Magazine*, April 13, 1969, 72, 76. Janet Lever and Pepper Schwartz, *Women at Yale: Liberating a College Campus* (Indianapolis: Bobbs-Merrill, 1971), 39, 42. Unofficial statistics from coeducation office, August 19, 1969, Brewster records, box 60, folder 16. "Facts on Women," 23.

25. "Facts on Women," 23. "Appendix A: Admission of Women Undergraduates for Sep-

tember 1969," in Elga Wasserman, "Report of the Chairman of the Planning Committee on Coeducation, 1968–1969," May 29, 1969, Brewster records, box 60, folder 16. Lever and Schwartz, 43–44, 45.

26. Kim, 18; Sherrie Selwyn '98, "The Social Scene in 1969," in Donadio, 16–17. Oberdorfer, 194–211. "Anti-War Protest: A Case of Suspended Horror," *Yale Alumni Magazine,* June 1972, 29. Wiseman, 34–39.

27. Lucy L. Eddy, "In the Blue," *Yale Alumni Magazine,* April 1970, 24–25. Katherine L. Jelly, "Coeducation: One Student's Views," Lisa Getman, "From Conestoga to Career," and Barbara Deinhardt, " 'Mother of Men'?," in *Women in Higher Education,* ed. W. Todd Furniss and Patricia Albjerg Graham (Washington, D.C.: American Council on Education, 1974), 62, 63; 64–65, 66; 66–69. Barbara Packer and Karen Waggoner, "Yale and the New Sisterhood," *Yale Alumni Magazine,* April 1970, 26–31, 27. Liva Baker, *"I'm Radcliffe! Fly Me!": The Seven Sisters and the Failure of Women's Education* (New York: Macmillan; London: Collier Macmillan, 1976), 15–64.

28. Ruth Jarmul '71 and Cynthia Pincus, director of the Information and Counseling Center for Women, "The Educated Woman," *Yale Alumni Magazine,* December 1971, 16–19; "LEVI Reports Results of Second Questionnaire," *Yale Alumni Magazine,* July 1971, 36; "The Shape of Things to Come," *Yale Alumni Magazine,* April 1969, 34–35. "Coeducation 1969–70," 1–6, 11–17; Appendix A: Admission Statistics, charts 1–4, 18–19; and Appendix G: Correspondence, 1, 15–17.

29. "Trustees Vote to Increase the Number of Women," *Yale Alumni Magazine,* January 1973, 30. Kim, 20. "Facts on Women," 23. Appendix A: Admission of Women Undergraduates for September 1969, in Wasserman, "Report of the Chairman." "Coeducation 1969–70," 1–5; 11–17; and Appendix A: Admission Statistics, charts 1–4, 18–19. "R. Inslee Clark, Jr., Dean of Admissions, Resigns to Become Horace Mann Headmaster," *Yale Alumni Magazine,* February 1970, 16; Jeffrey Gordon, "Inky's Era," *Yale Alumni Magazine,* March 1970, 32–37; and "Henry Chauncey and John Muyskens Take Top Admissions Posts; Appointments Also Fill Other Administrative, Faculty Positions," *Yale Alumni Magazine,* June 1970, 19. In the fall of 1972, Yale accepted 194 African Americans, 94 Asian Americans, 50 Mexican Americans, 25 mainland Puerto Ricans, and 3 American Indians.

30. Table 1: "Bachelor's Degrees Conferred in Institutions of Higher Education by Race, Ethnicity, and Sex: Institution, State and Nation 1975–76," in U.S. Department of Health, Education, and Welfare, Office for Civil Rights, *Racial, Ethnic, and Sex Enrollment Data from Institutions of Higher Education* ([Washington, D.C.], April 1978),1:41, 10. Robert A. Dahl, "The Dahl Report," and "President Brewster's Statement," *Yale Alumni Magazine,* May 1972, 20–26, 23, 24, 26; 26–27. "Whither the Dahl Report on Yale College? A Postscript," *Yale Alumni Magazine,* June 1972, 28–29. In 1975, Harvard and Radcliffe adopted an equal access policy and established a new Harvard-Radcliffe Office of Admissions and Financial Aid.

31. President Brewster's "Background Memorandum on Coeducation Admissions Policy," cited in "Trustees Defer Decision on Future of Coeducation," *Yale Alumni Magazine,* December 1972, 30–31; "Trustees Vote to Increase the Number of Women," 30; "Transfer Admissions Shrink," *Yale Alumni Magazine,* January 1973, 34.

32. Chart: "Institutions Recently Coeducational, Princeton University," in *The Casebook on Coeducation at Amherst College,* II C/10 and II C/3–5.

34. "Commission on the Future of the College," *Princeton Alumni Weekly,* November 10, 1970, 5; "Highlights from the Report of the Commission on the Future of the College," May 1973; and Chapter 3, "The Size of the College, Coeducation and the Composition of the Student Body," 92–95; 71–95, 122–125, of "The Report of the Commission on the Future of the College," April 1973, HSF Commission on the Future of the College, box 127. "Princeton," pp. II E/33–36, and "A General Conclusion," pp. II E/44–46, *The Casebook on Coeducation at Amherst College.*

The 436-page "Report of the Commission on the Future of the College," submitted to President William G. Bowen (1972–1987) in May 1973 outlined "seven principles." The first was a late-twentieth-century version of "Princeton in the nation's service":

1) Higher education should serve both social and individual purposes; it should simultaneously equip a student to realize his full human potentialities and to contribute to the life of his community and nation.

2) Princeton should influence student outcomes in four principal areas: knowledge, skills and tastes; career and profession; values and attitudes; and character and personality.

In assessing its strength, the report cited "Princeton's great achievement" as having "managed to become a major research university while still preserving that dedication to undergraduate teaching." The seventh principle committed Princeton to encouraging "a high degree of diversity in its academic and extra-curricular programs and in the composition of the student population." Four groups received "special consideration in the admission process": engineering candidates, targeted at between 160 and 185 freshmen; alumni children, averaging between 13 and 20 percent of freshmen; minority students; and "applicants with unusual athletic ability." Generally "satisfied with the present applicant pool," the Bressler commission recognized that more well-qualified women needed to be persuaded "to *consider* Princeton as an option." It also recognized, however, that blacks and women experienced minority status on campus and needed "role models" among administrators and faculty.

34. William G. Bowen, "Coeducation at Princeton," report of the president, April 1980, 3–32, 32, 4, 5 (Chart I: "Fall Term Opening Enrollments, Men and Women Students in the Undergraduate College, 1969–1979"), 6, 8, 9–12, 16–19 Horton collection, box 2, folder 9; also in *Princeton Alumni Weekly,* April 21, 1980, ibid. Earle E. Coleman, "Enrollment," in Alexander Leitch, *A Princeton Companion* (Princeton: Princeton University Press, 1978), available online at *http://mondrian.princeton.edu/Campus WWW/Companion/enrollment.html;* Alexander Leitch, "Women," in *A Princeton Companion,* at *http://mondrian.princeton.edu/ CampusWWW/Companion/women. html.* Selden, 8–9.

35. "Women Admits Hit Record High," *Princeton Weekly Bulletin,* April 22, 1985, 1. "At Princeton, a Bid to Draw More Women," *New York Times,* November 5, 1986, clipping; Maureen Nevin Duffy, "Princeton Reviews Policies on Women," *New York Times,*

March 15, 1987, HSF Coeducation clippings, box 125, folder: Coeducation 1974–1987. Dori Kornfeld, "Survey to Evaluate Campus Experience for Female Students," *Daily Princetonian,* October 16, 1997, 1, 15. Bibbins, Chiang, and Stephenson, 56.

36. In the Class of 1983, women accounted for 38 percent; for the university as a whole, women made up 36 percent. In 1989, 1,740 women enrolled, about 39 percent of the undergraduates; women were 32 percent of the graduate students (Sally Freedman, "Celebration of Coeducation at Princeton," *Princeton Weekly Bulletin,* April 10, 1989, 1–2). By one estimate, women constituted 45 percent of Princeton's 4,524 undergraduates in 1996 (Don Henry III, "Privilege, Diversity Meet," *Trenton Times,* March 10, 1996, A1, A14). In 2000–01, the 4,554 undergraduates included 2,171 women (about 48 percent) and 2,383 men (52 percent). In May 2002, Princeton's Women's Center estimated the enrollment of undergraduate women at 49 percent, women graduate students at 37 percent, and engineering students at 31 percent. Women were 28 percent of the faculty and 16 percent of the tenured faculty (Princeton University Women's Center, "Facts about Women at Princeton," 2002, at *www.princeton.edu/~womenctr/why.html*).

37. Fred M. Hechinger, "More Negroes Accepted by Ivy League Colleges," *New York Times,* April 14, 1968, clipping, Horton collection, folder 11, box 2. "This Year's Freshman Class Has 41 More Women and Six Fewer Blacks" and "Admissions Office Starts Rolling with Earlier Acceptances," *Yale Alumni Magazine,* October 1971, 35. Yale's tabulation of "University Wide Minority and International Student Enrollment by School 1984–85 to 1999–2000," Table 5, indicated that minority student enrollment in Yale College reached a high of 33.7 percent in 1995–96; it was 31.3 percent in 1999–2000. Minority enrollment throughout Yale University has averaged over 37 percent between 1996–97 and 1999–2000 (Yale University, Summary of Yale College Admissions, 1979–2001, in Beverly Waters, ed., *A Yale Book of Numbers, 1976–2000* [New Haven: Yale University Office of Institutional Research, November 2, 2000], at *www.yale.edu/oir/*). Julie Thermes, *Essor et declin de l'affirmative action: Les étudiants noirs à Harvard, Yale et Princeton,* preface by Andre Kaspi (Paris: CNRS, 1999), 383. "Yale's Minority Student Recruiting: An Uneven Record, but Improving," *Yale Alumni Magazine,* May 1972, 37; "Admissions: 'An Element of Humanity and Order,' " and "Excerpts from the Chauncey Speech on Admissions Reform," *Yale Alumni Magazine,* August 1972, 22–24; Mitchell F. Crusto, "Selling Yale," *Yale Alumni Magazine,* April 1973, 20–23.

38. Hechinger. Chart: "Institutions Recently Coeducational, Princeton University," *The Casebook on Coeducation at Amherst College,* II C/10, II C/3–5. Thermes, 385.

39. Cathy Trower and Richard P. Chait, "Forum: Faculty Diversity. Why Women and Minorities Are Underrepresented in the Professoriate, and Fresh Ideas to Induce Needed Reform," *Harvard Magazine,* March–April 2002, 33–37, 98; see Table I: "Student Diversity, 2000–2001," and "Tenured Women Faculty Members at Select Elite Institutions, 1999," 35, available in online version. "A Princeton Profile, 2001–02: Seniors and Alumni." See Yale University Office of Institutional Research (OIR), "Factsheet," at *www.yale.edu/oir/.* In the fall of 2001, Princeton enrolled 4,611 undergraduates: 2,380 men (51.61 percent) and 2,231 women (48.38 percent); Yale enrolled 5,253 undergraduates: 2,661 men (50.65 percent) and 2,592 women (49.34 percent).

40. Vanita Gupta '96, "Unity, Not Homogeneity: Women's Studies at Yale"; Adria Imada

'93, "New Spaces, New Voices: Asian-American Women's Group"; "Coeducation at Yale College: A Brief Chronology"; and Katherine Gergen '96, "Pools of Strong Women: Sculpting the Rocks of My Identity," in Donadio, 38–39; 48–49; 66–71; 55–57. Packer and Waggoner, 27. Mark Alden Branch, "Beyond Women's Studies," *Yale Alumni Magazine,* December 1998. Nancy Cott joined the Harvard history department in 2002 as a tenured professor and as director of the Schlesinger Library on the History of Women.

41. Munford, 13. Bibbins, Chiang, and Stephenson, 96–108, 104–5. Margaret M. Keenan, "The Controversy over Women's Studies," *Princeton Alumni Weekly,* April 21, 1980, 12–15, 17–18; Ann Waldron, "The Holden Collection on Women's History," *Princeton Alumni Weekly,* April 21, 1980, 16, Horton collection, box 2, folder 9. Miriam Y. Holden, who died in 1977, had belonged to the National Woman's Party and was a friend to Gerda Lerner, a pioneering scholar in American women's history. In 1978, Harvard's Faculty Council had established the Committee on Women's Studies but did not approve an undergraduate degree program offering a joint concentration until 1986, making it "the last Ivy League institution to approve such a program" (Peggy Lim, ed. *The Women's Guide to Harvard* [Cambridge, Mass.: Harvard-Radcliffe Women's Leadership Project, 2002], 88). Women's studies advocates found support in a 1980 Brown University project report, "Men and Women Learning Together: A Study of College Students in the Late '70s," which indicated that women's sense of self-worth and grade point average declined from high school through college, perhaps because of stereotypes limiting their aspirations (Mandeville, "Women and the Ivies," *Columbia,* October 1982, 12–19, 18–19).

42. Sally Moren, "Women's Studies Comes of Age," and Ann Waldron, "Career Path Parallels Ascendancy of Women's Studies," *Princeton Weekly Bulletin,* April 22, 1985, 1–3; 3, 7; "Princeton Fostering Women's Studies," *New York Times,* June 16, 1985, clipping; Princeton University, "Program in Women's Studies," brochure, HSF Coeducation Clippings, box 125, folder: Coeducation 1974–1987. Bibbins, Chiang, and Stephenson, 36–37.

43. Leitch, "Women"; Outar, 1–3; Carlo H. Balestri, "Breaking Down Barriers: The First Four Years," *Daily Princetonian,* October 11, 1994, 1, 6. Eleanor O'Sullivan, "Princeton Pioneer Recalls Breaking All-Male Barrier" and "Graduates Say Education Has Paid Off," *Asbury Park Press,* June 8, 1983, C12. "O Pioneers," *Princeton Living,* September 1994, clipping; Jed Seltzer, "The University's First Women Recall Challenging Campus Status Quo," *Daily Princetonian,* April 7, 1998, 1, 6–7, 10, HSF Coeducation Clippings, box 125, folder: Coeducation 1988–. David Sigmund, "Princeton Marks Quarter Century of Coeducation," *Trenton Times,* April 2, 1995, A3. David Newhouse, "25 Years of Women's Achievements," *Trenton Times,* April 7, 1995, A12. Bibbins, Chiang, and Stephenson, 118. Ron Southwick, "Second Generation: Women at Princeton Come Full Circle," *Trenton Times,* May 31, 1998, A1, A9. Elsi Heilala, "A Sense of Belonging: Nugent Rises through Princeton Ranks," *Daily Princetonian,* November 18, 1994, 1, 8–9. Melissa Kiser Mesrobian '75, " '73 Coed Returns as First Alumna Professor," *Princeton Alumni Weekly,* April 21, 1980, 14, box 2, folder 9, Horton collection. Judith Cummings, "Once All-Male Princeton Graduates 1,027, with 2 Women Leading Class," *New York Times,* June 11, 1975, 37. Selden, 8–9.

44. Bowen, "Coeducation at Princeton," 24–26; Bibbins, Chiang, and Stephenson, 126–127, 170; Selden, 8–9, 13, 15. Tricia Cortez and Mike Fischer, "Gender Imbalances Exist in Many Student Organizations,"and "Gender Imbalances Service and Services," *Daily Princetonian,* October 10, 1994, 1–3; 2.

45. Preethi Krishnamurthy '96, "Women in the Political Union"; "Coeducation at Yale College: A Brief Chronology"; and Richard C. Levin, "To the Yale Community," in Donadio, 54; 66–71; 5.

46. Patrick Healy, "Monumental Win for Lin," *Boston Sunday Globe,* June 2, 2002, B5. Folk; Alexis Wolff, "Movie Shows First Days of Yale Women," *Yale Daily News,* March 22, 2001. "Coeducation at Yale College: A Brief Chronology," 66–71; Gergen, 57. Kathy Newman GRD '96, "Overlooking Women," and Neomi Rao '95, "Nature or Nurture" (abridged from the *Yale Free Press,* February 1995), in Donadio, 27–30, 28, 29; 60.

47. Leitch, "Women"; Selden, 9–12. Bowen, "Coeducation at Princeton." "O Pioneers"; Carmelita W. Reyes, "President Goheen Returns to Discuss Coeducation's Birth," *Daily Princetonian,* April 7, 1995, HSF Coeducation clippings, box 125, folder: Coeducation 1988–. Bibbins, Chiang, and Stephenson, 50, 51. Newhouse, "25 years of Women's Achievements," *Trenton Times,* April 7, 1995, A1. "Princeton Athletics: Striving for Equality," *Daily Princetonian,* November 18, 1994, 2. Emily Goodfellow '76 became the first player to win 12 varsity letters, four each in field hockey, squash, and lacrosse. From 1980 to 1982, she was the only woman writer for ABC's *Wide World of Sports* and baseball programming, and from 1991 to 1995 she coached the Princeton women's squash team (Malena Salberg, "Goodfellow Refuses to Let Athletic Success Define Her," *Daily Princetonian,* November 18, 1994, 1, 12–13).

48. Folk; Wolff. "If You Think Frailty's Name Is Woman, Take a Second Look at Yale's Newest Athletes," *Yale Alumni Magazine,* March 1972, 34–35. "Coeducation at Yale College: A Brief Chronology," 69, 70; Tisha Neufville '97, "Claiming the Field: Women's Athletics," in Donadio, 53.

49. "Woman to Direct Physical Education," *Yale Alumni Magazine,* April 1973, 35; Bruce Fellman, "Great Moments in Yale Sports," *Yale Alumni Magazine,* March 2001, 75–78, 77, 78. James L. Shulman and William G. Bowen, with Lauren A. Meserve and Roger C. Schonfeld, *The Game of Life: College Sports and Educational Values,* In Collaboration (Princeton: Princeton University Press, 2001), 118, 128–29; see fig. 6.1: "Percent of Athletes Reporting That Being 'Recruited' Was a 'Very Important' Reason for Choosing This Specific College (by Cohort, Gender, and Division)," 129. For Yale Athletic Teams in 2001–02, see OIR, "Factsheet."

50. "Coeducation at Yale College: A Brief Chronology," 66–71; Kirby Lunger '95, "Women's Fraternities," in Donadio, 52. Bibbins, Chiang, and Stephenson, 53, 167–68.

51. Kris Millegan, "What Hath Women Wrought," *Conspiracy Theory Research List,* February 2001, available at *www.ctrl.org/boodleboys/wrought.html;* Molly Ball and Emily Bell, "Behind the Sacred Walls of Yale's Secret Societies," *Yale Herald,* Summer 2002.

52. "The Dispute over Mory's: 'Male, Yale and Wet'?," *Yale Alumni Magazine,* December 1971, 23; "Mory's: One Step Closer to Going Dry, or, God Forbid, Female?," *Yale Alumni Magazine,* March 1972, 33; "More on Mory's: A $20 Assessment Stirs Up a Storm," *Yale Alumni Magazine,* May 1972, 33. Arthur Greenfield, "The People vs. Mory's," *Yale Alumni Magazine,* June 1973, 25–29.

53. Bibbins, Chiang, and Stephenson, 59–62, 71, 73–74, 78–80. Howard Gertler and Steven Piccirillo, "Struggling against Misunderstanding," *Daily Princetonian,* November 4, 1994, 1, 3; Steven Piccirillo and Howard Gertler, "Fighting for a Place at the 'Street,' " *Daily Princetonian,* November 8, 1994, 1, 7.

54. Bowen, "Coeducation at Princeton," 26–29; Selden, 9. Meg Tuttle, "Behind a Militant Mask," *Weekly Nassau,* November 9, 1979, 3; Duffy. Balestri and Yessios, 8; Piccirillo and Gertler, 1, 7. Paige MacLean and Debbie Lewis, quoted in Bibbins, Chiang, and Stephenson, 7, 67.

55. Jessica Moss '95 and Shira Weinert '95, "The Women's Center: Still Crazy after All These Years," and Precious Williams '97, "A Story of Sisterhood: The Black Women's Caucus," in Donadio, 31–33; 50–51.

56. Packer and Waggoner, 27. "Coeducation at Yale College: A Brief Chronology," 66–71; Gergen, 55–57. "Sexual and Other Harassment Is Illegal," March 12, 2002, at *www.library.yale.edu/1hr/policies/sexual harassment.html.* "Committee to Review Yale's Policy on Faculty-Student Relationships," *Yale Bulletin and Calendar,* April 7–14, 1997, at *www.yale.edu/opa/ybc/v25.n27.news.01.html.* "Yale College Grievance Board for Student Complaints of Sexual Harassment," [2002], at *www.yale.edu/yalecol/pages/shcomplaints.html.* Ben Smith, "The Yale ACLU," *Yale Herald,* September 22, 1996, at *www.yale.edu/aclu/news/herald.html.*

57. Balestri and Yessios, 1, 8. Bibbins, Chiang, and Stephenson, 109, 110, 113, 117; 111–116, 120–123, 170. "At Princeton, a Bid to Draw More Women." Duffy. Kornfeld, 1, 15.

58. Gertler and Piccirillo, 1, 3. Craig A. Hardesty, *The Gay, Lesbian, and Bisexual Students' Guide to Colleges, Universities, and Graduate Schools* (New York: New York University Press, 1994), 80–83, 142–143. Michael Boucai, "Gay Students Should Come Out, Break the Silence," *Yale Herald,* October 19, 2001, 11, citing "To Be Gay at Yale," *Rolling Stone,* October 11, 2001.

59. Bibbins, Chiang, and Stephenson, 9–12, 169, 170; 171–75. Their project received financial support from the Office of the Dean of Students, the Office of the President, the Women's Studies Program, the Undergraduate Student Government, the Women's Center, and different classes.

60. Ibid., 157, 160–61, 162; 45, 47, 48–50.

61. Harold Shapiro, Robert Goheen, and William Bowen, quoted in Freedman, 1–2. "Gender and Education: Symposia Commemorating 20 Years of Undergraduate Coeducation at Princeton," reported in *Princeton Weekly Bulletin,* April 10, 1989, 1–2, HSF Coeducation clippings, box 125, folder: Coeducation 1988–; Robert F. Goheen '40, "A President Recalls Coeducation," April 13, 1989, *Daily Princetonian,* box 125, folder: Coeducation 1988–. For the 25th anniversary commemoration, April 6–13, 1995, see also Sigmund, A3, and Newhouse, A1, A12. Reyes; "Celebrating Women at Princeton: 25 Years and More . . . ," brochure, April 6–13, 1995, HSF Coeducation clippings, box 125, folder: Coeducation 1988–.

62. Rao, 58, 59–60.

63. "Around the Campus: 9/20/01," *Yale Daily News,* September 20, 2001; Naomi Massave, "Women in Universities Is Gender Panel's First Topic," *Yale Daily News,* September 21, 2001. Bruce Fellman, "Where We Stand," *Yale Alumni Magazine,* 36–41, 39.

64 Yale University OIR, "University Faculty by Gender and Ethnicity, 1982–1999," and

"Women and Minority Ph.D. Recipients, The Graduate School of Arts and Sciences, 1978–1999," November 20, 2000, available at *www.yale.edu/oir/*. See also OIR, "Factsheet." Rick Klein, "University Bases Affirmative Action on 'Open, Honest' Faculty Searches," *Daily Princeton*, April 11, 1996, 1, 3–5; see the charts "Number of University Faculty, Fall 1995," 1, and "Number of University Administrative and Support Staff, Fall 1995," 4. Trower and Chait, 33–37, 98; see esp. "Tenured Women Faculty Members at Select Elite Institutions, 1999," 35. Massave. Enrolling 1,853 degree candidates, Yale awarded 267 Ph.D. degrees and 132 master's degrees in 2000–01. In 1999–2000, 144 women and 18 minorities (6 percent) were among Yale's 317 Ph.D. recipients.

65. Massave. "Coeducation at Yale College: A Brief Chronology," 67, 68. "Two Women Are among the Four New Yale Trustees," *Yale Alumni Magazine*, July 1971, 34. For list of trustees, see Yale University website, *www.yale.edu*. In 1971, the Princeton board of trustees had selected Mary St. John Douglas (1972–1988), wife of John W. Douglas '43 and daughter of Fordyce B. St. John '05, and Susan Savage Speer, wife of T. Guthrie Speer Jr. '50 and daughter of William L. Savage '20. Leitch, "Women." Selden, 8–9, 13–14. "A Princeton Profile, 2001–02: Trustees of the University," available at *www. princeton.edu/pr/facts/profile/ 01/44.htm*. Freedman, 1–2.

66. Selden, 9, 13, 15; Leitch, "Women." Balestri and Yessios, 8. In June 1994, Rodin was selected as the University of Pennsylvania's first woman president and the first in the Ivy League (Ted Anthony, "First Woman Nominated Head of Ivy Institution," *Boston Globe*, December 7, 1993). Associated Press, "Yale University Names Woman Anthropologist to Position of Provost," *Boston Globe*, February 26, 1994. For administrative appointments, also see Yale University website.

67. Freedman, 1–2. Bowen, "Coeducation at Princeton," 32, 4, 5 (Chart I) 6, 8, 9–12, 16–19. Leitch, "Women." Selden, 8–9. Jennifer Gennari Sheperd, "A Lab of Her Own," *Princeton Alumni Weekly*, March 8, 1996. "Shirley Tilghman Named Princeton University's 19th President," press release, May 5, 2001, available at *www.princeton.edu/pr/news/01/ q2/0505-tilghman.htm*. Shirley Tilghman, quoted in Sally Jacobs, "In a League of Her Own: Princeton's First Female President Wants to Add Color to Campus and Tackle the Tenure," *Boston Globe*, July 10, 2001. Patrick Healy, "Harvard Loses Scholar West to Princeton," *Boston Globe*, April 13, 2002, and "Princeton Leads, 4–0," *Boston Globe*, May 19, 2002. David Abel, "Princeton Goes Head-to-Head with Harvard: N.J. Rival Trying to Lure Cambridge's Black Stars," *Boston Globe*, February 11, 2002. To its Nobel laureates in the sciences, Princeton added the 1993 Nobel Prize–winner in literature, Toni Morrison, then the Robert F. Goheen Professor in the Humanities.

68. Jennifer Greenstein Altmann, "Thriving in the Presidency," *Princeton Weekly Bulletin*, May 20, 2002. "A Princeton Profile, 2001–02: Finances and Officers of the University," available at *www.princeton.edu/pr/facts/ profile/01/28.htm*. Steven Schultz, "Princeton Signs Pledge on Gender Equity," *Princeton Weekly Bulletin*, February 12, 2001; "Tilghman Establishes Gender Equity Task Force," *Princeton Weekly Bulletin*, October 1, 2001. Abel. Karen W. Arenson, "More Women Taking Leadership Roles at Colleges," *New York Times*, July 4, 2002, available at *www.nytimes.com/ 2002/07/04/education/04PRIN. html*. In addition to Provost Gutmann, Nancy Weiss Malkiel served as dean of the college and was reappointed to a five-year term in June 2002; Kathleen Deignan was dean of undergraduate students; and Karin Trainer was librarian. Underscoring her

commitment to science, Tilghman appointed William B. Russel, a Princeton chemical engineering professor, as dean of the Graduate School. Men were also appointed as deans of the faculty and the School of Architecture and as vice president for research. Among the eleven officers of the Yale Corporation were four female vice presidents, for campus life, facilities, human resources, and information technology. Four years earlier, men had been nine of the officers of the corporation and 10 of the 13 academic officers.

69. Natalie Bender '98, "Generation Gap," in Donadio, 34–35.

70. Southwick, A1, A9. By 2000, women were more than 15,000 of Princeton's 72,000 living graduates and almost half the undergraduates. Yet some women were still "trying to claim and be a part of a tradition that didn't include you," observed Kruti D. Trivedi, class of 2000 (quoted in Selden, 15). Despite feeling "unwelcome at a school that is supposed to be their own," women were "happy with their decision to come to Princeton."

Masculine Cultures and Traditions

The chapters in this section discuss the difficulties of introducing coeducation at institutions that have had a strong masculine tradition. While it might seem that all former men's colleges have had such traditions, other factors beside an all-male student body can make the culture more or less strongly masculine.

In Chapter 6, Forcier compares two private institutions: Dartmouth, which like Yale and Princeton is a prestigious Ivy League institution, and Lehigh, a university in Pennsylvania that used to be regional and technical. Dartmouth's geographical isolation, small size and long history contributed to its entrenched masculinity and delayed the admission of women; at Lehigh, a curricular emphasis on engineering had similar effects. The reasons these institutions decided to become coeducational, and the difficulties that women faced within them, are also related to these same factors. Forcier discusses, for example, the social reasons for Dartmouth's admission of women, in comparison to Lehigh's desire to become a true university.

Not only is the South in general traditional, but postsecondary coeducation spread from the west to the east, and former British colonies were slower than other states to admit women, as Ihle explains in Chapter 7. The University of Virginia, the state's flagship campus, resisted women's admission, except in special circumstances, until a lawsuit in 1969 resulted in mandatory coeducation. Ihle traces the effects of coeducation on the university today, noting the mostly positive ways it has improved academics and students' social lives.

Boston College's masculine tradition developed not only because it was founded in the mid-nineteenth century as a means of educating the sons of Irish immigrants but also because it is a Catholic, Jesuit institution. As Higgins shows, when the Catholic hierarchy agreed to let women into parts of the college—first the nursing school and then the school of education—it did not provide the women with even minimally adequate services. Until 1970, women were admitted to parts of the college only out of fear that their morals would be compromised if they were educated in secular institutions. Yet once the Catholic hierarchy decided to make Boston College fully coeducational, it was able to implement this decision more rapidly and completely than in the case of institutions with less centralized authority structures.

6

"Men of Dartmouth" and "The Lady Engineers"

Coeducation at Dartmouth College and Lehigh University

Mary Frances Donley Forcier

To gain a fuller understanding of the coeducation movement at formerly all-male colleges and universities in the 1960s and early 1970s, it is essential to investigate the developments taking place at men's colleges and universities from the end of World War II. These developments include concerns about faculty recruitment and retention, about the healthy psychological development and proper social behavior of college men, and about the role of the humanities and the function of intellectual engagement in undergraduate academic and social life. To develop a more comprehensive understanding of how the coeducation movement arose and was implemented, this chapter will explore changes in two institutions in the immediate postwar period. Dartmouth College and Lehigh University, though differing in size, institutional identity, and geography, share a common quality: they are institutions in which masculinity has played a powerful and durable role in the organizational saga. As a result, they are institutions where distinctive cultural trends of the postwar period are easily visible.

Discussion of coeducation in the modern era began at both institutions in the mid-1950s. At Dartmouth, social issues were key, as the "civilizing" influence of women was seen as an important factor in the healthy psychological and social development of young men. At Lehigh, institutional aspirations to become a "true" university coalesced during the 1950s; these aspirations ultimately prompted serious consideration of coeducation. Both Dartmouth and Lehigh faced the challenge of integrating women into an overwhelmingly male undergraduate culture.

Dartmouth College, 1950–1971:
Men in the Wilderness

On November 22, 1971, Dartmouth College's board of trustees voted by a significant majority to admit women to the undergraduate program in the fall of 1972. This action marked the culmination of the trustees' consideration of coeducation, which began officially in February 1969. Dartmouth students and faculty had been discussing coeducation openly since the late 1950s, however, and the board had discussed the issue privately as early as the mid-1950s. Three elements of Dartmouth's culture would shape the college's consideration of coeducation: its small size, geographic isolation, and masculine character. Dartmouth's size had been essential to its identity since its founding in 1769, becoming enshrined in institutional memory with the Dartmouth College case of 1816. When the New Hampshire legislature passed legislation to transform Dartmouth from a college to a university, Daniel Webster, representing the college's alumni, argued successfully before the U.S. Supreme Court on behalf of the inviolability of the school's original charter. This case not only reinforced Dartmouth's identity as a college, rather than a university; it also cast the alumni body in a powerful role as the defender of the college's traditional nature. These two elements would figure strongly in the college's eventual consideration of coeducation.

Despite the influence of the university movement in the late nineteenth and early twentieth centuries, Dartmouth successfully preserved its collegiate culture. While President William Jewett Tucker (1892–1909) brought elements of the university model to Dartmouth, he also developed traditions, designed a campus, and stressed values that reinforced Dartmouth's view of itself as a small country college.[1] As Dartmouth grew in prestige and popularity—attributed in part to the attractive image of rugged collegiate life in the wilderness—it became one of the first colleges in the United States to implement a selective admissions process. Dartmouth responded to its sudden national prominence by deliberately remaining small and increasing selectivity and quality.

As at many men's colleges, the stresses of World War II brought up the question of coeducation *for* Dartmouth, but the question appears not to have arisen *at* Dartmouth. As the college celebrated its 175th anniversary in 1944, the Des Moines *Evening Tribune* lauded its all-male environment. "When Dartmouth College celebrated its birthday on Dec. 13, it also celebrated several traditions which have been unbroken in the 175 years since its founding. Dartmouth characterizes as 'not the least' among them the fact that it is still a 'college for men.'. . . Well, right or wrong, we can't blame them for crowing a bit. 175 years is a long time to hold out against the onslaughts of the female."[2] Yet a few months later, the *Boston Herald* lamented the war's effects on enrollment at men's colleges, suggesting that coeducation might become a necessity, even at Dartmouth. In the fall of 1944, Harvard president James Bryant Conant had taken the well-publicized step of allowing Radcliffe women access to Harvard classrooms, and coeducation was apparently a topic of concern for the *Herald*'s editorial board.

> The figures recently published showing the civilian enrollment in our men's colleges is sad reading. With an average shrinkage to 15 percent of pre-war enrollment, colleges without a considerable endowment and a body of well-to-do alumni are hard put to survive. . . . In such a situation, the co-educational institutions fare much better. . . . Doubtless there is many an old grad, shall we say of Williams or Amherst, who would almost rather see his college closed than opened to the 'weaker' sex. . . . Neither barber shops nor smoking cars are sacred to the male animal any more, but the Gothic halls of undergraduate Yale and the brick simplicities of rugged Dartmouth are still a refuge.[3]

The *Herald* editorial generated two replies from Dartmouth alumni. One, from a 1912 graduate, was amazingly prescient in anticipating how coeducation would be linked with year-round operation. "Dartmouth has an ideal location for year-round operation on a quarterly term basis; 12 terms in four years to graduate with one's entering class," wrote Joseph L. Richards of Harvard. "It needs the feminine touch. It would become more democratic rather than suffer a diminution of democracy by widening its clientele and making more intensive use of its facilities. . . . The writer has advocated co-education at Dartmouth since soon after he arrived there in the fall of 1910." The response of alumnus A. H. Bacon of Boston was probably more typical, however, both in its alarm at the prospect of coeducation and in its assessment of the loyalty of alumni:

> The Dartmouth spirit is a virile affair not afraid to champion any cause however unpopular, if it is in the public interest so to do. There is no feminine attribute in it. The winter carnival at Hanover furnishes all the feminine touch the undergraduates need. As to Dartmouth ever needing financial assistance, all President Hopkins has to do is send out the SOS call and the funds will come rolling in from the most loyal alumni in the USA.

These discussions of coeducation as a wartime expediency were not unexpected, given the impact of the draft on male college enrollments between 1941 and 1945. However, the end of the war and the influx of veterans into institutions like Dartmouth would soon make any discussion of coeducation, for the moment, irrelevant. As the November 1945 term began, Dartmouth found itself with not only a new president (John Sloan Dickey '29) but also 300 veterans. Another 700 veterans enrolled in March 1946, and trustees raised the enrollment limit from 2,400 to 3,000 students to accommodate the demand. The veterans' presence prepared Dartmouth for the consideration of coeducation—particularly in the transformation of prewar expectations for undergraduate social and sexual behavior. The GIs, while serious students, were nonetheless accustomed to the "adult" recreational activities of military life. Administrators found it difficult to apply traditional restrictions regarding women and alcohol to battle-weary veterans, many of whom were significantly older than traditional undergraduates. Many veterans also brought their wives; during the first term, 50 women lived on the Dartmouth campus with their husbands, bringing sanctioned sexuality to what had been, before the war, a male undergraduate preserve. Dormitories were renovated, and two apartment developments were quickly constructed on campus.[4] Veterans' wives were not permitted to enroll in classes; however, a series of lectures was hastily organized in response to women's requests for access to Dartmouth's resources.

The immediate postwar period witnessed a reexamination of expectations for undergraduate behavior, as well as a new focus on the psychological well-being of college students—a focus stemming from a larger effort on the part of colleges and universities to apply new psychological and counseling methods that had been developed as part of the war effort.[5] Dartmouth, for example, established its Office of Student Counseling in 1952. Out of this new concern for men's mental and emotional health grew the intimation in the mid-1950s that a college environment that promoted "normal" relationships between men and women might be the "healthiest" for men and for society.[6] In the spring of 1953, Dartmouth psychology professor Charles Leonard Stone asserted that the main purpose of a liberal arts education was to educate the "whole student." "If, as a result, the incidence of mental disorder, divorce and crime is somewhat reduced, even this small improvement will stand as a very worthy, indeed a great, achievement."[7] President Dickey also sought to set the moral tone for the young men in his charge. By 1951, when the student body had shifted from one composed primarily of veterans to one dominated by a more traditional 18-to-22-year-old population, Dickey stressed, "You are now at the stage in your biologic growth where today's standards of moral restraint in the relationship of the sexes may seem to you, as such things have seemed to many others at your age, to be arbitrary and senseless. . . . As yet, so far as I know, no experiment in freedom in matters of sex has ever escaped reckoning with the demands of responsibilities which go with the fact of the family relationship."[8]

Despite Dickey's admonitions, the behavior of Dartmouth men continued to be a cause for concern. Fraternities had long played a major role in Dartmouth's social life, providing weekend entertainment for not only Dartmouth students, but visitors from other campuses. Alcohol use and sexual activity in fraternities had been a concern for administrators as early as the 1930s; throughout the mid-twentieth century, as college women gained more freedom to visit men's colleges for the weekend without the presence of chaperones, administrators at those colleges felt an increasing need to take responsibility for the visiting women. In 1953, the president established the Commission on Campus Life and Its Regulation to address issues of conduct, particularly in regard to women guests and alcohol.[9] The commission reported at the close of the 1954–55 academic year, linking academic challenge with improvement in social behavior.

> A majority of the commission—indeed there was no opposition voiced—is convinced that there is one area of life at Dartmouth College, change in which would bring the most lasting improvement in "campus life," drinking problems included. This area is the curriculum, the work it requires and the challenge it offers. The faculty, in our view of the matter, could contribute to the quality and morale of campus life by putting more substance and work into its courses.[10]

The voting members also made a point of observing: "We wish to affirm as a basic principle that the presence of women guests in men's dormitory rooms is not an inalienable right, but a privilege of very special nature, open to serious misgivings on almost any basis, legal, moral, or societal."[11] Commission chairman Frank G. Ryder also suggested an area for further consideration in a July 5, 1955, letter to President Dickey: "One of several areas which we did not study, or did not treat adequately, or members have suggested for further examination: the academic and social advisability of an associated girls' school established in the vicinity"[12] Having compatible women in the vicinity, it was presumed, might curb those aspects of college life, which, though undesirable to the faculty and community, seemed to define the dominant myth of the Dartmouth man.

For some Dartmouth undergraduates, at least, the conflict between masculine roles led to confusion.[13] In the fall of 1957, senior Lincoln A. Mitchell, editor of the *Daily Dartmouth,* addressed the issue: "[The undergraduate] is torn by many things, confused by the different parts he is to play, and mystified by the seeming conflict between what he feels he should be and what he feels he is expected to be. This is most obvious in the freshman year. A man arrives at Dartmouth and naturally assumes that he is expected to act as—and be—a gentleman. Yet, he is also confronted with the role that has become traditional for the Dartmouth undergraduate: the hell-raising, hard-drinking, anti-academic, T-shirted, virile individualist of the North Country."

The development of the Hopkins Center—a cultural and performing arts center begun in 1955 and dedicated in 1962—was designed to bring a humanizing and civilizing influence to the Dartmouth campus, providing an alternative to the hard-drinking culture of fraternities and cultivating in Dartmouth men an appreciation for the arts. Not coincidentally, it also helped feminize the campus. In May 1957, Ann Hopkins Potter, daughter of President Hopkins, described her reaction to the architect's plans for the Hopkins Center.

This building is not designed primarily for the enjoyment of mothers and sisters and best girls and faculty wives and female residents of Hanover. However, as it is dedicated to so many other things, then it automatically becomes a place of the greatest enjoyment for a woman. . . . Dartmouth College, bless it, has always been fun, but there has never been a place where women were honestly welcome all the time. . . . [In the Hopkins center] she won't feel as if she's treading in all-male territory where she gets stared at and feels kind of conspicuous because "men only are supposed to be in here but on weekends it's thrown open for the ladies." That idea won't prevail at all; there will be no time when there isn't just as much room for the women as there is for the men. It will be a great day for Dartmouth when this becomes true! . . . On our strictly male campus it seems good to me that when the college men go into the Hopkins Center there are going to be plenty of women around. . . . After all, the world is made that way, so why not have some part of the campus give forth this normal state of affairs? It's just about time and it's *just great.*[14]

In the 1950s faculty recruitment and retention would also affect Dartmouth's consideration of coeducation. Dartmouth was not alone in its concern: throughout the 1950s, worries about the quantity and quality of professors preoccupied college presidents throughout the nation. One of Dickey's first priorities as president had been the rebuilding and rejuvenating of the Dartmouth faculty, which by 1945 was composed largely of professors who had been hired in the early 1920s. Before World War II, Dartmouth had prided itself on its faculty's emphasis on undergraduate teaching, even to the exclusion of research and scholarship; President Dickey found himself in the position of recruiting essentially an entirely new faculty (as of October 1963, approximately 60 percent of the faculty had been hired during the past ten years) whose values were vastly different from those of the relatively insular prewar faculty. To attract and retain quality professors, Dartmouth also increased faculty compensation, which had been at a dangerously low level. This increase helped contribute, by the late 1960s, to an increasingly tenuous financial situation, which also made coeducation more appealing.

Administrators sought to attract and retain quality faculty by improving not only the academic quality but also the intellectual orientation of their undergraduates. Throughout the 1950s, private colleges and universities increasingly emphasized "quality" to differentiate themselves from the growing public institutions; at Dartmouth, trustees fought to limit the size of the student body to 3,000 throughout the 1950s, arguing that Dartmouth's intimate size was essential to its identity, and that by limiting size it could improve its quality. Quality students would ensure a contented, high-quality faculty, administrators asserted. "There is nothing, literally nothing, that could so quickly raise and compound both the quantitative and qualitative productivity of our existing fine teaching force as a more intellectually motivated American student," Dickey told alumni and friends in 1958.[15] Faculty expressed their concern about the lack of intellectual liveliness in their students, and in 1957 a major revision of the curriculum was undertaken, encouraging undergraduates to take more responsibility for their own education and to grow intellectually. The revision replaced the two-semester, five-course system with three three-course terms.[16]

A study of the Dartmouth campus culture in the early 1960s described the stereotypical "Dartmouth man": "middle- or upper-middle-class, enthusiastic about sports, loyal to his fraternity and his college, and generally satisfied with the 'Gentleman's "C." ' . . . [His] motivation, however, seemed to be for grades rather than the joy of learning." This study found that in 1960–61, 63 percent of undergraduates said they would definitely choose Dartmouth again, while 30 percent were not sure, and 7 percent would not: an indication, the report's authors noted, that "37 percent are unhappy in some way." Those identified as the "higher intellectual types" were most dissatisfied. Students did suggest a solution for their ennui, however: half of those dissatisfied indicated that they would prefer a coed institution.[17] Coeducation, in fact, was suggested in this study as a solution to several perceived ills of the 1950s and early 1960s: the presence of women would improve the intellectual life on campus by contributing to class discussion and enhancing the campus experience for males of the "higher intellectual type." In addition, women would bring an element of moderation and civilization to the rough male preserve.

The issue of coeducation finally had emerged in 1958 after several years of furtive discussion. At a "Community Press Conference on Religion" in March 1958, two deans spoke in favor of the addition of women students, whether in a coordinate college or as full Dartmouth undergraduates, noting that coeducation should be considered in an attempt to make students "more responsible." However, President Dickey held firm against the idea, citing prohibitive costs, as well as the "history, tradition and locale of the college." One local newspaper noted, "The question of girl students has been current at least for the last five years, as various college groups have studied Dartmouth student social life and pondered ways of coping with Hanover's isolation. Remoteness leads to frequent student weekend trips to girl colleges and accompanying danger of highway accidents." In May, a petition was signed by 300 students and 127 faculty members in support of a "serious study of the principles of coeducation."[18] The *Valley News* lent its cautious support to the idea: "the petition . . . brings out in the open a proposal which has been widely discussed by faculty and students for quite a few years."[19]

Coeducation was discussed openly by 1959, and in 1961 the first full-time female graduate student enrolled at the college. The establishment of Dartmouth's summer program, designed to complement the new three-term system, brought coeducation to Dartmouth for at least one term per year. President Dickey noted that Dartmouth felt it could not open its doors to students from other schools and exclude women. When the summer program began in 1963, it attracted an equal number of men and women and was viewed by many at the time as the beginning of undergraduate coeducation at Dartmouth. The headline in the *Hanover Gazette* read "Co-Ed Enrolls at Dartmouth," as an article reported, "a Middlebury College sophomore will be Dartmouth College's first undergraduate coed."[20]

Exchange programs throughout the 1960s brought undergraduate women to campus for increasingly extended periods of time. The first, in November 1960, was sponsored by the Jewish Life Council; 30 Smith girls came to Dartmouth for a study-mixer weekend.[21] The "Great Day" experiment took place in March 1967, as more than 400 women from New England women's colleges took part in a discussion of "great books." The first "Coed Week" followed in 1968, and in 1969 the Twelve College Exchange Program was established, with 68 women enrolled at Dartmouth as regular students. Reaction on campus was decidedly mixed. While more than half of the undergraduate men at Dartmouth were against coeducation, 86 percent of the faculty were either "strongly" or "mildly" in favor. A 1965 interview with dean of the college Thaddeus Seymour sharply illustrated the contradictions of the day.

> "No one has talked about educating women," he said, "Every discussion about coeducation at Dartmouth has asked, 'Would coeducation make this a better men's school?' To be talking about it in those terms is to totally miss the point of coeducation. This issue is this: does Dartmouth have an obligation to offer its resources equally to men and women? And in taking the step, the institution should ask itself, 'Do we morally have the obligation to educate women?' . . . Guys are always taking about coeducation in terms of whether it would enable *them* to get a better education. I think most women would be quite insulted by most of the discussion of coeducation that goes on up here."[22]

Yet Seymour showed a paternalistic side—perhaps the last gasp of 1950s chivalry—that would seem remarkably dated just a few years later. "The one probably unique asset of Dartmouth is its tradition of close male fellowship. And you can't offer this to a girl. . . . Once an institution becomes responsible for girls, social regulations become strict. One of the great advantages of a men's community is its liberal attitude."

The call for greater student participation in college governance was a key issue on campus in the late 1960s, and in the fall of 1968, President Dickey and the board of trustees responded with the establishment of the Dartmouth Campus Conference, a group of trustees, faculty and students that would consider major campus issues, including coeducation. Following a recommendation from the conference, the board established a Trustee Study Committee in February 1969 to undertake a "comprehensive and concrete" study of coeducation, considering college and community opinion, land acquisition, strategic site planning, educational facilities, housing and boarding, financial resources, and "heritage."

The process of institutional decision-making at Dartmouth was changing dramatically. The 1968–69 academic year was a major watershed, as parietal regulations regarding women's presence in men's rooms were finally abolished; the Afro-American Society issued demands to the administration; an occupation of the administration building, led by Students for a Democratic Society, concluded with the arrest of 56; and female exchange students filed a letter of complaint with the Equal Employment Opportunity Commission, alleging discrimination against women.

The postwar era had in many ways come to an end, and with its passing John Dickey announced his decision to retire from the Dartmouth presidency. In 1970, mathematics professor John Kemeny was named president, and the change in leadership made it possible for Dartmouth to chart a new course in dealing with the prospect of coeducation. In the spring of 1971, the trustees recommended the establishment of a coordinate college for women, rather than full coeducation. The faculty, however, rejected the idea, passing a resolution that supported "integrated coeducation" as preferable to the "associated school" concept and called for the matriculation of women by September 1972. Soon after, the Committee on Year-Round Operation of the College was established to develop a plan for "integrated coeducation" in line with the faculty resolution: that the size of the student body should be increased to admit women, that the summer term should be the academic equivalent of the other three terms, and that approximately 3,000 undergraduates should be in residence on campus in the fall, winter, and spring.

In November 1971, the trustees announced their decision, adopting the "Dartmouth Plan" of year-round operation in conjunction with the admission of women. By adopting the Dartmouth Plan, the institution could admit 1,000 more undergraduates (women), thereby allaying alumni fears that Dartmouth would be preparing fewer male leaders in order to admit women. David Weber '65, who served as a trustee from 1971 to 1980, in recalling the decision, identified the role of institutional size in the trustees' deliberations: Dartmouth's "mystique, its essence," was not only tied to maleness, it was tied to its small size. "The trustees thus sought a way (1) to add women, (2) to maintain male enrollment and (3) to keep the college small—simultaneously. Year-round operation offered an ingenious and promising solution to this riddle."[23] In the fall of 1972, 177 women enrolled as freshman students; 74 women enrolled as transfers and 100 as exchange students; the undergraduate male-to-female ratio was 9:1.

Lehigh University, 1950–1970:
"Man, the Servant and Interpreter of Nature"

In May 1970, Lehigh University's board of trustees voted by a significant majority to admit undergraduate women in the fall of 1971. This action marked the culmination of the trustees' consideration of coeducation, which began officially in December 1968 (although coeducation had been discussed by Lehigh students and faculty since the mid-1960s). An analysis of coeducation at Lehigh, given the university's traditional strength in science and engineering, is particularly useful for the insight it provides into the relationship between coeducation and curricular change: the institution's tenuous identity as a "university" was seen as hinging on the admission of women to ensure Lehigh's strength in the arts and humanities.

Since its founding in 1865, Lehigh's masculine identity influenced the university's development. The life of its founder, coal and railroad baron Asa Packer, represents an archetype of the "self-made man" of the mid-nineteenth century. "Man, the servant and interpreter of nature"—the new university's motto—was an apt description of Packer. His goal in founding a university was to develop human capital for the Lehigh Valley's emerging railroad and steel industries: industries in which there was no role for women. Yet from the beginning, his mission for the university was broader than merely that of a technical school. The establishment of Lehigh, with its classical and technical programs, can be seen as a bridge between the earliest classical colleges with engineering programs—Union College (1841) and Rensselaer Polytechnic Institute (1824)—and later research universities based on the German model, such as Johns Hopkins University (1867) or the University of Chicago (1890).[24] The development of engineering as a profession in the 1880s and 1890s also helped to define Lehigh's male identity. Even though women were admitted to the graduate program in 1918 and to the summer school in 1929, Lehigh maintained its essentially conservative, male nature. During the 1930s, Lehigh's strong undergraduate male identity was clearly evident in its promotional literature. A Lehigh promotional brochure featured a full-page photo of Awards Day with the caption, "A Man's College," and described the institution: "Lehigh is not co-educational. Boys, treated as men, quickly measure up to the intellectual, social and moral standards required of them at college. Neither wealth, nor creed, nor social position differentiates Lehigh students—each man is measured by what he *is*."[25]

Despite the fact that Lehigh attracted vocationally oriented young men, it was not immune to a general "liberalization" of student views that took place on many campuses in the 1930s. The editors of the student publication *Lehigh Review*, for example, broached a controversial topic in December 1939, when "The Review Student Poll" asked: "Would you like to see Lehigh go coeducational?" Sixty-nine percent of students polled responded "no," while 31 percent were in favor of a coed Lehigh.[26] Despite the *Review*'s interest in co-education, the entrance of the United States into World War II brought more pressing concerns. The student newspaper, the *Brown and White,* appears to have taken up the banner for coeducation during the bleakest wartime years of 1943 and 1944. "Lehigh university [*sic*] needs co-eds. Education [f]or life, education to make the world a better place to live in, is incomplete unless shared directly with women." The *Brown and White* made several arguments. First, without "wholesome contact with women," men are unprepared for marriage; coeducation would produce more rounded graduates (particularly engineers); and the wartime exigencies made the time right for admitting women—since the men in the Army ASTD program were vacating the dormitories, women could move in. Finally, the paper noted, the American definition of "democracy," coupled with the gains in equality that women were making as a result of war-time conditions, mandated greater access to higher education for women.[27]

The faculty response, according to the *Brown and White,* was positive: 66 percent were in favor of admitting women to the arts college; 52 percent were in favor of admitting women to the business college.[28] Evidently, administrators took the *Brown and White*'s concern seriously enough to bring it to the attention of alumni. In April 1944, the newspaper's editor (in an article for the *Alumni Bulletin*) called for coeducation, proposing to admit 350 to 400 women to the arts school, 100 to the business school, and 100 to engineering. He wrote, "We do not look upon coeducation as a war-time expediency designed to bolster the University's financial position and keep the faculty together . . . instead we look upon co-education as the logical and sound educational policy for war and peace," which would broaden engineering education in particular, lead to more well-rounded graduates in general, and foster happy marriages among Lehigh alumni. While several young alumni expressed their support, the June 1944 issue of the *Bulletin* brought a sharp rebuke from the Philadelphia Alumni Club, whose members were in "total and complete disagreement with the thought expressed." This would be the last public word on coeducation at Lehigh until the 1960s.

As Lehigh emerged from World War II and the "veteran" era, it was firmly grounded in its masculine identity. "Presented in a man's way in a man's world," proclaimed Lehigh's major admissions marketing piece in 1952. "One of the most important features of the Lehigh program is its limitation to carefully selected men. . . . Living together, competing with each other on a man-to-man basis, exchanging ideas, they develop the quality of self-reliance."[29] The G.I. Bill, with its infusion of veterans and cash, had helped Lehigh rebound from its desperate wartime straits. A major postwar building program focused on needs that had been postponed since the late 1920s. The university, in an attempt to bring its students under greater control, built additional residence halls and helped to subsidize the building of well-appointed fraternity houses on a forested hill above the academic center of campus. Fraternity life, bolstered by new homes designed as much (if not more) for entertaining than for studying, became the center of Lehigh's social life in the 1950s. The dominance of fraternities, as well as new residence halls that sought to replicate fraternity life, helped to strengthen male bonds and male identity. The university's near-religious devotion to intercollegiate wrestling was perhaps its most visible expression of the value placed on "competing with each other on a man-to-man basis." Wrestling expressed the importance of the individual—"the quality of self-reliance"—more than other team sports, and at Lehigh during the 1950s, wrestling was king.

Despite the strengthening of the university's male identity in the late 1950s, there were several signs of the changes that would occur in the 1960s and 1970s. The first was the increased size and scope of the institution. The size of the student body had expanded dramatically as a direct result of the G.I. Bill. Before the war, undergraduate enrollment had been set at 1,500; during the war, it fell from a high of 1,780 at the beginning of the fall 1942 semester to a low of 288 in the spring 1945 semester. By the fall of 1946, 2,723 undergraduates were enrolled, of whom 65 percent were veterans. In the immediate postwar period, Lehigh grew to accommodate the influx of veterans. Following the "veteran period," however, the institution in the mid-1950s faced the result of the nation's low birth rate during the depression and early World War II: fewer college-age men from which to draw quality students.

Nationally, applicants for the classes of 1955 to 1967 (entering colleges between 1951 and 1963) were drawn from the cohort born from 1933 to 1945, years in which the birth rate remained relatively low. At the same time, a higher percentage of young Americans were choosing to pursue higher education, spurred by the lasting effects of the G.I. Bill and the development of less expensive public institutions. As a result, private colleges and universities became increasingly concerned about "quality" as a means of differentiating themselves from public institutions. Admissions efforts became more aggressive, and increasingly sensitive to student and parent preferences. In 1954, Lehigh's board recognized these trends as they discussed the possible impact of the growth of public higher education, coupled with the expected growth in the college-aged population, on Lehigh's programs and enrollment. Trustees estimated that unless private colleges and universities expanded, by 1970, 75 percent of students would be enrolled in public schools. Trustee E. F. "Coxey" Johnson '07, vice president of General Motors, "expressed his opinion that this is an unhealthy situation for the future welfare of this country, and suggested that private institutions should begin now . . . to prepare for the problems of expansion in future years in order to maintain a reasonable balance between private and public school enrolment." [30] However, President Martin Whitaker, in his 1953–54 presidential report, asserted Lehigh's desire to remain a small

institution, citing the decision in the immediate "post-veteran period" to reduce the student body to 2,500 undergraduates in an effort to maintain both
the quality of students enrolled and the quality of the academic program.[31]

Lehigh's undergraduate enrollment remained relatively stable during the
mid-to-late 1950s at approximately 2,650 (admitting a freshman class of 700
each year), but at its October 6, 1961, meeting the board approved a recommendation by President Harvey Neville that the undergraduate enrollment be
gradually increased to 3,200.[32] Beginning in the fall of 1962, the freshman class
would be increased by 25 each year, until it was stabilized at 800 in the fall of
1965.

The Lehigh of the early 1960s stood in sharp contrast to the insular, intimate prewar Lehigh; in 1922, for example, 1,500 undergraduate men, most of
whom lived in off-campus fraternities, were taught by 97 faculty members, 49
of whom were Lehigh graduates. For Lehigh alumni from the 1920s (including several trustees), the institution was completely different from the small,
personal community they had known as students.

The second major development at Lehigh during the 1950s was the growth
of the Graduate School, which increased enrollment approximately 10 percent
each year during the decade.[33] This growth, encouraged by the national emphasis on advanced-degree programs in science and engineering, had several
consequences. First, it reinforced the internal identity of the institution as a
university, rather than as a technical school with liberal arts "service" colleges
or as a liberal arts college with an attached technical institute. For faculty, in
particular, Lehigh's identity as a university would be an important factor in
evaluating the potential value of coeducation. Second, as at Yale and Princeton,
the growth of the faculty to meet the needs of a growing graduate program
would result by the late 1960s in an excess educational capacity that was greatly
underutilized, particularly in the College of Arts and Science.[34] This excess of
faculty resources would come as a surprise to those studying the feasibility of
coeducation at Lehigh; it could and would allow Lehigh to add women without substantially increasing faculty size. Its neighboring competitor Lafayette
College responded to these same trends by reducing the number of men and
maintaining the existing size of the institution.

A third trend at Lehigh, which emerged in the late 1950s, was faculty dissatisfaction with undergraduates' intellectual orientation (or lack thereof).
As at Dartmouth, the aged, dispirited faculty of the 1940s had been replaced
by a host of young, ambitious faculty—particularly in the College of Arts and
Science—whose ambition was not limited to their own academic careers but
extended to the university at large. To their disappointment, however, their
students did not always share their enthusiasm for intellectual engagement. In
June 1960, the faculty Committee on Student Life issued a report entitled "The
Climate of Learning." It criticized the university for its "apparent tolerance of

weak or indifferent students," as well as for not providing "enough intellectual excitement for the superior student. . . . [O]ur claim to prepare men for positions of leadership might be better documented if a Lehigh education also taught initiative in setting and solving problems and in assuming greater responsibility for one's own academic growth."[35] The frustration that faculty members and "superior students" expressed in this report would be echoed in the student protests of the late 1960s, as the "stag" culture of anti-intellectualism at both Lehigh and Dartmouth was criticized as an institutional liability.

At Lehigh, as at Dartmouth, a fourth trend of the late 1950s was increasing concern about men's behavior and a simultaneous protest by students against administrative constraints on student life. The semiannual bacchanal known as "Houseparty" had been a Lehigh tradition since the 1920s. By the 1950s, it had become a liability for the university, as student behavior grew increasingly unacceptable—particularly in regard to women visiting for the weekend. By requiring all freshmen to live on campus after 1949 and by moving fraternities on campus throughout the 1950s, the university had assumed increased responsibility for student behavior at a time when faculty were increasingly removed from student life outside the classroom—and at a time when the first cracks appeared in college students' traditional codes of sexual behavior.[36] The answer, from the administrative point of view, was to impose a set of intricate and closely monitored rules regulating student behavior. By the mid-1950s, students began to protest against what they viewed as inordinately controlling parietal rules and freshman regulations; as a result, they gained increased responsibility for self-government, two early expressions of the type of student protest issues that would coincide with the move toward coeducation ten years later.

The late 1950s also brought dramatic change in trustee leadership. In 1956, Eugene Gifford Grace, president and chairman of the Bethlehem Steel Corporation, retired as the trustees' chairman after a remarkable 43 years on the board, 22 as president. His retirement marked the end of an era in several key respects. For many years Bethlehem Steel's relationship with the university had been a mutually beneficial one, yet one marked by Grace's considerable force and autocratic style. His successor, Monroe Jackson (Jack) Rathbone '21, was president of Standard Oil of New Jersey—at that time, the world's largest corporation, far more removed and cosmopolitan than neighboring, cloistered Bethlehem Steel. Not only did the shift in power mark a transformation in Lehigh's identity as an emerging national (rather than a regional) university, but it also indicated a departure from Grace's traditional view of Lehigh as, first and foremost, an engineering school, in which the arts and business colleges were primarily service departments. Rathbone served as chairman of the board during the years in which coeducation was studied, debated, and adopted. By all accounts, his broad, global view of education, business, and the rapidly changing social and economic order was a driving force behind Lehigh's adoption of coeducation.

The period from 1960 to 1965 has been described as "the calm before the storm," as the university enjoyed its new emphasis on research and graduate work, and student protest was still in the future. At the annual "dean's meeting" with incoming freshmen in the fall of 1962, Glenn J. Christensen, vice president and provost of the university and dean of the College of Arts and Science, addressed the class of 1966. Christensen's talk reflects the official view of the university's role in the lives of young men, as he related a parable in which nobles prepared their sons for manhood by sending them to live with "the lord of the neighboring manor." "For the next four years," Christensen said, "Lehigh will be to you the lord of the neighboring manor." It is Lehigh's task, he said, "to make you men. . . . We accept wholly our responsibility to teach you the use of the mid-20th century equivalent of horses, armor, and arms, and to give you the knowledge of the ways of the world which will enable you to walk those ways with confidence." Despite its fraternal tone, Christensen's parable *did* include a role for women: "In the afternoons and evenings, the lady of the manor and her attendants undertook to make the bold rough young warrior and huntsman into an acceptable indoor person. They taught him his manners, how to dress for polite occasions, how to carry his part of a conversation, how to play a musical instrument, to sing, to write verse, to dance—in brief, to be a gentleman in society as he was expected to be a nobleman in the field."[37] In the years to come, many who advocated the admission of women to Lehigh would echo unconsciously his description of the role of women and the humanities in the shaping of young gentlemen.

The role of the arts and humanities was a pivotal issue affecting the admission of women to Lehigh. The College of Arts and Science had grown dramatically during the 1950s. In 1953, the arts college enrolled 14.2 percent of undergraduates, while in 1963 it enrolled 32.2 percent of undergraduates, with a corresponding growth in the number and visibility of arts college faculty. By the late 1950s and early 1960s, the humanities were gaining increased respect from prospective employers, as well; in a backlash against the "man in the grey flannel suit" and the "organization man," industry began arguing for broadening the education of specialists. At Lehigh, a key role for the arts college was to prevent engineers from falling into the trap of vocational education by fulfilling the same humanizing and refining function that some observers expected their college-educated wives to perform.[38]

The growth of graduate programs in the 1950s and early 1960s brought more women to campus as graduate students, research assistants, and teaching assistants. A turning point occurred in 1965, as Lehigh hired its first female assistant professor. A February 1965 *Alumni Bulletin* article focused on women at Lehigh, noting that the combination of more women seeking graduate education and the growing demand for professors at rapidly growing colleges and universities had led to a dramatic increase in the number of women in the Graduate School. The rising emphasis on graduate programs resulted in a 50 percent increase in graduate enrollment by 1964, with a corresponding growth in the number of graduate women: in 1964–65, of approximately 1,200 graduate students, 252 were women. In addition, women were admitted to advanced undergraduate courses on an ad hoc basis, beginning in the early 1960s.

Deming Lewis's appointment as Lehigh's president in 1965 also represented a major change for the institution. He brought strong project-management and consensus-building skills—developed during his tenure as director of communications systems research for Bell Labs—to the question of coeducation. Compared to Lehigh's previous presidents, whose primary interests lay in undergraduate engineering education, his experience in corporate research provided him with a broader view of the university's mission. Lewis faced significant challenges as he took office, including the continued concern over the fiscal health of private colleges and universities, as well as their ability to compete with the public sector for quality students and faculty. The emphasis on recruiting and retaining students of quality extended throughout the university, as energetic young faculty members hired during the immediate postwar years—particularly in the arts college—sought to increase both the quality and prestige of the institution.

The university's emphasis on attracting the best students led to the development of a wider "catchment area" for finding those students. The process of moving from local to regional to national "markets" was shaped by several factors: the increasingly national orientation of major universities (spurred by Harvard's development of the national scholarship system in the 1930s), the impact of the G.I. Bill (which increased the social, ethnic and geographic diversity of the student body), and increased opportunities for travel and geographic mobility. By the 1960s, Lehigh's emphasis on maintaining and even increasing the quality of students admitted—as measured by SAT scores, as well as high school class rank and GPA—had become an essential part of the institutional identity and a key factor in the admission of women. Colleges and universities were increasingly interdependent, as competition for the best and the brightest became an even more important factor in institutional decision-making. Other institutions' decisions to consider coeducation were reported in the pages of the *Alumni Bulletin* and the *Brown and White.* As a major competitor, Lafayette College, began taking steps in April 1968 to admit women, Lehigh students, administrators and faculty gained a new impetus for the serious consideration of coeducation.

In 1968, a student activist organization, the Committee for Undergraduate Responsibility in Education (CURE) demonstrated on campus, issuing a list of proposed changes in university life and governance. The implementation of undergraduate coeducation was twelfth on the list.[39] As a result of CURE's activities, the Joint Commission on University Life (JCUL) was formed, much as the Dartmouth Campus Conference had been, to provide a structure for communication among and between students, faculty, administrators, and trustees. In January 1969, under the auspices of JCUL, the Coeducation Study Committee was formed with international relations professor Carey Joynt as chairman.[40] In October 1969 the committee issued its preliminary report, favoring coeducation. On January 15, 1970, the board of trustees considered the question at an all-day special session, at which the final report of the Joynt committee was presented. A February 27 letter from Chairman Rathbone to all alumni summarized the meeting; while assuring alumni that Lehigh's "top-flight reputation in engineering and science must be preserved and enhanced," Rathbone shared with them the university's concern about attracting quality undergraduates—particularly to the arts and business colleges.[41] He cited a decline in applications for the past three years and noted that the percentage of students accepting offers of admission (a figure later termed the "yield") was also declining. The increase in applications at recently coeducational Yale, Princeton, Franklin and Marshall, Lafayette, and Colgate, he argued, was evidence of the drawing power of coeducation. He also noted the importance of the arts and business colleges to the education of engineers and scientists, arguing that coeducation would have the greatest impact on the arts college, thereby ensuring Lehigh's status as a quality university.

Rathbone also discussed other advantages of coeducation, citing the widespread dissatisfaction with Lehigh's social life and the "widely held view" that the addition of women would enhance the atmosphere. He addressed the financial cost of coeducation, using a model that forecast the gradual addition of 800 women to the student body by 1976–77. "We believe that the proportion of female undergraduates should never be permitted to exceed the level of 20 percent," he noted. While coeducation would provide a net operating budget advantage, the capital cost would be approximately $7.3 million, $2.5 million of which would be dormitory costs financed by the state or federal government. The remainder—$4.8 million—would need to be provided by "gift money" during the early 1970s.

Student protest had continued sporadically at Lehigh throughout the 1967–68 and 1968–69 academic years, becoming most visible during the late spring of both 1968 and 1969. However, April 1970 brought campus unrest to its most intense point. The trustees were scheduled to meet on April 9 to make a final decision on coeducation, as well as to address the student and faculty demands for participation in decision-making. At this meeting, President Lewis presented to the trustees a plan for coeducation: admitting 800 women over a period of four years: 100 each in the fall of 1971 and 1972; 200 in the fall of 1973, 1974, and 1975, without a reduction in the number of men. As of the January meeting, Lewis said, he had felt "fairly neutral about the question," but during the spring of 1970 "the weight of evidence has convinced me that it is indeed in Lehigh's best interest to become coeducational . . . a negative decision in the light of the highly competitive environment in which Lehigh as an emerging university finds itself would seriously inhibit . . . further progress."[42] Lewis noted that the growth of research and graduate programs during the recent past had largely favored the engineering college over the arts college. "We are in danger of retrogressing, toward the position of an institute of technology and away from that of a university," Lewis warned, noting that the admission of women would improve the size and quality of the College of Arts and Science, thereby guaranteeing Lehigh's status as a "true University."[43]

In the debate over coeducation at Lehigh, the admission of women and the full utilization and continued strength of the arts college were inextricably linked in terms of becoming a "true" university. Throughout their deliberations, policy-makers went to great lengths to emphasize—particularly in communications with alumni—their concern for maintaining Lehigh's strong engineering and science programs. Their framing of the question illustrates the importance of Lehigh's engineering identity to its alumni and trustees. While the rank-and-file Lehigh alumni had little actual voice in policy-making, the board of trustees was reflective of the institution's traditional strengths. At the time of the coeducation question, the board was composed entirely of alumni and dominated by executives of heavy industry who had begun their careers as engineers, including the chairmen of U.S. Steel, Standard Oil of New Jersey, and Alcoa. Their view of Lehigh's strengths, coupled with the traditional academic conservatism of engineers, made it imperative for policy-makers to frame the question in terms of the continued strength of the engineering program and the future quality of Lehigh. The arts college was also heavily subsidized during the 1960s by the engineering college; in order to make the arts college economically viable on its own, policy-makers found the solution: a new market composed of women students.

In May 1970, immediately following the Kent State crisis, the board of trustees approved a plan to admit 100 women in the fall of 1971 and another 100 in the fall of 1972, with a review at the end of two years. Later, citing budget pressures from inflation and the need for additional tuition revenue, President Lewis requested of both the board and the Forum (Lehigh's newly established joint student/faculty governmental body), that the university be allowed to admit 1,050 students instead of the originally approved 900 men and 100 women (the additional 50 would be either men or women). In the fall of 1971, 169 women entered Lehigh (19 more than the agreed-upon maximum of 150), and in the fall of 1972, 362 women enrolled, 112 more than the maximum of 250.

Transformations at Dartmouth and Lehigh, 1970–2002

While Lehigh's primary considerations were the sustained viability of the arts college and the balance of quality students among its three undergraduate colleges, a key consideration at Dartmouth was the improvement of what seemed to be an "intolerable" social situation for men. We can expect to see, therefore, the impact of coeducation most clearly at Lehigh in the changing nature of academic programs and at Dartmouth in the changing nature of campus social life.

Lehigh administrators were surprised by the enrollment patterns of the first women who enrolled, an example of how assumptions of the 1950s and 1960s needed to be revisited based on women's actual choices. Although most women, as expected, did enroll in the College of Arts and Science, fewer women seemed interested in elementary- and secondary-school teaching, while more than expected chose to enroll in the sciences and mathematics, as well as in the business college.

The patterns of male and female enrollment by college from 1970–71 through 2000–01, illustrate the impact of coeducation on the institutional nature of Lehigh's undergraduate colleges. Table 6.1 shows that in 2000–01, Lehigh undergraduates were distributed more evenly across the three colleges than in 1970–71 or 1980–81, indicating that Lehigh was much less defined by its engineering college than it was before coeducation. The overall enrollment at Lehigh in 2001 (4,490) was about 42 percent higher than it was in 1970 (3,166).

Table 6.1. Lehigh's Undergraduate Enrollment, by College, 1970–2001

	Arts & Science (%)	Business (%)	Engineering (%)	Total
1970–71	32	17	51	3,166
1980–81	32	19	49	4,441
1990–91	43	22	34	4,544
2000–01	39	28	33	4,490

Source: Office of the Registrar, Lehigh University.

Table 6.2. Lehigh's Male Undergraduates, by College, 1970–2001

	Arts & Science		Business		Engineering		Total
	N	%	N	%	N	%	N
1970–71	1,037	32	530	17	1,591	51	3,158
1980–81	853	25	585	18	1,864	56	3,295
1990–91	946	33	642	22	1,297	45	2,885
2000–01	790	29	758	28	1,173	43	2,721

Source: Office of the Registrar, Lehigh University.

Table 6.3. Lehigh's Female Undergraduates, by College, 1970–2001

	Arts & Sciences		Business		Engineering		Total
	N	%	N	%	N	%	N
1970–71	0	0	0	0	0	0	0
1980–81	548	48	280	24	318	27	1,146
1990–91	1,022	61	377	23	260	16	1,659
2000–01	964	54	512	29	293	17	1,769

Source: Office of the Registrar, Lehigh University.

Table 6.4. Lehigh's Undergraduate Enrollments, by Gender, 1980–2001 (%)

	Arts & Sciences		Business		Engineering		Total	
	M	F	M	F	M	F	M	F
1980–81	61	39	67	33	85	15	74	26
1990–91	48	52	63	37	83	17	63	37
2000–01	45	54	60	40	80	20	60	40

Source: Office of the Registrar, Lehigh University.

While Lehigh's overall enrollment has increased, Table 6.2 shows a decline of approximately 14 percent in the number of male undergraduates, from 3,158 in 1970–71 to 2,721 in 2000–01. The percentage of male undergraduates in engineering has declined slightly (from 51 percent to 43 percent) over the same years that the percentage in business has increased (from 17 percent to 28 percent).

Table 6.3 indicates that the number of women undergraduates increased the most between 1980–81 and 1990–91 (from 1,146 to 1,659) and then leveled off, with only 110 more women in 2000–01 than in 1990–91. The number of women undergraduates in 2001 was almost 1,000 less than the number of male undergraduates (1,769 compared to 2,721). Women were much more likely than men to be in the College of Arts and Science, about equally likely to be in business, and much less likely to be in engineering. Over time the number of both men and women majoring in engineering has decreased.

The data in Table 6.4 illustrate the "gendered" nature of each of the three undergraduate colleges over time. Business and, especially, engineering have remained "majority male" colleges, while the arts college has moved toward parity. In 1990–91 and 2000–01, the majority of students in the arts college were women.

Since the mid-1980s, in particular, Lehigh has had to grapple with the significant shift away from its traditional identity as an engineering school. The athletic teams, for example, changed their name from the "Engineers" to the "Mountain Hawks" in the 1990s (the women's teams had been known as the

"Lady Engineers"). This symbolic shift reflects the transformation that had taken place within the institution as it shed the industrial culture that had shaped it since its founding in 1865.

While Lehigh's academic priorities altered dramatically after coeducation, Dartmouth's most challenging adjustment was in its traditional social and residential life. At Dartmouth, as at most formerly all-male campuses, the social integration of women proved to be a challenge that administrators were slow to grasp fully, steeped as they were in the formal "dating" culture of the 1950s. The adjustment from an environment where women visited campus for "social" or sexual purposes to an environment in which women were viewed as competitors in the classroom was a long and sometimes painful process. Open hostility and sexual harassment, often fueled by alcohol, was a public spectacle at both institutions during the 1970s and 1980s, although on balance it appears as though women encountered better-organized, more deeply held, and longer-lasting resistance at Dartmouth. The veneer of "good manners" that characterized the 1950s, as well as the protective paternalism exemplified by Dartmouth's Thaddeus Seymour, had been swept away by the changing mores of the 1960s.[44]

Two incidents are often cited as the most vicious instances of incivility to women at Dartmouth. In the spring of 1973, the windows of the first floor of Woodward Hall, a women's dormitory, were broken, as each resident had an obscene and threatening letter slipped under her door that described women as the "enemy" to be sexually conquered by Dartmouth men. In the spring of 1975, a fraternity entered the annual "Hums" song competition sponsored by the college on a major weekend. Their song, "Our Cohogs," (a derogatory term for Dartmouth women), containing the line "our cohogs, they play four, they are all a bunch of whores," was judged by Dean Carroll Brewster as one of the winners. The hostility directed at the women of Dartmouth led to organized resistance to the prevailing culture. The women's studies program was inaugurated in 1978, and in 1979 the first Take Back the Night march was a response to fraternity aggression and incivility. In 1980, the Committee on the Quality of Student Life recommended that residential life be completely redesigned, with all residence halls becoming coed, and the Collis student center undergoing a major expansion.

In 1987, 15 years after the college became coeducational, the Women's Resource Center was established. Battles over the nature of Dartmouth fraternities, however, as well as over the relations of men and women on campus, continued well into the late 1990s, even as the institution neared gender parity (in 2001, the class of 2005 became the first entering class with equal numbers of men and women).[45] The traditional alma mater, "Men of Dartmouth," which some found reassuringly traditional and others found alienating and insulting, was replaced in 1988, 16 years after coeducation, by "Dear Old Dartmouth."

The debate surrounding "Men of Dartmouth" represents the larger process of institutional change in the wake of coeducation. For some, today's Dartmouth represents a particularly egregious example of the excesses of "political correctness"; for others, it represents the type of patriarchal and oppressive institution that must be transformed in the interest of justice and fairness.

Perceptions of Alumnae and Current Women Students

Women's experiences at both Dartmouth and Lehigh are highly individual and vary widely; taken as a whole, they reflect the complexity and ambiguity inherent in identifying "coeducation" as a historical or educational construct. In preparing for the twenty-fifth anniversary of coeducation at Dartmouth, for example, more than 2,000 alumnae replied to a questionnaire regarding the kind of recognition that might be appropriate. Gianna Munafo, the director of Dartmouth's Women's Resource Center, recalls:

> Asking what "Dartmouth's women graduates" want was rather like asking more generally—as that naïve Dr. Freud infamously did—what women want. The first survey I opened said, roughly, "I can't wait for the commemoration of coeducation, as long as there are opportunities to tell the hard truth about the resistance to women being admitted and all of the painful things that were said and done once we arrived." The second more or less said, "I am relieved Dartmouth has finally put aside all of the complaining and moaning about coeducation and is ready to celebrate our success—no more hand-wringing and sad stories, please!"[46]

Despite the wide variation in individual women's experiences, several broad characterizations can be drawn. The first, as we have seen, involves the differences in the two institutions' motivations for the admission of women. At Dartmouth, coeducation was identified as primarily a "social" problem, rather than an academic issue. The admission of women was expected to add a measure of civility to Dartmouth's legendary social scene. It was unreasonable and unfair to expect that women's admission alone would transform such a dominant culture; some Dartmouth men felt compelled to cling to their familiar "Animal House" ways, defending their existing position of power by harassing, intimidating, and bullying women. Women's responses were varied and, in many ways, divisive: some women joined coed fraternities or sororities, replicating the existing social system rather than transforming it. Others rejected the traditional institutions, joining faculty in calling for an end to Greek life.

At Lehigh, social issues were significant yet, in terms of institutional decision-making, were subordinate to the academic issues of parity for the arts college. Lehigh's fraternity system has frequently exhibited many of the same characteristics as Dartmouth's, and women have responded in much the same way. While some Lehigh women found Greek life (whether as "little sisters" at fraternities or as sorority members) to be a supportive, enjoyable part of campus life, others rejected the campus' emphasis on the Greek system as the main source of social life. Alcohol abuse, as well as incivility between women and men, remains as much—if not more—of a concern at Lehigh as it was in the late 1950s. The institution, since the early 1980s, has attempted to address issues of alcohol abuse, date rape, and development of a "healthier" and more civil social life; however, student interest in alternatives to the traditional fraternity parties on the "Hill" frequently has been less than enthusiastic. The admission of women did not solve those issues of "stag" culture that so troubled the faculty of the 1950s; it did, however, transfer greater ownership of those issues to the university, since women at Lehigh are now women *of* Lehigh. At Lehigh, debate over the nature of campus life has certainly focused on Greek life, alcohol use and abuse, and gender issues; however, in recent years the debate has been less volatile and high-profile, compared to Dartmouth.

One possible explanation is that Dartmouth students (and the Dartmouth culture) tend to view the undergraduate experience as an end in itself, while Lehigh students (and the Lehigh culture) focus on the undergraduate years as preparation for the future. This difference is rooted in the two institutions' very different histories, and it directly affects women's experiences at these institutions. Lehigh, since its founding, has had a strong emphasis on preparing engineers and professionals for "useful employment." Although it has, with the admission of women, become a "true university," its students still see their undergraduate education, first and foremost, as preparation for a career. In 2000–01, for example, 28 percent of Lehigh undergraduate degrees conferred were in engineering, while another 29 percent were in business and marketing. At Dartmouth, only 5 percent of degrees conferred in 2000–2001 were in engineering, while no undergraduate business majors are offered; most undergraduate degrees were in social sciences and history (33 percent) and English (10 percent).[47]

This distribution affects the institution in a number of ways related to women's experiences. First, women at Lehigh, regardless of major, are part of the institutional culture that focuses on career, and they are more likely to interpret their undergraduate experience as preparation for the future rather than as an end in itself. While this interpretation does influence some programming for women (a 1979 survey of Lehigh undergraduate women and alumnae, for example, called for more programs on career choices, balancing work and family, and preparing for a job search), it may detract from efforts to improve women's experiences *at* Lehigh. Lehigh women frequently evaluate their undergraduate experience by how well it prepares them for the workplace. "We stood out on campus just as women in business and the law professions tend to stand out today [in 1981]," recalled attorney Janet Scagnelli '75, one of the first Lehigh women admitted in 1971. "Lehigh proved to be a good assimilator for me."[48]

In contrast, for much of Dartmouth's history, the "Dartmouth experience" has been held up as a defining and unique four years in one's life. Essential to this experience is bonding with one's peers, enjoying the outdoors, and taking part in campus traditions—all of which have been greatly altered by the admission of women, and all of which matter greatly to undergraduates. Participating fully in the "Dartmouth experience," then, is vitally important to Dartmouth women as an end in itself.

In addition, both women and men at Dartmouth are more politically aware and active than most Lehigh students. Whether this is a function of the liberal arts environment, the fact that Dartmouth has traditionally emphasized educating "leaders," or the traditionally contentious nature of Dartmouth culture, cannot be determined. As a result, however, gender issues have become politicized to a much greater extent on the Dartmouth campus. The advent of the neoconservative *Dartmouth Review* in the 1980s is just one example of the extreme polarization that has surrounded gender and racial issues on the Dartmouth campus and made Dartmouth a cause célèbre for activists at each end of the ideological spectrum.

The gender composition of the two institutions' faculty also affects the nature of coeducation on the two campuses. In 2001–02, women represented 21 percent of Lehigh's 393-member full-time faculty; at Dartmouth, women made up 34 percent of the 446-member full-time faculty.[49] This difference may be explained in part by Lehigh's programs in business and engineering, where women are still greatly underrepresented at the Ph.D. level. What does this mean for women at these two institutions? The higher visibility of female faculty members at Dartmouth may generate a stronger emphasis on women's issues. Yet, despite studies that show the absence of female faculty role models to be detrimental for female students, Lehigh women in engineering and business cite both their female and male professors as valuable mentors. Ironically, engineering and other traditionally male fields, with their emphasis on meritocracy, may give women a sense of competing on a "fair playing field" based on ability and achievement. A 1979 Dartmouth graduate, a full-time working mother with young children, recalled her Dartmouth years with anger and frustration. She adds, however, "I went to law school right after Dartmouth. There, I came into my own. There, I found a positive outlet for my independence and my desire to be 'one of the boys.' In law school, women were equals. . . . I woke up to life, and found, to my surprise, that there was a hell of a lot more to it than fraternities and beer."[50]

Conclusion: How Much Can We Expect of Coeducation?

In examining coeducation in the modern era, it is essential to consider the context in which it was first suggested: the American college and university during the 1950s and 1960s. The admission of women was tied to postwar concerns about faculty recruitment and retention, the healthy psychological development and proper social behavior of college students, and the role of intellectual engagement in undergraduate academic and social life, issues that continue to resonate on campuses today.

Coeducation was expected to resolve these issues. Some institutional expectations have been realized: the admission of women, by many accounts, has enhanced the intellectual climate on both campuses while fostering new, more personal models of teaching and learning that rely on a partnership between faculty and students. Other expectations for coeducation did not fare as well. Did women truly "civilize" men at Dartmouth or Lehigh? Was it fair to expect them to take on that institutional responsibility in addition to their own educational goals?

If we look at the lives of alumni and alumnae from both institutions, however, there are indications of positive change. With the advent of coeducation, women gained additional access to undergraduate education—particularly in engineering and business—which has proved to be highly valuable personally and to society. A generation of men and women at these institutions came to know each other as competitors, team members, lab partners, and neighbors. Discussion about the complementary and sometimes conflicting roles of men and women has emerged in the public arena. As they face choices about combining work and family, careers and marriage, community life and individual achievement, Dartmouth and Lehigh graduates call upon the lessons—many of them difficult and even painful—learned during their undergraduate years.

Notes

1. Scott Meacham, "Charles Alonzo Rich Builds the New Dartmouth, 1893–1914" (M.A. thesis, University of Virginia, 1998); Marilyn Tobias, *Old Dartmouth on Trial* (New York: New York University Press, 1982).
2. "Look What They Missed!" *Evening Tribune* (Des Moines), December 13, 1944.
3. "The Co-Eds," *Boston Herald,* April 7, 1945.
4. Charles E. Widmayer, *John Sloan Dickey: A Chronicle of His Presidency of Dartmouth College* (Hanover, N.H.: Dartmouth College, 1991), 25.
5. Rebecca Lowen, *Creating the Cold War University: The Transformation of Stanford,* (Berkeley: University of California Press, 1994), examines Stanford's implementation of psychological services in the 1950s as part of the university's application of wartime research to peacetime campuses.
6. A 1949 *Life* magazine article, which contrasted women's experiences at the University

of Missouri and at Smith College, appeared to endorse coeducation as the "modern," healthy alternative. "Missouri vs. Smith," *Life,* May 9, 1949, cited in Daniel A. Clark, "The Two Joes Meet—Joe College, Joe Veteran: The G.I. Bill, College Education, and Postwar American Culture," *History of Education Quarterly* 38, no. 2 (1998): 185.

7.   Charles Leonard Stone, "Education for What? A Better Design for Living," *Dartmouth Alumni Monthly,* March 1953, 17–20.

8.   "A Free Man Is Answerable," convocation address by John Dickey, *Dartmouth Alumni Monthly,* November 1951, 19.

9.   President John Sloan Dickey to Professor Ryder, December 12, 1953, Dartmouth College Archives, Rauner Special Collections Library (hereafter DCA).

10. Report of the Commission on Campus Life, June 10, 1955, DCA.

11. Commission on Campus Life, "Regulations pertaining to women guests, etc.," June 10, 1955, 7, DCA.

12. Frank G. Ryder, chairman, Commission on Campus Life and Its Regulation, to President John Dickey, July 5, 1955, DCA.

13. Lincoln A. Mitchell, "The Undergraduate Chair," *Dartmouth Alumni Monthly,* November 1957, 30–31.

14. "An Open-Arms Aspect . . ." Ann Hopkins Potter, *Dartmouth Alumni Monthly,* May 1957, 28.

15. *Dartmouth Alumni Monthly,* March 1958, 24–26.

16. Dartmouth was growing concerned about cost and price issues during the 1950s, as were most private colleges and universities as they sought to compete with public institutions for faculty and students. The three-term (and, later, four-term) academic year was designed not only to provide a more intellectually challenging and independently driven academic experience for undergraduates but also to make the most efficient use of campus facilities and human resources.

17. Robert Sokol and Carla A. Sykes, "The Dartmouth Student," a summary report of studies carried out from 1958 to 1963 under the sponsorship of the Lincoln Filene Human Relations Research Program, Dartmouth College Special Collections, Rauner Special Collections Library.

18. "College Faculty Members, Students Want Coed Study," *Valley News* (Lebanon, N.H.), May 22, 1958.

19. "Dartmouth Squaws?," *Valley News,* June 6, 1958.

20. "Co-Ed Enrolls at Dartmouth," *Hanover Gazette,* February 14, 1963.

21. "Coeducation: A Limited Experiment," *The Dartmouth,* November 21, 1960, 2.

22. "Seymour Raises Seldom-Considered Points," *The Dartmouth,* April 15, 1965, 1–2. Emphasis in original.

23. David R. Weber to Mary Oronte, June 27, 1997, Dartmouth College Special Collections.

24. W. Ross Yates, *Lehigh University: A History of Education in Engineering, Business and the Human Condition* (Bethlehem: Lehigh University Press, 1992), 25, 30.

25. Untitled promotional pamphlet, c. 1935, 16, Special Collections, Lehigh University Libraries (hereafter Lehigh SC). Emphasis in original.

26. "The Review Student Poll," *Lehigh Review,* December 1939, 10–11.

27. "For Students, Faculty, Lehigh, Let's Have Co-eds," *Brown and White,* March 1, 1944, 2.

28. "Faculty Comments on Coeducation Question," *Brown and White*, March 8, 1944, 1.

29. *Lehigh*, admission publication, 1952, 4, Admission Office files, Lehigh SC.

30. Meeting, Lehigh University Board of Trustees, June 11, 1954, "Trustees Minutes" files, vol. 3, pt. 2, 1101, Lehigh SC.

31. Lehigh University Annual Report 1953–54, vol. 28, no. 5, 25, Lehigh SC.

32. Meeting notes, Lehigh University Board of Trustees, January 19, 1962, "Trustees Minutes" files, vol. 4, 1839, Lehigh SC.

33. "Report to the Graduate Faculty," June 2, 1958. Faculty Meeting minutes files, Lehigh SC.

34. Roger Geiger, *Research and Relevant Knowledge: American Research Universities since World War II* (New York: Oxford University Press, 1993). Geiger notes the development of "excess capacity" at Yale and Princeton and cites, in particular, Princeton's Patterson report on coeducation as evidence that adding women would allow the university to admit more and better quality students while providing additional tuition income. The Patterson report served as a resource for policy-makers at other all-male institutions as they contemplated coeducation.

35. "The Climate of Learning," report of the Committee on Student Life, June 1960, faculty meeting minutes, Lehigh SC.

36. Beth Bailey, "Sexual Revolution(s)," in *The '60s*, ed. David Farber (Chapel Hill: University of North Carolina Press, 1994), 242, provides a compelling analysis of middle-class adolescent and young-adult sexual mores during the 1950s and 1960s. Bailey argues that the "overelaboration" of parietal regulations at colleges and universities during the 1950s and early 1960s suggested that the system of control was weakening. Nonetheless, parietals helped to preserve "the distinction between public and private, the coexistence of overt and covert, that define[d] mid-century American sexuality" for middle-class men and women. The movement to bring sexuality into a more "natural" and "open" context, which took place between 1965 and 1970, influenced greatly the discussion of coeducation.

37. Glenn J. Christensen, "The Lord of the Neighboring Manor," *Lehigh Alumni Bulletin*, October 1962, 10.

38. "Men in Industry are at last being set free," wrote Gilbert Doan '19, retired manager of metallurgical research for Koppers Company, in the June 1962 *Lehigh Alumni Bulletin.* "Top management today urges each man to develop his family and community life fully, rather than neglect them for his job . . . he must make up his lost education at home . . . thus he escapes from the brainwashing of the vocational college and the narrow job." Gilbert E. Doan, "The New American," *Lehigh Alumni Bulletin*, June 1962, 10.

39. "CURE Submits List of Ideas," *Brown and White*, May 10, 1968, 1.

40. Joynt, who had joined the faculty of the College of Arts and Science in 1951, had served in the late 1950s on a committee that critically examined the fraternity system and student behavior. His selection as chairman of the study committee was a judicious choice: he had remained "above the fray" in the discussions of university governance in the mid-1960s, and his reputation as a highly principled and diplomatic member of the faculty would serve him well as chairman of the policy study group.

41. M. J. Rathbone to the Alumni of Lehigh University, February 27, 1970, C. B. Joynt personal files, private collection.

42. "Remarks to be made to Trustees introducing presentation on the subject of coeducation," W. Deming Lewis, April 9, 1970, 1, Joynt files.

43. Ibid., 3.

44. Bailey, 256, describes the public use of graphic sexuality, sexual images, and language during the revolutions of the 1960s as a political instrument against parental and institutional authority. In the early 1970s, men who resented women's presence at formerly male institutions also used profanity and sexual imagery as a political tool, unrestrained by the social controls that would have limited earlier generations of middle-class men.

45. Mary Kelley, "Claiming Their Rightful Place: Coeducation at Dartmouth: 1972–1997," 1998, Dartmouth College Special Collections; Kelley originally delivered this as an address during the 25 Years of Coeducation Celebration Weekend at Dartmouth College in 1997. Janelle Ruley, "Substantially Coeducational: The Transformation of an Institution; Dartmouth College, 1970–2000," senior fellowship project paper, 2000, Dartmouth College Special Collections. "Entering Class Characteristics," *Fact Book, 2001–02,* Office of Institutional Research, Dartmouth College.

46. Gianna Munafo, quoted in Kelley, 1.

47. Common Data Set, 2001–02 (CDS-J), Office of Institutional Research, Dartmouth College, and Office of Institutional Research, Lehigh University.

48. Janet Scagnelli, quoted in *Lehigh: The Annual Report of the University,* November 1981, 7.

49. Common Data Set, 2001–02 (CDS-I).

50. Marjory D. Robertson, quoted in Kelley, 18.

7

Women's Admission
to the University of Virginia
Tradition Transformed

Elizabeth L. Ihle

Virginia cherishes its heritage as a preserver of tradition. It is the site of the first permanent English colony in North America, the home to eight U.S. presidents, and the location of both the second oldest college in the country (William and Mary, founded in 1693) and the most traditional of state universities. The University of Virginia, founded by Thomas Jefferson in 1819 in Charlottesville as an "Academical Village," has always reflected the state's reverence for tradition. The old part of the university is still covered in cobbled walks and contains numerous buildings designed by Jefferson himself. Indeed, the most honored student housing, offered only to outstanding student leaders, is on the Lawn and the Ranges, a series of rooms with working fireplaces (with wood provided by the university), distant bathrooms, and a succession of tourists traipsing by.[1] The university has a burial ground for students killed in the Civil War. No one would dream of commenting on the beauty of the campus because the university does not have one; instead it has "the Grounds."

Tradition is also a state of mind and a daily practice. The honor code is revered. Two literary societies, begun in the 1820s and 1830s, still flourish. Students are never referred to freshmen, sophomores, juniors, or seniors, but rather as first, second, third, and fourth-year students.[2] Even today students wear coats and ties or dresses to football games. The university still has a number of secret societies that wield enormous influence. Professors have generally been called *mister*, as gentlemen ought to be; the term *doctor* is vocational and inappropriate to this haven of good breeding.

Since Jefferson's proposal for public education in Virginia, "A Plan for the General Diffusion of Knowledge," did not suggest education for females beyond the elementary years, it should come as no surprise that Mr. Jefferson's university was created as the capstone of the state's system of education with only males in mind. In this chapter, I argue that the state's reverence for tradition delayed women's admission to the university, as it struggled with the question for nearly ninety years; coeducation transformed the university but tradition as a whole still flourishes. This reverence for tradition is the reason that Virginia was the last state of the former Confederacy and indeed the last state in the nation to admit women unreservedly to its flagship state university.

Overall, the South embraced coeducation later than the rest of the nation, although under special circumstances women occasionally were admitted to southern, all-male institutions in the late nineteenth century. The adoption of coeducation moved through the South from west to east. The westernmost states of the Confederacy, those that had the least amount of tradition, either simply created a policy of coeducation when they founded their state universities or adopted coeducation early in their history. The first three to do so were Arkansas in 1872, Mississippi in 1882, and Texas in 1883. Then came both Alabama and Tennessee in 1893 and Louisiana in 1905. The holdouts were in the east. Florida maintained coeducation until 1905, then was sex-segregated until 1947, and then resumed coeducation. The last Southern states to admit women were the former British colonies: the Carolinas, Georgia, and Virginia. Georgia admitted women in 1918. North Carolina maintained separate schools for each sex until after World War II. South Carolina, under a Populist governor "Pitchfork" Ben Tillman, made its liberal arts college at Columbia coeducational in 1894, despite the wishes of the academic community. However, the college provided no facilities for women, not even toilets, and their reception was so hostile that few women enrolled before the 1920s.[3] Georgia admitted women in 1918 and North Carolina integrated Chapel Hill in 1945. Virginia, however, established separate and inferior colleges for women and maintained them until the 1970, giving it the dubious distinction of being the last state in the nation to admit women to its flagship university.

Early Attempts to Admit Women

The question of women's education arose at the University of Virginia when John W. Mallet, a chemistry professor, moved in October 1880 to establish a committee to investigate the ways the university could sustain the highest education of women. In December the committee recommended that the university take more responsibility for teacher training and the liberal arts education of women either by the adoption of coeducation or the establishment of a coordinate college. The faculty endorsed the committee's resolutions but later changed its mind when it saw no practical way of implementing either plan.[4]

The issue of women's admission to the university was not raised again until May 1892, when a woman petitioned to be examined in mathematics.

The faculty agreed to her plan. Although she was tutored privately and passed the examination with high marks, the faculty developed reservations about extending this privilege to all women. It decided in 1894 to withdraw examination privileges for women, noting that they did not have a right to attend the university and that the institution's education was unsuitable to the female sex because it would make women boisterous, bold, and even aggressive, and it would limit their reproductive abilities. The board agreed with the faculty's decision, adding that coeducation was not in character with the University of Virginia and had not been intended by Thomas Jefferson.[5]

A nursing school for women was added, though, in 1901, apparently as a means of getting nursing help for the university's medical school. Four women entered this two-year training program; hours were arduous, and they received no academic credit. The program was kept entirely separate from the university.[6]

By 1900 the state offered four options for white men to earn college degrees at public state colleges or universities. In addition to the University of Virginia, they were Virginia Polytechnic Institute, the Virginia Military Institute, and the College of William and Mary, which had just turned from private to public hands. All the state had for its white women, however, was the Women's Industrial and Normal Institute established at Farmville in 1884. It offered teacher training that hardly exceeded a high school education today.[7]

Little further action was taken on the issue of women at the university until the early 1900s. However, as the state began to get serious about improving public elementary and secondary education after 1905 and decided that knowledgeable teachers were a necessity, the movement had some positive indirect benefits for women's public higher education. The summer normal school at the university was opened to women in 1906.[8] In 1908 the legislature established three more normal schools for women; these offered approximately the equivalent of two years of high school work and two years of college.[9]

During the 1910s, pressure to improve women's public higher educational opportunities in the state increased so much that it made national news and was debated in every legislative session of the decade. Although some people supported coeducation at the university because it would bring additional revenue into the university treasury, most preferred the establishment of a coordinate college for women, an arrangement similar to that of Harvard and Radcliffe, Brown and Pembroke, or Tulane and Sophie Newcomb. Under most coordinate arrangements, men and women would have separate classes but would share faculty, laboratories, libraries, concert series, and other facets of student life. University of Virginia president Edwin Alderman, who had supported women's education in North Carolina, warmly endorsed a coordinate college because he disapproved of coeducation in the undergraduate and professional schools but thought that completely separate women's education did not prepare women for modern life.[10] Also supporting a coordinate college for women were the university rector, the governor, Harvard president Charles W. Eliot, and Princeton president Woodrow Wilson. Groups such as the Virginia Federation of Labor, the Farmers' Co-operative and Education Union, and the Virginia Department of Public Instruction also went on record as supporting the idea.

Women, too, argued in favor of the coordinate plan, either out of genuine agreement with it or out of knowledge that coeducation at the university was still unthinkable. They pointed out that women also needed a capstone to Jefferson's education plan and observed that a coordinate college would be less expensive than an entirely separate one for women. They also observed that twice as many girls in Virginia finished high school as boys and speculated that men were afraid to meet women in the classroom for fear of being found deficient.[11]

The main opponents of the coordinate plan were students and the powerful alumni. The students opposed the coordinate plan saying not only was it contrary to Jefferson's ideals but also it would lower men's respect for women as they sought an equal footing with their male companions.[12] The Richmond alumni chapter spearheaded the opposition to the coordinate college. They argued that such a plan would lead to coeducation, that women would destroy the university's honor system, that they would increase the expenses of the school, and that they would change the exclusively male atmosphere of the university.[13] The argument that men needed to have a place of their own to "find themselves, grow and develop amid surroundings that inculcate manliness and men's high ideal" was reminiscent of the arguments used against coeducation elsewhere in the South.[14]

Throughout the decade of the 1910s both the university and the legislature argued the issue. In 1911 Alderman and the faculty recommended the establishment of a coordinate college as a matter of justice. In December, 1913, the board of visitors, the university's governing body, held an open hearing to discuss the matter, and both the women and the alumni presented their cases. With Alderman's support the board voted to recommend to the legislature the establishment of a coordinate college, although such a bill had already been decisively defeated in the 1912 legislature. Alderman's position on this issue alienated him from some of the students and alumni and cost him trust that he never completely regained. The board retained its position supporting a coordinate college until 1917, when it decided not to continue pressing the issue so long as the nation faced the specter of international war.

Meanwhile, the legislature, under pressure from the alumni, consistently rebuffed the board. Although a bill to establish a coordinate college passed the Virginia senate in 1916, it was defeated in the House of Delegates by one vote. Similar bills offered in 1910, 1912, 1914, and 1918 also met defeat. However, the pressure for expanding women's public higher education options did re-sult in two improvements. First, in 1916 the rank of the four normal schools at Farmville, Harrisonburg, Radford, and Fredericksburg was raised to that of college, and the schools were authorized to grant Bachelor of Science degrees in education; then in 1918, as men enlisted in military service and enrollment plummeted at the College of William and Mary, women were offered admis-sion, thus giving them their first access to a Bachelor of Arts degree at a public institution.[15]

The debate about women's access to the University of Virginia, while not a success, did have some positive outcomes for women. In 1919 and 1920, with-out legislative approval, the university began to admit women to the Gradu-ate School and to some of the professional schools, though an unwritten rule seemed to say that "women had to be better than men in every way in order to be admitted."[16] Even after admission, the first seventeen women did not have an easy life. T. Braxton Woody, class of 1922, later recalled, "It was a great shame and humiliation the way the students and the faculty treated those women—ab-solutely unbelievably brutally. Their lives were made unbearable. When coeds would walk into class, the men would rock the house—bang, bang, banging their feet on the floor."[17] Women soon organized a Women's Self-Government Association and established a few sororities. Also in the 1920s the university appointed a woman to its board for the first time.

In the late 1920s and early 1930s the idea of a coordinate college was raised again, but this time the enthusiasm of the board of visitors for such a plan had waned. It passed a resolution requesting that such a college not be located in Charlottesville. The Halsey commission, established by the legislature in 1928 to investigate the possibility of establishing a coordinate college, decided that the State Female Teachers College at Fredericksburg, sixty-five miles away from the university, should be converted into such a school. Despite support from the legislature, alumni, students, and board, Governor John Garland Pollard vetoed the resulting bill in 1932, on the grounds that the state could not afford such expenditure during an economic depression. Possibly because of this defeat, in 1936 the legislature gave the four normal schools power for the first time to offer Bachelor of Arts degrees.

In 1944 the Fredericksburg institution, now known as Mary Washington College, was given coordinate status with the university, and Radford College (now university) was made coordinate with the Virginia Polytechnic Institute and State University.[18] In both cases, the board of visitors of the male institution was given control over the female one. The fact that neither of these women's institutions was close to the men's indicates that coordination was largely a designation, not a reality. Neither Mary Washington nor Radford ever achieved the same distinction as their coordinate partners. As a 1969 lawsuit pointed out, Mary Washington remained inferior to the university in student-faculty ratio, faculty quality, finances, enrollment, and curricular offerings. After World War II, all the traditionally female normal colleges began admitting men, at least as day students

The Final Campaign

By the 1950s, the University of Virginia enrolled several hundred women annually, but almost none in the College of Arts and Sciences, the heart of the undergraduate program. The main exception was transfer students from Mary Washington in their third and fourth years. A few women entered the university as education majors, using that as a "back door" for classes in the college. One mathematics professor, with a job offer from the University of Minnesota, agreed to stay at Virginia, so long as his daughters could attend. By the end of the decade, wives and daughters of faculty members gained college admission.[19]

By the mid-1960s amid nationwide civil and student unrest, the issue of women's admission to the university arose again. A 1965 report from the Virginia Higher Education Study Commission noted in the section on Mary Washington College that its relation to the university offered few advantages and several disadvantages. The report speculated that "There is suspicion in some quarters that the main interest of the University in maintaining Mary Washington College as a branch with enrollment limited to women students is to prevent pressure for a coeducational program in undergraduate arts and sciences at Charlottesville."[20] When the board met to review the report on January 8, 1966, it discussed several recommendations affecting the university but made no comment on the one that the university should consider becoming coeducational.[21]

By 1967, the enrollment of 7,800 included 834 women. Although the College of Arts and Sciences remained almost exclusively male, women could be admitted after two years of college elsewhere to all programs except those leading to a Bachelor of Arts degree. Women could be admitted to the Bachelor of Science programs in chemistry and physics.[22] Most women, however, were enrolled in various professional programs like nursing, education, architecture, law, medicine, engineering, and the Graduate School of Arts and Sciences. Two women had even been elected to the Student Council in 1966, and both students and the community discussed the possibility of coeducation more frequently.

Another year and a half passed before the topic of coeducation surfaced again with the board of visitors. On April 8, 1967, the board passed a resolution empowering university president Edgar F. Shannon Jr. to conduct a study to determine the need for admission of women to the College of Arts and Sciences. If such a need existed, he was then empowered to conduct a study of its feasibility and to present the findings of both the needs study and the feasibility study.[23] One reason for the board's action was that many visitors realized that if the university did not voluntarily admit women to the college, the courts would probably make them do so.[24] At the June 2 board meeting Shannon reported the establishment of the Committee to Study the Admission of Women.

Eighteen months later, in December 1968, the committee, popularly called the Woody committee after its chair, French professor T. Braxton Woody, issued its report. The seven-member committee had polled faculty, students, and alumni. The former two groups were generally in favor of women's admission. Letters sent to 40,000 university alumni, however, elicited only 98 replies, two-thirds of which opposed coeducation. The years had not altered their opposition. As one alumnus wrote: "In spite of all the forces pressing upon us to the contrary, should we not seek here at the University to maintain the College's predominantly masculine character and its moderate size, as essential to preserving our traditions and fulfilling our Founder's intentions for us as the capstone of Virginia's education system, and as an institution of high national and international repute."[25]

The committee concluded that there were several advantages to coeducation. Supported by statements from Yale, Princeton, and Vassar, it argued that mixed classes would enhance the educational process. Increasing the size of the university would offer more opportunities and assist it in its quest for academic excellence. The committee suggested that opening the college would benefit the Schools of Nursing and Education, as well as the various departments within the college. Moreover, coeducation would help with the "weekend problem," which occurred as university men traveled to other colleges and universities each weekend to party.[26]

The committee also noted some possible disadvantages. There was the possible effect of women on the university's honor system. The Honor Committee had examined a study that contended that an honor system at a coeducational institution was slightly less than half as effective as one at an all-male institution. Presumably chivalry might interfere with justice in the case of a female defendant. On the basis of that study, the Honor Committee had recommended against coeducation.[27] The committee also noted coeducation's possible effect on enrollment in the state's women's colleges, alumni and student opposition, diminished opportunities for separate education, and the direction of the development of the university.[28] Despite the disagreement of the alumni and the Honor Committee, the Woody committee voted six to one to recommend that the university proceed with making the college coeducational.

The one dissenting vote was cast by Julian Bishko. He thought that the admission of women would not

reverse the deterioration in dress, manners, social behavior and personal ideals prevalent on the Grounds in recent years. On the contrary, I fear that the abandonment of much that has made Virginia unique among leading American universities, much that can be summed up as our ancient dislike of conformity with the patterns commonly and pejoratively associated with the typical large American state university—"State U-ism"—will eventuate, not to our gain but to our regrettable loss.[29]

The board received the committee's report and then requested the president to proceed with studies of the feasibility of implementing the recommendation. Also at that meeting the board heard via the president requests from Martin F. Evans, president of the Student Council, that 500 women be admitted to the College of Arts and Sciences in 1970 and that female high school seniors from the area be admitted to the College of Arts and Sciences beginning in September 1969. However, the board took no action.[30]

In February, the board tackled the problem of women's admission again. After the Woody committee's report, President Shannon had turned to the board's Education Committee to examine the issue of the feasibility of the admission. The committee discussed the issue on February 14 and had decided to bring the issue to the full board the next day without a recommendation. On February 15 the full board dropped the ban against women in the college but approved their admission with caution. It did not want women to take the place of qualified men and did not want the faculty to be overburdened with more students; therefore, it insisted that the general assembly had to provide additional funding to take care of increased enrollment. It also wanted to make sure that women's admission took place in an orderly and controlled fashion. It did not want enrollment at the state women's colleges, especially at Mary Washington, to suffer. Despite the conservative nature of the board's acceptance of women's admission, the vote was not unanimous, and several board members wrote statements concerning their objections. Most of those expressed a concern that the alumni had not been satisfactorily polled on the topic.[31] In a separate resolution it approved the admission of wives of students and wives and daughters of staff members. It was estimated that about twenty women would enter the university under these circumstances.[32]

While some alumni might have thought the university was moving much too fast on the subject of coeducation, other elements thought it was moving too slowly. In May, 1969, the American Civil Liberties Union (ACLU) and the National Student Association filed a lawsuit in the U.S. District Court for the Eastern Division of Virginia on behalf of four women, and all other women similarly situated, against the board, president, governor, other state officials, and the Virginia State Council for Higher Education.[33]

The leading ACLU lawyer for this case was John Lowe, a 1967 University of Virginia Law School graduate, who had set up practice in Charlottesville. Lowe had hired a local high school graduate, Virginia Anne Scott, as his assistant. Scott's mother had died without completing her degree and had told her daughter that everything would be all right if she could just finish school. Scott, however, had no money to attend a college elsewhere.[34] Therefore, she agreed to be one of the plaintiffs.

The plaintiffs maintained that their constitutional rights were denied because the university had precluded their admission. "The policies and practices of the officials of Virginia in maintaining a system of sexual discrimination and degradation is an archaic vestige of the 18th century concepts of education and not in keeping with any modern theory of education," noted the ACLU.[35] Depositions were taken in August.

Since the preliminary hearing was set for September 29, too late to accommodate the September 19 registration deadline, U.S. district judge Robert R. Merhige Jr. ordered the university on September 8 to consider the four women's applications without regard to their sex and to admit them if they met the requirements. Because the women would lose all academic credit and their tuition if they eventually lost the case, three of the women chose not to enroll, but Scott was the exception and became a first-year student in fall 1969. She later recalled that a number of students made her life unpleasant, although another group of students was supportive of the effort to admit women.[36]

In a deposition, rector of the board, Frank C. Rogers, a Roanoke attorney, testified both to his personal dislike of coeducation and to his responsibilities as rector:

> Well, as Rector, I was influenced by many factors, like that it was inevitable and that times had changed and whether I like it or not it had to come. Now personally I regret it very much, the necessity of doing it, just as I have regretted the necessity for most of the changes that have taken place. I like the good ole days. I don't like any of these changes, but I hope that as Rector I have been willing to act responsibly and not influenced by my own personal likes and dislikes.[37]

President Shannon, father of five daughters, offered a similar opinion in his deposition, but his views may not have been so conservative as the alumni would have liked to think. He later recalled, "I felt that the University, as the state's leading educational institution, certainly ought to admit women to the undergraduate program. As a state university, we did not have a legal leg to stand on."[38]

The plan presented to the court was developed by Frank Hereford, at that time vice president and provost of the university, and later university president from 1974–85. As it was originally proposed, the university would admit 250 first-year women and 150 third- and fourth-year in September 1970 and then increase women's numbers through 1980, when 35 percent of the total college enrollment would be female. The rationale for the low percentage was to lessen the impact on enrollment at the traditionally female state colleges.[39]

When the constitutionality of a state law is challenged in a federal court, a three-judge panel must be convened to hear the case. Thus, on September 29, 1969, a three-judge court comprised of U.S. circuit judge J. Braxton Craven Jr. and district judges Robert R. Merhige Jr. and John M. Mackensie listened to testimony from both sides. Hereford was one of those subpoenaed. "I somehow or other was chosen to be the person to testify for the University. It was a long day," he later recalled.[40] The university's dean of women, Mary E. Whitney, also testified, reporting that men and women graduate students taking courses at the university stayed in the same dormitory and no problems of any consequences had developed. Shortly afterward, possibly as a result of her testimony, she was notified that her position at the university was being eliminated and that her services would not be needed the following year.[41]

The panel indicated its concern about the constitutionality of the university's previous policy in restricting the admission of women to the College of Arts and Sciences, but it did not order any immediate resolution. It referred to the university's plan as "speculation" and to the goals for women's admission as "quotas." It asked the president of the university to file with Judge Merhige by October 31, 1969, another plan for the implementation of coeducation in the College of Arts and Sciences and a report of progress and implementation of such plan.

Therefore, issues concerning women's admission dominated the October 3 board meeting. The board changed its proposal and resolved:

> that the restrictions heretofore placed on the admission of women to the undergraduate schools at Charlottesville be and they hereby are unconditionally removed, so that there be no restriction of admission of women applicants to the University of Virginia at Charlottesville, including, without limitation, its College of Arts and Sciences and other undergraduate schools, other than the same restrictions imposed upon male applicants for admission to such schools, provided, only, that the number of women may be limited during such temporary transition period as may be determined necessary by the Board for the implementation of this resolution; and that all such applicants shall be considered irrespective of their sex.[42]

The visitors directed the admission of 450 women in September 1970 and 550 women in 1971, with no limitation on the number of women admitted after that.

On February 9, 1970, the three-judge federal panel ruled against the university's original position and approved the board's new plan to admit women over a two-year period. It decided also that, in spite of the university's violation of the Fourteenth Amendment and several civil rights laws, no one was to be assessed damages.

In the following September, 450 first-year students were admitted and 550 a year later. Raymond C. Bice, who had a long and distinguished career at the university, first as an assistant professor of psychology, then dean of admission, dean of the college, and finally as university historian, reminisced about women's arrival on campus. He said that the *Cavalier Daily,* the student newspaper, predicted that the university was going to have to make some changes, like fewer potatoes in the cafeteria, frilly curtains in the classrooms, fewer courses in science and math, and the addition of courses in child care.

> Well, of course, what happened is that when the women arrived, they loved potatoes, and there were no frilly curtains. The women enrolled in math and science like it was going out of style. They were very much involved. All these fears they had turned out to be wrong. Once the women got here, the students changed their minds very quickly. Amazing things started to happen. First of all, the library, which was usually very empty at night, suddenly became a very popular place to study; men and women studied there together. Before women were here, the men used to take off for the weekend, now they stayed here. The academic performance went way up.[43]

Corks and Curls, the University of Virginia yearbook, acknowledged in the spring of 1972 that coeducation had changed the university but had not destroyed it. In fact, it had turned out to be a pleasant change:

> It has been hard to some of Virginia's gentlemen to accept the women. Many just weren't sure how to act. Two hundred leering potential rapists camped outside the women's dorms in early September did not make for good public relations. Seeking dates with co-eds only on off weekends, or days when the weather was too poor to roll, was not good for morale. Chauvinistic letters to the CD [*Cavalier Daily*] demanding more cooperation from the feminine gender did not lead to faith in the home base boys. But the men are learning: the incision has been healed, the rib has settled comfortably back into place, and surprisingly though for many, the operation wasn't all that painful.[44]

After September 1972, the university offered equal admission to all qualified students regardless of sex. In 1972, the first year of no restrictions on women's admission, 45 percent of the entering first-years were women. Changes to the facilities had not kept up, and for a few years houseplants grew in some urinals.[45]

Women were soon admitted to most campus organizations and honor societies. The only holdout, the Jefferson Literary Society, which had planned to remain all male, relented in the face of a potential lawsuit.[46] Women were soon awarded rooms on the Lawn and the Ranges.

The university quickly established various sports for women. One of the first was the women's basketball team. In 1976 it held an Invitational Basketball Tournament, and five years later it was nationally ranked. That same year, 1981, the university also had women's track and field hockey teams, and photos of cross country and volleyball teams appear in the 1986 yearbook.

Virginius Dabney, great great grandson of one of the university's earliest presidents and son of a faculty member, looked back on the 1960s and 1970s, which saw the addition of hundreds of African-American students and thousands of women. He summed up the period by concluding, "the institution's faculty, academic standards, and intellectual level were sharply upgraded, and the students manifested a greatly augmented concern for the less fortunate elements of society."[47]

Women at the University Today

Women continue to enroll in the university and to excel scholastically. Today, women make up nearly 60 percent of the students entering the college, a rate somewhat higher than women's enrollment in higher education nationally. Their numbers have also increased in the university's overall enrollment, thus signaling growth in women's enrollment in the graduate and professional schools. In terms of GPA and the number of students graduating in four years, they have excelled men (see Tables 7.1–7.3).

Women's athletics began in 1973. Currently the university supports twelve teams for each gender. Men constitute 436 of the athletes or 55.3 percent, while women have 372 participants or 44.7 percent of the total.[48]

Recognizing that women faced difficulties in life on the Grounds, in 1986 the university established a Taskforce on the Status of Women. As a result of its work, in 1989 the university established a Women's Center to help serve women

Table 7.1. Student Body in the College of Arts and Sciences by Gender

	Female		Male		
	N	%	N	%	Total
Fall 1981	4,133	51.6	3,883	48.4	8,016
Fall 1991	4,491	54.0	3,815	46.0	8,306
Fall 2001	5,524	59.6	3,740	40.4	9,264

Source: University of Virginia Institutional Assessment and Studies, "Historical Data," available at *www.web.virginia.edu/iaas/data_catalog/institutional/historical/historical.htm.*

Table 7.2. Women's Enrollment throughout the University of Virginia

	Female		Male		
	N	%	N	%	Total
Fall 1981	7,566	46.1	8,854	53.9	16,420
Fall 1991	8,688	48.3	9,318	51.7	18,006
Fall 2001	9,834	52.1	9,014	47.9	18,848

Source: University of Virginia Institutional Assessment and Studies, "Historical Data," available at *www.web.virginia.edu/iaas/data_catalog/institutional/historical/historical.htm.*

students, faculty, and staff. The following year the university created the Studies in Women and Gender Program, which offers both a major and minor. Over the years, the Women's Center has consulted with several university entities including the Darden Graduate School of Business Administration and the School of Medicine and helped them make substantial changes. Some of the changes simply had to do with the climate, while others affected safety issues like parking lot and laboratory security. The tenure clock in medicine is now ten years with clinical, research, and teaching tracks.[49]

In 1999 a Task Force on the Status of Women issued a report that called for the establishment of a Women's Leadership Council. The Council's goals are to increase the diversity of those in leadership positions among administrators, faculty, and students, so that by 2010 their diversity in gender and race matches the diversity of the population the university serves.[50]

The university has been rather progressive in its response to sexual orientation. Since 1972 it has had a Gay Student Union that is also Charlottesville's oldest gay, lesbian, transsexual, and bisexual organization. Today it is called the Queer Student Union. It works with the Lesbian, Gay, Bisexual and Transgender Resource Center sponsored by the Office of the Dean of Students. Since 1991 the university has had a policy of barring discrimination on the basis of sexual orientation. The Alumni Association has an LGBT affiliate group called the Serpentine Society. Even with all these groups, many lesbian students prefer to channel their activism through women's rights groups on campus.[51]

While the proportion of women in the student body grew easily, the number of female faculty did not keep pace. In 1970 less than 5 percent of college faculty was female. Of the 23 women on a faculty of 483, only ten were at the assistant professor level or above, and only six had tenure. In 1983 women's representation had increased to 18 percent, but only 15 of the 106 women were tenured. In 1990 the 122 female faculty members comprised nearly 20 percent of the total, but only 36 of them were tenured as associate or full professors.

Table 7.3. Cumulative GPAs and Four-Year Graduation Rates

	Average GPA	Female GPA	Male GPA	Four-year graduation rate (%)	Female (%)	Male (%)
Fall 1984[a]	2.912	2.935	2.893	76.4	78.7	73.9
Fall 1991	3.028	3.060	2.997	79.8	81.1	78.6
Fall 2001	3.12	3.16	3.069	83.0	86.2	79.2

Source: University of Virginia Institutional Assessment and Studies, "Historical Data," available at *www.web.virginia.edu/iaas/data_catalog/institutional/historical/historical.htm.*

a. First year this data was recorded.

Women held only 10 of the 200 endowed professorships. Three women were serving as department chairs.[52] Today the number of tenured women remains low, and the low number serving as department chairs and deans remains a key issue.[53] Outside the College of Arts and Sciences, women appear to have made more progress in being hired into full-time instructional and research positions. They have been even more successful in being hired as lower-level administrators (see Tables 7.4–7.6).

While women may have made significant progress in gaining some administrative and managerial positions, they have made little inroad into the board of visitors, which is appointed by the governor. Although the first woman was appointed to the board in 1920, there have never been more than two women serving together on the board of 16 or 17 people (see Table 7.7).

Things change slowly in the Old Dominion, as the 90-year struggle for

Table 7.4. Total Fulltime Instructional and Research Faculty

	Female		Male		
	N	%	N	%	Total
Fall 1981	223	15.5	1,213	84.5	1,436
Fall 1991	322	19.5	1,331	80.5	1,653
Fall 2001	530	27.1	1,423	72.9	1,953

Source: University of Virginia Institutional Assessment and Studies, "Historical Data," available at *www.web.virginia.edu/iaas/data_catalog/institutional/historical/historical.htm.*

Table 7.5. Executive, Administrative, and Managerial Employees

	Female		Male		
	N	%	N	%	Total
Fall 1981	190	41.0	273	59.0	463
Fall 1991	261	45.3	315	54.7	576
Fall 2001	236	50.1	227	49.9	463

Source: University of Virginia Institutional Assessment and Studies, "Historical Data," available at *www.web.virginia.edu/iaas/data_catalog/institutional/historical/historical.htm.*

Table 7.6. Gender Composition of the University Administration and Deans

	Female		Male		
	N	%	N	%	Total
1981–82	3	13.0	20	86.9	23
1991–92	1	4.8	20	95.3	21
2001–02	6	26.1	17	73.9	23

Source: University of Virginia Institutional Assessment and Studies, "Historical Data," available at *www.web.virginia.edu/iaas/data_catalog/institutional/historical/historical.htm.*

Table 7.7. Gender Composition of the Board of Visitors

	Female		Male		
	N	%	N	%	Total
1972	1	6.3	15	93.7	16
1982	1	6.3	15	93.7	16
1992	2	12.5	14	87.5	16
2001	2	11.8	15	88.2	17[a]

Source: University of Virginia Institutional Assessment and Studies, "Historical Data," available at *www.web.virginia.edu/iaas/data_catalog/institutional/historical/historical.htm.*

a. The seventeenth board member was a male student. Previous years had no student representation.

women's unrestricted admission to the university indicates, but few people today would wish to return to a single-sex system. Had Mary Munford, the leader of the efforts to establish a college for women in Charlottesville in the 1910s, been able to see the eventual result of efforts, she would be gratified. Virginia Anne Scott, the first woman admitted in 1969 as a result of the ACLU, must take pride in seeing the accomplishments of the thousands of women who have succeeded her. Mr. Jefferson's university not only survived women's admission to its sacred Grounds but also seems to have thrived from the academic vitality that the women brought. It is consistently named one of the top public universities in the nation. The single-sex tradition at the university was challenged and destroyed, but today women and men can take pride in the many other traditions that still make the University of Virginia a unique and special institution.

Notes

I am indebted to research assistance from graduate assistants Jacqueline McCormack and Patrick Cooper of James Madison University and student John Blair Reeves Jr. at the University of Virginia.

1. Susan Tyler Hitchcock, *The University of Virginia: A Pictorial History* (Charlottesville: University Press of Virginia, 1999), 32.

2. Jefferson believed that learning ought not be quantified as having been completed by such titles as freshman, sophomore, and so forth, but rather by the amount of time each student had spent learning.

3. Daniel Walker Hollis, *The University of South Carolina*, Vol. 2: *College to University* (Columbia: University of South Carolina Press, 1956), 172–73.

4. Philip Alexander Bruce, *History of the University of Virginia, 1819–1919: The Lengthened Shadow of One Man* (New York: Macmillan, 1922), 4:67.

5. Ibid., 4:67–69.

6. Hitchcock, 125–26.

7. Virginia was one of the first southern states to extend a limited form of public higher education to African Americans under the Morrill Act with the establishment of the Virginia Normal and Collegiate Institute in Petersburg in 1882. It offered a curriculum similar to the women's normal school in Farmville, probably about two years of high school and two years of college work. With the rise in popularity of Booker T. Washington's industrial training, the collegiate program was dismantled in 1902 and not resumed until 1922.

8. "Shall Jefferson's University Admit Women?," *New York Times Magazine,* February 6, 1916, 15.

9. These normal schools are now James Madison University in Harrisonburg, Radford University in Radford, and Mary Washington College in Fredericksburg; the school founded in Farmville in 1884 is now called Longwood University.

10. Dumas Malone, *Edwin A. Alderman: A Biography* (New York: Doubleday, Doran, 1940), 390.

11. "Co-Education in Virginia," *American Educational Review* 32 (1911): 411.

12. Ibid.

13. Bruce, 5:95–97.

14. Murray M. McGuire, "Some Objections to the Co-ordinate Women's College," *University of Virginia Alumni Bulletin* 14 (January 1914): 12, as quoted by Mary E. Whitney, "The Struggle to Attain Coeducation," *Journal of the National Association of Women Deans and Counselors* 34 (fall 1970): 40.

15. Women applied to William and Mary in such great numbers that in 1925 its board declared that no more than 40 percent of the student body could be female. The cap remained in place until the mid-1960s.

16. Whitney, 40.

17. As quoted by Julie Young, "Coeducation," *UVa Alumni News,* July–August, 1990, 12.

18. Virginia Tech began admitting women to programs not open to them anywhere else in the state in the early 1920s; however, women's enrollment remained quite small until the 1970s.

19. Hitchcock, 153.

20. John Russell Dale, "Control and Coordination of Higher Education in Virginia," State Council for Higher Education in Virginia, Richmond, 1965, 15, Special Collections, University of Virginia.

21. Minutes of the University of Virginia Board of Visitors, box 1 (October 1965–June 1969), January 8, 1966, 53, Special Collections, University of Virginia.

22. "Board of Visitors Studies Possibility of Women at U," *The Bullet,* April 17, 1967.

23. Visitors' minutes, vol. 13, April 8, 1967, 244.

24. Virginius Dabney, *Mr. Jefferson's University: A History* (Charlottesville: University Press of Virginia, 1981), 490.

25. President's Special Committee, "The Admission of Women to the College," November 1968, 49, as quoted in Whitney, 42, Special Collections, University of Virginia.

26. T. Braxton Woody, "Report of the Special University Committee on the Admission of Women to the College of Arts and Sciences of the University of Virginia," November 1968, Special Collections, University of Virginia.

27. The study was William J. Bowers, "Student Dishonesty and Its Control in College,"

Bureau of Applied Social Research, Columbia University, 1964, as cited in Dabney, 491.

28. Woody, iv. By the early 1970s most of the state's women's colleges, named at the time Longwood College, Radford College, and Madison College, accepted men as day students.

29. Ibid., 51.

30. Visitors' minutes, vol. 13, December 14, 1968, 426, Special Collections, University of Virginia.

31. Visitors' minutes, vol. 13, February 15, 1969, 439–43, Special Collections, University of Virginia.

32. Frank Walin, "U.Va. Plan to Admit Coeds Approved," *Richmond Times-Dispatch*, February 10, 1970.

33. *Kirstein v. Rector and Visitors of the University of Virginia*, 309 F.Supp. 184 (1970).

34. Kathleen F. Phalen, "John Lowe: Lightning Rod for Civil Liberties," *UVA Lawyer*, winter 1996, 33.

35. As quoted in the *Richmond Times-Dispatch*, February 10, 1970.

36. Except for comments in Phalen's article about John Lowe, Scott, who still lives in Charlottesville, has consistently refused interviews about her experience.

37. Deposition of Frank W. Rogers given on August 22, 1969, in Charlottesville, Virginia. As quoted in Mary E. Whitney, "Women and the University," 2d ed., 2000, Special Collections, University of Virginia, 116.

38. As quoted in Phalen, 34.

39. *Cavalier Daily*, September 23, 1969, as quoted in Whitney, "Women," 121.

40. As quoted in Young, 14–15.

41. Frank Walin, "U.Va. Ruling Expected Today," *Richmond Times-Dispatch*, September 30, 1969; Whitney, "Women," 117.

42. Visitors' minutes, box 2, vol. 14, October 3, 1969, 686–88, Special Collections, University of Virginia.

43. Raymond Bice, University Historian, interview by Elizabeth L. Ihle, University of Virginia, September 14, 1994. See Table 7.3 on women's academic performance.

44. *Corks and Curls*, 1972.

45. Hitchcock, 188.

46. Dabney, 492.

47. Ibid., 467. The university accepted its first African-American male graduate student in the College of Law in 1951 and its first undergraduate in 1960.

48. Jane Miller, Associate Senior Director of Athletics, e-mail communication, October 30, 2002; "Table 1: Athletics Participation," Equity in Athletics Disclosure Act Reports, 2002, available at *www.virginia.edu/uva/EADA2002/Table%20/*.

49. Sharon Davie, Director of the University of Virginia Women's Center, interview by Elizabeth L. Ihle, University of Virginia, September 20, 2002.

50. *www.virginia.edu/insideuva/2000/07/equity.htm*

51. Claire Kaplan, Coordinator of University of Virginia Sexual Assault Education Office, interview by Elizabeth L. Ihle, University of Virginia, April 5, 2003.

52. Hitchcock, 212.

53. Davie.

8

Coeducation but Not Equal Opportunity

Women Enter Boston College

Loretta Higgins

As a single-sex institution, Boston College was no different from the majority of Catholic schools in the late nineteenth and early twentieth centuries. Coeducation was not only frowned on, it was considered dangerous, as Pope Pius XI stated in his encyclical, "Christian Education of Youth," published in 1929. The hierarchical structure of the Catholic Church precluded individual Catholic schools from making decisions such as whether to become coeducational. Boston College, founded by the Jesuits, was no exception. It gradually adopted coeducation over a 50-year period, marginalizing women at first but finally allowing them full university citizenship.

Boston College, a premier Catholic university, had humble origins that date to 1863 when the Jesuit order founded what was little more than a glorified high school for the sons of Irish immigrants. Its roots as a school for men were deep and never questioned until 1919, when it established a graduate program in education that also admitted women. Father Augustine F. Hickey, supervisor of Boston Catholic schools, saw this program as a way to continue the education of the teaching nuns and proposed to Boston William Cardinal O'Connell, that Boston College offer 20 Saturday morning, off-campus lectures at Cathedral School Hall in Boston.[1] Cardinal O'Connell gave permission, beginning the slow and uneven path to coeducation at Boston College. The program exceeded all expectations when 700 nuns attended the classes, but it took until 1923 for Boston College to award college credits for the courses.

Over the next several decades, Boston College increased the presence of women, but only at the margins of university life. In the 1920s, in a complete break from tradition, the Jesuit authorities in Rome permitted women to take graduate education courses at the main campus, called the Heights. The first class began in June 1924, and although all the women were nuns and the classes were held in the summer just for women, it was a remarkable event. Although little noticed, on June 16, 1926, Boston College awarded a Master of Arts degree to Margaret Ursula Magrath, an alumna of Mount Holyoke College, who became the first woman to earn a degree from Boston College.[2] That the official bulletin of the Graduate School of Education described the school as "for men only" was an indication of the ambivalence toward education for women that continued at Boston College for the next five decades.[3]

The marginalization of women at Boston College reflected a conservative gender ideology prevalent in Catholicism, as well as much of American society, in the early twentieth century. When women won the vote in 1920 the doors of equal opportunity were not suddenly opened for them. Rather, women continued to be expected to marry and to give birth to replenish the loss of so many lives during World War I. Boston College administrators expressed many of these conservative views. For example, in a 1929 address to the League of Catholic Women at Emmanuel College, a local Catholic women's institution, Father Jones I. J. Corrigan, S.J., a Boston College ethics professor, castigated women who supported the Equal Rights Amendment and the National Woman's Party. "Nature," he asserted, "clearly meant woman to be man's partner, not his thwarted competitor," and "Not equal but superior rights for women is the highest social law." He said that those in favor of the amendment were "infected with the homehating virus of Russian Sovietism."[4]

As it expanded in the 1930s and 1940s, Boston College opened somewhat to women, but, as before, places women were allowed were peripheral to the main identity and location of the institution. In 1929, Boston College added an all-male law school, which in 1940 became coeducational.[5] The decision to admit women was puzzling, as Jesuit education was a predominantly male enterprise and the nearby Portia Law School was for women. Female attorneys were still rare; they had been denied entrance to the Massachusetts bar just a few years before, and the courts were upholding the exclusion.[6] The law school, apparently, admitted women in order to sustain enrollment during World War II.[7] After women were admitted, however, very little changed. Only one woman of the ten admitted in 1941 graduated. According to one publication, the women found the all-male environment uncomfortable, if not intolerable.[8] In 1936, Boston College established another postgraduate coeducational school: the School of Social Work. The motivation for the establishment of the school was the need for professionally trained social workers who would synthesize the "principles of Christian philosophy . . . with the various methods and techniques that had been developed in social work." It was hoped that the school would establish Catholic leaders in the field.[9]

Women, Nursing, and the Gender Ideal

A momentous event for the position of women at Boston College occurred in 1947, when the School of Nursing opened as the first undergraduate day school to admit women. Archbishop Richard Cushing of Boston was the power behind the nursing school, but the idea for it probably sprang from an undated, unsigned report that lamented the fact that the only two schools in New England providing college degrees in nursing were Yale and Simmons.[10] According to the report, the nursing profession was becoming more complex, and nurses needed to be educated in ethics as well as in physical care. The author worried that if Catholic nurses were not well educated, "they would no longer be an influential and important factor in the nursing situation in this area."[11] Women who were educated in non-Catholic schools, the report stated, faced a danger to faith and morals.

The opening of the School of Nursing under the direction of Anthony G. Carroll, S.J., the regent, barely caused a ripple in the university. In the fall of 1946, the student newspaper, *The Heights,* announced that a nursing school would be located on Newbury Street in downtown Boston, and it continued to report on the development of the new school with no fanfare or controversy.[12] According to the nursing school dean, Rita Kelleher, the Jesuits were generally supportive of the school and its students, while the lay faculty and undergraduates were less so.[13]

This muted response of the college community to the nursing school, from students to the board of trustees, seems surprising. The easy acceptance, however, was probably due to three factors that maintained separate spheres for men and women at Boston College. First, because nursing was a profession, it could not be incorporated into the College of Arts and Sciences. Second, the new school was off the main campus; the female students would not be seen around the Heights except for the few hours a week when they took their science laboratories. Third, nursing was a "female" occupation, not competitive with male pursuits. While perhaps not envisioned at the time, the opening of this school presaged a different direction for this once all-male institution.

Dean Kelleher saw some advantage in having a separate campus for the nursing school: although the students might have missed being at the Heights, the Newbury Street campus provided a cohesiveness and sense of community among the students and faculty.[14] One of the graduates of the first class, Geraldine Dowd, recalled that being downtown helped the students develop a sense of unity that made them feel like a big family.[15]

This distancing, however, extended to university activities, and nursing school administrators became advocates for women. In 1946, Father Carroll complained to the president of the university that nursing students were excluded from a variety of activities, including debating, the literary magazine, and the newspaper. He knew that Stephen Mulcahy, S.J., dean of the College of

Arts and Sciences, opposed female students' participation, but he argued that as many of these activities as possible should be made available "at least until the school is sufficiently large to support its own activities."[16] Father Carroll also sought equal privileges for female students. In 1947 he complained that nursing students were the only undergraduates who did not receive tickets to athletic contests.[17] In addition to being discriminatory, Father Carroll argued, this policy made the students feel as thought they were not "true students of Boston College." This was one opportunity for the university to make the female students less marginal. "Since . . . there are many University activities in which, as girls, they cannot participate but here is certainly one wherein they can be active without any difficulty being involved."[18]

Father Carroll also protested the marginalization of women in the campus media. On the surface, the media proclaimed that women were to be welcomed as equals. A January 1949, *Heights* editorial preached, "Let us think of Boston College as a university. . . . The students should make it a unified body of men and women."[19] In February an editorial entitled "Boston College—An Organism" stated, "Thus we should think of ourselves as sons of Boston College and the women in the School of Nursing as her daughters."[20] The sentiment was commendable, yet the editorial still implied a "we the men" and "they the women" attitude.

Women were marginalized in terms of staffing the campus media as well. Although the students' annual $24 fee included the *Boston College Stylus,* a literary magazine, as well as *The Heights,* the students complained that these publications seldom carried any news about the nursing school. A year later, in an issue of *The Heights* dedicated to the incoming freshmen, the deans of the College of Arts and Sciences and the School of Business Administration, the president of the university, and the student counselor—but not the dean of the School of Nursing—published welcome letters.[21] To compensate, some female students started their own newspaper and yearbook.[22] Since they could not join the University Glee Club, they had to pay for their own glee club. Because the activities fee did not support nursing school Catholic charity groups, those too were carried by the school.[23]

At the close of the 1940s Boston College had survived the crisis of World War II and had opened its first undergraduate day school for women. There is no indication administrators gave much thought to the impact of the nursing school on the university or whether the university was indeed making a commitment to the education of women. As the moving force behind the event, Archbishop Cushing was less interested in championing the education of women than he was in Catholic nurses taking leadership in Boston health care.[24] Administrators saw the School of Nursing as a separate academic unit, not merely geographically but also philosophically. The new regent and dean had more than enough to keep them busy developing a curriculum that would reflect a truly academic focus, rather than simply a three-year diploma school grafted to some liberal arts courses in a university setting. When nursing students faced exclusion, the nursing school fostered its own co-curricular activities. In an era before students exhibited militant attitudes, protests to injustices were seldom expressed or, if they were, often were dismissed. Militancy would have to await a new generation.

Women, Proximity, and the School of Education

"I was called in at a meeting, I believe of the Father Prefect of Studies and President, and told, just told, that we were going to start a School of Education," recalled Charles F. Donovan, S.J., the first dean of the new school.[25] That the decision was made in the early 1950s to open such a school was at once perfectly understandable and quite surprising. Boston College had long been involved in the education of teachers both at the graduate and undergraduate levels. Administrators believed that with the war over, education was going to be very important, and established the School of Education in time to graduate teachers who would serve the postwar "baby-boom children."

There is evidence that many students and faculty were against the School of Education. Six months before the decision to found the School of Education was publicly announced, a *Heights* reporter found that his peers were overwhelmingly against coeducation at Boston College. The students seemed to believe that coeducation would promote inattention to studies, and one said that "Women have their place in life and it's not at B.C."[26] There is no way of knowing how widespread these anti-coeducation feelings were, but such opinions were published with virtually no dissenting responses in subsequent issues of the paper. In addition to an environment that was opposed to coeducation, some believed that a school of education was inferior to a school of arts and sciences. Father Donovan recalled that there were more negative feelings about the value of a school of education than there were about having women students.[27]

While Father Donovan was an advocate for "this new type of student," he was also greatly concerned about the "reputation" of the women students. Because he saw as one of his roles the protection of these students from the antipathy of other faculty members, he became very strict about rules. Bobby sox and sneakers, for example, were an anathema, in that people from other schools on campus would sometimes ridicule "the bobby-soxers from the School of Education."[28] The length to which Father Donovan went to keep the school free of stain is exemplified in the following story. A group of women, sophomores in the School of Education, had gone to a school in a nearby town to observe a classroom. On the way home, they made what turned out to be an unwise decision: they stopped at a bar for a drink. Father Donovan learned about the indiscretion and made a difficult but speedy decision to dismiss all the young women involved. The unpopular decision stood in the face of much parental pressure.[29]

While some faculty had reservations about the presence of women, many were won over by the academic ability of the education students. In order to establish an excellent reputation for the fledgling school, these students were screened as no group ever was before. They received individual attention and the faculty carefully scrutinized their progress. The teachers who were graduated had to be "the most professionally competent" group. Even the lay faculty, whose members had more trouble accepting the new students than the Jesuit professors, became respectful of the academic ability of the education majors when they began taking electives in the College of Arts and Sciences. English professor John Fitzgerald believed that nothing as "drastic or wonderful" had happened at Boston College since the founding of the School of Education brought women to the Heights. The students, commented another faculty member, were "as good or better than the boy English majors."[30]

Women at the Fringes of Campus Culture, the 1950s and 1960s

Some attitudes on campus served to thwart the cause of women's equality and prolonged the acceptance of women as partners in education. Women were portrayed as sex objects, mindless playthings for the amusement of men, which did not fit with the image of an idealistic Catholic institution. A German professor praised the "coeds" in the Schools of Nursing and Education and told the men that the women would make fine wives.[31] He discussed how important the education of women was for society, but even this staunch advocate never talked about the benefits of education for the individual woman.[32]

Male student reaction was mixed. Some were supportive, some contemptuous; sometimes they expressed their feelings with tinges of sexual anxiety. The student weekly newspaper published a number of sexist articles; "How to Date a Co-ed" numbered the dating procedure from one to six with number one selecting a "specimen." The beginner was advised to begin with a "not-too-beautiful specimen" and progress to prettier ones as basic skills improved. *The Heights* reprinted "an analysis of the creature known as woman seen through the eyes of the chemist" that originally appeared in the *Chem Bulletin.* It described woman as an "unstable element."[33] Students sometimes expressed outright hostility toward women. One male student, queried by a *Heights* reporter about the women on campus, said that having girls at the university would be detrimental in the long run because "our prestige will suffer from it. We'll come to be known as just another college." He continued that it was not in the Boston College tradition to "have these mantraps draped all over the campus." Others said that they would not have gone to BC had they known that women were to be admitted.[34] These comments in the school newspaper prompted a flurry of responses both pro and con to the polemic about women on campus.

When the School of Education opened in September 1952, a honeymoon period ensued. The dean of women believed that the university community was happy to have the teachers as part of it.[35] The women in the School of Education did not have all the privileges accorded to the male students in the other undergraduate programs, but they were so pleased to be at Boston College that their school spirit was high and they were happy with the institution.[36] The School of Education's Women's Council, comprised of three students from each class, began to publicize problems that concerned female students. They complained that women were subjected to "cat-calls and warhoops" in all areas of the campus. The men put laboratory specimens on the women's lunch trays. They played practical jokes.[37] Even the issue of cheerleading took on symbolic importance, and women deans discussed whether female cheerleaders would hurt the image of Boston College women.[38]

Women were being integrated slowly into activities. A breakthrough of sorts occurred in the spring of 1955 when, for the first time in the history of *The Heights,* a woman became an editor. She joined the managing board as co-feature editor, and her election made front-page news in an article that sounded upbeat and positive.[39] However, one year later it was back to the status quo with an all-male board. Even though they were generally greatly outnumbered, women were beginning to be represented on the committees that planned class and school activities. In 1955, the junior week chairmen consisted of one woman and eight men; by 1957 the ratio was four women to fifteen men. Similarly, the prom committees of the other classes reflected inroads made by women.[40]

These modest gains were tempered by the lack of integration of female students in many of the university activities. Each school had its own glee club, though the clubs occasionally gave joint concerts.[41] It was not until 1956 that the Schools of Nursing, Education, and Intown were represented in the yearbook, the *Sub Turri.* For years, the Drama Society had to call on women from surrounding Catholic women's colleges to play women's parts in productions. Needless to say, when women became part of the Boston College day community, they were invited to become members of the society. It was School of Nursing dean Rita Kelleher's perception, however, that her students were more involved in making costumes and in backstage work than in acting.[42]

In addition to the problem of slow integration into campus activities, women at Boston College were faced with the larger problems that loomed as insurmountable barriers to equality for many years. Their housing was subpar and it was difficult for them to take part in liberal arts courses. These problems were recognized in the mid-1950s, but their solutions would wait for many years.

While insufficient housing at Boston College remains a problem to this day, in the 1950s and 1960s women were most affected by inadequate or unavailable living facilities. Dean Kelleher described female students' housing, located in apartments about a half-mile from campus, as "terrible, terrible." Since they were all that Boston College was offering, the students had a choice of commuting, not going to Boston College, or living in the apartments. Kelleher believed that the inadequate housing for women hurt School of Nursing recruitment efforts and that many of the potential students probably ended up at the Georgetown University School of Nursing, "our competitors." As for those who did come, Kelleher commented, "They wanted to go to BC very badly to come up and put up with the housing up here."[43]

As an alternative to university housing, female students were sometimes placed in private homes owned by women who lived alone and rented rooms, sometimes as far as a mile from the campus. Alumnae later laughed at the Boston College recruiting materials that described a "brisk walk," which was a path around a reservoir, windy even in the best of weather.[44]

In addition to housing problems, the dean of the School of Nursing had ongoing problems with finding suitable teachers for her students. While appointing faculty for the nursing courses in the nursing major was not a problem, it was difficult to find faculty to teach the liberal arts courses that were required. Until 1954, the regents of the various schools were responsible for securing faculty from the College of Arts and Sciences to teach necessary courses for their students. When the regent system ended, it became the responsibility of the dean to obtain teachers. It had been the custom for the professors to teach courses for nursing students at the Newbury Street campus. The students went to the main campus only for their science laboratories. According to Dean Kelleher, the Jesuits at the highest levels of administration were always helpful and supportive, but the chairmen of departments and even the dean of the College of Arts and Sciences could be obstructionist. She had to negotiate individually with each one of them for the teachers that she needed. The chemistry and sociology departments were particularly uncooperative, leaving the responsibility to find part-time teachers to the dean. When she complained to a faculty member about the sociology department not caring about the qualifications of the person teaching sociology to nursing students, the professor did not think it was a problem because he did not consider the degree from the School of Nursing a true Boston College degree.[45] One woman who was a nursing student in the 1960s recalled that "everybody knew that the School of Nursing" received "the worst or the beginning English teachers."[46]

Despite the problems surrounding women's education, the mood was optimistic. Mary Kinnane, dean of women from the mid-1950s to the mid-1960s, recalled that the faculty and students in the School of Education developed a close bond "of a family nature." She described those early years as a "pioneering period for all women at BC." She believed that although women were unhappy at times because of inequitable treatment, they could not afford to dwell on the negative aspects because that would interfere with moving forward. Women "built where they could . . . a lot of it was discrete, waiting for the right time. . . . One could not impose anything, and one worked within the system."[47]

A Brief Coeducational Experiment

It is unclear if the university administrators were unaware of the problems that were confronting the women on campus or if they discounted the seriousness of the issues. Rather than dealing with those issues, the university experimented with coeducation when it announced in 1959 that a limited number of highly qualified female undergraduate students would be admitted to the School of Education and take courses in the College of Arts and Sciences. Ultimately, however, this brief experiment would fail when Jesuit authorities outside the university ordered that it end.

There was initial jurisdictional controversy over the coeducational experiment. William R. E. Casey, S.J., dean of the College of Arts and Sciences, queried the rector, Michael Walsh, S.J., regarding who would have jurisdiction over the "talented girls in the SOE [School of Education]." The women were to be registered under the auspices of the School of Education because Boston College did not have permission to enroll women in liberal arts.[48] Apparently, Father Donovan was concerned that the university was using the School of Education to introduce coeducation surreptitiously into the College of Arts and Sciences. He also feared that the best applicants to the School of Education would be "raided" by the "Special Program."[49] In response to these concerns, the president stipulated exceedingly strict criteria for the admission of women into the special programs and to the honors program. No more than 15 percent of the women entering the School of Education in any one year were to be selected for special programs. Their scores on the College Board entrance examination would need to be 650, or over 700 for admission to honors.[50]

Poor housing continued to plague Boston College women. The director of admissions expressed anger that there was a problem with housing for women. He complained to the president that "[T]wo very brilliant girls" had applied and he was fearful of losing them for lack of housing. He suggested that the women be admitted directly into the College of Arts and Sciences and that someone should be appointed to position of director of women's housing.[51] While squabbles over the jurisdiction of the women and adequate housing continued, a new obstacle appeared, one that would ultimately undermine the brief experiment with coeducation: disapproval from authorities in the Jesuit hierarchy.

While the small experiment in coeducation was disguised in part by technically registering the students in the School of Education, the alert New England provincial, James E. Coleran, S.J., recognized that this posed a challenge to the tradition of educating men. Rev. Coleran wrote to BC president Michael Walsh, S.J. and expressed his grave concerns. President Walsh responded that he had intended to ask the father general for permission and reassured Rev. Coleran that "this variation concerned only six girls" and that he had planned to write for Coleran's approval in the fall.[52] Furthermore, Father Walsh apologized that the "matter got somewhat out of hand" but said he "would appreciate it very much if we could allow these young ladies to follow the arrangement we have made because of the commitments Father Walsh made to them." He pleaded that in the future Boston College be allowed to admit women into the College of Arts and Sciences honors program.[53]

In a subsequent letter, the president sent the provincial a formal request for permission "to allow Boston College to accept a limited number of academically talented Catholic young women into the College of Arts and Sciences." President Walsh then referred to Pope Pius XII, who had expressed his belief that talented and influential Catholic women had an important part to play in the public, intellectual, and professional life of a nation. He used the same arguments that had been used in the late 1930s by some of the members of the Jesuit Educational Association.[54] Boston College, he argued, often received inquiries from women about enrolling in the College of Arts and Sciences. These were women who did not want "a specialized vocational school" (the School of Nursing), nor did they want to take education courses. Because they were interested in careers requiring a strong mathematical or science background, other Catholic institutions in New England were not suitable. Lastly, since students in the School of Education were already taking courses in liberal arts, why not just make it official, Father Walsh asked?[55]

In a subsequent letter, Father Coleran dealt the crushing blow: in no uncertain terms, the provincial ended the plan for women before it began. He agreed that the women who had already been accepted for September be admitted but warned that the program must discontinue. Father Coleran made it clear that he would not discuss the issue with the Jesuit general, but suggested that if Father Walsh desired to do so he would not stand in the way, although he doubted it "would do any good."[56]

So did the program for women in the College of Arts and Sciences end. Had it continued, the official integration of women might have occurred sooner than 1970. The correspondence of the Jesuit administrators at Boston College showed that while some Jesuits at Boston College were in favor of experimenting with coeducation, the provincial was not, and without the strong hierarchical support needed for approval of such decisions, the issue of coeducation was halted.

Women, Coeducation, and the 1960s

Although the 1960s would bring dramatic changes to campus culture and university life and begin a move toward greater equity for women at Boston College, the decade began with several lingering inequities, particularly in housing, health care, and the in loco parentis policy.

Housing for women was a recurring challenge that plagued the university. The inequities were enormous. Professor Mary Kinnane, then dean of women, recalled that she and nursing dean Rita Kelleher "made our annual pilgrimage to Father Michael Walsh to try to establish housing for women." During one period of its history, the School of Education was housing its women students in 28 different places, but "we built residence halls for men."[57] The dormitory issues continued to be aired in the pages of *The Heights*, where stories exposed the lack of privacy, no place to entertain guests, inadequate bathroom facilities, poor food, cold rooms, and no option to live in off-campus housing that was not controlled by Boston College.[58] Another reporter stated that, "A BC girl is, in all things, supposed to be incapable of taking care of herself."[59]

Health services for women were inequitable. During the day, nurses and doctors cared for both men and women. If a woman was ill, however, she was not admitted to the infirmary, she was sent back to her "mini dorm" where the housemother cared for her. If a student became ill at her residence, transportation to the Boston College Health Center sometimes became a problem.[60]

As at many other institutions, the in loco parentis policy was more for women than for men, seemingly in an attempt to protect them from danger and to reinforce the popular standards of womanly behavior. A mid-1960s handbook for resident women provides a picture of the rules and regulations that governed the lives of Boston College women. The introduction stressed that the rules were to keep the women safe, ensure optimal study conditions, and protect them from "untidy or thoughtless housemates." The student was admonished to "maintain standards of conduct befitting a Catholic college woman."[61] Some rules did not seem to make sense. Women, for example, had ten o'clock curfews with "lates" given for basketball games but not for studying at the library.[62] At a Jesuit Educational Association Workshop held in 1965 the speaker said that women needed "sensible house rules which make it possible for them to be comfortable rather than feel that they must always be on their guard at every moment."[63]

The Boston College administration took a step toward placating women students when they hired Ann Flynn as assistant dean of women. Flynn was an activist who criticized Boston College for segregating women in the nursing and education schools. She changed some of the unpopular residency rules, tried to improve the women's food situation, and worked, with some success, to improve the dormitory situation for women.[64] Most women had been moved out of private residences to apartments located about one mile from campus.[65]

The Path to Coeducation

Female students took the initial step toward full coeducation at Boston College. In 1966 two women from the School of Education circulated a petition asking that women be admitted to the College of Arts and Sciences.[66] By March 1967, the organizers of the drive to make Boston College totally coeducational placed the 1,500-signature petition in the president's hands. *The Heights* supported such a change: "The official policy of the college of Arts & Sciences is still based on a medieval distinction between the sexes. We have moved into the 20th century in theology and philosophy, but biologically we are still in the middle ages. The capabilities of women have elsewhere long been proved, but at BC they have yet to be recognized."[67]

Others on campus supported coeducation. In a letter to *The Heights,* Boston College's soon-to-be-famous feminist author and philosopher, Assistant Professor Mary Daly, supported coeducation in the College of Arts and Sciences. It was absurd, she pointed out, to have female professors in a school where female students were not allowed. She criticized a culture that erects "artificial barriers" for certain people while congratulating those who have managed to overcome those same barriers, giving the appearance of liberalism but in reality perpetrating oppression. She hoped that the university would embrace coeducation, which would promote understanding between the sexes and move beyond a "dehumanizing biologism and toward the recognition of personalist values, not in words and images only, but also in fact."[68] The Education Policy Committee of the College of Arts and Sciences recommended the admission of "girls" to the college in the near future. Their report suggested that commuter "girls" be admitted, thus "dismissing one of the major obstacles to admission of girls by next fall."[69]

While many students and faculty were supportive of education, there were others who were not. The Education Policy Committee acknowledged several arguments against the admission of female students: "men are better alumni donors, men whose spaces are taken by girls are subject to the draft, and educational performance is better without the distractions created by having girls in the classroom."[70]

In spite of the arguments against full coeducation, in March 1969 the University Academic Senate approved a motion "that Boston College be completely co-educational in all undergraduate schools with the entering class in the fall of 1970."[71] To the surprise of many, including members of the senate, the decision caused no dissent on campus.[72]

The university was suddenly swept along by the tide of coeducation. Boston College purchased the rented apartments that had served as dormitories and students began rallying for coeducational dormitories.[73] This seemed like an incredibly radical idea at a university where only a few decades before many opposed men and women sharing classrooms.

Women were very eager to attend Boston College. The immediate result of full coeducation was an applicant pool twice the size that it was before coeducation. The percentage of women students grew from 27 percent the year before full coeducation, to 31 percent in 1970, 52 percent in 1975 and 55 percent in 2000.[74] These increased numbers meant a more highly selective student body. In addition, the number of dormitory beds tripled during the next 20 years. It was a welcome change, but Boston College struggled with questions of propriety relating to coeducational dorms and the fast-fading philosophy of in loco parentis.[75]

Coeducation, Militancy, and Feminism

As the 1970s began, Boston College was no exception to the spirit of militancy on college campuses. The conflict in Vietnam became both symbol and catalyst. The students had won the battle for coeducation and now were ready to fight for other issues. In 1970, after full coeducation, the homecoming queen contest was abolished on the grounds that it was sexist.[76] The college fired the popular dean of women who stated that "Women pay the same tuition as men do but Boston College doesn't provide the same services."[77] The firing seemed to mobilize women, who protested by occupying the offices of the vice president for student affairs and the dean of students.[78] At a subsequent rally, the speakers reiterated the demands that had been made to the president:

1.   Another counselor for women, to raise the total to two for 1810 women.
2.   The faculty locker and shower room would become a facility for female faculty and students.
3.   More lights on middle and upper campus.
4.   A bus for nursing students to an inner city hospital.
5.   An experimental gynecological clinic to be financed from the present infirmary budget.
6.   A slot for a woman in Student Affairs Administration.
7.   A library of material pertinent to women's rights.
8.   Facilities for women at the recreation complex.[79]

Nursing school dean Rita Kelleher recalled that although she "thoroughly disapproved" of many of the things that the protesting students were doing, they were able to accomplish what had eluded her for years.[80]

To address the changing roles of women on campus, Boston College administrators created two committees, the Women's Affairs Committee and the Committee on the Role of Women (COROW). The COROW report, published in 1972, reiterated what a good number of the concerned members of the Boston College community had been saying for a long time: that in the area of physical facilities, the university was eminently more suited to male than to female students. The athletic facilities, infirmaries, dormitories, and washrooms were inadequate and improperly equipped for women. The committee hypothesized that the institution's history as all male probably helped explain these inadequacies.[81] With the exception of athletic scholarships, which were not available to women, no discrimination was found in financial aid. The report listed a group of university services in which women were underrepresented. Among them were the counseling services, the placement office, health services, and athletics. Few women appeared as officers in student organizations. There was a disproportionate number of women in nursing and of men in management.[82]

In retrospect, the opening of the Women's Center in 1973 was a watershed event. Its purpose was to provide a place for students, faculty, and staff to go for "general advice, information, reading material, or a place to talk and work with other women."[83] More than 200 members of the Boston College community attended the first-day festivities. The optimism accompanying that event was short lived, however. The center began to experience harassment: pornographic literature was slipped under its door, its public notices were destroyed at night, and pictures demeaning to women were cemented to the door of the center.[84]

Boston College Absorbs a Catholic Women's College

When colleges and universities that had previously been for men, started becoming coeducational, Catholic colleges for women began a decline. Applications decreased as more women chose to go to coeducational schools. The demise of women's colleges was occurring at a rapid rate between the years 1960 and 1975. Newton College, formerly Newton College of the Sacred Heart, became one of those statistics when it was acquired by Boston College. According to Marie McHugh, who was chair of the humanities division at Newton at the time, the news of the takeover was a "shock." "Because no one had any inkling, at least below the higher administrative level, that it was going to happen."[85] The two institutions, separated by only a mile, had not had a thriving relationship. The students at Newton were very loyal to their school, considering it a better place than Boston College.[86] The secrecy surrounding the acquisition continued during the integration of the Newton students. The department chairs at both institutions were told not to contact each other because all negotiations were to be done at the presidential level. The lingering impression about the takeover was that Boston College was thrilled to be acquiring 735 dormitory beds and that "the facilities were the most important part of the College."[87] Mary McCay, a feminist professor of English at Newton, compared the closing of the college due to lack of funds to Virginia Woolf's analysis in "A Room of One's Own" of women's difficulties in remaining independent.[88]

The First Generation of Coeducation

Coeducation advanced rapidly as the number of women students rose quickly. In 1975, the entering class of Boston College comprised 1,069 women and 962 men, with the student body at 4,779 women and 5,065 men; this, in just five years of full coeducation.[89] The numbers at BC followed national trends, with more women than men enrolled in colleges and universities.[90]

In academics, authors of a study of Boston College concluded that the university was acting as Jo Freeman's "null environment." According to Freeman, a null environment in education "neither encourages nor discourages students of either sex." Women experience disadvantages in such an environment because they need encouragement to counteract their previous socialization that women's roles are limited. The men and women had identical grade point averages, but women reported less involvement in class discussions. The men, even when totally unprepared for class, held forth and counted on "improvisation, luck, and gall to get them through," unlike the women who talked in class only when they had prepared and were convinced that they were right.[91] There was little indication that women were actively discouraged from seeking careers, but neither was there an atmosphere of strong support or encouragement for such goals.

Women students have assumed leadership of major organizations such as the Undergraduate Government of Boston College since 1981 when Joanne Caruso became the first female president. Since 1993 women have led that organization as president about 30 percent of the time, and as editors of *The Heights*, about 30 percent of the time. Women have almost exclusively been editors or co-editors of the yearbook, *Sub Turri*.[92]

Other indicators that women were becoming an integral part of campus life were the increase in the number of varsity sports for women. In 1976, there were 7 women's and 12 men's teams; by 1978, there were 12 varsity teams for women, compared to 14 for men. In 2000, there were nine women's varsity teams and eight men's teams. More men than women participated in athletics, however. In 2000, 451 men and 318 women were varsity athletes while 3,638 men and 703 women played intramural sports.[93]

Through the years as the number of women students increased, so did the number of women faculty members, but not dramatically. In 1976, women made up 25 percent of the faculty. In 2000, that had increased to 34 percent.[94] As at other universities, women's representation increased at the lower faculty ranks: 18 percent of full professors, 29 percent of associate professors, 48 percent of assistant professors, and 36 percent of instructors.

Over time, women are advancing into the ranks of Boston College administrators. In 1981, women were only 2 of 11 assistant and associate deans; in 2002, women were in the majority at 9 of 14. The chief academic officers, including deans and the university librarian numbered 11 in 1981, of whom three were women. In 1994 two of ten chief academic officers were women; and in 2002 three out of ten officers were. Although the number of vice presidents increased from seven in 1981 to ten in 2002, the number of women holding these positions has not risen above two in any given year.[95]

Women's representation on the board of trustees has increased somewhat. For over two decades the Board of Trustees of Boston College has comprised approximately 40 members, with the number of women staying fairly constant at 14 to 17 percent since 1993, increasing from 13 percent in 1983 and 6 percent in 1988.[96]

The iconography on campus is predominantly male. Many of the older buildings of Boston College are named after Jesuits who had served as president. For example, Gasson Hall, named for the thirteenth president under whose administration the Chestnut Hill site became the new home of Boston College. Bapst Library was named for the first president of Boston College. Many of the newer buildings are named for benefactors of Boston College—Robsham Theater, Vanderslice Hall, Cushing Hall. Still other buildings are named for those whom Boston College wished to honor. At least two of more than 80 buildings are named for women. Bourneuf House honors economist Alice E. Bourneuf, who was the first woman faculty member in the College of Arts and Sciences, hired in 1959.[97] The Thea Bowman AHANA Center was named for Sister Thea Bowman, who was granted an honorary degree by Boston College in 1989 because of her work as a black Catholic leader.[98]

Since 1973 the campus has also become more diverse. Boston College has significantly increased the number of applications and enrollments of minority students.[99] From 1999 to 2002 they grew 10 percent each year; in 2003 they rose by 16 percent. As at many other Catholic campuses, Boston College does not fully recognize or support gay and lesbian groups. Boston College's anti-discrimination statement does not include sexual orientation. This has been a bone of contention between gay and lesbian students and the administration. In addition, Boston College has denied several petitions by the organization of Lesbian, Gay, and Bisexual Community at Boston College to gain official status as a student organization, but in 2003 the Gay-Straight Alliance was accepted as an "official" university group. A group of faculty and administrators led by the dean for student development meets regularly with students to support gay students.[100] The undergraduate student government has a Gay, Lesbian, Bisexual, and Transgender Issues Department, which focuses on educating and informing the college community on the issues facing gay, lesbian, and bisexual students.[101]

Women's issues receive attention through the women's studies program and the women's center. Boston College offers an interdisciplinary minor in women's studies, consisting of two required courses plus four additional courses chosen from an array of more than 40 courses representing many different disciplines. Approximately 15 students are enrolled as "minors," but many more take women's studies courses.

The Women's Resource Center celebrated its thirtieth anniversary on March 12, 2003. It is located in the student union building and, since 2002, has its first permanent director. Previously, a graduate student who worked part-time and usually had the position for one year held the position of director, leading to fragmentation of programming. The center has changed through the years. In the 1990s it was seen as a place that was friendly only to angry feminists. The staff tried to make it more welcoming to all women and to interest more women of color in its programs. The center has a large advisory board made up of people from all aspects of campus life, men and women alike, although predominantly women. The center holds classes, hosts support groups, does community service, and often co-sponsors speakers with other campus groups.

In the twenty-first century, women seem to have conquered the Heights. They have held the highest offices in the student government; are excelling in varsity athletics; are active in every area of the university including the arts, volunteering, assisting with faculty research; and have achieved success in all disciplines.

It took 107 years for Boston College to become fully coeducational. The struggle often extended beyond the college walls and into the Catholic hierarchies. When the university admitted women, there were few plans for integrating them into the life of the institution and no declaration of beliefs about the rights of women to equal education. Despite the lack of planning and in spite of objections from the Jesuit hierarchy and Catholic beliefs about the role of women, it is likely that Boston College provided a great service to women.

Notes

1.   David R. Dunigan, *A History of Boston College* (Milwaukee: The Bruce Publishing Company, 1947), 247.
2.   *The Pilot* (Boston), 30 September 1983, 4.
3.   Dunigan, 248.

4. "Father Corrigan, S.J., Deplores the National Woman's Party," *The Heights*, February 19, 1929, 1.

5. Todd F. Simon, *Boston College Law School after Fifty Years: An Informal History, 1929–1979* (Boston: Boston College Law School, 1980), 1–7.

6. Ibid, 19.

7. Charles F. Donovan, interview by Loretta Higgins, Boston College, February 17, 1984.

8. Simon, 19.

9. Walter McGuinn, "Boston College Announces the Opening of a School of Social Work," April 4, 1936, file 11.17, Boston College Archives (BCA). Charles F. Donovan, David R. Dunigan, and Paul A. FitzGerald, *History of Boston College: From the Beginnings to 1990* (Chestnut Hill, Mass.: University Press of Boston College, 1990), 170.

10. "Brief Concerning the Establishment of a Catholic School for the Higher Education of Nurses within the Area of Metropolitan Boston," Nursing box A 12, file 11.20, BCA.

11. Ibid.

12. "Mary Maher Appointed Dean of School of Nursing," *The Heights*, February 7, 1947, 1, 5.

13. Rita P. Kelleher, interview by Loretta Higgins, Hingham, Mass., February 14, 1984.

14. Ibid.

15. Geraldine Dowd, "Being a Graduate of the First Class in the School of Nursing," interview by Rita Kelleher, 1975, Audio-cassette number 712, Kennedy Resource Center, Boston College School of Nursing.

16. Anthony G. Carroll, "Letter to Father Rector," September 20, 1946, Nursing box A 12, file 11.20, BCA.

17. Anthony G. Carroll to William L. Keleher, September 16, 1947, Nursing box A 12, file 11.20, BCA.

18. Ibid.

19. Editorial, *The Heights*, January 28, 1949, 4.

20. "Boston College—An Organism," *The Heights*, February 18, 1949, 1.

21. *The Heights*, September 15, 1950, 1.

22. Kelleher interview.

23. Anthony G. Carroll to Treasurer of Boston College, June 3, 1948, Nursing box A 12, file 11.20, BCA.

24. Dowd interview.

25. Donovan interview.

26. Jack Moylan, "Should BC Go Co-Ed?" *The Heights*, February 26, 1951, 5.

27. Donovan interview.

28. Ibid.

29. Ibid.

30. John J. Fitzgerald, interview by Loretta Higgins, Chestnut Hill, Mass., November 22, 1985.

31. Bill Dextrage, "An Interview with Rev. Paul McManus," *The Heights*, November 6, 1953, 5.

32. Ibid.

33. Phil Dobbyn, "Exchange News," *The Heights*, March 11, 1955, 3.

34. Leon Lewis, "The Question," *The Heights*, November 7, 1952, 5.

35. Leon Lewis, "The Question," *The Heights*, October 31, 1952, 5.

36. Fitzgerald interview.

37. Anne Marie Faria and Ann Dewire, "Wee Men, Wee Minds," *The Heights*, November 8, 1957, 5.

38. Kelleher; Mary Kinnane, interview by Loretta Higgins, Boston College, February 12, 1986.

39. "Kay Donovan Elected First Woman Editor," *The Heights*, March 25, 1955, 1.

40. *The Heights*, April 22, 1955, 1; April 13, 1956, 1; April 20, 1956, 1 and 3; 27 April 1956, 1.

41. Sheila Mullen, "Tower to Town," *The Heights*, March 29, 1957, 4.

42. Kelleher interview.

43. Ibid.

44. Donovan interview.

45. Kelleher interview.

46. JoAnne Regan, interview by Loretta Higgins, Boston College, October 10, 1984.

47. Kinnane interview.

48. William V. E. Casey to Reverend Father Rector, November 4, 1958, box 11, file 3.22, BCA.

49. Charles F. Donovan to Michael Walsh, November 8, 1958, box 11, file 3.11, BCA.

50. Michael Walsh to Edmond Walsh, November 28, 1958, box 11, file 3.11, BCA.

51. Edmond D. Walsh to Michael P. Walsh, April 14, 1959, box 11, file 3.22, BCA.

52. Michael Walsh to James E. Coleran, June 2, 1959, box 11, file 3.22, BCA.

53. Michael Walsh to James E. Coleran, June 10, 1959, box 11, file 3.22, BCA.

54. Michael Walsh to James E. Coleran, July 15, 1959, box 11, file 3.22, BCA.

55. Ibid.

56. James E. Coleran to Michael Walsh, August 14, 1959, box 11, file 3.22, BCA.

57. Kinnane interview.

58. Elizabeth Donnelly, "Case for Apartments," *The Heights*, October 8, 1965, 10.

59. Michael Egger, "As I See It," *The Heights*, December 3, 1965, 5 and 7.

60. Tom Hughes and Denis Vaughn, "The Women's Residence Situation at Boston College," *The Heights*, April 17, 1963, 4.

61. George L. Drury, Edward J. Hanrahan, and Marion A. Mahoney, *Resident Women's Handbook* (Chestnut Hill, Mass.: Boston College, 1966–1967), 4.

62. Hughes and Vaughn, 4–5.

63. Mary Alice Cannon, "The Place of the Woman Student on the Jesuit Campus," in *Jesuit Educational Association Workshop Proceedings*, ed. G. Gordon Henderson (New York: Jesuit Educational Association, 1965), 427.

64. Janet Cameron-Barry, interview by Loretta Higgins, Marlborough, Mass., August 21, 1984.

65. Kevin Lynch, "Woman with a Problem," *The Heights*, July 19, 1968, 4.

66. Janice M. Basile, "Education Coeds Seek Admission into A & S," *The Heights*, October 21, 1966, 1 and 8.

67. "20th Century Biology," *The Heights*, October 28, 1966, 6.

68. Mary F. Daly "Letter to the Editor," *The Heights*, November 4, 1966, 8.

69. Vern Humbert, "Girls in A & S, Where Are They Now?" *The Heights*, March 3, 1967, 5.
70. Ibid.
71. Michael Berkey, "UAS: Yes to Girls, Theo Cut—No to Motion on Dr. Daly," *The Heights*, March 25, 1969, 1.
72. "Report of the Senate Committee on Admissions and Academic Standards," Boston College, April 11, 1969, RG 16, SG 16-26, BCA.
73. "Liberate the Latent Cell Blocks," *The Heights*, September 23, 1969, 6.
74. *Boston College Fact Book*, 1969, 1970, 1975, 2000, BCA.
75. Donovan, Dunigan, and Fitzgerald, 368.
76. Dave Muething, "UGBC Votes Homecoming Queen Contest Sexist," *The Heights*, October 28, 1970, 5.
77. Chris Campos, "Ann Flynn Fired; Dean of Women Position Abolished," *The Heights*, March 9, 1971, 8.
78. Mary Lou Doherty, "Women's Action Committee Occupies VP, Dean's Offices," *The Heights*, March 19, 1971.
79. "Little Women," *The Heights*, March 19, 1971, 4.
80. Kelleher interview.
81. Jolane Solomon and James L. Bowditch, "Report to the President of the Role of Women at Boston College," 12–15, BCA.
82. Ibid., 5 and 7.
83. Maureen Dezell, "Commentary: Women's Center," *The Heights*, February 27, 1973.
84. Maureen Dezell, "Women's Center Harassed," *The Heights*, March 18, 1974, 5.
85. Marie McHugh, interview by Loretta Higgins, Chestnut Hill, Mass., February 21, 1984.
86. Ibid.
87. Ibid.
88. Mary McCay, "Closing of Newton Limits Women's Choice in Education," *The Heights*, March 24, 1975, 4.
89. *Boston College Fact Book*, 1982–1983, 16, BCA.
90. Christopher Jencks and David Riesman, *The Academic Revolution* (Garden City, N.Y.: Doubleday, 1968), 301.
91. Sharlene Hess-Biber and Joan McGregor Gosselin, "Career and Lifestyle Aspirations of Boston College Undergraduates," 1982, 5, in author's possession. Jo Freeman, "How to Discriminate Against Women Without Really Trying," in *Women: A Feminist Perspective*, ed. Jo Freeman (Palo Alto, Calif.: Mayfield, 1975).
92. *Sub Turri*, 1992–2002, BCA.
93. Boston College self-study for accreditation, January 1997, Appendix C, n.p., Office of the President of Boston College.
94. *Boston College Fact Book*, 1976, 15, 35; 1978–1979, 11, 22, BCA; 1992–93, 2000, and 2001, available at *http://www.bc.edu/publications/factbook/*.
95. *Boston College Catalog*, 1981–82, 136; 1987–88, 122; 1994–95, 125; 1998–99, 341; 2002–03, 341, BCA.
96. Ibid.
97. Donovan, Dunigan, and FitzGerald, 458.

98. Ibid., 514.
99. See Alex Timiraos, "Nursing AHANA Numbers Increase for 2007," *The Heights*, February 25, 2003, 1.
100. Personal files, Loretta P. Higgins, associate dean, Boston College School of Nursing, Newton, Mass.
101. Office of the Dean for Student Development, *Boston College Student Life Guide, 2002–2003*, 36.

Structural Issues

Although coeducation seemed to be "in the air" by the late 1960s, some men's colleges found it easier than others did to make the decision to admit women. In Chapter 9, Poulson compares two institutions that differed in this regard: the public university, Rutgers, in New Brunswick, New Jersey, and the Catholic university, Georgetown, in Washington, D.C. Poulson shows how the need at Rutgers to placate internal constituencies, particularly those associated with the university's women's college, Douglass, slowed decision-making. At Georgetown, in contrast, the centralized administration, and the fact that the other four undergraduate colleges at the university already admitted women, facilitated the 1968 decision to admit women to the liberal arts college. Poulson's discussion of changes in the two campus's climates once coeducation was established makes it clear that although there are similarities from one type of institution to another, there are also differences depending on such factors as whether the university is religious or secular, private or public.

Hamilton College was a conservative men's college for more than 150 years before it decided in 1968 to found an innovative women's college, Kirkland, as its coordinate. In Chapter 10 Miller-Bernal discusses the reasons for this seemingly surprising development, as well as the consequences for women when, a decade later, Hamilton College took over its coordinate to become a coeducational college. The sense of identity and entitlement that women, both faculty and students, developed in their own college enabled them to press for and obtain concessions in the newly coeducational Hamilton. Thus coordination, established in large part to appease male students and alumni by avoiding full coeducation, had unanticipated positive benefits.

9

A Religious and a Public University

The Transitions to Coeducation at Georgetown and Rutgers

Susan L. Poulson

Like many other colleges and universities in the country, Georgetown and Rutgers Universities admitted women to their Colleges of Arts and Sciences for the first time in the late 1960s and early 1970s. Yet the reasons they adopted coeducation differed because of their public and private status and their internal constituencies. Their preparation for coeducation, however, was largely similar in that both had a narrow conception of how to welcome women. The history of coeducation is filled with examples of admitting women with little change to an existing campus culture, but at Georgetown and Rutgers the arrival of women students during a period of changing gender ideals in American society spawned a student culture that blurred traditional gender norms and roles.

The Reasons for Going Coed

Georgetown and Rutgers felt the same pressures to admit women that prevailed throughout American higher education in the 1960s and 1970s. The political climate made it increasingly unpopular to exclude any group merely on the basis of social distinction. The civil rights movement prompted many Americans to question the traditional social order. As one Rutgers College professor commented: "It is wrong for blacks to be segregated from whites, and it is just as wrong for whites to be segregated rom [*sic*] whites. Women should have the right to attend any college, and not be discriminated against because of their sex."[1] Faculty members favored coeducation for another reason: tuition benefits for their daughters. They enjoyed free tuition for their offspring, but the single-sex nature of the institution meant that only their sons could gain access to the colleges.[2]

Administrators were aware that the majority of male students wanted coeducation. A 1968 poll of male secondary students indicated that 78 percent favored coeducational colleges while only 5 percent preferred single-sex schools. A 1969 Notre Dame study of its own students found that nearly a third of students who were accepted but did not enroll cited its single-sex status as the reason, and 72 percent of Notre Dame students indicated that they had thought about transferring to a coeducational school.[3] When pollsters asked Princeton students "If Princeton were to remain all-male, would you advise an academically qualified younger brother to accept admission?," 22 percent of the freshman class and 56 percent of the senior class said "no."

Finally, in the perennial quest for academic prestige, people at Georgetown and Rutgers saw that even elite institutions were coeducational. Rutgers administrators and faculty watched nearby Princeton as it first debated and then adopted coeducation in the late 1960s.[4] Georgetown was in the midst of becoming a nationally competitive, highly regarded institution, drawing students from beyond its traditional Catholic constituency. While the Catholic tradition had a long heritage of single-sex education, Georgetown's peer institutions outside the Catholic system of higher education were considering admitting women or were already coeducational.

Beyond these similarities, however, Georgetown had an additional reason for adopting coeducation that Rutgers did not. Financial pressures weighed heavily on Georgetown. Caught between rising costs and stagnating revenue, it sought to expand its largest source of income: tuition. In 1968, the academic vice president, Rev. Thomas Fitzgerald, S.J., wrote that the administration was "anxious" to admit at least 50 girls to the college in 1969 and to increase slightly undergraduate enrollment "to support the large number of academic programs already in existence and to help assimilate the operating costs of the new Library."[5] As a state-supported university, Rutgers felt no such pressures. It had the financial backing of the state legislature, which at the time placed no pressure to cut costs.

The Paths to Coeducation

While Rutgers and Georgetown adopted coeducation during the same period of time, there was little similarity in how they made the decision. The differences stem from the nature of the institutions. As a multifaceted state university, Rutgers had to accommodate internal constituencies. At Georgetown, which had a centralized administration and no internal constituencies opposed to coeducation, the decision to adopt coeducation was relatively easy.

In the 1960s, Rutgers University was one of the few state institutions in the country that still retained single-sex education. In the mid-eighteenth century, when the Dutch Reformed Church established Rutgers as a college "for young men destined for study in the learned languages and in the liberal arts," its all-male status was normal. In the mid-nineteenth century, Rutgers began a gradual transition to state university status, first in 1864 when it became a state agricultural school, then in the late nineteenth century when it received federal funds, and finally in the early twentieth century when it ended all association with the Dutch Reformed Church.[6] In the late nineteenth century, there were two unsuccessful attempts to introduce women's education at Rutgers. In 1881, the trustees rejected a Rutgers faculty proposal for coeducation. Fourteen years later, the trustees rejected a proposal that the college associate itself with the Rutgers Female Seminary in New York City.[7]

The all-male nature of Rutgers College became further entrenched with the establishment of all-female Douglass College as a part of the Rutgers University. The New Jersey College for Women, later named Douglass College in honor of Mabel S. Douglass who helped found the institution, opened in 1918. It enjoyed relative autonomy with its own faculty, dean, and board of managers. Douglass College fared well during its early history. It expanded the size of its student body, ran a budget surplus, and acquired properties for further expansion. By 1960, Douglass was a well-established, high-quality liberal arts college whose student body had higher qualifications than the all-male Rutgers College across town. The remaining four undergraduate colleges—agriculture, arts and sciences, engineering, and education—were collectively called the "Colleges for Men." They had an integral relationship, sharing facilities, a common dean of students, and supporting services from the central administration.[8]

In the 1960s Rutgers College faculty initiated two attempts at coeducation. In the early 1960s, Rutgers faculty proposed that newly acquired property adjacent to the university be used to create a two-year coeducational college that would feed students in to the single-sex, upper-division schools of Rutgers and Douglass Colleges.[9] Douglass faculty effectively opposed this attempt, and the site was developed into Livingston College, a separate coeducational institution. In 1968, the Rutgers College faculty made a second attempt to institute coeducation, this time with a plan that would keep Douglass a women's college, but admit women to Rutgers College at a ratio of one woman to two men. This would provide for an even number of men and women on the two campuses. Rutgers students supported the idea. Asked whether "I favor the initiation of coeducation at Rutgers," three out of four responded positively.[10]

Douglass representatives vehemently resisted the prospect of coeducation at Rutgers College. Douglass dean Margery S. Foster, who led the fight, believed that coeducation at Rutgers threatened the survival of Douglass as a women's college. Not only would Rutgers attract many highly qualified women applicants away from Douglass, but "[t]here would be pressure for change from internal feelings," she argued, "both from students and faculty."[11] Foster also noted that Rutgers was not adopting coeducation for the benefit of women and asked the university president that "a study should be made of the effect of women of Rutgers taking in women before accepting a recommendation based primarily on the uses of women for the education of men." Coeducation, she believed, would create peer pressure "to conform to the Madison Ave. sex role definition of empty headed fluffy women and strong all knowing men. Whereas in single-sex institutions more individuality is allowed and perhaps even admired."[12] "On a coeducational campus women find themselves pandering to the notion that men are superior. . . . If a woman has no chance for leadership in college we are undercutting her potential for contributing to society."[13] Rutgers, she added, "doesn't want a woman student council president or a woman editor of the newspaper or yearbook."[14]

In addition to this classic defense of coordinate education, Foster developed other arguments against coeducation at Rutgers. Many men, she wrote, develop at a different pace socially and intellectually from women, and a single-sex college may offer a better opportunity for women to grow at their own pace and sort out their identity. "More studying takes place with some separation," she asserted. Women would not do as well on the Rutgers campus because it was crowded and men "seem to require less college housing." Perhaps the most unusual reason Foster cited for her opposition to coeducation was the "population bomb." Coeducation, she believed, tends to promote early marriage, "the pressure of peers and parents alike on young women to produce an engagement ring by graduation is strong indeed and those enthusiasts who would advocate these premature alliances tend to ignore the increasing numbers of unhappy couples who discover too late that they have very little in common with which to build a lasting relationship."[15]

The majority of Douglass faculty members opposed coeducation as well. In April 1970 the Douglass faculty voted by a three-to-one margin to "reaffirm its commitment to coordinate education."[16] A coalition of older faculty and younger feminists favored single-sex education. Many of them feared that Rutgers would consume Douglass, which would then lose its unique identity. One professor commented, "If it became co-ed it might just be an uptown Rutgers."[17]

Douglass student opinion of coeducation at Rutgers College was mixed. An opinion poll conducted in the spring of 1966 indicated strong student support for coeducational classes.[18] Shortly after the Douglass faculty voted to continue as a single-sex institution, an editorial in the student newspaper, the *Caellian*, criticized the decision for "keeping this College's antiquated, provincial autonomy. The faculty vote . . . will not discourage those who truly believe in coeducation—those who know that coeducation is the only realistic way of realizing the actualities of life in the outside world."[19] Yet there was also evidence of strong opposition to coeducation among Douglass students.[20] A 1967 student government reported that "it is very important for Douglass to retain its own identity as a women's college continuing its high standards and fine education."[21] Some Douglass students voiced their opposition to coeducation in campus newspapers, arguing that an all-female environment permits a valuable and unique atmosphere in which women may discover and develop their capabilities.

> After approximately eighteen years of male dominance, including the effects of at least twelve years of coeducation, a girl needs the opportunity to develop as an individual as a woman, not a man's idea of a woman. A woman's college is not a luxurry [sic]; it is a necessity. Contrary to popular opinion we are not here to preserve our virginity. We are here to develop our identity. . . . [W]e feel that coeducation will make it even easier to preserve the myth of feminine inferiority. After all most of us went to coed grammar and high schools. If men have failed in twelve years to realize that we are their equals we doubt that another four years will convince them.[22]

An influential Rutgers alumni association also opposed the admission of women to Rutgers College. Shortly before the board of governors was to have a crucial vote on the issue of coeducation, the Rutgers Alumni Association Executive Committee resolved that it "vehemently opposes any attempt at making Rutgers College a coeducational institution." They asserted, "no sound foundation has been established for such a move," the "financial and space implications" have not been considered, and coeducation "would further limit the admission of highly qualified male applicants to the College."[23]

The opponents of coeducation at Rutgers briefly prevailed. In October 1970, the board voted against coeducation by seven to one.[24] They stated that the current structure allowed students single-sex and coeducational courses through intercollegiate registration.[25] Several alumni board members supported the tradition of single-sex colleges.

Undeterred, the Rutgers College faculty formed a committee to pressure the governors to reverse their decision. They contacted the Women's Equity Action League and the American Civil Liberties Union to explore legally forcing the college to admit women. They also encouraged the Rutgers Parents Association to appear before the board of governors to argue on behalf of coeducation. In September 1971 the board approved coeducation at Rutgers College. It reversed its earlier decision to make the transition smoother for the incoming president.[26]

Georgetown's path to coeducation is a much simpler story. In its decision to adopt coeducation, Georgetown differed from Rutgers in two significant ways. First, the impetus for coeducation came from the administration, which wanted to expand the student body to meet rising costs. Second, there were no internal constituencies in the university opposed to coeducation. The other four undergraduate colleges—the School of Business Administration, the Schools of Foreign Service, the Institute of Language and Linguistics, and the School of

Nursing—already admitted women. The alumni had relatively little influence on the decision, and the Georgetown administration made no attempt to survey alumni opinion beyond consulting a few key alumni.

The actual decision for coeducation was quick. In the spring of 1968, Father Thomas Fitzgerald and Father Royden B. Davis began a series of meetings with various campus constituencies to discuss the possibility of coeducation at Georgetown. The board of directors supported the idea and the executive faculty approved a proposal that 50 to 100 female students be admitted each year.[27] The faculty and male students expressed virtually no opposition to coeducation.[28] Coeducation came to Georgetown after 179 years when, in August 1968, the board voted unanimously to admit women.[29]

The Admission of Women: Numbers and Academic Qualifications

The number of women admitted grew rapidly at both campuses. To prevent the perception that women were misplacing men, Georgetown administrators initially planned a slight increase in the enrollment of men while admitting a small number of women. Yet in the first three years, Georgetown enrolled about fifty fewer men. Thereafter, however, when the issue of women's admission became less eventful, the drop in men accelerated and was replaced by a proportionate increase in women.[30] By 1978 Georgetown was majority female.[31]

The admission of women to Rutgers College and the opening of coeducational Livingston College at the New Brunswick campus dramatically increased the number of women at Rutgers University. As predicted, total undergraduate enrollment in New Brunswick more than doubled between 1964–65 and 1975–76. While enrollment at Douglass College rose 40 percent, Rutgers College enrollment rose an astounding 68 percent.[32] The newly established Livingston College opened in 1969 with 769 students and admitted 3,488 just six years later.[33] The percentage of women students in New Brunswick expanded dramatically. In the early 1960s women accounted for one of every three students; by the mid-1970s, they made up nearly half. The total number of women grew by 325 percent, from 2,604 to 8,471.

By doubling the pool of potential applicants through coeducation, Georgetown and Rutgers expanded their student body size *and* increased the academic quality. As Richard McCormick, dean of Rutgers College from 1974 to 1977, later recalled, coeducation "took the heat off the numbers question."[34] The Rutgers admissions office reported that "because of the limited number of spaces for women, most of the women applicants tended to be outstanding students."[35] In its first years of coeducation, Georgetown received ten times as many applications as it had openings, which meant that it could be very selective.[36] Yet the university also broadened its admissions criteria:

The Committee on Admissions chose not to select [women] by the usual criteria, with academic factors dominating. Had they done this, a class could have been selected whose members would all have ranked in the top 5 percent of their classes, with Verbal scores of at least 675 and Math scores of at least 650. Instead, the Committee set an academic standard which allowed class ranks of some students to be as low as the top 10%, and allowed the College Board scores of others to be as low as 550. Once this group of about 200 candidates was selected, the Committee recommended that we choose those who had shown outstanding qualities of leadership, involvement and diversity. Strong weight was placed on recommendations from guidance counselors, teachers, alumni interview reports, and on-campus interview reports.[37]

The first group of women at Georgetown had academic qualifications that were, on average, significantly higher than the men's, averaging in the ninety-second high school percentile rank for women, while men averaged in the seventy-eighth.[38] During the first four years of coeducation at Rutgers, the average class rank of all students rose from the eighty-seventh to eighty-ninth percentile. Douglass, in contrast, dropped during the same period of time, from the ninetieth to the eighty-sixth percentile.[39] As at Georgetown, the academic qualifications of the first women applicants to Rutgers College were "very high," according to the director of undergraduate admissions to Rutgers College.[40]

A Cultural Revolution

During the early years of coeducation, there was a cultural revolution on campus that affected settings, rituals, and ideals at the universities. In physical terms, the campuses changed very little, but in cultural terms, there was a revolution in the relationship between students and the university and in gender norms.

Settings
On the eve of coeducation, one of the most noticeable features of both campuses was sexual segregation. In the classroom, housing, and the daily ordering of campus life through the in loco parentis policy, male and female students had relatively little contact.

When the few women at Rutgers who cross-registered were on campus, their presence became a spectacle. "Why were so many Rutgersmen cutting their Wednesday classes and spending the day loitering around the campus?," the student newspaper, the *Targum*, asked. "Why were students deliberating for hours over a cup of coffee in The Ledge, or milling around the lounge there? Why did the campus suddenly look so much better? The answer is simple—girls."[41] Not surprisingly, many women students found this uncomfortable.

Prior to coeducation, the sexually segregated housing reflected and supported traditional gender identity. With the admission of women, however, the most immediate concern at both institutions was finding a place to house them. Most Georgetown College men resided in dorms surrounding "the Yard," an open brick square at the center of campus. Male School of Foreign Service students lived on the "East Campus" two blocks away. All women students, regardless of which undergraduate school they attended, lived at the northern end of campus in two single-sex dormitories. Coeducation would not necessarily undermine this segregation; at first, Georgetown administrators did not consider coeducational housing. However, in the 1960s both Georgetown and Rutgers began mixing the sexes in coeducational housing and thus undermined sexual segregation.

Georgetown's male students greeted the first experiment in coeducational housing with surprise and a sense of humor. "If girls do commandeer Copley's third floor next year," one *Hoya* editorial proclaimed, "we would like to make one suggestion. Either alumni be given ample warning or those little frilly things which inevitably mark a girl's room must be kept away from the windows."[42] According to the student newspaper, the reaction among both men and women was "surprisingly limited." "Most of the guys are just kind of interested." Rev. William C. McFadden, S.J., resident Jesuit of Copley dormitory said, "I can't imagine that [the administration] would have [allowed women into Copley] if they weren't forced into it. Regardless, it is going to be done, and right now they are searching for reasons to justify it." Male students who resided in the dormitory designated to become coeducational were initially shocked and then generally receptive. Only one of the sixteen members of the dormitory council expressed any reservations, and the president of the council felt that the women would add something, "especially to any social event we try to hold."[43]

Coeducation at Georgetown and Rutgers coincided with a change in a central feature of traditional campus life: the in loco parentis policy. It was a policy by which the university controlled student behavior, and it was not gender neutral. Reflecting a conservative Catholic ethos, the in loco parentis policy at Georgetown was extensive. Throughout most of the 1960s, administrators introduced students to the myriad rules that regulated student life in two separate books: *The "G" Book* for men and *Miss "G" Goes to Georgetown* for women. *Miss "G"* more fully regulated women's lives and endorsed the ideals of cleanliness, modesty, and sexual restraint. "Your bed must be made and your room in order by 11 A.M.," the 1967 *Miss "G"* instructed. "Room checks will be made twice weekly and demerits assigned for disorderly rooms by a member of the Residence Staff."[44] *The "G" Book* was much milder in its regulations, essentially leaving the standards to individual interpretation. The 1967 *"G" Book* advised that "Georgetown gentlemen are expected to keep their rooms neat and orderly."[45]

Georgetown strictly regulated women's clothing to ensure a standard of female modesty and decorum. The 1966 *Miss "G"* declared "Personal pride is a quality inherent in the weaker sex, and clothing plays an important part in the coed's plans for college." The regulations forbade sports attire; shorts and pants outside of the dorms, except on Saturday; and warned of demerit points for "careless grooming, [and] wearing of inappropriate attire."[46]

At night, curfews kept men and women separate. First year women at Georgetown were required to be in residence by 10:30 p.m.; the rest were to be in by twelve midnight. The curfews for men were a half-hour later than the women's, presumably to give an escort time to return to his dormitory. Men and women were responsible for the behavior of their guests. Women were advised that "Each woman student is responsible for the behavior and conduct of her male guests. Discretion and good taste should be displayed at all times. Public display of affection (prolonged kissing or embracing) or any action that may appear to be such, is considered in poor taste . . . [and] is subject to sanction by the Residence Council or the Dean of Women."[47] "Poor conduct on the part of your date" resulted in ten demerits for women and "public display of affection anywhere in proximity to the dormitory" received the strongest sanction of fifty demerits.[48]

Students pressed Georgetown University to dismantle the in loco parentis policy even before the admission of women to the college. By the end of the 1960s, the university greatly reduced social regulation and the "G" books disappeared after 1971. Curfews became more liberal. Freshman women, for example, were permitted to stay out until 12 midnight (2 a.m. on weekends) and upperclass women obtained the ability to sign out for the evening if they returned by 9 a.m.[49]

Male students at both campuses tried to change the more controversial part of the in loco parentis policy: intervisitation. Influenced by the sexual revolution and by the knowledge that students were successful at changing these policies at other colleges and universities, students were increasingly impatient with a policy they felt too intrusive. At Rutgers, women could visit on specified weekends, usually when a major social event occurred, with the stipulation that the doors remain open. At Georgetown, men were not permitted above the first floor of the women's dorm, and women were not allowed in the men's dorms "unless accompanied by a Jesuit."[50] Students at both campuses used formal and informal tactics to challenge the policy. Representative student organizations pressed for liberalization, while students themselves undermined the policy through noncooperation. Impatient with the incremental changes to the intervisitation policy, students began to demand nothing short of twenty-four-hour visitation with closed doors. Under the pressure of students, administrators at both campuses agreed.

As men and women students socialized more with each other, the "mystique" of the other sex lessened. As former dean of women Patricia Rueckel commented in 1975, "There is no longer a mystique about male and female qualities because students like to know one another as persons, friends, class-mates, not as future mates and sex objects. Living near one another has helped young men to change their attitudes about 'womanhood' and young women to be more realistic about 'maleness.' "[51]

Students, too, recognized the benefits of gender integration. One male student, according to the *Targum,* said it is "good to be able to expect a smile back" in explaining the aura of relaxed friendship that has dispelled the usual "avoiding eyes" between men and women on campus in previous years.[52] Women students expressed similar sentiments to a *New York Times* reporter. "Last year, when you walked on the campus, the fellows eyed you," one student commented. "Now you can walk around without feeling that they're grading you." Another woman student agreed: "Last year, the men would hardly say hello to a woman on campus. This year, they are friendly and less defensive. It's a lot more normal."[53]

Women sometimes experienced gendered expectations and harassment in the classroom, especially when their numbers were few. Laurie Goodman of the first class of women at Rutgers recalled that during lab instruction she was expected to clean up after a mess in the laboratory. Phyllis Anderson-Wright, another student in the first coeducational class, recalled that when she walked into a General Microbiology Lab "there were a pair of bikini panties on the blackboard . . . and on the blackboard it said, 'welcome to Rutgers . . . home of men' or something like that and but then afterwards you'd come in and there would be little things on the blackboard, lewd pictures, you know a penis, a big penis, or something. . . . One of us would go up and rip it off."[54] Other women shrugged off any discomfort. Maria Angermeier, the first woman to graduate from Georgetown, indicated that although she sensed some subtle hostility, it did not bother her. "Some of the fellows did tease me about being the first woman accepted," she said, "and I sometimes got the feeling some of the upper-classmen didn't especially like the idea, but there was nothing directed toward me in particular. I really can't make any generalizations about the experience."[55] The presence of hostility toward women varied by course and by professor. It waned over time, as women became more numerous in the classroom and as feminist objections to the chilly climate in the classroom became more wide-spread.

Rituals
Rituals, or prescribed forms and methods for social customs and occasions, also had been highly gendered. They tended to give men initiative in social-izing and employment and to encourage dependency and attention to physical beauty for women. Coeducation would dramatically alter the patterns of social interaction.

Prior to coeducation, dating at Georgetown and Rutgers followed specific patterns. Georgetown men often sought dates from a network of women's Catholic colleges in the area, including Immaculata, Dunbarton, Marymount, and its unofficial counterpart, Trinity College. The back of the *"G" Book* in the early 1960s listed the various women's schools, and each year Georgetown students nominated a representative from each college to the Homecoming Court. In a series of articles in 1964–65, the *Hoya* reviewed the "reputation" of the girls at each campus.[56] At Rutgers, some men could find dates more easily by attending mixers at Douglass because of its proximity. Others returned home to date women in their area.

At both institutions there were stigma against dating female students from the other parts of the university. "They are not the kind you want to get serious with," commented a Georgetown male student, "but the kind you see around and really have a ball talking to."[57] A female student complained that "being in the College makes you a dating anathema."[58] "Debbie Douglass" was the negative stereotype of Douglass students. She had "strong middle-class hang-ups" and was "99% stuck up." The Douglass stereotype was also sexually reserved: "Debbie Douglass—mucho studious, mucho frigid!!!" "They never smile." "Glasses, overweight, and a bun." "I'm glad Rutgers is going co-ed next year," a Rutgers student commented in 1971, "Douglass girls will finally have some competition and maybe they'll come down off their pedestals."[59]

Coeducation greatly altered dating patterns. As the numbers of women increased, men no longer had to travel to surrounding colleges to meet women. In addition, the dating taboo against Georgetown or Rutgers woman lessened. The social network among Catholic colleges in the capital area collapsed as students stayed on campus to socialize. The campus media rarely mentioned the other women's colleges, and the frequent travel between campuses ended. Georgetown's social life increasingly became an island unto itself. Rutgers, too, became more self-sufficient as the number of women approached parity with men. Men no longer needed to take the 20-minute bus ride across town to meet women. Social mixers and media coverage of social events on each other's campuses were not as frequent as before coeducation.

The social calendars at Georgetown and Rutgers underwent a dramatic transformation in the 1960s and 1970s. In the early 1960s the social calendars at both institutions were dotted with events that celebrated female beauty. One popular event was the military ball. Each year the Reserve Officer Training Corps (ROTC) programs planned a weekend to honor the cadets with parades, reviews, and a dance with a queen. At Rutgers, the queen was chosen on the basis of grace, poise, verbal expression, grooming, good taste, and beauty. The judges were a mix of military men, administrative officials, and on at least one occasion, a religious leader.[60] In the early 1960s, the Rutgers student newspaper created the "Miss Beautiful Secretary on Campus" contest "to honor . . . our industrious secretaries."[61] Judged on the basis of beauty and personality, the winner was awarded an air conditioner and rug for her office and a modest pay raise. In 1964 the queen had to share the spotlight with a "Miss New Jersey Bond Issue," chosen to publicize the upcoming Bond Issue Referendum that was to finance the proposed Livingston College.[62] Three criteria for her selection were beauty, speaking ability, and a strong interest in the bond issue.[63]

Homecoming was the most important social occasion at Rutgers College, and judges selected a queen on the basis of beauty, personality, and charm. To nominate a young woman, the Rutgers College student would submit her portrait photograph, a full-length snapshot, her name, address, height, weight, school or occupation, and "vital statistics," the measurements of her breasts, waist, and hips. The judges were various administrative officials from the university. One year, for example, the judges were the assistant director of student aid, the assistant to the dean of men, an assistant director of athletics, and a female resident counselor at Douglass.[64]

In the 1970s, social events that celebrated female beauty with a contest of some sort almost completely disappeared. The Miss Beautiful Secretary contest and Miss New Jersey Bond Issue contests never reemerged. Mostly because of growing antimilitary sentiment on campus, the military balls ended.

Ideals

In response to coeducation and the influence of the feminist movement, the ideal image of what men and women should look and behave like would undergo dramatic change in the late 1960s and 1970s. These ideals could be physically represented, as in campus media, or they could be ideals in action. Some of the most salient changes in ideals were in advertisements, athletics, and ROTC. They are similar because the impetus for change originated outside the institutions.

In response to Title IX of the Education Amendments Act, colleges and universities across the nation were forced to provide more equitable treatment for women athletes. Before Title IX women's athletics was largely intramural, with as much emphasis on getting exercise as on the dynamics of competition and winning. For example, in the 1968 Georgetown yearbook, entitled *Ye Domesday Book,* the author, presumably from the Women's Athletic Association, invited women to participate, for "sheer love of sport," or to "rid yourself of excess flab." "Not only have the men graciously assented to let us use their gym for 'early' morning classes," the *Ye Domesday Book* quoted a female athlete as saying in 1968, "but they have also given us two evenings a week, provided there is no men's basketball game."[65] Title IX changed all this. Women gained better equipment, equitable access to facilities, and a larger coaching staff. A competitive, nontraditional ethos for the female athlete developed that celebrated strength, skill, agility, and a winning spirit.

Even more striking was the opening of the ROTC program to women. This, too, was in response to forces beyond campus walls. The military decided to open the program to women, who began to train alongside men for positions well beyond the traditional nurse. Many were shocked. "They actually take girls in ROTC!," a Georgetown campus publication commented. "Everybody has heard of women scholarship cadettes, but nobody ever saw one before. Do you know what it's like to find out that the guy next to you in line is a girl? I mean, it's not easy to tell in those baggy green fatigues the Army issues. The last great bastion of manhood crumbling like a stale oatmeal cookie in a box of C-rations!"[66]

The depiction of women in the pervasive campus media also perpetuated gender ideals. In the many advertisements that promoted cultural ideals of masculinity and femininity, three themes are salient: that men attract women with their income potential and prestige; that producers viewed their audience as having heterosexual male sensibilities and used female sexuality to promote their products; and that some advertisements appealed to men by displaying male dominance.

Men were attractive to women if they earned a good income. The McDonnell corporation listed "Ten reasons She will want you to take a job at McDonnell," including "stability and security," and the fact that "McDonnell is a name in aerospace." The ad featured an attractive young woman gazing at a partially obscured man, presumably impressed by someone working at the company. The Equitable Life Assurance Society advertised the attractiveness of financial security. In a series of sketches, a "hip" young woman, with a mini-skirt, high heels, and long beads ignores a conservative, collegiate-looking young man in horn-rimmed glasses until he asks if she "wouldn't be interested in someone like me who has landed a good-paying job that will let his family live well and who, in addition, has taken out a substantial Living Insurance policy from Equitable that will provide handsomely for his family if, heaven forbid, anything should happen to him." The woman responds by giving him a big smile, hooking his arm and saying, "How's about showing me that pipe collection, swinger?"[67]

Advertisers appealed to heterosexual male sensibilities by using female sexuality. An advertisement for the Dodge Charger, for example, featured a young woman dressed in mini-skirt and go-go boots. She was Joan Parker, "the new Dodge Fever Girl . . . A new girl for girl-watchers to watch." Other ads displayed an ethos of male dominance. An ad for a store selling drafting equipment featured a young woman in leotards and high heels facing away from the camera, but twisting back with a smile, under the headline, "At Your Service, Men!" Old Spice advertisements featured a woman under the bold print "Masculine," indicating she was attracted to "an untamed male." An ad for Studd fragrance products featured an attractive young woman with a tear in her eye. The ad stated, "So make her cry a little . . . " In the 1970s these advertisements featuring overt male dominance and traditional role modeling began to disappear as the mostly national corporations responded to criticisms about sexist stereotyping.

The emerging gender ideals on campus created new boundaries for acceptable male and female behavior. As more women entered athletics and ROTC and received recognition, they appropriated the traditionally male qualities of aggression and team play. Advertisements that overtly featured traditional roles for men and women, including male dominance, began to disappear. For men and women arriving on campus in the mid-1970s, gender roles were no longer so clearly defined.

Women in Early Coeducation

In the early years of coeducation, Rutgers and Georgetown were caught unprepared for the kinds of changes necessary to make women welcome. At the same time that many women students, faculty members, and administrators were accomplishing "firsts" for women, being the "first" to hold a position or increasing their representation in some areas, some women expressed frustration at the slow pace of change.

In the initial years of coeducation, many women broke barriers when they entered positions never before held by women. At Rutgers in 1974, for example, three women formed the first sorority, and Tau Epsilon Phi, a coeducational fraternity, elected a woman president. Margaret Kelleher became the first female ROTC cadet commander, a position usually awarded to two seniors. Women also made up half of the news staff on the *Targum*. A year later, women students began an all-female choir as a counterpart to the all-male Rutgers Glee Club.[68] At Georgetown, Ellen Pollan became the first woman to be student producer for the student theater in 1973.[69] A year later, a woman headed the security force for the first time in Georgetown history.[70] In 1977 students elected the first woman as student government president.[71]

Both institutions hired more women to the faculty. In 1972, the first year of coeducation, Rutgers hired women to fill half of 40 new faculty positions. Female faculty members not only influenced students by becoming role models but also taught courses that focused on women's experiences, including, at Rutgers, Women in Literature, Sociology and Sex Roles, Biology and Feminism, and Sexuality and Society. One professor who expanded her contemporary political science course to include a section on feminism found that "when we talked about the radical feminist movement, the men students became very upset. The women who had been docile to that point reacted to the men's hostility. Looking back, I think it was an experience where both gained insight."[72]

Georgetown and Rutgers adopted more gender-neutral administrative posts. Both institutions replaced the offices of the dean of men and dean of women with the more generic forms of administration, such as the dean of student affairs at Georgetown. Rutgers hired some women for administrative positions. In 1972, Alice Irby became the first woman to hold a university-wide post when she became the vice president for student services.[73] Over the summer of 1972, the board of governors elected its first female chairman, Claire Nagle.[74] In 1973, Georgetown hired Dr. H. Rosaline Cowie to become the first female dean, at the assistant level, of the College of Arts and Sciences.

Women in these positions sometimes showed greater sensitivity to the needs of women. Dean Cowie, for example, not only recognized "a need for women in professional positions to serve as role models for both male and female students," but she also made a special effort to encourage female students, whom she believed had a more difficult time building self-confidence. Her convictions may also have come from her previous position at a women's college: she had been on the faculty at Newton College, a small single-sex women's Catholic college, until it had been absorbed by Boston College, a nearby, recently coeducational Jesuit institution.[75] Georgetown dean Patricia Rueckel wrote that:

> the assumption that women students can occupy corridors or entire residences which were previously all male is naive. We must make plans to insure that attitudes and subtilties [sic], as well as the facilities themselves are changed.... I would feel more comfortable trying these experiments in a setting which was less traditional than Georgetown University; one in which the facilities had been planned for this purpose, and campus sentiment was supportive.[76]

While women were making many breakthroughs and gender ideals were evolving, for some women at Georgetown, change in women's lives was neither as fast nor as far reaching as they desired. One result was a growing feminist presence on campus. In 1969, the first year of coeducation, women formed the Georgetown Women's Liberation Movement (GWLM) "to join with other women in redefining woman's role in society."[77] The GWLM wanted to raised women's consciousness by writing pamphlets and offering courses in the recently opened Free University. In the fall of 1971 a group of women students formed the Women's Caucus "to draw out any anger and resentment among women and to redirect it, to learn to understand other women and to discover that personal problems are not always isolated problems."[78] The Women's Caucus pursued a number of feminist goals: to investigate the admissions and scholarship policies of the university, to set up a writer's workshop, to explore creating an on-campus day care center, to pressure the university to hire a gynecologist at the Student Health Service, and to work to repeal the District of Columbia's abortion law.

In this era of increasing feminist consciousness, some women in staff positions became more assertive. In 1972, Rutgers secretaries and lab assistants unionized under the American Federation of State County and Municipal Employees and negotiated with the university for a contract that called for new grievance procedures, more benefits, and greater job security.[79] In the spring of 1972, Georgetown's dean of women, Valerie Berghoff, invited more than 2,000 women associated with the university to a women's conference. The purpose was "to explore new dimensions of consciousness for women." About 250 women attended, many more than expected. Students represented a small percentage of those who attended; most were women over 25 years of age and worked for the university.[80]

At Rutgers University, feminism emerged earliest and strongest at Douglass College. Before the institutional support of women's studies programs and centers, feminism emerged on campus through the activities of individual faculty. Professors Elaine Showalter and Mary Howard chaired an ad-hoc committee on the Education of Women that had several feminist results: they issued a report highlighting the need for more women administrators and faculty members, and they later proposed curricular changes to make Douglass more feminist. In 1971, Douglass created the new major of women's studies, and in 1973 it opened a Women's Center. Douglass students formed an early women's liberation group, named XX, after the female chromosome structure. In the early 1970s XX called for curricular changes, offered self-defense workshops, and protested when a recruiter for AT&T guided women applicants into lower-level jobs.

By the mid-1970s, various women's groups and other organizations brought feminist speakers to the Rutgers and Douglass campus, further spreading feminist awareness. At a Rutgers Symposium on Women, William O'Neill, author of the 1972 book entitled *Everyone Was Brave: A History of Feminism,* began a lecture by asking the women present: "Have you really come a long way baby?"[81] In the fall of 1973 women's groups sponsored a Women's Film Festival that showed films with feminist themes.

The institutional development of women's programs was much slower at Georgetown. While some professors incorporated feminist pedagogy and content into their courses, a women's studies minor was not available until 1986.[82] Georgetown opened its first Women's Center in 1990 after a group of women students pressured the administration.[83]

Coeducation after Thirty Years

The presence of women has made Georgetown and Rutgers very different places from what they were 40 years ago. A visitor from that era may experience a sense of cultural vertigo. Neither institution adopted coeducation expressly for the purpose of improving women's lives and opportunities but rather from concerns of institutional viability and prestige. Administrators at both campuses made relatively few plans to assimilate women, not out of an intention to alienate them but out of ignorance of the need to do so. Administrators who recognized that the universities should make cultural adjustments were few and far between. It was a classic case of a dominant culture that did not discern the needs of a subordinate culture because it had never needed to.

Reflecting nationwide trends, female students became predominant in both student bodies. At Georgetown women have been the majority in every class since 1977. Women made up 55 percent of the student body on the entire Rutgers University campus in 1999, which gives Rutgers the third highest percentage of women among all public institutions. The student bodies of Rutgers and Georgetown have also become more diverse over the years. In 1998, for example, with 32 percent minority students, Rutgers had the sixth highest percentage of minority students of all large universities in the country. Asian students represented 13 percent of the student body; African Americans, 10 percent; and Latinos, 8 percent.[84] The diversity is reflected in the numerous organizations and events that center around ethnic identity, including clubs for Haitians, African Americans, Native Americans, West Indians, Palestinians, Chinese, Hindus, Latin Americans, Poles, Cantonese, Koreans, Turks, and Armenians.

Both institutions recruited more women faculty over time. By the turn of the century, women were 31 percent of the faculty at Rutgers and 30 percent at Georgetown. The relatively recent arrival of women to tenure-track positions means that women are in higher proportion in descending order of rank. At Rutgers, for example, women were 18 percent of all full professors, 38 percent of associate professors, 41 percent of assistant professors, and 42 percent of instructors.[85] Ten years earlier, in 1990–91, women were 15 percent of full professors, 25 percent of associate professors, and 38 percent of assistant professors.[86] The representation of women faculty, of course, varies by department. At Georgetown, women were 20 percent or less in the departments of chemistry, philosophy, economics, and government. They were at least half in the departments of art, music and theatre, biology, English, sociology, public policy, history, linguistics, and the languages.[87]

Extraordinary breakthroughs for women at the top levels of administration occurred at Georgetown in the 1990s. Jane McAuliffe became the first woman dean of Georgetown College, and Dorothy Brown became the first woman provost.[88] "I have always found Georgetown a good place for women," Brown commented. She noted that appointing women to positions is only a part of leadership; subordinates must be willing to accept leadership. She also found that the university faculty accepted female leadership more than students did.[89] Georgetown recently took a step that ultimately makes the presidency of the university accessible to women. Historically, only members of the Society of Jesus became president of Jesuit institutions. Recently, however, Georgetown was the first Jesuit institution to appoint a lay member president, thereby also opening the door to women. To a lesser extent, the university's board of directors has expanded the number of women. In 1970, the board had one woman of 21 members, or less than 5 percent; today the number stands at just 6 of 49 members, or 12 percent.[90]

Both campuses have active women's studies programs. Georgetown developed a women's studies program that first offered a minor in 1987 and a major in the mid-1990s. In 1990 a group of students pressed for and received funds to open the Women's Center, which provides referral services and sponsors various events about women at home and abroad.[91] The university currently supports the Women's Center with a full-time director and a location accessible to students. Rutgers University has developed a cluster of feminist academic organizations: the Department of Women and Gender Studies, the main source for academic teaching on women's issues; the Center for American Women and Politics, a unit of the Eagleton Institute of Politics that seeks to enhance women's influence and leadership in public life; the Institute for Research on Women, which fosters interdisciplinary research on women and gender around the world; the Center for Women's Global Leadership, to develop and facilitate women's leadership for human rights and social justice worldwide; and the Center for Women and Work, which addresses the needs of working women. The Department of Women and Gender Studies is thriving. Established in 1973, it is now one of the largest and strongest programs in the country. The department has a faculty of 27 and 76 affiliated faculty who together teach over 100 courses that annually enroll about 1,300 students. About 200 students are in the major and minor program. The program also offers masters and doctorate degrees.[92]

In the 1990s, there was somewhat of a backlash against feminism on the Georgetown campus. Some women students formed the Independent Women's Forum in 1992. While supportive of women's careers and aspirations, it wanted to offer a more traditional, nonfeminist orientation for women. This philosophy received even greater attention when two female students published a pamphlet called "The Guide: A Little Beige Book for Today's Miss G." Asserting that "the fight for equality is largely a thing of the past," the pamphlet touted "individual responsibility, independent thinking and initiative to reach our potential." "Call us New Traditionalists with a mission." The authors discounted some published assertions about the frequency of rape and eating disorders, as well as unequal pay for women. They also called for a return to traditional dating and sexual restraint.[93] It is difficult to measure the appeal of "The Guide," but it received a lot of attention on and off campus, including a televised interview of its two editors by Barbara Walters.

As a Catholic institution, Georgetown has restrained the growth of organizations that serve gay and lesbian students. After Georgetown administrators refused to fund or recognize a gay student organization called Gay People of Georgetown in the late 1970s and early 1980s, the group sued the university, alleging that it had violated the D.C. Human Rights Act. In 1987, the D.C. Court of Appeals found that the university must fund the group, now called GU Pride.[94] Despite official resistance by the university, many faculty and administrators are sympathetic to gay issues. In 1998, they helped organize Safe Zones, a program that trains faculty and staff to assist and guide gay students to appropriate resources should they seek their help. There are currently about 150 of these faculty and staff "allies," who display a Safe Zone sticker in their offices to alert students to their membership. Most recently, the university has refused to support a resource center that was proposed for gay, lesbian, bisexual, and transgender (GLBT) students. The proposed center would offer various services to GLBT students, including referrals to mental health specialists, collecting data on harassment of GLBT students, and sponsor events that raise awareness of GLBT students.[95]

Feminist organizations at Georgetown are sometimes a source of controversy as well. In the late 1980s, when a group called the Women's Caucus supported pro-choice positions on abortion, it alienated some pro-life feminists, conservative students, and the administration. It resolved the controversy by forming a second group, Hoyas for Choice, which was openly pro-choice but did not receive university funding. Conservative student groups and organizations, such as the satirical journal *The Georgetown Academy*, often ridicule the Women's Center and its programming.[96] The center walks a fine line trying to serve female students while not provoking controversy. For example, after a female student recently complained that the center staff belittled her inquiry about becoming a nun, the center further trained its staff for handling such referrals and placed information about religious vocations in the center. When the center's initial sponsoring of *The Vagina Monologues* became controversial, it did not sponsor it the following year but left it to a broad coalition of students to do so.[97]

Campus media at Georgetown and Rutgers is more equitable than in the past. Both give extensive coverage to women's sports in the newspapers and the yearbooks. In the 1990 edition of the Rutgers yearbook, for example, athletic coverage was organized by the sport, without labeling the teams as "men's" or "women's." The men's and women's basketball teams each received four pages of coverage.[98] In the 1990s, the campus media at Rutgers University was an interesting mix of gender patterns. Only in 1990 and 1995 was there a female editor of the yearbook; the Douglass newspaper, *The Caellian*, had only women editors; and women outnumbered men two to one in holding positions as the editor-in-chief and managing editor of *The Targum*.

An Ongoing Process

Women and feminism have changed Georgetown and Rutgers, not only as places but also as processes, for education is ultimately a process of personal and social change. Students come to these institutions from various families with their own gender ideals, usually more traditional than those on campus. Once on campus, students are in an environment where some are challenging traditional gender norms. Many students alter their ideals, sensibilities, and life plans.

The presence of women adds weight to the influence of feminism on and off campus. The presence of women in the student body gives rise to the need for more women faculty; the presence of women in the women's studies courses sustains them, which in turn sustains women's studies programs and staffing. These institutional organizations then attempt to spread the feminist ethos throughout the campus and sometimes beyond. Female students and feminist organizations on campus are in a mutually sustaining relationship. Coeducation has helped academia in America, directly and indirectly, to become one of the most dynamic promoters of women's status and progress.

Notes

1. "A History of the Coeducation Controversy: Is It Over Yet?," *Targum*, December 1, 1969, 1.
2. Royden B. Davis, S.J., Dean of College of Arts and Sciences, Georgetown University, interview by Susan Poulson, May 19, 1986; Remigio Pane, Rutgers College faculty member, interview by Susan Poulson, Piscataway, N.J., February 1989.
3. "Poll Shows Co-Education Favored," *The Observer,* January 15, 1969, 1.
4. Richard P. McCormick, interview, Piscataway, N.J., February 9, 1989.
5. Rev. Thomas R. Fitzgerald, S.J., to Patricia Rueckel, October 29, 1968, University Archives, Laninger Library, Georgetown University (hereafter GUA).
6. Richard McCormick, *Rutgers: A Bicentennial History* (New Brunswick, N.J.: Rutgers University, 1966), 3, 117–18, 155.
7 . Ibid., 169.
8. Richard McCormick, *Academic Reorganization in New Brunswick, 1962–78: The Federated College Plan,* (n.p.: n.p., 1978), 2.
9 Report of Arts and Sciences Planning Committee, February 18, 1963, Richard B. Schlatter Papers, University Archives, Alexander Library, Rutgers University, cited by McCormick, *Academic Reorganization,* 5. McCormick has characterized these intentions as "quite frankly imperialistic" (McCormick interview).
10. "A History of the Coeducation Controversy," 3.
11. "Administrators on Coed: How and What For?," *Targum*, December 1, 1969, 4.
12. Foster to Gross, July 2, 1970, 1, 4, Papers of Margery Foster Summers, Alexander Library (hereafter referred to as MFS).
13. "Administrators on Coed," 4.

14. "Foster Sees No Co-Education, but More Coed Classes," *Targum*, March 17, 1970, 1.

15. Ibid., 4, 8, 4–5.

16. The resolution continues "that during the next five years the college will implement this undertaking by adopting programs designed to achieve these ends." At the same time, the faculty voted by 85 to 39 (with two abstentions) to oppose a resolution stating "that if Rutgers College becomes coeducational, Douglass College should become coeducational also provided that the autonomy of the College within the structure of the Federated College Plan is maintained" (Douglass College Faculty minutes, April 14, 1970, University Archives, Alexander Library, Rutgers University [RUA]).

17. "Douglass Faculty Members Offer Opinions: 'Coordinate versus Coeducation' Question," *Caellian*, April 24, 1970, 1.

18. "Rutgers-Douglass Mix? Vote on Coed Classes Could Bring Change," *Targum*, October 3, 1966, 1.

19. "The Vote on Tuesday," *Caellian*, April 17, 1970, 4.

20. "96 Per Cent Want Coed Option; Coopies Agree," *Targum*, February 18, 1966, 1.

21. "Coed Classes Caught in Quandary," *Targum*, February 3, 1967, 1

22. Cheri Connell, Kathryn Conner, Janet Cottrell, and Barbara Oettle, "Letter to the Editor," *Targum*, December 10, 1969, 6. Two Rutgers students replied to this letter accusing these women of "female paranoia," arguing that one cannot develop fully and realistically in a single-sex environment (David Szonyi and Frank Yacenda, "Letter to the Editor," *Targum*, December 11, 1969, 3). Another male student wrote that a woman's college was like a nunnery and advised the four women students not to "matriculate with the idea that outside the gates of your Female Haven the world, too, is a marshmallow of gentle curves and clouds of softness" (Nathan Edelstein, "Letter to the Editor," *Targum*, December 12, 1969, 2.

23. Vincent Kramer to Karl Metzger, October 8, 1970, Papers of Arnold B. Grobman, University Archives, Alexander Library, Rutgers University (hereafter ABG). The committee reaffirmed its opposition a year later, even after the board of governors approved coeducation (Grobman to Bloustein, October 21, 1971, 2, ABG).

24. Board of governors minutes, October 9, 1970, RUA.

25. "Governors Spurn Girls," *The Home News* (New Brunswick, N.J.), October 10, 1970, 1, 12.

26. McCormick interview.

27. Rev. Thomas R. Fitzgerald, S.J., to Daniel J. Altobello, July 26, 1968, GUA.

28. Davis.

29. Board of directors minutes, August 6–8, 1968, Office of the University President, Georgetown University.

30. Enrollment statistics, Records of the Office of Admissions, Georgetown University.

31. "Class of '78 Is First Class to Claim Female Majority," *Hoya*, September 13, 1974, 3.

32. This includes Douglass, Rutgers, Livingston, and Cook Colleges by 1975–76.

33 Final Enrollment Reports for Rutgers, The State University, 1964–76, Office of the University Registrar, Piscataway, N.J.

34. McCormick interview.

35. "Coed Applicants Have Higher Academic Record," *Targum*, February 9, 1972, 1.

36. "Georgetown Admissions Office Swamped by Female Applicants," *Standard*, March 13, 1969, GUA.

37. Georgetown University Office of Admissions, "Annual Report," July 1969, 7, 6–10, GUA.

38. SAT verbal scores were also significantly higher for women, but SAT math scores were somewhat lower than those of the entering men.

39. From 1971 to 1976, mean verbal and math SAT scores declined at both Douglass and Rutgers, as they did across the country. Interestingly, verbal scores declined more at Douglass than at Rutgers, and math scores declined more at Rutgers than at Douglass. One possible explanation for this is that as more women were admitted to Rutgers, their better performance in verbal scores and poorer performance in math scores were reflected in the Douglass and Rutgers mean scores. Data provided by Ian A. Hodos, Senior Associate Director of University Undergraduate Admissions, Office of University Undergraduate Admissions, Rutgers University, New Brunswick, N.J.

40. "Coed Applicants Have Higher Academic Record," 1.

41. "Men Flock Outdoors to Welcome Visitors," *Targum*, November 19, 1964, 1.

42. *Hoya*, February or March 1969, clipping in GUA.

43. *Hoya*, February 1969, clipping in GUA.

44. *Miss "G" Goes to Georgetown*, 1967, 16–17, GUA.

45. *The "G" Book*, 1967, 33, GUA.

46. *Miss "G" Goes to Georgetown*, 1966, 32, GUA; *Miss "G,"* 1967, 9–10. Until the mid-1960s, freshman women were required to take a physical education class, presumably to ensure that they maintained a certain level of exercise necessary for health.

47. *Miss "G,"* 1967, 8.

48. When students were to spend an evening off-campus, they were required to inform the residence hall administration of their whereabouts. The 1967 *"G" Book* required freshmen men to get written authorization from parents or guardians. "If such leave is to be spent in Washington or the vicinity," it states in bold print, "the student must also present a letter of invitation from an adult host who maintains a home here." Upperclassmen were required to sign out with their prefect.

49. *Miss "G" Goes to Georgetown*, 1971, 33, GUA.

50. *The "G" Book*, 1967.

51. "Life in a Coed Dorm: Young Adults Sharing Responsibility," *Georgetown*, May 1975, 7.

52. "Women in College See Pros, Cons, of Dorm Life Here," *Targum*, September 11, 1972, 1.

53. "Rutgers College Is Graduating First Women" *New York Times*, May 27, 1973.

54. Phyllis Anderson-Wright, interviewed by Tamara Xavier, April 25, 1993, cited in Jean Pachucki, "The Women's Movement at Rutgers University from 1967–1976," Spring 1994, RUA.

55. "First Woman Accepted to College Is Graduated," *Georgetown Today*, September 1972, 33.

56. See "Ye Trinity Maiden: Vanguard of Idealism," *Hoya*, April 24, 1964, 7; "Dunbarton Damsels Lonely Glamourines," *Hoya*, May 1, 1964, 8; "O, Farewell Visitation!," *Hoya*,

May 15, 1964, 13; "Immaculata Seeks Companionship," *Hoya*, October 8, 1964, 7; and "Marymount Misses: 'Just Show Us a Good Time,' " *Hoya*, March 4, 1965, 7.

57. "Freshman Girls Call GU Gentlemen Most Elusive Problem on Campus," *Hoya*, October 13, 1966, 2.

58. Anonymous student to Father Davis, October 11, 1972, GUA.

59. Stereotypes cited in an article by Diane Kiesel, "The View from Across Town," *Caellian*, December 10, 1971, 8.

60. "Meg Schoen Chosen Mili Ball Queen," *Targum*, May 10, 1962, 2.

61. "Miss Beautiful Secretary Contest to Be Held Soon," *Targum*, [1962], clipping in RUA.

62. "Queens to Be Crowned Saturday for Homecoming and Bond Issue," *Targum*, September 28, 1964, 1.

63. "Bond Issue's Beauty Queen to Be Named," *Targum*, September 22, 1964, 1.

64. "Linda Dancer—Homecoming Queen," *Targum*, [1962], clipping in RUA.

65. "Women's Athletic Association," *Ye Domesday Book*, 1968, 143.

66. "Women Liberate ROTC Confines," *Georgetown Voice*, October 30, 1973, 17.

67. *Targum*, October 20, 1966, 3.

68. "First Female ROTC Cadet Commander Assumes Post," *Targum*, February 12, 1974, 7; "Delta Beta Psi to Be First Rutgers Sorority," *Targum*, May 7, 1974, 1; "RU Women's Chorale formed," *Targum*, February 24, 1975, 7.

69. Joseph P. Joyce, "Georgetown Theatre: More than a 'Passing Fancy,' " *Georgetown Today*, November 1973, 9.

70. "Georgetown's Security Chief: Another First," *Georgetown Today*, January 1974, 16.

71. Ann LoLordo, "A Woman Whose Time Has Come," *GU Today*, July 1977, 22.

72. "Rutgers College Is Graduating First Women."

73. "Woman Nominated for Vice-President," *Targum*, April 10, 1972, 1.

74. "Female Board Chairman Is Rutgers First," *Rutgers*, September 10, 1973, 6.

75. "Named First Woman Dean in College," press release, June 6, 1973, Office of the University President, Georgetown University.

76. Patricia Rueckel to Charles Hartmann, dean of students, June 24, 1969, GUA.

77. "Women's Lib. Can't Be Ignored," *Georgetown Voice*, September 29, 1970, 8.

78. Wendy Jordan '73, "Women Organize," *Georgetown Voice*, October 26, 1971, 8.

79. "Secretaries Get First Contract with Rutgers," *Targum*, November 12, 1973, 1.

80. "GU Women's Conference Attacks 'Male Superiority,' " *Georgetown Voice*, February 20, 1972, 2.

81. "Weeklong Symposium Begins Tonight on Women's Issues," *Targum*, September 18, 1972, 2.

82. Jonathan Iwasko, "Women at Georgetown," *The Academy*, February 1992, 5.

83. Nicole Wallace, "Women's Center Activities Underway," *The Georgetown Voice*, Septermber 20, 1990, 12.

84. *Rutgers, The State University of New Jersey, Fact Book*, 2000–2001, 14.

85. Ibid., 68.

86. Paul L. Leath, provost, "Annual Report: New Brunswick Campus, 1990–91," 7, RUA.

87. "Building the Future: Georgetown University Self-Study Report for the Middle-States Commission on Higher Education," March 24, 2002, 47.

88. In addition, by 2001, women held the positions of dean of policy studies, vice president and general counsel, vice president for human resources, dean of the School of Nursing and Health Studies, vice president, and treasurer, among others ("Women in Top Administration," *Blue and Gray,* April 23, 2001, 1).

89. Debbie Hwang, "Provost Says GU Gender-Sensitive," *Georgetown Voice,* November 30, 2000, 7.

90. Georgetown University Undergraduate Bulletin, 1970–71 and 2000–01, GUA.

91. Kyle Sproul, "The Underrepresented: Women's Struggles for a Larger Voice in the Curriculum, the Classsroom and the Student Body," *The Georgetown Voice,* 30th Anniversary Issue [March 1999], 34.

92. See *www.georgetown.edu/department/women*; *www.rci.rutgers.edu*; and *http://women's-studies.Rutgers.edu/home/about.*

93. Bryanna T. Hocking and Dawn Scheirer, *The Women's Guild* (n.p.: n.p., 1997).

94. Kathryn King, "Gonzalez: Center Impossible for GU," *The Georgetown Voice,* February 14, 2002, 7.

95. Ryan Michaels, "No," *The Georgetown Voice,* February 8, 2002.

96. Any Yang, "Women's Center Generates Debate and Controversy," *Hoya,* September 19, 2000, 14.

97. "Considered a Valuable Resource to Some Students, Women's Center Is Unknown or Pointless to Others," *Hoya,* September 19, 2000, 10.

98. *The Scarlet Letter,* Rutgers University yearbook, 1990.

10

Coeducation after a
Decade of Coordination

The Case of Hamilton College

Leslie Miller-Bernal

Coordination between a men's and a women's college has existed in the United States since 1879 when the "Annex," later called Radcliffe, enabled some women to receive instruction from Harvard professors. While only a few institutions of higher education have ever had a coordinate structure, in the mid-1960s there were still some well-known coordinate colleges, including Pembroke and Brown, Barnard and Columbia, Radcliffe and Harvard, Sophie Newcomb and Tulane, and Douglass and Rutgers. In 1966 Hamilton College, a small, private liberal arts college for men in Clinton, New York, announced that it was establishing a women's coordinate college. This decision did not seem particularly unusual for the time, but the type of women's college that was founded—a progressive or innovative college—was more exceptional. After only ten years of operation, Hamilton College absorbed this women's college, Kirkland, and Hamilton became coeducational in the more typical sense. This chapter discusses how and why Hamilton College decided to found Kirkland and the reasons Hamilton became coeducational a decade later. It seems that coeducation, after even a brief period of coordination, can have benefits for women students, despite coordination and coeducation being instituted primarily with men's interests in mind.

Hamilton as a Traditional Men's College

Founded in 1812 and loosely affiliated with the Presbyterian Church during most of the nineteenth century, Hamilton College had a reputation for being academically sound and conservative. Like at other small, private liberal arts colleges for men, many of Hamilton's early graduates became ministers, but by the early twentieth century, a majority entered secular professions. The curriculum at Hamilton was traditional, with an emphasis on the classics, but gradually broadened to allow students to choose electives, within limits (even as late as 1968, Hamilton offered neither sociology nor performing arts majors). The student body was homogeneous, consisting mostly of white middle-class Protestants of northern European ancestry. Social life at Hamilton centered on fraternities, and football and ice hockey were popular sports. Hamilton seemed similar to many tradition-bound men's liberal arts colleges in the northeastern United States.

World War II and its aftermath affected even this rural, idyllic campus. A lay president during the war years tried without much success to introduce some innovations in Hamilton's curriculum. But the biggest changes occurred during the halcyon years of the 1960s, when the federal government and foundations gave money to encourage the growth of higher education. Hamilton College faced the issue of how to grow without losing the advantages of smallness. President Robert McEwen also wished to stimulate Hamilton in order to keep up with the modern world.[1]

The Idea for a Coordinate Women's College

In the early 1960s, Hamilton's trustees established their first ever Long-Range Planning Committee. One educational concept that appealed to trustees and administrators was the "cluster" concept, in which a college established other colleges nearby that had somewhat unique focuses or specialties. Members of the planning group traveled to Oxford University, College of the Pacific, and Santa Cruz to learn more about clusters.[2] President McEwen was particularly enamored of this idea and proposed that Hamilton establish a cluster of about five colleges in order to have a "lively impact" on Hamilton. Each college was to be separately organized, with its own faculty, president, trustees, and definition of purpose. In that way, Hamilton would remain small but would still achieve "educational flexibility."[3]

For about seven years, Hamilton engaged in a great deal of planning around the college cluster idea. A key question to be settled was which type of college should be established first. An early planning document discussed many possibilities but saw problems with all but a women's college. A denominational college for Friends or Presbyterians, for example, was dismissed because religious bodies would probably not be interested in establishing a college that "would basically be subordinate to Hamilton." A progressive or experimental college, dubbed "College John Dewey," was likewise rejected because it would be "prickly—perhaps exasperating—as a neighbor" and besides, why not just pick and choose the better features of the experimental college for Hamilton itself?[4] Given Kirkland's later experiences as a progressive women's college, these sentiments about "College John Dewey" would seem to have been prophetic.

Planning for the college cluster proceeded on the basic premise that the new colleges should benefit Hamilton and that Hamilton should remain the dominant institution "although the College might not state it this bluntly and in public." To ensure Hamilton's dominance, the satellite colleges would have fewer students; to benefit Hamilton, the colleges had to be liberal arts with high admission standards and have a curriculum that made up for Hamilton's "deficiencies" in such fields as sociology and economics.[5] A women's college seemed like an obvious first choice. Women's enrollments in higher education were rising faster than men's, and the experiences of coeducational institutions in the Northeast, such as Middlebury and St. Lawrence, showed that it was relatively easy to find highly qualified young women who wished to attend a coeducational college. In fact, as David Ellis, an alumnus faculty member on the faculty planning committee, wrote to the trustees' Long-Range Planning Committee, it would be easier to recruit 350 first-rate women students than another 300 men of top quality.[6]

The interim report of the trustees' planning committee, released in spring 1963, recommended growth through the "coordinate colleges option," with the first coordinate institution being a liberal arts college for women. The report pointed out how this arrangement would result in "better students for Hamilton" since trustees believed that some of the best men students were not applying due to Hamilton's "isolated male character." The report detailed the many ways in which the women's coordinate college would be separate from Hamilton (with its own trustees, faculty, president, classrooms, curriculum, dormitories, and dining facilities) but argued that Hamilton would benefit from an increased diversity of curricular offerings since students would be able to cross-register.[7] While the trustees and administration of Hamilton seemed to believe that a women's coordinate college was the best option, alumni were not necessarily convinced. President McEwen wrote to the alumni, reassuring them that "newspaper reports to the contrary, the board did not agree that the first of these colleges would be for women . . . [it was] merely one of the many possibilities that the committee has studied for the past eighteen months and will continue to study."[8]

Despite this public posture of uncertainty, more and more planning occurred based on the assumption that the first college in the cluster would be a women's college. Hamilton sought advice from educators from other institutions, as well as from recent graduates of prestigious women's colleges. By summer 1963, reports of various planning groups began to incorporate rhetoric that indicated that they believed that the new college for women should also be experimental or progressive. A group that included the president and dean of Hamilton and the president of Goucher College argued that the college for women should develop its own "distinctly characteristic" goals, its own methods of teaching and evaluation, perhaps omitting grades entirely, which would enable it to "escape some of the conventional inherited practices of older institutions."[9]

Even though the new college was increasingly being conceived as an innovative institution, planners made some traditional assumptions about women students and their needs. The second wave of the women's movement had not yet developed to the extent that these assumptions were consistently challenged. Planners viewed women as different from men and assumed that they would have life trajectories that included a "black-out" period devoted to their families. It therefore seemed appropriate to plan a new institution that was more flexible than conventional colleges, with easier ways for women to leave college and reenter at various times in their lives. The planners were explicit about the type of women they envisioned enrolling in the new college. As one summary of a two-day planning meeting in New York City in 1964 expressed it, the women should be like Hamilton students in being "of superior academic ability"; at the same time, they should "not be exceptional," meaning that they should "not think exclusively in terms of a career." While it was acknowledged that women needed education to fit them for "important roles as leaders in society," planners also believed that "an essential part" of women's education "must be" to enable a student to "understand the 'black-out period' of child bearing and child-rearing and emerge as a vital individual ready and able to use her later, productive years effectively."[10]

The second chair of the trustees' planning committee, Walter Beinecke, developed this theme of women's family roles even further when he sent a final report on the educational philosophy of the women's coordinate college to the board of trustees in fall 1964. He wrote, "No one would deny that a married woman owes her first allegiance to her husband, her children and her home; nor that she finds her greatest happiness and the fullest expression of her talents in meeting her responsibilities to them." Beinecke listed four goals for the "Hamilton Coordinate College for Women": (1) to produce a woman who enjoys the "process of learning"; (2) to educate a "wife" who could "grow" with her husband "while inspiring her children"; (3) to enable women to see themselves as "fully capable . . . to meet the needs of society in ways that are beyond the abilities of men"; and (4) to give women the academic tools necessary to carry on careers appropriate to the "varying stages of their lives—before marriage, on a part-time basis during motherhood, and on a full-time basis after their children are grown."[11]

Given the number of people involved in planning for the new women's college, both within and outside Hamilton, it is not surprising that the planning documents contained contradictory statements about the appropriate relations between the founding college, Hamilton, and its "offspring," Kirkland. Most planners seemed to think in terms of how Hamilton College would benefit from the women's college. Thus the curriculum of the new college was seen as a way of expanding Hamilton's course offerings in areas where the men's college was deficient (the social sciences and performing arts, for example). Yet, other planners recognized the danger in this and argued that the new college's curriculum should be planned with women students' needs and interests as the guiding principle. A planning group chaired by Dr. Millicent McIntosh, past president of Barnard College, argued that the women's college's course offerings should have "an integrity and purpose of their own" and not be developed "to round out delinquencies in the short course list of Hamilton."[12] When Kirkland opened, however, the curriculum did reflect an imbalance that could be explained by the needs of Hamilton College. Ironically, less than a decade later, some Hamilton administrators pointed to Kirkland's lopsided curriculum as a reason for disbanding the college, saying that it had "questionable standards and a bent to push 'arts and crafts.' "[13]

The Women's College Opens

In 1968, before construction of the new campus was completed, Kirkland College opened with 172 women students. The college was built across the street from Hamilton and right from the beginning it depended on Hamilton, both for 60 acres of land and a million dollar interest-free loan. While the colleges were separate in terms of having most of their own classrooms, faculty, president, and board of trustees, they did share a library and a few other facilities. From a student's perspective, coordination entailed being able to take courses at the other college. In the early years, however, this was not so easy for Kirkland students since some Hamilton faculty distrusted their academic qualifications. When a Kirkland student wanted to take a course at Hamilton, the dean of Kirkland would bring the student's record to the Hamilton faculty member in order to get permission for her to enroll.[14]

Kirkland College contrasted with Hamilton physically and in practically every other way. Its president, Samuel Babbitt, was young, Yale-educated, and progressive; he combined academic respectability with innovative ideas that he developed during his time in the Peace Corps. Kirkland had a high percentage of Jewish students, and Kirkland students' attitudes toward social issues were decidedly left-wing.[15] Kirkland students saw themselves as "pioneers" in an exciting academic adventure, responding to President Babbitt's invitation to enroll in order "to find your own paths and to learn and to grow with a new college."[16] Another way in which Kirkland differed from Hamilton was in its high percentage of women on its faculty—slightly more than 25 percent, which was much less than the hoped-for target of a half but much greater than the single woman Hamilton had on its faculty in 1968.[17]

Given that Kirkland opened during the period of student rebellions, it is not surprising that it was more innovative than its planners had intended. From the beginning, Kirkland's educational philosophy was strikingly different from Hamilton's conventional approach. Kirkland students helped run the college by participating in long, intensive discussions with faculty and "Sam" (what most faculty and students called President Babbitt) in the major governing body, the student-faculty assembly. Students voted to have complicated, unwieldy rules for men's visits in the dorms; although these rules were later modified, they demonstrate how much control over their college lives Kirkland students were given. Courses were ungraded; instead, students received written evaluations for their work, which meant that class sizes had to be kept small to enable instructors to cope. Kirkland faculty and students had close, relatively nonhierarchical relationships, fostered by the small class sizes and their participating together in many meetings. Two of the words most frequently used to describe the atmosphere at Kirkland were "intensity" and "community." One student praised the college as a "very, very family kind of thing."[18] A faculty member noted the frequent "squabbling" at Kirkland's many meetings but also talked about the underlying commitment to the "spirit of Kirkland."[19]

Problems Faced by the College

Almost from its beginning, Kirkland found itself hampered by a shortage of money. Like most women's colleges, it had been founded with much less money and a smaller endowment than the average men's college.[20] Hamilton did not share its endowment with Kirkland, and the new college was not allowed to use Hamilton's constituencies for fund-raising. As is typical of small institutions, particularly innovative ones that require low student-faculty ratios, Kirkland had high costs when computed on a per student basis. Although President Babbitt was quite successful at attracting foundation gifts and in obtaining donations from supporters, the new college's debts kept rising. As early as 1971, President Babbitt talked about the need for funds from "as yet untapped private sources" for the "very survival of the college." Three years later he characterized the situation as a "time of retrenchment." Babbitt realized the critical importance of building the endowment so that he would not have to spend as much time in "incredible annual fund-raising."[21]

Hamilton College's power over Kirkland hindered coordination. As the word implies, coordination requires two parties to work together. Yet, many administrators, faculty, and students at Hamilton believed that theirs was the superior institution and dealt with their counterparts at Kirkland as if they were subordinates. Several structural and cultural features reinforced this hierarchical relationship. Not only was Hamilton a much older, larger, and richer institution, but it had founded Kirkland and loaned it additional money, which meant that Kirkland was dependent on it.[22] As a women's college, Kirkland suffered from the general cultural view that women's activities and institutions are intrinsically inferior to men's. Moreover, many people viewed Kirkland's innovative teaching practices as insufficiently rigorous and hence less prestigious than Hamilton's traditional approach. Similarly, Hamilton faculty and administrators criticized Kirkland's curriculum for being imbalanced, as it stressed the "easy" and feminine subjects of performing arts, social sciences, and, in the natural sciences, botany and the history of science. Even though Kirkland's curriculum had been created to overcome Hamilton's weaknesses, its origins were generally overlooked, with the college's detractors viewing its curriculum as another indication that Kirkland was the weaker academic institution. Critics of Kirkland also pointed out that over time, the academic gap between Hamilton and Kirkland students had increased, as measured by the SAT scores of entering students.[23]

Kirkland people did not accept the view that their college was inferior and that coeducation was preferable to coordination. Sam Babbitt, in particular, eloquently defended Kirkland time and again, disagreeing publicly with the president of Hamilton, J. Martin Carovano, who viewed coordination as financially and administratively inefficient. Babbitt argued that the differences between Hamilton and Kirkland led to "creative friction" and that coordination had a richness that a single-approach coeducational college could not have. Babbitt believed that Kirkland had been given too little money from the outset and that, despite successes in fund-raising, it needed more money from Hamilton to fulfill the promises of coordination.[24] Babbitt also disputed the idea that Kirkland students were weaker than Hamilton students. Yes, their SAT scores might not be quite as high, he said, but Kirkland students did as well as men in courses they took at Hamilton, and as seniors, Kirkland women performed better than Hamilton men.[25] Babbitt and others acknowledged the validity of the criticism of Kirkland's curricular imbalance but believed that this could be overcome. The deans of Hamilton and Kirkland had been working on a plan to introduce changes at both institutions that would avoid reinforcing gender stereotypes. Kirkland, for instance, would expand its offerings in such traditionally male subjects as computer science and statistics, and Hamilton would reduce its offerings in these areas.[26]

Although over time Kirkland students became less politically radical and more integrated with Hamilton students, both in college organizations and even in mixed-sex dormitories, the women continued to feel that they were not accepted as equals. One Kirkland student wrote an op-ed piece titled "Anatomy of Disillusionment" for the student newspaper; it described how for a "long time" both Kirkland students and faculty had been "condescended to."[27] This perception was also confirmed by the first dean of Kirkland who said that the men students viewed the women as "second-class citizens," which she felt contributed to the high attrition rate of the first cohorts of Kirkland students.[28] As alumnae, Kirkland women bitterly recalled how Hamilton students believed that Kirkland courses were not academically rigorous and assumed that women students were "promiscuous."[29]

The End of Kirkland and the Establishment of Coeducation

In 1977, less than a decade after it opened, Kirkland faced an insurmountable financial crisis. The college was unable to meet its operating expenses, and since it was involved in a capital campaign to raise $20 million, borrowing more money was not feasible. Hamilton refused Babbitt's request for sufficient money to enable Kirkland to survive—a guarantee of up to $600,000 a year for five years. Hamilton's President Carovano had never been convinced of the benefits of coordination, which, after all, had been his predecessor's idea. President Carovano also seemed unsympathetic to progressive education; he was reputed to have characterized Kirkland as a "remnant of the '60s without present validity."[30] Hamilton's trustees at first seemed receptive to giving Kirkland the money it needed. Faced with President Carovano's opposition to coordination, however, the trustees ultimately changed their mind. On June 10, 1977, the Hamilton board of trustees voted unanimously (with three abstentions) in favor of the following statement:

> The Hamilton Trustees recognize the substantial contributions Kirkland has made to education on the Hill and are prepared to commit immediately all of Hamilton's resources, financial and otherwise, to an educational program for men and women that will reflect and preserve the present strengths of each College; The Hamilton Trustees believe that the current arrangement of two independent colleges is no longer financially feasible and, accordingly, will not agree to Kirkland's request for up to $3 million in unconditional support over the next 5 years nor to any other requests for unconditional financial assistance beyond that already agreed to for the 1976–77 academic year; and The Hamilton Trustees believe that the educational program should be redesigned within a structure that will include ultimately one chief executive officer and a single faculty.[31]

Thus the trustees concurred with the president that it was "very unlikely" that the women's college would become "financially independent in the foreseeable future" and were willing to extend Kirkland only limited support.[32] Although at first reluctant to do so, by August 1977 Kirkland trustees and administrators had accepted that if they were not going to "close immediately," they had to agree to consolidate with Hamilton.[33]

During its short life, Kirkland inspired great loyalty. When President Carovano announced the decision that it would be consolidated with Hamilton, a great storm of protest erupted. Students, faculty, alumnae, trustees, and friends (some of whom belonged to the Hamilton community) held rallies, demonstrated, circulated petitions, held interviews with the press, and organized letter-writing campaigns. Hamilton trustees refused to change their minds, however, and in some respects became even more hard-line over time. Negotiations over the fate of Kirkland faculty broke down. In a decision that made it clear that all-male Hamilton saw its college as superior, all of Kirkland's tenured faculty members were required to go through another tenure review at Hamilton. Untenured Kirkland faculty members were given two-year appointments. Some refused to be so humiliated and left. In the opinion of the faculty member at Hamilton who at the time was chair of the Committee on Appointments, Kirkland instructors were right to feel "knifed in the back." Because Kirkland emphasized teaching more than publishing, Hamilton lost some excellent faculty and "caused a great deal of grief."[34]

Even though Kirkland students were treated better than its faculty, with guaranteed admission into the new, coeducational Hamilton and the option of graduating according to either Kirkland or Hamilton requirements, many of them were deeply distressed at the imminent end of their college. During the 1970s, Kirkland students had become more aware of the benefits of attending a women's college, and now this "room of . . . [their] own" was being taken away from them. One Kirkland student wrote about her fear of losing a "firm sense of female identity" and "solidarity" that had come from "being a woman's school in conjunction with—and opposed to—a men's college." She tried to maintain her optimism by saying that the new challenge would be to "prove receptive to the specific problems that attend being a woman in a male-oriented culture." She insisted, however, that given women's loss of leadership positions in other formerly women's colleges, coeducational Hamilton would need a women's resource center—"a must."[35]

Kirkland's Legacy at Coeducational Hamilton

Hamilton benefited in many ways from its takeover of Kirkland in 1978. No longer could it be considered a stuffy college with a strong but limited curriculum. Now it had a fine performing arts center, other modern buildings, and an innovative curriculum that soon included women's studies (as a minor in 1981 and a major in 1984). Hamilton had expected to experience a half a million dollar budget deficit as a result of taking over Kirkland and its debts, but in fact, more success with fundraising and increased enrollments resulted in a lower deficit ($300,000). Women formed an increasing proportion of applications and enrolled students: over one-third of the students in the first coeducational class were women, and within five years, they represented over 40 percent. Numerical representation of women on Hamilton's board of trustees also improved, from having no women in 1977 to having five women (out of 35 members) by 1980. Women on the faculty did not change nearly as dramatically but did increase slightly, from 19 to 22 percent.[36]

The time period, as well as the generally feminist consciousness of the Kirkland constituency, predisposed the newly coeducational Hamilton to respond to women's concerns. By 1978, many other men's colleges in the Northeast (for example, Williams, Amherst, and Dartmouth) had already become coeducational. As peer institutions, they served as models for Hamilton. The women's movement was also strong, with concepts such as sexism and male chauvinism a new part of the lexicon. Scholars were beginning to examine the disadvantages of coeducation for women, recognizing that being educated with men did not necessarily mean receiving equal treatment. Hamilton's women students benefited from these trends. The women's center established by Kirkland students continued as part of Hamilton. In addition, Kirkland's endowment, about three-quarters of a million dollars, was used to create a foundation to endow scholarships for women and programs of special interest to them. In the second year of coeducation, this foundation underwrote a two-day conference on women and education, with the well-known feminist author Florence Howe as one of its speakers. Hamilton also engaged in various assessments of women's students' experiences. In the first year of coeducation, a planning subcommittee of trustees, students, faculty, and administrators visited three comparable colleges (Middlebury, Vassar, and Williams) to evaluate the adequacy of Hamilton's extracurricular activities as a coeducational institution. Later the college assessed the classroom climate for women students, reaching the unsurprising conclusion that men students were more vocal in most classes.[37]

Hamilton's fraternities created the most difficulties for women. Shortly after Hamilton became coeducational in 1978, a self-study report prepared for the Middle States Association devoted a long section to fraternities, concluding that they were intrinsically discriminatory, as women had fewer residential and dining options than men. Moreover, women had no say in planning the part of the campus's social life sponsored by the fraternities. "Women become strictly invitees, never the ones to do the inviting," the report noted.[38] One response to the dominance of fraternities was to establish a few sororities, but they never achieved the prominence of the fraternities. Heavy drinking and incidents of sexual harassment connected to the fraternities continued to plague the campus. Among 36 alumnae from the class of 1988 who were surveyed about their college experiences, practically the only negative comments concerned fraternities and heavy drinking as key parts of the college's social life. As one alumna wrote, "I hated the frat scene and the mob atmosphere."[39]

Toward the end of the twentieth century, Hamilton College took steps to curtail fraternity influence. In 1995 the college announced a major change in its residential life: all students were required to live and eat on campus. While fraternities were not abolished, the college bought all the fraternity houses. As experiences of other colleges have also shown, however, it is not easy to end fraternity influence. Fraternity rushing still occurred at Hamilton, and according to a former dean of faculty, Bobby Fong, "fraternity-like" behavior entered the dorms, facilitated by block housing that enabled groups of students to live together. Moreover, four Hamilton fraternities sued the college on antitrust grounds, arguing that their options for living and dining had been curtailed.[40]

In these and other ways, Hamilton College has demonstrated awareness of its past, brief association with a women's college and has made serious attempts to ensure that women students' experiences with coeducation are positive. What Hamilton has not tried to preserve are the progressive aspects of Kirkland. No one attempted to change the forms of evaluating students, for example, or to break down the boundaries between academic disciplines. As a faculty member at Hamilton who previously taught at Kirkland perceptively noted, "We tried to make something of the women's college stay more than we tried to make something of the innovative college stay."[41]

Women's Position at Hamilton More Recently

Since the 1980s, women have become a larger proportion of students, faculty, and board of trustees at Hamilton, as Table 10.1 shows. Women are now over half of Hamilton undergraduates, and with the appointment in 2003 of Hamilton's first woman president, Dr. Joan Hinde Stewart, half of the top administrators are women, too. The number of women on the board of trustees has increased, but they remain slightly less than one-third (excluding life trustees, which are overwhelmingly men). There are also more women on the faculty, but their proportion has remained less than 40 percent.

Women students are about as likely as men students to hold top leadership positions in student organizations. For the four time periods shown in Table 10.1, three men and one woman were editors-in-chief of the student newspaper; three women and one man were presidents of the student government.

Table 10.1. Women's Presence at Hamilton College, 1989–2003

	1989–90	1994–95	1997–98	2002–03
Undergraduates (%)	46	46	47	52
Faculty (%)	32	37	36	36
Top administrators (%)	17	17	17	50
Board of trustees (%)	14	28	24	29
Editor-in-chief				
of student newspaper	M	M	F	M
Student government				
president	F	M	F	F

Source: Hamilton College Catalogs, 1989–2003; *The Spectator,* 1989–2003.

Women have also done well academically. Of the student awards given in 2002 and noted on the Hamilton College web page, 10 of 14 went to women; similarly, in 2001, 7 of 11 awards went to women. Another indication of women's academic success was their representation on "Alexander Hamilton's List" in spring 2003. The list comprised 165 students whom the faculty recognized for "their achievements in writing"; of the 149 whose gender was apparent from their first names, 86, or 58 percent, were women.[42]

Women and their past history at Kirkland College are visible to the Hamilton College community in other ways as well. Alumni gatherings have some events for Kirkland alumnae, and in 2002, the former president of Kirkland, Samuel Babbitt, returned to campus to give the first "Chuck Root" lecture, honoring a former Kirkland trustee. An institute called the Kirkland Project, which focuses on the intersections of gender, race, class, and sexual orientation, is increasingly active. Each year it sponsors a series of lectures on a particular theme; in 2002–03, the subject was "masculinities" and in 2001-02 it was "the body in question." With a $150,000 Hewlett Pluralism and Unity Grant, matched by the college, the Kirkland Project has provided faculty members with stipends to incorporate gender, race, class, sexuality and other aspects of human diversity into the curriculum. The project now offers its own first-year interdisciplinary seminar on "Coming of Age in America," and it is starting to develop follow-up sophomore seminars. Additionally, it gives brown bag presentations, produces a newsletter, supports a couple of summer student interns who are engaged in "socially useful, unpaid work," and sponsors a few faculty and students for three days of education and work in economically deprived areas of the nearby city of Utica.[43]

Conclusion

Although no documents from the planning period for Kirkland indicate that coordination was seen as a stepping-stone to coeducation at Hamilton, this was how some people at Hamilton later interpreted the decade of coordination. No matter the intentions, the result seems to have been more equitable coeducation than most other colleges achieved by adding women directly into a historically men's college. Faculty and students from Kirkland who entered Hamilton in 1978 had a model of what an independent women's college was like. They resolved to preserve that heritage and ensure that Hamilton used funds from Kirkland in ways that benefited women. Women's influence there remained strong because of the era, with its well-established national women's movement, and because there were available models of formerly men's colleges that had become coeducational.

At Hamilton today, the women's studies program is large and active for a small liberal arts college. One faculty member has an appointment entirely in women's studies and one faculty member has a shared appointment in women's studies and psychology. There are also two visiting professors of women's studies. Moreover, the Kirkland Project is active and has somewhat overlapping areas of concern with women's studies.

It would be naïve to believe that Hamilton has achieved complete gender equality through the coordinate college route to coeducation. Fraternities still cause problems; men's sports get more attention than women's sports in the student newspaper; women make up less than 40 percent of all faculty and less than 30 percent of full professors; and the board of trustees is less than one-third women. Moreover, the way in which Kirkland was taken over by Hamilton has caused long-standing resentments. Some faculty and students have worn black armbands at Hamilton's commencements to symbolize their opposition to the hostile takeover of Kirkland. The Hamilton College campus continues to be seen as divided into two parts—the historical, fraternity-dominated Hamilton side and the more modern, politically progressive Kirkland side.[44] Hamilton College has attempted to unite the campus architecturally, by building a bridge connecting the two sides that ends in a new student center, but it remains to be seen whether it is possible to eradicate the split that easily.

Considering that Hamilton College was a conservative men's college for more than 150 years, its transformation to a coeducational college in which women students' interests are well represented is quite remarkable. Today, women at Hamilton represent more than 50 percent of the student body, and a woman appears to be at least as likely as a man to head the student government association. Kirkland's legacy has come to be better recognized on an official level, with its own alumnae gatherings and an institute bearing its name. President Robert McEwen undoubtedly did not foresee this outcome when in 1961 he began to explore ways of sparking some life into a rather stodgy college, but coordination and a national women's movement proved to be a powerful combination that benefited Hamilton women.

Notes

1. Leslie Miller-Bernal, *Separate by Degree: Women Students' Experiences in Single-Sex and Coeducational Colleges* (New York: Peter Lang, 2000), 143.
2. Richard Couper, Letter to Frank Lorenz (April 29, 1997), Couper file, Hamilton College Archives, Burke Library (HCA). Richard Couper '44, was the first trustee chair of the Long-Range Planning Committee; in 1962 he became the first administrative vice president at Hamilton and Walter Beinecke became the planning committee chair.
3. Robert McEwen, memo to Hamilton Long-Range Planning Committee, August 1961, Historical Documents of Kirkland College, HCA.
4. Hamilton Long-Range Planning Committee, "The Cluster," n.d., HCA.
5. Ibid.
6. David Ellis, memo to the Hamilton Long-Range Planning Committee, 1963, HCA.

7.   R. W. Couper, "Interim Report of the Long-Range Planning Committee," April 20, 1963, HCA.

8.   Robert McEwen, letter to Alumni, 1963, Historical Documents of Kirkland College, HCA.

9.   "Notes on a meeting at Hamilton College, July 1 and 2, 1963," Historical Documents of Kirkland College, HCA.

10. Winton Tolles "Summary of a Two-Day River Club Meeting in New York City, March 25–26, 1964," Historical Documents of Kirkland College, HCA.

11. Walter Beinecke, "Final Report on the Educational Philosophy of the Women's Co-ordinate College for Hamilton," September, 1964, Historical Documents of Kirkland College, HCA.

12. Tolles, "Summary of a Two-Day River Club Meeting."

13. Dean Gulick to President Carovano, February 21, 1977, HCA.

14. Inez Nelbach, interview by Peggy Farber, August 1977, HCA.

15. Miller-Bernal, *Separate by Degree*, 149. Kirkland students gave more liberal answers than college students nationally to such questions as whether colleges had been too lax in dealing with student protesters and whether a college had the right to ban extreme speakers from campus.

16. Samuel Babbitt, *Kirkland College Catalog* 1969–70, HCA.

17. Miller-Bernal, 150.

18. Connie Strellas, interview by Peggy Farber, April 16, 1978, HCA.

19. Eugene Putala, interview by K. G. Russell, summer 1992, HCA.

20. For a discussion of early women's colleges, see Helen Lefkowitz Horowitz, *Alma Mater* (Boston: Beacon Press, 1984); Mabel Newcomer, *A Century of Higher Education for Women* (New York: Harper and Row, 1959); and Barbara Miller Solomon, *In the Company of Educated Women* (New Haven: Yale University Press, 1985).

21. Samuel Babbitt, President's Reports, 1970–71, 1974–75, HCA.

22. In the mid-1970s, Hamilton students made up close to 60 percent of the total enrollment of around 1,650 for Hamilton and Kirkland combined. See Miller-Bernal, 168.

23. Ibid., 160.

24. Samuel Babbitt to Francis H. Musselman, March 1, 1977, HCA.

25. Samuel Babbitt, memo to the Hamilton Board of Trustees, May 5, 1977, HCA.

26. Catherine Frazer and Walter Lawrence Gulick, "Academic Coordination," April 7, 1977, HCA.

27. *The Spectator*, March 3, 1978, HCA.

28. Nelbach interview.

29. Robin Krasny, "Kirkland College Today: An Experiment Stabilized" (B.A. thesis, Princeton University, 1973), HCA.

30. Samuel Babbitt to Kirkland trustees, May 12, 1977, HCA.

31. Minutes of the trustees of Hamilton College 1976/77, June 10, 1977, HCA.

32. J. Martin Carovano, letter to Hamilton students, June 23, 1977, HCA. At one point in the negotiations, Hamilton administrators offered money to Kirkland on condition that they were given the right to approve Kirkland's budget. Babbitt was unwilling to turn over control of Kirkland's "basic policy document," however. He believed, as did

at least one member of the Hamilton board of trustees, that at the heart of the money issue was Hamilton's desire to "control" Kirkland. See Miller-Bernal, 161.

33. Samuel Babbitt to Kirkland people, August 1, 1977, HCA. The legal term for what happened to Kirkland is not consolidation, actually, since that would require dissolving both institutions' charters and establishing another one for a new institution. The term for what actually occurred is "amalgamation" of Kirkland with Hamilton, with Kirkland's dissolution and Hamilton's assuming its assets and debts. See Miller-Bernal, 162–63.

34. Jay Williams, interview by K. G. Russell, summer 1992, HCA. This treatment of the Kirkland faculty caused the resignation of an alumnus member of Hamilton's board of trustees, Dr. Maurice Clifford '41, and led a couple of Hamilton alumni to write letters to the student newspaper saying that they were withdrawing their support from Hamilton. See Miller-Bernal, 163.

35. Leslie Elion, *The Spectator*, September 23, 1977, HCA.

36. Miller-Bernal, 164–68.

37. Ibid., 164, 327.

38. "Self-Study for the Commission on Higher Education of the Middle States Association," 1980, 55, HCA.

39. For information about how these surveys were administered, see Miller-Bernal, 289–90.

40. Ibid., 326–27.

41. Nancy Rabinowitz, interview by K. G. Russell, July 1992, HCA.

42. The list is available online at *http://hamilton.edu*.

43. Ibid.

44. As one student wrote about these divisions, the Kirkland side of the campus, now referred to as the "dark" side, is known for "artsy-fartsy intellectual snobs" who "sit under trees and write poetry," whereas students on the "light" or Hamilton side are known for being "forever adorned in J. Crew apparel . . . in a perpetual drunken bliss" ("Breaking Down the Stereotypes: The Light Side and the Dark Side," *The Spectator*, September 12, 1997, 10, HCA).

Coeducation beyond Liberal Arts

The chapters in this section describe educational institutions that are often overlooked in discussions of higher education: military academies and for-profit technical colleges. Both chapters focus on women's experiences at these schools and use interviews with students—women, and in some cases men—as a primary source of information.

The United States Military Academy at West Point became coeducational in 1976 as a result of a federal law mandating women's admission, whereas Virginia Military Institute (VMI) did not admit women until 21 years later, following a protracted legal battle. Diamond and Kimmel describe the different approaches each military institution used in dealing with women cadets—integration at West Point, which allowed for some physical differences between men and women, and assimilation at VMI, which required women to meet exactly the same physical standards as men. Regardless of the approach, however, women cadets faced hostile receptions at both institutions. Interviews with cadets reveal how the young women dealt with hostility and how, over time, both their modes of adapting and men's reactions to them changed.

The last case study concerns women's entrance into technical fields, such as computers and electronics, at for-profit technical colleges and community colleges. Women were never formally barred from these programs, but neither were they encouraged to enroll before the 1970s. Deil-Amen's study of women students, a high percentage of whom were minority students from low-income families, in two for-profit technical colleges and six community colleges, reveals the importance of women receiving encouragement in their pursuit of nontraditional majors. In the right environment, women can succeed, even if they are somewhat older than traditional age college students, have not done well in secondary school, and have other responsibilities, such as, childcare and jobs. Women's confidence is key, and that confidence is directly affected by an educational institution making it easy for them to enroll and feel comfortable.

11

"Toxic Virus" or Lady Virtue

Gender Integration and Assimilation at West Point and VMI

Diane Diamond and Michael Kimmel

> It would be ridiculous to talk of male and female atmospheres, male and female springs or rains, male and female sunshine. . . . [H]ow much more ridiculous is it in relation to mind, to soul, to thought, where there is as undeniably no such thing as sex, to talk of male and female education and of male and female schools.
> —Susan B. Anthony and Elizabeth Cady Stanton

The first women who trained in such traditionally masculine fields as law, medicine, and the military had to prove that they could succeed in a male environment in the face of strong opposition to their presence. This chapter examines the experiences of women at the United States Military Academy at West Point and the Virginia Military Institute, two formerly all-male institutions that became coeducational only under duress. In their metamorphosis from all-male institutions to coeducational ones, West Point and VMI progressed through a succession of stages, not unlike those of the grieving process following the death of a loved one. This is understandable, since for many people in the military communities this transformation was the death of the institution as they knew it.

West Point had long been recognized as a bastion of stereotypic masculine culture.[1] The first women at West Point, who entered in 1976, encountered "an institution that had been designed exclusively by and for men and that exemplified masculinity."[2] Similarly, VMI, which women first entered in 1997, had established its reputation as a place where boys underwent ordeals to achieve manhood, as reflected in an aptly titled book on the history of VMI, *Drawing Out the Man: The VMI Story.*[3] Given that both institutions' identities were firmly rooted in their male-only status, it is not surprising that both initially struggled against coeducation. While many faculty and administrators came to accept the inevitability of coeducation, male cadets continued to resist the admission of women vociferously.

This chapter examines West Point's and VMI's initial resistance to admitting women, the women's reasons for attending, the male cadets' reactions to the admission of women, and the women's modes of adaptation.[4] Before we discuss coeducation, however, we present a brief overview of each institution's history and discuss the fundamental differences in institutional approaches to incorporating women: gender integration at West Point versus gender assimilation at VMI. Finally, we describe changes that have occurred during more than a quarter century of coeducation at West Point and the current state of coeducation at VMI.

Brief Overview of West Point and VMI

West Point first came to prominence during the American Revolution, when strategic fortifications were constructed to block British advances up the Hudson River. Located on the west bank of the Hudson River 50 miles north of New York City, West Point has been continuously occupied by U.S. troops since January 20, 1778. George Washington established his headquarters there in 1779. In 1802, President Thomas Jefferson signed into law a bill of Congress authorizing the establishment of "a military academy to be located at West Point in the State of New York."[5]

West Point's mission is to educate, train, and inspire the corps of cadets. To become a member of the corps, a person must be nominated by a legal authority, who is most often a member of Congress or the Department of the Army. Securing a nomination does not guarantee an offer of admission, however. Admission is highly competitive, as recent statistics on first-year students indicate. In 2001, their average SAT score was 1268, and 50 percent were in the top 10 percent of their high school class.[6]

Each West Point graduate is expected to be a leader committed to the values of duty, honor, and country, who grows professionally during a career as an officer in the U.S. Army, and who gives a lifetime of selfless service to the nation. Academy graduates are awarded a bachelor of science degree and commissioned as a second lieutenant in the army, serving a minimum of five years of active duty. West Point has a long list of illustrious graduates, including two U.S. presidents, Ulysses S. Grant and Dwight D. Eisenhower; the president of the Confederacy, Jefferson Davis; such famous generals as Robert E. Lee, "Stonewall" Jackson, Douglas MacArthur, George S. Patton, Alexander Haig, and Norman Schwarzkopf; and astronauts Frank Borman, Edwin E. "Buzz" Aldrin, and Edward White II.

VMI was founded in 1839 and is located in Lexington, Virginia, in a valley between the Blue Ridge and Allegheny Mountains. For more than 20 years before the formation of VMI, its site was occupied by a military post of the Commonwealth of Virginia, serving as a storage point of arms. Shortly after the War of 1812, an arsenal was established on the town's outskirts. The townspeople felt that the arsenal guard of 20 soldiers lacked self-discipline when not on duty. In 1834 Lexington's leading citizens proposed that the arsenal be transformed into a military college, with the students protecting the arms while pursuing educational courses.

On November 11, 1839, 23 young Virginians became the first cadets at the newly established VMI. Initially VMI was open only to Virginians, but in 1858 it opened its doors to students from states outside the commonwealth. It remained a bastion for southern white men, however. Not until 1968 were five African-American Virginians admitted to VMI; women were admitted to VMI beginning in 1997. VMI is not as academically competitive as West Point. In 2001, first-year VMI students had an average SAT score of 1134, more than 100 points less than the average at West Point, and only 10 percent of VMI first-year students were in the top 10 percent of their high school class (compared to 50 percent at West Point).[7] VMI appears to be becoming more academically competitive, however, as indicated by its accepting a lower percentage of its applicants.

It is the mission of VMI to produce "citizen-soldiers, educated and honorable men [and women] who are suited for leadership in civilian life and who can provide military leadership when necessary."[8] Unlike West Point whose graduates are required to serve a minimum of five years of active duty in the army, VMI graduates have the option of seeking a commission in the armed services on graduation. VMI's most famous graduate is undoubtedly George Marshall, whose accomplishments include having been chief of staff of the U.S. Army in World War II, author of the "Marshall Plan" for European recovery, and winner of the Nobel Peace Prize. More recent relatively well-known graduates include best-selling author Harold Coyle and actors Dabney Coleman and Fred Willard.

The Struggles over Coeducation

The background for gender integration at both academies includes the dramatic influx of women into the workforce, the Equal Rights Amendment (ERA), and changes in the military during and after the war in Vietnam. Following that war, the United States shifted to an all-volunteer force. To maintain sufficient manpower, the military dramatically increased the number of women in the armed forces and expanded the assignments available to women. Between 1972 and 1976 the number of women in the armed services rose from 45,000 (1.9 percent) to 110,000 (more than 5 percent) of military personnel. Prior to

1975, the U.S. Army had a separate corps for women, the Women's Army Corps (WAC). In June 1975 the secretary of the army told Congress that the WAC was no longer needed and that its removal would ensure full integration of women into the army. Congress resolved that women could not be fully integrated unless it dissolved the separate corps status of the WAC.[9]

One general aim of the women's movement was to obtain women's access to previously all-male institutions. The service academies were no exception. In 1972, the U.S. Naval Academy denied admission to two women nominated by Senator Jacob Javits of New York and Congressman Jack McDonald of Michigan. The legislators responded by introducing several bills in both houses making it illegal for the services to deny admission to the academies on the basis of sex. These bills failed to pass, either because they were held up in subcommittee or Congress adjourned before action could be taken. In May 1975, however, Congressman Stratton bypassed the subcommittee where legislation to open the service academies to women had been held up and proposed an amendment to the Defense Authorization Bill of 1976 to admit women into the service academies. The issue was brought to the floor of the U.S. House of Representatives where, after a short debate, it passed 303 to 96. On June 6, the Senate followed suit and on October 7, 1975, President Ford signed the bill into law.[10] One hundred nineteen women entered West Point's first coeducational class in 1976, and 62 of those women graduated.

Both West Point and VMI initially opposed coeducation. Prior to the admission of women at West Point, army officials argued "the primary purpose of the United States Military Academy was to develop combat arms leaders and that since women were excluded from combat assignments, admitting women to West Point was incongruent with its mission."[11] Officials further contended that women would detract from the academy's mission; reduce unity, morale, and efficiency; and lower admission standards and the prestige of the institution. Before the congressional decision, West Point superintendent general Sidney Barry made clear his position on women at the academy. Recalled a West Point alumna,

> Before we got there, the superintendent had the entire corps come to an assembly, so to speak, in this big auditorium, have them close their eyes and raise their hand if they thought it was a good idea for women to be there. . . He said that he would resign before women went into the academy. He didn't resign. But what he did was he set us up . . . the commander of the academy. He's telling all these guys that he's in charge of, who are supposed to be emulating him, . . . their big leader, 'I'm resigning before this happens.' This is like the worst thing that could ever happen to the academy. . . . So then we come the next year. What are they supposed to think?[12]

It was into this highly charged environment that the first women entered the academy the following summer.

Fifteen years later, Virginia Military Institute, a state-supported military educational institution, began its own battle to remain an all-male institution. In court, VMI officials argued that the essential character of the institution would change with the admission of women, that women were not suited to VMI's "adversative" educational methodology, and that the presence of women would undermine the cohesiveness of the corps. When Major General Josiah Bunting, who would later become VMI's superintendent, gave a deposition on behalf of the Citadel, South Carolina's state-supported military educational institution that was also fighting in the mid-1990s to remain all-male, he called women "a toxic kind of virus" that would destroy the military institute.[13] Other opponents believed that women were too demure, passive, and noncombative to succeed, that ladies were still the virtuous "angels of the house" celebrated in antebellum advice books.

VMI's court battles were intimately linked to the struggle of the Citadel to remain all male. Their struggles coincided, in part, because one year after the Justice Department initiated its case against VMI, a high school student in South Carolina named Shannon Faulkner applied and was admitted to the Citadel, after removing identification on her high school records that she was a woman. The Citadel had previously been an all-male institution, so there was no place on its application form that asked the applicant's sex. When Faulkner was subsequently rejected because of gender, she brought suit against that institution, also a state-supported, all-male, military-type institution.

While the VMI and Citadel cases were heard in different district courts, they both landed at the U.S. Court of Appeals for the Fourth Circuit (in Richmond, Virginia) and therefore their adjudication was linked. Both schools rely on what they call the "adversative method," emphasizing "physical rigor, mental stress, absolute equality of treatment, absence of privacy, minute regulation of behavior, and indoctrination of values . . . designed to foster in cadets doubts about previous beliefs and experiences and to instill in cadets new values."[14]

VMI spent six years and $5 million fighting the admission of women before the U.S. Supreme Court ruled in 1996 that its all-male admissions policy violated women's constitutional right to equal protection. However, whereas West Point had been compelled to admit women, VMI could have voted to relinquish its state funding and become a private institution. Although privatization would have permitted VMI to preserve its male-only admission policy, it would have been a costly proposition. Cognizant of this fact, the VMI board of trustees voted (by a narrow margin of 9 to 8) to admit women into the institute's corps of cadets. Thus, in 1997, twenty-one years after the first women entered West Point as plebes, the first women entered VMI as rats.

Gender Integration vs. Gender Assimilation

In their efforts to incorporate women into the corps of cadets, West Point adopted a policy of gender integration. Such a policy acknowledged aggregate gender differences in physical, but not mental, realms and developed mechanisms for testing physical efficacy that accommodated those differences. By contrast, VMI adopted a policy of gender assimilation. Assuming that women's equality meant strictest adherence to exactly the same treatment, VMI changed neither its curricular nor physical training regimen for women. If they wanted to be "equal," they had to do exactly the "same" things the men did.

West Point's policy was governed by federal law, part of the 1976 Defense Appropriation Authorization Act that stated, "the commissioning of female individuals shall be the same as those required for male individuals, except for those minimum essential adjustments in such standards required because of physiological differences between male and female individuals."[15] Adhering closely to the letter of the law, West Point officials developed a system of "equivalent training," which took into account physiological differences between men and women. Some male cadets, however, did not accept this principle, insisting instead that women be held to the same physical standards as they were. In a survey administered a few months before the first women arrived, a cadet proclaimed, "their PE should be the same as the men's, and their scores on competitive PE tests should be averaged in with the men's, and *no special* increments. If they can't cut it on a two mile run, or a reveille run, they should be treated the way men are."[16] Such reactions did not quickly disappear. Even after women had attended the academy for almost a year, a study found that "a fairly high percentage [of male cadets] were still in favor of exactly equal physical standards for women," since some male cadets perceived the accommodations as "lower standards."[17]

Whereas West Point adopted an equity model, VMI espoused an assimilation model, maintaining a single standard (i.e., the male standard) for both female and male cadets. Paradoxically, throughout litigation the official VMI position was that men and women were inherently different with divergent needs and abilities. VMI defense witnesses testified that women were not capable of the physical demands made on the men. After hearing the case, a district court concluded, "If women were to be admitted, VMI would have to convert to a dual-track physical training program in order to subject women to a program equal in effect to that of men."[18] Yet once the Supreme Court decision was handed down, VMI voted to admit women and resolved that men and women would be treated the same, with no accommodations for physiological differences. VMI policy was guided by the direction from the Supreme Court: "VMI's implementing methodology is not inherently unsuitable to women. . . . [S]ome women are capable of all the individual activities required of VMI cadets . . . and can meet the physical standards [VMI] now impose[s] on men."[19]

While a single physical fitness standard may appear gender neutral, it is, in fact, based on a standard developed by and for men. In adopting a position of equality rather than equity, real differences are ignored. Male standards become *the* standard of analysis, with women evaluated only in relation to men. As sociologist Joan Acker explains:

> Understanding how the appearance of gender neutrality is maintained in the face of overwhelming evidence of gendered structures is an important part of analyzing gendered institutions. One conceptual mechanism is the positing of an abstract, general human being, individual, or worker who apparently has no gender. On closer examination, that individual almost always has the social characteristics of men but that fact is not noted.[20]

VMI male cadets favored a policy of gender assimilation over one of gender equity and integration. "I believe that if they decide to have women here, that they have to perform up to the standards that have been upheld," commented one male cadet. "You don't lower your standard. We don't lower our standard for anybody."[21]

However, the assimilation model for physical fitness testing (one based on the male body) places female cadets in a bind. Since the test is geared to male physical attributes, women are more likely to fail. If women voice opposition to the standards imposed by equality-as-sameness, they could be branded hypocrites, professing to want the VMI experience only to seek changes once they have arrived. In fact, VMI female cadets did not want the test modified. Their rationales for maintaining a single physical fitness standard focused on concerns that differential standards would lead to male resentment and a perception of women as weak: "If there were dual standards I think girls would get a lot more flak for it. You know, 'well you only passed the VFT [Virginia Fitness Test] 'cause they lowered the standards for you.' That type of thing. So I think having the single standard is good as far as relations go between guys and girls. It makes it a lot easier."[22]

Problems arose whether the institution adopted an integrationist or assimilationist model. West Point's equity model of integration, based on "equality of effort," proved difficult for many male cadets to understand. They resented what they perceived as lower standards for women, and their acceptance of female cadets remained largely predicated on the women's ability to keep up with the men in the physical fitness arena. Under the assimilationist model at VMI, male cadets could not complain that women were receiving preferential treatment. However, the model itself failed to acknowledge actual physiological differences, compelling the women to measure up to the male standard that was set as the norm. Such a policy represents formal equality, but it in fact promotes substantive inequality.[23] Also, in both models the standard itself is never questioned: women are expected either to measure up to pre-existing standards created by and for men or to justify accommodations made for bio-logically based differences. In either case, men remain the center of analysis, with women considered only in relation to them.

Men's Beliefs about Women at West Point and VMI

The first women to attend West Point in 1977 came for many of the same reasons as their male peers: they were looking for a challenge, knew of West Point's reputation for educational excellence, or came from families of West Point graduates. "I like risk, challenge, adventure. I wanted to do something different," recalled one West Point alumna.[24] "[I] was looking for something not everybody else did," declared another.[25] A survey of West Point's first coed class conducted on entry into the academy found that not only did "both sexes give similar reasons as important factors in wanting to come to West Point" but that "in commitment to a military career, cadets of both sexes are equal."[26] In fact, the largest differences between men and women in the first coed class at West Point were "associated with attitudes to sex roles, marriage, childbearing, and the prospect of being in a coeducational environment."[27] Unsurprisingly, whereas the women were more liberal in their attitudes and more enthusiastic about being in a coed environment, the men were more conservative and re-sponded negatively to the prospect of being in a coed environment.

At VMI in 1997, men and women in the first coed classes were also at-tending for many of the same reasons, including the challenge, the institution's prestige, and to prepare for a military career. Some women chose VMI because they wanted to attend "a small military school"; some had received full schol-arships; and some came because they had not been accepted to one of the federal service academies and they wanted to prepare for military careers.[28] The women were emphatic that they had not chosen VMI to be pioneers or rebels but were instead seeking the challenges VMI offered. "I wasn't much of the pioneering female [that] people actually associate with us. For me it was more of the military aspect of it. It was very attractive. I guess it was something new and challenging."[29]

Although male and female cadets at both West Point and VMI chose their institutions for similar reasons, many male cadets could not accept that the women were there for much same reasons they were. At West Point, some male cadets said that they did not understand why any woman would want to attend their academy. Exclaimed one male cadet, "Any woman who would even think of coming to West Point is not mentally straight."[30] Others thought women came to West Point to find a mate, as did the male cadet who asserted, "A lot of the girls who came to the Point came looking for a husband."[31] Still others believed that women came so that they could say they were one of the first women to attend. "Most girls or women whom I have talked to either are against women at West Point or if they want to come would do so only to be the first women at West Point."[32]

At VMI, more than 20 years later, some men also struggled to comprehend why any woman would want to attend their institute. "I try to put myself in their shoes, and I try to think about it like what if I wanted to go to an all-female school. . . . [W]hat kind of person would it be to do that and it would be kind of an effeminate guy who would want to do that and I just can't see why a girl would want to come here."[33] Several cadets voiced concern that some women were only attending to "prove something," or, in other words, to make a political statement as feminist radicals. Admitted one male cadet, "I think the male cadets look at [female cadets] and a lot of them have the impression that, well, if they're coming here, they've got something to prove, that they're coming here because they've got an agenda and they want to give us a speech on how they can do everything just as good if not better and that that's what they're here to do."[34]

However, a number of male cadets insisted that while some women had come to make a point, other women were there for the right reasons, and it was "obvious" which female cadet was which. According to this interpretation, the "quiet" women were at VMI for the "right reasons," while the women who were "always running their mouths" were attending in order "to prove a point."[35]

The men were correct insofar as many women had enrolled to prove something, but the women were there to prove something to *themselves,* not to the men. "I didn't really feel like I had to prove anything except maybe to myself, but I felt that it was the best opportunity considering my career goals. . . . I thought that VMI had what I was looking for."[36] Unaware of the irony, one male cadet condemned women for attending VMI to "prove something" and then offered the same motivation as his reason for attending: 'I came here to prove something, the fact that I could make it through it. . . . But still why, why come here as a normal girl?' "[37]

Even those female cadets who espoused what might be called a "feminist" motivation nonetheless selected VMI for much the same reason as the men.

> I'm just glad that I was born and I lived in an area where nobody told me, "you can't do this because you're a woman," and I think when I first heard about this place that's the first time I'd ever heard that you can't do something because you're a woman. I was like, "I've never heard that before." . . . [P]eople always ask at this school, "why did you come here?" I think that's a lot of the reason. I mean I wanted to go to military school. I didn't have the grades or anything to go to West Point, and I think that that was a big attraction, like people say, "did you come here to prove a point?" It's like, "I didn't come here to prove anything to *you.* But I came here because I wanted to do it and because I can."[38]

A particular type of person is drawn to a military education. Although men's and women's motivations for attending both West Point and VMI were more alike than different, many male cadets in the first coed classes could not accept that women were there for the same reasons they were.

Male Cadet Reactions to Coeducation

Just prior to coeducation at West Point, male cadet attitudes toward the admission of women ranged from extreme prejudice to ambivalence to acceptance. At the extreme end of the spectrum were the male cadets who held highly traditional views about women in general, believing that women had no place in a man's world, such as the military. "Women should spend more time at home raising their children than seeking jobs, especially those as demanding as an Army officer. Women are mainly responsible for the guidance of their children. . . . The world is really becoming morally messed up, and I believe it is because of the deterioration of the mother's guidance on her children and the deterioration of the family."[39] Some cadets went even further in wanting to run women out of the academy, even though they knew it was "already law" that women were to be admitted. One cadet said that he felt it was his "duty" to drive out as many women "as possible" because "it's either them or me."[40]

Other male cadets were more concerned that standards would be made more lax to accommodate the women. Recalling West Point's integrationist model of gender norming of physical standards, one male cadet asserted that, "females will receive special treatment—which is unfair."[41] "Too many things have been changed to make the system easier for women to come here,"[42] maintained another. Some male cadets steadfastly held to the army's initial arguments in opposition to coeducation, insisting that West Point was for training combat leaders and since women could not be combat leaders, they should not be in the corps of cadets. A few remained adamant that there be a separate academy for women, ignoring the fact that the decision had already been made and that women were to be attending West Point that summer. "I strongly believe that women should attend separate military academies. West Point is for the training of combat arms, and I don't feel that women should be in combat arms; however, I feel that the Army can use women as executives, but they can receive the necessary training at a separate academy."[43]

Still others employed religious arguments to support their opposition to women's admission. Said one male cadet, "I feel, in accordance with the Bible, that a woman's place is in the home."[44] Remarked another, "Since the inception of Christian society, the women's virginity and femininity have been cherished qualities, and her role in the home as the mother and homemaker have placed her on a plateau above the normal level of life. To make her the male's 'equal' would be to bring her down into the gutter of everyday life, the greatest fall since the fall of Eden."[45] Some male cadets feared a loss of "esprit de corps," viewing women as intruders in West Point, "one of the oldest, and most definitely, strongest fraternities in the history of the United States."[46]

Not all men opposed coeducation. Some cadets, although not happy about the imminent change to coeducation, accepted the admission of women as another task that an officer must carry out "whether he likes it or not." Such an attitude was sometimes combined with a view that coeducation would help to break the "closed-minded stubbornness" of the academy.[47] A minority of men went further, seeing coeducation as a change that would improve the institution, for cadets, and for the army more generally. Declared one, "Admission of women will be beneficial for West Point and the Army. Basically, West Point is supposed to develop Army Officers (some say combat officers). The Army's women ranks are increasing, and we may as well have qualified officers leading them."[48]

Some men recognized the irrationality of their fellow cadets' vehement opposition to the admission of women and had the foresight to realize that the greatest obstacle to the women's successful integration would be the attitudes of their peers. "I almost have to laugh at the harbingers of doom who predict that the Academy will crumble on its foundation when women are finally accepted next summer. . . . [T]he only difficulties I foresee in the transition will arise from the attitudes of those individuals who resist the move."[49] A few had insights into the motivations behind male resistance to the coeducation at West Point, as did the male cadet who remarked, "I feel that the real reason for the establishment not wanting women is that women are a threat to their masculinity!"[50]

Twenty-one years later, as VMI admitted its first female cadets, the male cadets were as opposed to coeducation as were their predecessors at West Point. Men at VMI most frequently mentioned "loss of tradition" as their reason for opposing coeducation. A reflective cadet said that "tradition" was the "primary reason" male cadets were wary of women at VMI.

> Over some hundred and thirty years we didn't have this. Now, all of a sudden, it was forced down to us through the Supreme Court, the federal government. . . . A lot of it I think goes back to the notion that women are not supposed to be in an environment like this. . . . [W]hen I talk to guys . . . there's still this picture of a mother's place is in the home supporting the father, raising the kids, barefoot, making oatmeal every morning. And to have a woman in a leadership position, having power, having responsibility, I think it threatens them.[51]

Reminiscent of the remarks made more than two decades earlier at West Point, a VMI male cadet commented on his peers' attitudes. "A lot of people have the view that women have no place in the military or at least not in combat situation and therefore no place where we're going to go through the toughest part of our life, the Ratline. 'I don't want a woman around. I want it to be just men.' So, of course I've heard that."[52]

Some men saw the presence of women as an "intrusion" in what was "still" a "male school."[53] Others said that the school was "ruined" since "everything ended when the girls got here."[54] Male cadets expressed concern that "some of the women are trying to change the institute" or were "just trying to make a statement."[55] Women were perceived as "breaking down the fraternity spirit we're supposed to have," thereby causing "breaks in the camaraderie."[56]

Although many VMI cadets opposed coeducation, as at West Point, a number of them exhibited more enlightened, or at least more tolerant, attitudes toward it. Some initially opposed the admission of women but learned to develop a better attitude: "Before I came here, when I was accepted and I was a senior in high school, I didn't want 'em here. I thought they'd just ruin the school. . . . But after I got here my feeling changed."[57] By training alongside the women, some male cadets came to realize the women were trying to achieve similar goals. "When you get to know that this female doing push-ups three people down from you is another person and you get to know her and her personality, it's kind of hard to dislike somebody after you've gotten to know them as much as it is you just hate the fact of who they are."[58] The presence of women sometimes became a source of motivation. Recalled one male cadet, "It's kind of weird. They were a motivating force to help me get through the first year because if she can do it—five-foot tall, 100 pounds soaking wet—if she can do it, I can do it."[59]

A major step toward accepting coeducation occurred when male cadets recognized that, at least "now," women were attending VMI for the same reasons they were—"to get the VMI experience."[60] Similarly, forming friendships with the women also helped reduce antipathy toward them, enabling male cadets to see their women friends as "real people" who are "here for good reasons, you know, the same reasons I'm here."[61]

A few men acknowledged some positive consequences of coeducation. Women were credited with making VMI "a lot more professional" and helping the corps "grow up a little."[62] Today, VMI more closely reflects the world these men will enter on graduation—a coed one. Although the vast majority of VMI male cadets maintained that the disadvantages of coeducation outweighed the advantages, a small proportion acknowledged that having women at VMI was preparing them for the future.

Female Cadets' Modes of Adaptation

During the early years of coeducation at West Point, female cadets reported that "resentment" was the reason integration was not yet successful. Even male cadets who might have supported coeducation responded to peer pressure, forming their opinion "on what the guy next to them said" and concentrated on their own "survival" by being quiet about any dissenting views.[63] When asked whether she had felt supported or resented by the male cadets, an alumna from one of West Point's first coed classes replied, "Very resented by most; supported privately by some; never supported publicly by any. They had to survive the system, too!"[64]

To survive and succeed within this sometimes openly hostile environment, the first female cadets adapted by blending in, not standing out. As an alumna explained: "The best way to get through something like West Point is to blend in and go with the flow. When you can't blend in you attract attention. Any attention is unwanted. It's never good attention—'My, look at how straight she is standing, fast she is running.'— It always turns to 'My, doesn't she need a haircut, why aren't her shoes more shiny?' "[65]

Blending in often entailed isolating themselves from other women. "We were still trying desperately to fit in," an alumna asserted, "and fitting in meant not making too much of women's solidarity."[66] In order to avoid notice and be accepted as cadets, many of the first female cadets at the academy downplayed their femininity. An alumna from the fourth coeducational class (class of 1983) contrasted the experience of women from the first coeducational class with that of women in her own class, noting the resentments that developed among cohorts of women as the modes of adaptation changed.

> They did what they had to do to not . . . stand out, very short haircut, they never wore makeup, they never wore their skirt, anything like that that would make them singled out. Well, our class [class of 1983] comes along and we want to wear makeup, and we want to wear our skirts. And I think to some extent, to some of these women, it bothered them. . . . There was some resentment from the first class. It was like we were doing it on our own terms. They did it on the men's terms, and they sort of, in a way, looked down on us because we wanted to be feminine, wanted to wear our skirts, and we wanted to be seen as women.[67]

To be accepted by the male cadets, the first female cadets at West Point found that it was not enough to be outstanding women; they had to keep up with the men in the physical arena. Those women who could keep up with the men were judged to be *not like* other women, and therefore acceptable. Rather than alter their conviction that female cadets could not succeed, male cadets considered female cadets who were successful, *exceptions to the rule.* But male cadets were not the only ones who were critical of female cadets who fell behind; female cadets were also disparaging of women who did not hold their own alongside the men. These female cadets feared that the failures of some women would be generalized to all women.

> Female cadets who were able to keep up physically (not fall out of runs, not fall back in road marches, excel in Physical Training tests, not be overweight) were treated similar to male cadets. It seems to me that although the formal grading

standards at the academy placed a high emphasis on academics, the informal grading and evaluations done amongst cadets was done primarily on a physical fitness scale. Those female cadets who could not keep up were looked down upon by male cadets because they did not have what it takes, while other female cadets also looked down upon them because it was felt that they made all women at the academy look bad.[68]

To succeed as cadets, women felt they had to change men's attitudes. "You won men over one at a time. . . . Most of the men had a preconception of how the women were or how women are, or what women were there for, or whatever."[69] At the same time, some male cadets began to look at female cadets as individuals who were at West Point for the same reasons they were.

> It's easy to be biased toward a group when you don't know people in the group. But once the guys knew the women, I think they realized we were like their mothers and their sisters and their girlfriends. We were just people. We were like them. We were trying to get through and we were trying to do everything they were trying to do and that it didn't become a he-she issue.[70]

However, male cadets could easily fall back into the old pattern of viewing women as a group rather than as individuals. In the eyes of many male cadets, success on the athletic field transformed some women into individuals and potential leaders.

> For the most part . . . they started looking at you as an individual, not just as a female cadet. But then it's also easy, they also would slip easily into the generalizations, "well women cadets, women cadets this. But not you . . . " And I was lucky because I was very athletic . . . that got rid of 90 percent of the grief right there. If you could keep up, if you could make the runs, if you could do this, if you could do all that stuff. . . . The next most important thing was the leadership. If you had some credibility and some bearing and that sort of thing. Academics . . . that wasn't important to your automatic credibility.[71]

The female cadets at West Point realized they had to walk a fine line, keeping up with the men physically while at the same time being neither too feminine nor too masculine, nor, for that matter, too successful, so that the men would not feel threatened by their achievements. Women who did achieve leadership positions were prone to resentment by their male peers. The same women whose physical aptitude had enabled them to excel, to be recognized as individuals and accepted by male cadets, were the ones most likely to be seen as threats to male authority, usurping leadership positions formerly held by male cadets. "Some men had trouble dealing with us first as peers or colleagues, and then if we were given rank, as authority figures. It came as no surprise that many of them were threatened by that; they were offended when a female was in authority."[72]

In spite of overwhelming obstacles, women were succeeding, and in the first four years of coeducation, male cadets' attitudes toward female cadets improved. Other researchers have noted that these changes in gender role attitudes at West Point occurred later than comparable attitudinal changes in the larger society, suggesting that the coeducation experience itself may have positively influenced the male cadets.[73] Another study found that contact between men and women helped ameliorate male cadets' negative preconceptions about women. Those male cadets who had the most contact with female cadets were the ones most likely to realize that the allowances for physiological differences between women and men were appropriate.[74] The first female cadets broke the initial barriers, paving the way for future generations of women at the academy. In fact, the success of the first female cadets surpassed the expectations of the researchers who had set out to study the integration process.[75]

At VMI, as at West Point, importance was placed on blending in. However, it was male cadets, more often than female cadets, who underscored the importance of blending in. When asked what advice he would give a perspective female cadet, a VMI male cadet replied, "Try and fit in with the rest of the guys. Don't try and be different. You may be female but just try and be one of the guys. Do everything they do and don't try and be different or single yourself out, and you'll fit in like everyone else; you'll do fine."[76]

A big part of blending in was not doing things that drew attention to oneself, and the women realized that they already stood out because of their gender. Acknowledged one female cadet, "there are so few of us, we stand out because we don't look like everyone else here."[77] As a result, the women tended to avoid anything that would draw additional attention to themselves as women. To many that meant downplaying their femininity in order to be accepted by their male peers. However, some women at VMI consciously chose to assert their femininity by wearing their skirts. The skirts became a medium for asserting gender identity and formed a contested ground both between women and men and between women and women. Some chose not to wear their skirts so that that the "guys" would not "resent" them so much, or because they believed that the goal should be uniformity.[78] "This isn't the place to wear skirts. It separates us even more. . . . I didn't come here to become a man. . . . I['m] still gonna keep my feminine side. I'm still gonna act like a girl, but I don't need to make it so pronounced."[79]

However, a number of women, while valuing unity, relished those opportunities where they could assert themselves as women. "I like to wear a skirt once in a while. I have no problem wearing the pants because I do like the unification aspect of it. . . . But sometimes you get tired of being in a group and being the same, and you kind of do want to stick out sometimes. But just because the first wave of females [are] still here I think they went through a lot for their approval, so they don't wear skirts. . . . It's not accepted yet."[80]

For a few, wearing the skirt became more than an act of preference—it became a symbol of resistance:

> The last year when we just got skirts and everybody was making a big deal about it like, "You know you can't wear your skirts. You wanted to come here, you know. You want to be the same as us. You can't wear skirts." I was like, ugh, well, I'm gonna wear mine to class. So I wore mine to class, and I walked in. I was so scared, I was like my heart was pounding, and I knew everybody was staring at me.[81]

Whether they chose to assert their femininity occasionally or downplay it, female cadets recognized that they needed to work within the system to gain the approbation of their male peers. As at West Point, the women at VMI found that acceptance was primarily a function of being able to keep up with the men physically. "If you can do the same things as a man physically, then they'll respect you more. But it doesn't matter if your grades are like ten times better or you're better at everything else. If you can keep up with them physically . . . a lot of times then somebody will be like, 'Oh . . . that's cool. Now I respect you.' "[82]

One consequence of this emphasis on the physical domain was that women were condemned—"slammed"—if they failed to live up to the men's standards.[83] Another consequence was that they often had to work twice as hard as the men in order to keep up with them. As one cadet explained, "You know, we have to run twice as much as the guys to be able to keep up and I think that we need to do that in order to show that we can make it."[84] Those who did not succeed were criticized for making all women look bad. The female cadets were aware that given how few of them there were, "everybody's watching you all the time."[85]

Similar to the reasons for change at West Point, when VMI men worked alongside women, they tended to develop cross-sex friendships and see women not as outgroup members but as individuals. Even some male cadets who would have preferred that VMI remain all-male tended to accept a particular woman once they got to know her, especially if they trained alongside her and saw her as a team player. "During the ratline, N. [a female cadet] and I were great friends. She'd come down to our room before formation and . . . we'd talk. . . . It helped us out a lot that she depended on us and we helped her out. . . . We didn't just say, 'Oh, you're a female' and push her by the wayside. She was accepted."[86]

Although VMI women who were successful, physically, academically, and militarily, were the ones most likely to be accepted by male cadets, difficulties sometimes arose when such women were appointed to a leadership position. Some male cadets wondered whether their appointments were deserved or whether, instead, they were politically motivated. As a male cadet explained, when the first woman was made battalion commander, rumors spread that she might have "made it a political issue with . . . high-ups of the administration and that's the reason she got her appointment to that position."[87] Some invoked tradition to explain the difficulty men had accepting the appointment of a woman to a leadership position. "It was explained to me by one of my brother rats that. . . . for centuries. . . . men have been the head of everything . . . like with VMI, it's been for such a long time . . . then to have a female take over that position, they're just not ready to see a female taking it over."[88]

By the time the first women graduated from VMI, male-female relations had begun to improve. Some men were beginning to accept women as fellow cadets rather than seeing them as outsiders invading male territory. At the same time, those women who graduated proved that they could accomplish the goals set for them. Like the first women at West Point, the first women at VMI were pioneers, laying the groundwork for subsequent classes of women.

A Quarter Century of Coeducation at West Point

Much has changed in the more than two decades since West Point admitted female cadets, and many of the problems initially experienced by the first women at West Point have been alleviated. When 119 women entered the newly coeducational West Point in 1976, women made up 0.5 percent of the faculty (3 out of 572 instructors). When the 62 women who remained after four years graduated in 1980, women's faculty representation had increased to just over 2 percent (14 out of 595). It might seem that the almost 48 percent attrition rate of women in the class of 1980 is fairly high. However, when considered in light of the almost 40 percent attrition rate of men in the same class, the percentage of women who graduated is actually quite impressive, especially given the extraordinary obstacles they encountered. By contrast, in 2000, there were 600 women in the corps of cadets (150 per class), and women were almost 13 percent of the faculty (75 out of 585). Whereas the first class of women made up 2 percent of the corps of cadets, women now represent approximately 15 percent. In addition, female cadets are well represented in leadership positions, with an equal percentage of men and women selected as first captains.[89]

Since 1976, several factors have helped to advance coeducation. First, the presence of female cadets has become naturalized—current cadets never knew West Point without women. Second, the number of female cadets, faculty members, and officers has increased. Third, women are now found at all levels of the institution, from upperclass leaders to professors to military officers. Fourth, West Point's chain of command is strongly supportive of women, sending the message that women are valued members of the community. Not only do these changes make West Point more hospitable to female cadets, they enable the women to be more comfortable expressing their femininity and associating with other women. When asked in 1997 to describe the changes since her attendance, an alumna from the first coeducational class responded:

> The highest level of the administration is clearly, clearly supportive. Clearly vocally, procedurally supportive of men and women. . . . Cadets don't know anything different. So the presence of men and women is just a natural thing. So that's a difference. And then the other thing that I see is that women are much more comfortable being a group of women together doing something than existed when I was a cadet.[90]

Female cadets who were attending West Point in 1997 confirmed that they received support from other, more experienced women who could serve as role models.

> When I was a plebe, the upperclass females in the company got us together and said, if you ever have a problem, either harassment, or just like a girl problem, or anything, that we should just go talk to them because they were familiar with the experiences. Guys in our chain of command weren't familiar with those kinds of things, so that was a comforting thing.[91]

While women may still need to win men over, today's men seem much more willing to accept women as cadets. Among current cadets, gender difference is downplayed and teamwork emphasized. Women still gain the respect of the men physically, by proving themselves on the field, however. Differential standards, the result of the West Point's intergrationist policy, have remained a point of contention, but female cadets have found that even if men will not admit it in front of their male peers, individually they will acknowledge that the differences are inconsequential. "The guys complain . . . that our standards are too easy or whatever but they're so comparable and usually you can get them to admit it. Never in a group will they admit to it, but if you're talking to them one on one they'll be like, [deep voice] 'well yeah, right, okay, I understand.' "[92]

Given the changes that have taken place at West Point over more than a quarter century of coeducation, is gender integration a fait accompli? Evidence suggests that although gender conflict today is more muted, it has not completely disappeared. In 2002, a group of female cadets described their experiences at West Point as generally positive and gender relations quite good. However, these women also had no difficulty offering up examples of gender bias, including receiving sexist emails and the common misperception among male cadets that female cadets tend to be overweight. In a survey administered by West Point's Office of Policy Planning and Analysis in 2001, graduating seniors were asked whether they had heard members of the corps of cadets make disparaging remarks about women at West Point; 99.2 percent of them said yes, and slightly more than half said "frequently."[93] Even if these remarks are spoken in jest, they nonetheless create a subtly hostile environment that serves to remind women of their marginal status.

Many feared that the admission of women would lead to the ruin of West Point, but that fear has not been realized. People worried that standards would drop, producing a watered-down version of the once rigorous West Point experience. Instead, standards are actually higher today than they were before women attended. Women today run the mile faster than male cadets did in the 1960s, for instance. The academy has changed, but instead of the cadet experience being inferior to what it used to be, it is actually better. This is not simply the canon preached by those who have a stake in championing women at the academy. It is the view espoused by those who have been at West Point since it was all-male. One cadet proudly recounted how her professor had said that "one of the best things that ever happened to West Point was women coming because it used to be a boy's school and now it's a school of leadership, it's a professional school."[94]

The Current State of Coeducation at VMI

Now in its sixth year of coeducation, VMI no longer has any cadets who were there when it was all male. Yet VMI is still in the early stages of coeducation, and much remains to be done before women are fully accepted. VMI still lacks many of the support systems that have made West Point more inviting to women. Although the chain of command now favors coeducation, it was not so long ago that the institute's superintendent vocally opposed having female cadets. Also, the number of female cadets has remained low, so that the presence of women has not become naturalized.

In 2000, women made up 10 percent of the full-time faculty, and 17 percent of the entire faculty at VMI (10 full-time and 14 part-time). That same year, women made up 5.2 percent of the corps, with a total enrollment of 68.[95] Although VMI has as its goal a corps of cadets that is 10 percent women, the institution is finding it difficult to attract and retain sufficient numbers of women. Perhaps this is because of VMI's steadfast resistance to gender norming and its unwavering reliance on the assimilationist model, which demands that women assimilate to what was defined previously as a male norm. It is hard for anyone to make it through VMI's daunting training regimen, but women face two obstacles that men do not: physical standards set to men's physiology rather than women's, and insufficient support from peers. Female cadets are still made to feel that they are interlopers invading male territory. In addition, VMI's adversative method, which is administered by upperclass cadets, may prove detrimental to cadets who are perceived of as outsiders, as women usually are, making them subject to greater scrutiny by upperclassmen.

As at West Point, there was concern that the admission of women to VMI would destroy the institution. Many feared that enrollment would drop, the school's status would diminish, and alumni giving would decline. In fact the opposite has been true. Between 1996 (the year before women first attended VMI) and 2001, VMI's applicant pool increased by nearly 50 percent with 1,436 applications received for the class of 2005, the second-highest total on record. VMI's acceptance rate has dropped to 61 percent, the lowest in a decade, allowing VMI to be more selective in its admission process. In *U.S. News & World Report* 2002 "America's Best Colleges," VMI significantly improved its ranking, moving into the second tier (upper half) overall. And after women were admitted, alumni giving actually increased. Far from leading to the demise of the institution, the admission of women to VMI seems to have helped reinvigorate it. Having weathered the initial storm, VMI must now address the barriers for women that remain.

Conclusion

The metamorphosis from tradition-bound, all-male military institutions to coeducational ones takes time. The greatest hindrance to that transition is the attitudes of male cadets. The first female cadets were pioneers who withstood the challenges to their worth with courage and dignity. Through their perseverance, women demonstrated that in spite of obstacles, they can succeed in traditionally male domains.

The transition to coeducation compels institutions, and those within them, to evolve. Closed-mindedness initially prevents many men from dealing with women as they actually are. Instead, these men hold fast to their preconceived notions of women and their capabilities. Women struggle to challenge the constraints that prejudice places on them, while concomitantly striving to prove their competence. As male cadets begin to accept female cadets, presumptions about women as a group are replaced with more flexible ideas about women as individuals. With time, the presence of women becomes more accepted and natural. By including women within their ranks, these institutions are reinvigorated, and their members are better prepared to face the challenges of the new world.

Notes

1. Robert Priest, Howard Prince, and Alan Vitters, "The First Coed Class at West Point: Performance and Attitudes," *Youth and Society* 10 (1978): 205–24.
2. Janice D. Yoder, "Women at West Point: Lessons for Token Women in Male-Dominated Occupations," in *Women: A Feminist Perspective,* ed. Jo Freeman (Mountain View, Calif.: Mayfield, 1989), 524.

3. Henry A. Wise, *Drawing Out the Man* (Charlottesville, Va.: University Press of Virginia, 1978).

4. Between 1997 and 2000, a total of 98 cadets, alumni, faculty, and administrators were interviewed. West Point cadets and alumni were volunteers provided by the United States Military Academy Office of Public Affairs. Alumnae from the first coed classes at West Point were selected through a snowball sampling technique, asking participants to refer others for interview. VMI cadets, faculty, and administrators were either volunteers provided by the Virginia Military Institute Office of Public Relations or individuals referred through VMI contacts. At West Point, 35 interview subjects were current or former female cadets, and 21 present or former male cadets. All but one of the male alumni were still on active duty in the army. At VMI, 20 were current female cadets, 15 current male cadets, 4 faculty, and 3 administrators. (The number of female cadets represents half of all female cadets to ever have been enrolled at the school at that time.) The semistructured cadet interviews ranged over a variety of issues, including their motivations for attending a military school, their social and educational experiences, and their perceptions of the barriers to women's full integration. The faculty and administrator interviews focused on their perspective on the process and progress of coeducation at VMI.

5. See *www.usma.edu/bicentennial*.

6. Data from *www.princetonreview.com/college/research/profiles/admissions.asp?listing =1023919&LTID=1*.

7. Data from *www.princetonreview.com/college/research/profiles/generalinfo.asp?listing =1022822&LTID=1*.

8. *United States v. Virginia*, 976 F.2d 890 (4th Cir. 1992), 893–94.

9. This section relies on Bettie Morden, *The Women's Army Corps, 1945–1978* (Washington, D.C.: Center of Military History, United States Army, 1990).

10. Janda Lance, *Stronger than Custom: West Point and the Admission of Women* (Westport, Conn.: Praeger, 2001), 26.

11. Alan G. Vitters, Nora Scott Kizer, and Robert F. Priest, "Women at West Point: A Case Study in Organizational and Interpersonal Change" (presented at the Inter-University Seminar National Biennial Conference, Chicago, October 20–22, 1977), 2.

12. West Point alumni and cadets were grouped into four cohorts: (1) the first five coeducational classes plus alumni from the last all-male class, coded WP1 (graduating classes 1979–84); (2) a cohort who attended West Point 8–12 years after women were first admitted, coded WP2 (graduating classes 1988–92); (3) a cohort who were attending West Point in 1997, 21 years after women were first admitted, coded WP3 (graduating classes 1997–2000); and (4) a cohort who were attending West Point in 2000, 24 years after coeducation began, coded WP4 (graduating classes 2000–04). VMI cadets were grouped into two cohorts, (1) the first two coeducational classes plus cadets from the last all-male class, coded VMI1 (graduating classes 2000–02); and (2) cadets in the third and fourth coeducational classes, coded VMI2 (graduating classes 2003–04). *M* or *F* at the end of the interview code indicates the subject's sex. All interviews by Diane Diamond, unless specified otherwise. WP1-4F, telephone, June 1997.

13. Cited in Valerie K. Vojdik, "Girls Schools after VMI: Do They Make the Grade?," *Duke Journal of Gender Law and Policy* 4 (1997): 76.

14. *United States v. Virginia,* 852 F.Supp. 471 (4th Cir. 1994), 6.
15. Public Law 94-106 of 1976 Defense Appropriation Authorization Act.
16. Robert F. Priest and John W. Houston, "Analysis of Spontaneous Cadet Comments on the Admission of Women," Office of the Director of Institutional Research, United States Military Academy, May 1976, 8.
17. Robert F. Priest, Alan G. Vitters, and Howard T. Prince, "Coeducation at West Point," October 1977, 7, United States Military Academy Special Collections and Archives.
18. *United States v. Virginia,* 852 F.Supp. 471 (4th Cir. 1994), 11.
19. *United States v. Virginia,* 116 S. Ct. 2264, 2284 (1996).
20. Joan Acker, "From Sex Roles to Gendered Institutions," *Contemporary Sociology* 21 (1992): 568.
21. VMI1-2M, VMI, October 1999.
22. VMI2-2F, VMI, October 1999.
23. Alison Jagger, "Sexual Difference and Sexual Equality," in *Theoretical Perspectives on Sexual Difference,* ed. D. L. Rhode (New Haven: Yale University Press, 1990).
24. WP1-7F, email, January 1998.
25. WP1-4F, telephone, June 1997.
26. Robert F. Priest, Howard T. Prince, Teresa Rhone, and Alan G. Vitters, "Difference between Characteristics of Men and Women New Cadets Class of 1980," Office of the Director of Institutional Research, United States Military Academy, March 1977, 17.
27. Ibid., 18.
28. Quote from VMI1-1F, VMI, October 1999.
29. VMI2-2F, VMI, April 2000.
30. Priest and Houston, 6.
31. Robert F. Priest, "Content of Cadet Comments on the Integration of Women," Office of the Director of Institutional Research, United States Military Academy, August 1977.
32. Priest and Houston, 6.
33. VMI2-5M, VMI, April 2000.
34. VMI1-5M, VMI, October 1999.
35. VMI2-5M.
36. VMI1-5F, VMI, October 1999.
37. VMI2-1M, VMI, April 2000.
38. VMI1-9F, VMI, October 1999.
39. Priest and Houston, 7.
40. Ibid., 6.
41. Ibid., 9.
42. Ibid.
43. Ibid., 6.
44. Ibid., 9.
45. Ibid.
46. Ibid.
47. Ibid., 12.
48. Ibid., 11.
49. Ibid., 12.

50. Ibid., 11.

51. WP1-6M, telephone, February 2001.

52. VMI2-1M, VMI, April 2000.

53. VMI2-6M, VMI, April 2000.

54. VMI2-7M, VMI, April 2000.

55. VMI1-7M, VMI, October 1999; VMI1-2M, VMI, October 1999.

56. VMI1-3M, VMI, October 1999; VMI1-7M.

57. WP1-7M, email, March 2001.

58. VMI2-1M.

59. VMI1-2M.

60. VMI1-7M.

61. VMI1-4M, VMI, October 1999.

62. Ibid.

63. WP1-8F, email, January 1998.

64. WP1-7F, email, January 1998.

65. Ibid.

66. Carol Barkalow, *In the Men's House: An Inside Account in the Army by One of West Point's First Female Graduates* (New York: Poseidon, 1992), 85.

67. WP1-5F, telephone, June 1997.

68. WP1-6F, email, January 1998.

69. WP1-4F.

70. WP1-1F, telephone, June 1997.

71. WP1-5F.

72. Barkalow, 94.

73. Yoder, 531.

74. Jerome Adams, "Report of the Admission of Women to the United States Military Academy at West Point: Project Athena IV," United States Military Academy, 1980, 49.

75. Ibid.

76. VMI1-4M.

77. VMI1-8F, VMI, October 1999.

78. VMI2-2F.

79. VMI2-7F, VMI, April 2000.

80. VMI2-3F, VMI, April 2000.

81. VMI1-9F.

82. Ibid.

83. VMI1-4F, VMI, October 1999.

84. VMI2-7F.

85. VMI1-10F, VMI, October 1999.

86. VMI2-2M, VMI, April 2000.

87. VMI2-3M, VMI, April 2000.

88. VMI2-7F.

89, Office of Public Affairs, United States Military Academy; "Women at West Point," *www.usma.edu/PublicAffairs/WomenWP/WomenWP3-1.htm.*

89. WP1-2F, telephone, June 1997.

90. WP3-2F, West Point, March 1997.
91. WP3-4F, West Point, March 1997.
92. "First Class Survey," Office of Policy Planning and Analysis, United States Military Academy, 2001.
93. WP3-4F, West Point, March 1997.
95. "VMI Common Data Set," 2000, Office of Institutional Research, Virginia Military Institute, available at *http://admin.vmi.edu/ir/cds0001.htm.*

12

Women's Movement into Technical Fields

A Comparison of Technical and Community Colleges

Regina Deil-Amen

Most historically male colleges and universities had charters that forbade the admission of women. In other institutions of higher education, however, the absence of women has been assumed rather than enforced. The two for-profit technical colleges considered in this chapter fall into this category. The programs they offer, such as electronics, engineering, information technology, and various other computer-related technical fields, were originally designed for men students. It was not until the enormous growth in the labor market demand for people trained in these areas, and the second wave of the women's movement in the 1970s, that these technical colleges experienced a significant enrollment of women students.

Enrollments in for-profit colleges nearly quadrupled in the last two decades of the twentieth century, rising from 111,714 students in 1980 to 430,199 students in 1999.[1] Much of this increase is due to the growth in the number of for-profit institutions, which has far out-paced growth in the public and nonprofit sectors. During the 1990s, the number of two-year degree-granting for-profit colleges rose 78 percent, while the number of two-year public institutions grew only 9 percent and the number of two-year private nonprofits declined by 6 percent. Among four-year colleges, the number of for-profits increased 266 percent, while the number of four-year public and private nonprofit colleges grew by only 3 and 4 percent, respectively. For-profit colleges now represent 28 percent of the two-year college market and 8 percent of the four-year market.[2]

For-profit students have always been more likely to be women, since, historically, many of these schools have tended to specialize in training in female-dominated service occupations such as cosmetology, health support, and office support.[3] The more technology-oriented for-profit colleges continue to enroll predominantly men, and only recently have women's enrollments in these programs become substantial. Working and lower-class women have been especially eager to enroll in order to gain access to traditionally male technical fields.

This chapter compares women's recent experiences in two for-profit technical colleges with women's experiences in comparable vocational fields in six community colleges. Community colleges have always had a high enrollment of women, but not in technical programs. The chapter discusses how women's experiences in these educational institutions support, extend, or contradict existing theories about gender and the integration of women into traditionally male educational domains. The particular question addressed is whether female students' confidence about their ability to do schoolwork and to get a degree varies with institutional context and whether staff activities explain this institutional influence.

The focus on these colleges is distinctive in three ways. First, it examines gender integration issues for middle- and lower-achieving students, many of whom come from lower-class backgrounds. Second, it considers the integration of women into applied technical support fields via technical colleges and community colleges—segments of higher education that have been largely ignored in academic discussions about the inclusion of females in postsecondary education.[4] Third, unlike frameworks that tend to apply either a psychological or a sociological perspective to the study of gender, this approach incorporates both psychological theory and institutional analyses to study the experiences of women in historically and majority-male technical colleges.

The For-Profit and Community College Sectors: Histories of Transformation

For-profit colleges, commonly referred to as "proprietary" or "trade" schools, suffer from a negative image caused by past scandals. The majority of these private, profit-motivated institutions traditionally offered programs of one-year or less in business, marketing, cosmetology, and crafts in urban areas, serving mostly low-income students who qualified for Pell Grants and guaranteed student loans. These schools developed a reputation as degree mills, offering a poor education at a high price and churning out thousands of students into saturated markets where job salaries were too low for the graduates to pay back their student loans.[5] Yet recent changes in Title IV federal student loan assistance programs have resulted in drastic improvements among colleges in the for-profit sector. Tighter regulations prompted the for-profit sector to increase standards and make significant changes in their programs.[6] As a result, over 1,500 of the shorter term and lower quality "trade schools" have closed, and the percentage of for-profits that are accredited to award associate's, baccalaureate, and higher degrees has grown.[7] These "accredited career colleges" have improved their curriculum and faculty.[8] Newer colleges have also been created with standards that ensure national or regional accreditation.[9]

These accredited career colleges are characterized by a service-oriented approach and offer programs that provide students with an education in a specific career field, most often in the technical or business arena.[10] They constitute nearly 22 percent of the postsecondary educational institutions in the United States, yet they tend to be small, enrolling only about 8 percent of all college students.[11] Approximately 85 percent of accredited career colleges grant associate's degrees and close to 15 percent grant baccalaureate degrees.

Like their trade school counterparts, career colleges retain their focus on serving students who have done poorly in high school, many of whom are low-income.[12] However, the tuition at for-profit colleges is rather comparable to average tuition at two- and four-year nonprofit colleges, in the mid 1990s averaging $7,302 per academic year at the two-year for-profits and $9,153 at the four-year for-profits.[13] These tuitions allow these schools to buy more equipment and technology than is found at most public educational institutions.

Community colleges first appeared around the turn of the century as "junior colleges," preparing students to transfer to senior, four-year colleges by providing the first two years to commuter students at low cost. Since the 1960s, junior colleges have been transformed from their traditional transfer mission into institutions offering many more vocational programs.[14] The number of community colleges nationwide grew from 39 in 1919 to 345 in 1960, and now more than 1,200 community colleges exist, enrolling nearly 40 percent of all undergraduates.[15] Today's community colleges are public, two-year open admissions colleges, offering two-year associate's degrees and one-year certificates. As comprehensive institutions, community colleges offer a range of educational opportunities, including baccalaureate transfer, applied career programs, precredit remedial programs, basic literacy, GED test preparation, English language proficiency, and a variety of continuing education classes and short-term vocational training courses. Over half of all community college students are enrolled in occupational programs.[16]

Although community colleges and for-profit colleges tend to offer degrees in some of the same fields, community colleges offer degrees in liberal arts and sciences, while for-profit colleges typically do not. Furthermore, community colleges tend to require more general education classes; for-profits either require a reduced number of such courses or tailor their general education classes to make them directly relevant to students' applied program. Compared to community colleges, career or for-profit colleges have higher percentages of full-time students and slightly more minority students, with black and Latino students constituting nearly one-quarter of career college enrollments and about one-fifth of community college enrollments.[17]

The Colleges Studied: History and Current Enrollments

The two for-profit colleges focused on in this chapter are among the accredited career colleges described above and will therefore be referred to as "technical career colleges." They are regionally and/or nationally accredited and offer associate's degrees of similar quality to community colleges, as well as accelerated bachelor's degrees.

The first, Technical Institute, includes one urban campus in a large Midwestern city and another campus in a nearby suburb. Tech Institute's campuses, however, are not stand-alone institutions. They are part of a national system of nearly 20 campuses across 14 states and Canada. Tech Institute was established in the 1930s but first received associate's-degree-granting status in 1957 and bachelor's-degree-granting status in 1969. During this time, the enrollments were nearly all male, and the faculty and administration were likewise comprised of mostly men. Students were enrolled mainly in electronics engineering technology programs. From the beginning, Tech Institute, like other technical career colleges, enrolled students who had not done well in high school and who did not have privileged backgrounds. Today, Tech Institute's program offerings lead to associate of applied science in electronics and bachelor of science degrees in accounting, business administration, computer information systems, electronics engineering technology, information technology, technical management, and telecommunications management. Tech Institute has been accredited since the 1950s. It has held the same regional accreditation as community colleges since 1980. Each of the two Tech Institute campuses included in this study enrolls over 2,800 students in a given term.

The administrative structure of each Tech Institute campus is similar to more traditional nonprofit colleges in that its leadership includes a president under which several deans operate, including the dean of academic affairs, dean of students, and a dean for each major the college offers, plus a dean of general education. In addition to these deans, there is a dean of career services who oversees an associate dean, four career counselors, and three support staff. Tech Institute also has a dean of information technology and a dean of evening/weekend studies. Like other colleges, Tech Institute has registrar, admissions, business, and student finance offices.

ABC Technical College (ABC Tech) is located in the suburbs just outside the same large Midwestern city. Like Tech Institute it is just one of many "technical institutes" that are part of a larger for-profit college system focused on technology-oriented programs of study. This larger system operates 70 technical institutes in 28 states, which provide career-focused, degree programs to approximately 31,000 students, and has been actively involved in the higher education community in the United States since the late 1960s.

The particular ABC Tech campus focused on here is accredited by the Accrediting Council for Independent Colleges and Schools (ACICS) to award diplomas, associate of applied science degrees, and bachelor of applied science degrees in computer-aided drafting and design technology, computer and electronics engineering technology, and information technology. It is a small institution, with just under 400 students in a given term.

The campus's administrative structure is less traditional than Tech Institute in that it includes a director of education, a director of finance, a director of recruitment, a director of career services, a dean of academic affairs, two financial aid administrators, and a special services coordinator. Each of the three program areas is led by a program chair who is also an instructor.

Although, historically, each of the two for-profit technical colleges was predominantly male, neither ever had a formal "men only" policy. However, in 2000 ABC Tech's enrollments were still only about 7 percent female, mainly because women are much less likely to enroll in computer and electronics programs.

Women began enrolling in larger numbers at Tech Institute only after 1979, when it offered a degree in "computer science for business," and then in more significant proportions during the 1980s when it added degrees in accounting and business. An administrator at Tech Institute noted, "When I worked at [Tech Institute] in 1980, they had built the new . . . facility with the majority of restrooms for men. As female enrollments grew, some of these were reassigned and we had urinals in at least one of the 'Women's' for a number of years. We used to joke about putting potted geraniums in them!"[18] In the early 1980s the student body was still 90 percent male, but by 1995, female enrollments had reached 29 percent.[19] By 2002, female enrollments at Tech Institute were an impressive 36 percent.[20]

Women constitute between one-quarter to one-third of the teaching staff at Tech Institute, and, surprisingly, 60 percent of the administrators are female. In fact, three of the seven people that make up Tech Institute's "senior management group" are women. Just over half of the administrators and directors at ABC Tech are women, but only 15 percent of the instructors are women.[21]

The six community colleges are all located within a 20 mile radius, in and around a large Midwestern city. Two of the colleges were among the first "junior colleges" and were originally established in 1911 and 1934. Four of the six, like most of the community colleges in the United States, were built in the post–World War II era. This was the time when community colleges proliferated so that more people would have access to college, while allowing four-year colleges and universities to remain elite in their status and admissions criteria.[22]

Each of the six community colleges studied offer a full array of classes and services, so that the majors focused on here actually constitute only a portion of each college's overall enrollments. These majors are electronics, engineering technology, computer technology, computer information systems, computer networking, computer-aided drafting, business, and accounting.[23]

Women are the majority of students at the community colleges. They represent 56 to 61 percent of the enrollments, which vary from college to college, ranging from 3,500 to 12,500 students taking courses for college credit each semester.[24] In fact, all but one of the six community colleges have enrollments above 7,000. Female representation is, however, somewhat lower in business and accounting and drastically lower in the technical programs. Women are well represented among community college administrators and full-time faculty; 47 to 68 percent of administrators and 42 to 56 percent of *all* full-time faculty members are women. Although women are well represented in business, their representation among technology faculty is much lower, with the exception of computers.

The technical career colleges have adapted to the needs of adult working students. Traditional academic content is blended with applied learning concepts, with a significant portion of students' programs devoted to practical study in a lab environment. Advisory committees, made up of representatives of local businesses and employers, help each program periodically assess and update curricula, equipment, and laboratory design. Students attend classes year-round with breaks provided throughout the year. Classes are typically available in the morning, afternoon, and evening, depending on student enrollment. This class schedule offers students flexibility to pursue part-time employment opportunities. For a three-quarter academic year, the tuition at Tech Institute is approximately $14,000 (about $4,700 per term); at ABC Tech, it is approximately $11,000 (about $3,700 per term). Many of the students who enroll qualify for need-based Pell Grants of up to $3,300. In addition, each of the technical colleges offers institutional academic scholarships from $1,000 to full tuition, and they provide extensive personalized financial aid assistance to help students secure federal and state loans. Many students receive tuition reimbursement from their employers as well.

The community colleges offer classes on a more traditional semester system, yet many students continue their studies during the summer semester. Although the programs are also applied, lab time is significantly less and general education courses make up a larger proportion of degree students' credits. Tuition is much lower at the community colleges, with in-district tuitions for a two-semester academic year ranging from $1,140 at the urban community colleges to about $1,300 at one of the suburban colleges ($570 to $650 per term respectively).

Women students at both types of institutions are fairly similar. Table 12.1, which presents information from a sample of women at the two for-profit

Table 12.1. Women Students' Characteristics by Type of College

	For-Profit Colleges[a]	Community Colleges[b]
Race (%)		
Black	28.3	16.6
Hispanic	22.7	21.8
Asian	16.4	16.3
Middle Eastern/S.Asian	1.9	2.9
White	30.0	4.4
Parents' education (%)		
High school	54.1	53.6
Some college	32.5	29.5
B.A. or graduate	13.4	8.8
Family income (%)		
$29,000 or less	43.5	43.9
$30,000–60,000	42.7	36.1
$60,000+	13.8	1.1
Financially supported by their parents (%)	38.6	43.2
Number of children (%)		
None	53.8	56.3
One or more	46.2	7.7
High school GPA (%)		
Mostly As	8.3	10.6
As/mostly Bs	42.7	48.6
Bs/mostly Cs	40.7	37.2
Cs and below	8.3	3.7
Average age	24.6	25.7
Worked while enrolled (%)	74.7	75.7

Source: Data were collected in surveys distributed by the author at various times from 2000 to 2002.

a. N=290 women. The exact number of women varied slightly from question to question since not all women answered every question. Includes business, computers, and technology curricula.

b. N=435 women. The exact number of women varied slightly from question to question since not all women answered every question. Includes business, computers, and technology curricula.

technical colleges and women students enrolled in the programs listed above at the six community colleges, shows that they represent a less privileged sector of American women than is found at most liberal arts colleges. The women are also older, on average, than traditional college students. More than half of them have parents who have no more than a high school education; over two-fifths have family incomes under $30,000; about 45 percent have children; fewer than 11 percent received mostly "A" grades when in high school; nearly three-quarters of them are working while enrolled; and their average age is about 25 years old. A slight majority of women at the two for-profit colleges are black or Hispanic; the community colleges have about the same percentage of Hispanic women students (about 22 percent), but fewer black women, so their overall percentage of these minority students is less, 38.4 percent compared to the 51 percent at the for-profit colleges. In several aspects, women students at the vocational colleges appear to be less advantaged than those at the community colleges: somewhat fewer of them are financially supported by their parents (38.6 percent versus 43.2 percent); fewer have family incomes of $60,000 or more (13.8 percent, compared to 20.1 percent of the community college women); and more of the women at the vocational colleges received Cs and below as high school grades (8.3 percent versus 3.7 percent).

Theories to Explain Women's Underrepresentation in Technological Fields

Psychological and Social Psychological Explanations
Traditionally, theories and causal models of female underrepresentation in male-dominated mathematics, science, and technology (MST) fields and courses of study have taken a psychological approach, arguing that female students' prior socialization has led them to be less interested, not as highly motivated, or not as confident as male students. Theories of motivation are perhaps the most frequently employed to understand variations in women's perceptions of their ability to enter and succeed in male-dominated fields. Some research has found that students' academic goals, performance, and learning are characterized by the degree to which they attribute educational outcomes to effort and ability. Students have implicit theories about their ability to do well in school. "Helpless" or maladaptive individuals appear to focus on ability and its adequacy, while mastery-oriented students appear to focus on mastery through strategy and effort.[25] Helpless individuals tend to view challenging problems as a threat to their self-esteem, whereas mastery-oriented students usually view challenges as opportunities for learning something new. Helpless students are therefore *extrinsically* motivated, pursuing performance goals, while mastery-oriented students are *intrinsically* motivated, pursuing learning goals. If an individual

attributes academic success to internal causes, his or her self-esteem is enhanced. However, if a failure is attributed to internal causes, feelings of shame result, making it less likely for such an individual to pursue similar academic endeavors in the future.[26]

One comparison of men and women's achievement in mathematics found that male students are more likely to attribute their grades to such intrinsic characteristics as ability and effort; they are also more likely than women to enroll in additional math courses.[27] These findings could also be applied to differences among women, however, meaning that women who see their achievements as due to intrinsic characteristics should be more likely to enroll and succeed in traditionally male fields.

Some research has investigated the influence of social psychological factors in women's willingness to pursue male-dominated MST fields. This type of research looks at characteristics of the social groups in which an individual is embedded in terms of their effects on the person's motivation. Studies have found that fathers, male peers, and siblings play a strong role in facilitating girls' interest in MST. Teachers, also, are important, both directly, in terms of encouraging or discouraging women to be interested in these male-dominated fields, and indirectly, in terms of teachers' attitudes, which influence the overall school climate.[28]

This survey of women students at the vocational and community colleges included a measure of students' locus of control, that is, whether they attributed their success to intrinsic characteristics (their ability to work hard, for example)—an internal locus of control—or whether they saw their success as a matter of luck—an external locus of control. Students were presented with four statements and asked to indicate their extent of agreement with them, on a five-point scale, from "strongly agree" to "strongly disagree." The four statements were "Good luck is more important than hard work for success," "Every time I try to get ahead, something or somebody stops me," "Planning only makes people unhappy because plans hardly ever work out," and "When I make plans I usually carry them out." Disagreement with the first three statements and agreement with the fourth indicates internal locus of control. The hypothesis was that women with a more internal locus of control would have greater confidence about their ability to get a degree and to do schoolwork.

The survey also examined the effect of faculty and staff members' encouragement of women students. Students were asked: "In the past year, have these people encouraged or discouraged you to stay in college?" Six types of people were then listed (including "teachers" and "college staff"), and the students could give responses ranging from one for "strongly encouraged" to five for "strongly discouraged." The issue of encouragement is considered later in both the quantitative and qualitative sections of this chapter.

Institutional Explanations

When theories and empirical studies have deviated from a focus on psychological or social factors, they have typically proposed institutional explanations as to why women have not succeeded in nontraditional fields, often neglecting psychological factors altogether. For example, reproduction theory states that mainstream or dominant cultural characteristics of a society are maintained by its structures of class, production, and power. Education is the product of an arbitrary cultural scheme that is based on existing relations of power. Reproduction of culture is achieved through an education system that excludes the cultural skills and dispositions of students in nondominant cultural groups.[29]

Empirical research based on the reproduction of cultural patterns in college settings has investigated the effects of curriculum, gender stereotypes, the composition of school faculty, and supports for learning. Women are more likely to study male-dominated fields if an institution has a mentoring system that involves successful women as industry role models, allows for course scheduling flexibility for single parents or students with full-time jobs, and makes gender- and ethnic-bias free software accessible to students.[30]

Other research suggests that advanced mathematics requirements or emphasis on the "scientific method" act as barriers, which are not central to expertise in science and are therefore artificial but serve to dissuade minority and female students from studying science.[31] Equal access to science and engineering, let alone to the most fundamental elements of computation, requires accepting multiple ways of learning, knowing, and thinking, a practice that is currently not broadly upheld in institutions of higher learning.[32] Gender stereotyping and intimidating behaviors on the part of faculty and staff are also prevalent institutional factors that prevent the full participation of women and minorities in MST fields.[33]

This study departs from most of the psychological research tradition in that it looks at institutional differences in female student success. Qualitative research, based on interviews and examination of college publications, focuses on how institutional practices encourage women's involvement in technical fields. Women's confidence is examined in terms of institutional factors as well as differences in students' socioeconomic background and personality. Thus the research is based on a combination of psychological and institutional theory.

Institutional Encouragement of Women Students at Technical and Community Colleges

The two for-profit vocational colleges encourage the enrollment of women. One method they use is to include women in visual representations of the colleges. At Tech Institute, for example, the 2001 college catalog features 114 photos of students, staff, and instructors. Forty-five percent of the students pictured are female, despite the fact that only slightly more than a third of the college's enrollment is female. This visual overrepresentation of women is a deliberate attempt to both recruit women and contribute to a female-friendly environment at the college.[34] In addition, Tech Institute is involved in a partnership between higher education, high schools, and industry designed to expose young women to technology careers. ABC Tech's website prominently features women in technology with links to multiple articles and additional websites about how women can benefit from technical careers. Their website also highlights specific links to the student testimonials of three women who got degrees at ABC Tech in electronics engineering technology, computer network systems, and computer aided drafting technology.

Other admissions techniques also encourage women to enroll. The technical colleges use a direct, one-on-one recruitment approach that welcomes all students who express interest to come to visit the campus and talk with an admissions counselor. For women, who are more likely to doubt their ability to pursue a technical education, this experience, which enthusiastically invites them to become a student at the college, reinforces their choice and reduces self-doubt. One female student at ABC Tech explained how the aggressive admissions process facilitated her decision to enroll: "All I did was send them an e-mail and just said that I was a little bit interested. Within a day I had a call back from an admissions counselor. He was fantastic, made me feel so at ease. His name was Mike. I can't remember his last name, but I still see him at school."[35]

Another ABC Tech student, Maria, knew she was interested in technology but was unsure about the type of college she wanted to attend. Following a college fair at her high school, she was phoned by staff at several colleges and asked to visit their campuses, but ABC Tech was the most successful at scheduling a personalized campus tour immediately. Maria and her mother visited the campus, and they were swayed by the friendly, personal attention they received and the college's technology equipment. Maria was able to decide on an initial program choice, fill out her financial aid forms, and enroll for classes all in one day.[36]

Among the community colleges, in contrast, only two single instances of website material addressed females specifically, including one college's deeply buried business course listing for career changers. Furthermore, community colleges have little budget money allocated to recruitment and advertising, and none of it was directed toward recruiting women into technology fields.

The for-profit technical colleges have a well-developed advising system that requires every student to see an adviser at least once a term, and sometimes more often. The ratio of advisers to students is 1 to 65 at ABC Tech. At Tech Institute, student services includes four counselors and two deans, while two administrators and four career advisers are devoted to helping students make the transition into jobs. That is about a 333:1 student to staff adviser ratio. Indeed, advisers initiate contact, and are particularly likely to do so if they feel the student needs support or assistance. The mandatory one-on-one advising offers extensive assistance at obtaining financial aid and career and job placement assistance. The vocational colleges have traditionally enrolled large proportions of middle- to low-income students and students who have done poorly in high school. They have therefore developed structures that address the needs of students who face obstacles to their educational success. Since women in nontraditional fields are more likely to face obstacles relative to men, these same structures may be working to the benefit of women.

The six community colleges, in contrast, have a less developed advising system than do the vocational colleges. Their system is modeled on that used at four-year colleges, which was devised for middle-class students. With an average of one counselor for every 1,000 students, access to guidance is quite difficult for students. Counselors are able to respond to students who seek help, but it often takes two or three months before students can obtain an appointment. Many students never see a counselor, and one counselor reported that if everyone sought an appointment, the school would not have enough counselors for them.

Kristin, who attended a community college before enrolling at Tech Institute, noted the difference in advising systems: "[At the community college] you have to go to them. Here, the first term, they make you see the first-term adviser, and help you through . . . they always offer help, which is good."[37] Apparently, the highly structured systems of advising give students clear direction in negotiating the college-going process. Most importantly, advising is initiated by the college rather than by the student.

The relatively small size of the for-profit colleges allows for a sense of community in which instructors have close contact with students. Since these two colleges tend to hire instructors who have extensive industrial experience in the area in which they are teaching, students have ready access to role models in their field. Previous literature highlights the importance of role models for women aspiring to careers in technology, yet it tends to assume that women students' role models are themselves women.[38] This research, however, revealed that female students readily targeted both male and female faculty members as relevant role models. The close-knit, family-like community within the schools nurtured these cross-gender relationships that may be less common in larger, more "anonymous" postsecondary contexts. Women students often commented on the importance of this sense of community, personalized attention, and access to role models. Carla explained the benefits of familiarity and close contact between administrators and instructors at ABC Tech, noting that they were role models for her or were people she wanted to emulate.

. . . and walking up and down the hallways, I've only been going there—this will be my third quarter—the dean knows me, the associate dean knows me, the financial aid people know me. I mean, all the instructors that I've had, they all know me, they say hello. . . . It's more like an extended family. I mean, the class sizes are small enough, and even with an influx of new students and it's still, it's so close knit. I love that. I almost feel like it's almost going to a job where you become familiar with your surroundings, with the people that you go there with all the time. It's wonderful, you know. . . . I have two classes right now where there's six kids in the class. So six kids to one instructor. I am really earning what I am paying just to have one [instructor]—I'd be lucky if I had that on a job, you know what I mean? Very lucky. So here, you have the complete personalized treatment. . . . But the other wonderful thing is the contacts. I mean, I don't have one instructor here who I can't ask, "Would you be willing to be a reference for me?" And they know me. They wouldn't, you know, it wouldn't be, "Oh, I hope that they remember me." . . . Anyone there, you stop them down the hallway, they'll advise you. I think that an important part of your education should be surrounding yourself with people who you want to emulate—people who you respect and admire. And that was another great boost for me, too.

Carla also spoke at length about how the feeling of community at ABC Tech made her view her status as a female in a positive rather than negative light. Because of all the support and close attention she received, she felt empowered rather than intimidated to enter her field:

If anything, I know [being female] helps just because of equal opportunity employment. I know I'm really not going to—as long as I keep my grades up and pay attention to what I'm doing—it's going to be beneficial to me to be one of the few women that are going into it. I know that's a plus, and then the reason why I looked at ABC Tech specifically, I was just researching it on the Web. My husband started at [another college] He hated it, there were just so many kids in a lab, there were so many students in a classroom, and it was just so hard to get personalized treatment. Here my instructors, I love them; they know you by name, they know your family situation, they know where you're coming from, they know what kind of job you have, they tease you about it! They're more like a friend. It's fantastic; I can't imagine going to a school where you're one of hundreds sitting in a lecture hall, and you don't get the personalized treatment. I just, I love it. I wouldn't mind the opportunity but [laughs] I kind of really like what I have going here.[39]

Maria explained how tightly linked the sense of community or family was with faculty role models: "Everyone is sort of family and they try to learn from each other. There's different personalities in the class and everything, but the teacher makes . . . comments about one being in the field and . . . most of them bring in their own experiences and they make me feel as if I'm in a position for doing the same thing as they are."[40]

In contrast, interviews with female students in technical fields at the community colleges revealed that although they did not sense hostility and knew that academic support was available from tutors and particular faculty members, they often felt as if they were isolated and left on their own to succeed or fail in a male-dominated field.

Women Students' Confidence

Confidence change is an interesting measure of success since it involves changes in how women feel about their educational achievement and future prospects. In this study, students' perceptions of their changes in confidence since they first began college were assessed through surveys of close to 300 women at the for-profit colleges and 435 women in comparable programs at the community colleges. Given the evidence of prior studies, confidence was predicted to have an impact on women's willingness to persist at college and their ultimate success in male-dominated fields. In this study, women students who had higher GPA were more likely to report that their confidence had increased since they first began college. It is, of course, not possible to tell which occurred first, their higher grades or their increased confidence. Undoubtedly, though, the two go hand in hand, so it is important to know what factors increase students' confidence.

The survey asked students to compare their present level of confidence with their confidence when they first began at their college in two areas: in their ability to do schoolwork and their ability to get a degree. Students placed themselves on a five-point scale where one represented "much higher" confidence now and five, "much lower" confidence. Their responses were recoded into two categories: those who indicated that their confidence was higher and those who indicated that their confidence was the same or lower. A slightly greater percentage of women at the for-profit colleges (72.7 percent) than at the community colleges (70.1 percent) reported increased confidence about being able to do their schoolwork. The difference in confidence about getting a degree was much larger, with 76.8 percent of women at the for-profit colleges compared to 64 percent of women at the community colleges reporting increased confidence in this area. What accounts for women's higher confidence at the for-profit colleges? One possible explanation is that these colleges offer a less demanding curriculum. However, the research does not provide any evidence for such an explanation. In fact, this study found that students at these colleges obtain similar or better jobs in their field than do students in comparable programs in community colleges, which suggests that either there are few differences in the academic rigor of the curriculum or that curricular differences do not necessarily affect students' ability to get good jobs.

Another explanation might be that a key institutional characteristic—

faculty and staff encouragement of women students—leads to different levels of confidence at these two types of colleges.[41] Women students at the for-profit colleges were much more likely than those at the community colleges to report being encouraged by faculty and staff (58.4 versus 42.6 percent). Such encouragement was important for their increased levels of confidence, as the results in Table 12.2 show. Moreover, attendance at the for-profit vocational colleges had an additional benefit. Women at the vocational colleges who reported *not* being encouraged felt about as confident about getting their degree as women at the community colleges who said that they were encouraged. In terms of confidence about their ability to do their schoolwork, women at the for-profit colleges were neither more nor less confident than women at the community colleges. At both types of institutions, women who reported having received encouragement from faculty and staff were the most likely to say that they had increased in confidence about their ability to do schoolwork.

To examine this institutional effect further, the data were analyzed by a method that permits examination of whether faculty and staff encouragement and institutional type (vocational colleges versus community colleges) have a significant effect on female students' increased confidence, after controlling for socioeconomic background, race, and a personality attribute (locus of control). Each form of confidence was analyzed separately.[42]

Women students experienced greater increases in confidence about their ability to do schoolwork if they were black or Latina. Asian students seemed somewhat more confident as well, but they were not more likely than whites to be confident. Parents' education and family income level had no effect on women's confidence about being able to do schoolwork. The psychological char-

**Table 12.2. Women Reporting Increased Confidence
by Level of Encouragement (%)**

	For-Profit Colleges	Community Colleges
Increased confidence about getting a degree		
not encouraged	69.5	57.4
encouraged	81.9	71.2
average	76.8	63.9
Increased confidence about ability to do schoolwork		
not encouraged	65.3	65.7
encouraged	77.1	73.2
average	72.7	70.1

acteristic, locus of control, also had a significant effect on students' confidence about being able to do coursework; that is, students who felt that life was under their control (an internal locus of control) were more likely to be confident about their abilities than students who had an external locus of control. Although attendance at for-profit colleges appeared to have a positive effect on students' confidence about their ability to do the schoolwork, this effect disappeared once faculty and staff encouragement was taken into account, suggesting that it is the additional encouragement that for-profit students receive that explains their higher levels of confidence.

Racial characteristics had a stronger effect on students' increase in confidence about getting a degree than they did on confidence about ability to do schoolwork. Black, Latina, and Asian students were significantly more likely than white students to report increased confidence that they would get their degrees. While family income level surprisingly had no effect on confidence about getting a degree, those students whose parents were more educated were slightly less likely to experience increased confidence about obtaining their college degrees. Again, women with an internal locus of control were more likely than those with an external locus of control to believe that they would complete their degrees. While staff and faculty encouragement was important to students' confidence, so was attendance at a for-profit vocational college. In other words, confidence about getting degrees was greater in the vocational colleges, even after taking into account how much encouragement students received. Presumably the smaller size of the vocational colleges and the greater attention overall they give to students help make women more confident.

Qualitative findings of this research support some other psychological studies, particularly with regard to the importance of locus of control. The women interviewed who were in technical programs tended to have psychological qualities attributed to *men* in previous research, including a mastery-oriented perspective and a strong internal locus of control. This was true of community college women, but it was even more pronounced among the women who were surveyed and interviewed at the for-profit colleges. These qualities are particularly interesting given these students' history of lower academic achievement. The students at the for-profit colleges interpreted their poor past academic performance to a lack of effort rather than a lack of ability. Carla noted that she was "lazy" in high school, and Kristin said that she missed many classes because she just didn't want to attend, admitting, "I didn't really go that much at all."[43] Furthermore, the women at the technical colleges tended to make statements about their postsecondary educational and career pursuits that typify a mastery-oriented approach to problems and challenges. Carla, for instance, offered an explanation for her motivation to pursue a career in computer design: "The other reason why I chose computers was because they intimidated me. I wanted to know everything about that stupid box; I didn't just want to use it as a glorified typewriter. I wanted to know what made it work. That's really where the interest lied [*sic*] in me."[44]

The qualitative part of the study also confirms the importance of institutional factors for women's success in male-dominated technical fields. Many studies have found that women's discomfort as a numerical minority inhibits their success. However, we found that the colleges' institutional culture welcomes women and enables them to feel competent *despite* their minority status. The large enrollment of older, nontraditional students means that deviation from the traditional student norm is commonplace. Many women mentioned that teachers and administrators were particularly understanding regarding their need to incorporate both job and family responsibilities into their college plans. Carla, who had attended a local four-year college before enrolling at ABC Tech, compared her experiences at the two institutions. At the four-year college, traditional-aged students were more numerous, and the college made few attempts to accommodate its older students. In contrast, at ABC Tech, Carla said,

> I'm going into the nighttime study, and usually, whenever you go to nighttime classes, it tends to be the older students that are already working full time and have a family. And that was the other thing that I really loved when we went to orientation is that they told us, they're like, "we understand—particularly for you that are going in the night program—that you probably have a family and a full time job that you're coming from." And they're like, "We understand and want to work with you." Which was practically unheard of [at my other college]![45]

Samantha, a student studying electronics at Tech Institute felt that her instructors have been particularly understanding and sympathetic to her needs as a single parent. She talked about how instructors did not make a fuss about having her children occasionally come with her to class:

> A couple times I had to bring my children to school with me, you know, they sat in the back of the class. . . . My instructor was like . . . actually all of 'em so far will go back and sit there and talk to the kids. . . . Usually I'll ask before, you know, like I think one day I had to bring them in. I couldn't get a babysitter, but I asked them right before class started. I'm like, "Okay, I don't have a babysitter. I can either go home, you just give me an assignment, and I'll go home or . . ." He was like, "no, stick 'em in the back."[46]

This type of support was not just a "feel good" issue. The colleges' accommodation of students' work and family demands helped to legitimate the factors motivating students' pursuit of their educational goals. Students discussed how the absence of such factors when they were in high school resulted in lower effort and academic success. Carla explained that she got low grades in high school because she was bored, did not bother to do much homework, and failed to see how high school would matter in her life. Now, Carla gets good grades at ABC Tech and feels more focused and driven because, as she says, "Once you have children . . . you're doing it for someone besides yourself."[47]

Conclusion

Obstacles to women's integration at traditionally male institutions are not only legal but also psychological and institutional. This study has found that women today are more interested in applying to traditionally male technical programs and that they can succeed, particularly if institutions adapt to their needs. Women's success does not require that they become a large numerical presence; rather, it depends on institutions making overtures to welcome them, counseling them frequently, giving them explicit encouragement, and developing teaching schedules that permit women with jobs and children to manage classes despite these constraints. Small institutions also seem to have an advantage in terms of making women, especially those who have not previously done well academically, feel comfortable.

Previous research has highlighted psychological and socialization explanations for women's lack of success in the male-dominated fields of mathematics, science, and technology. While this study supports the idea that psychological factors—in particular, locus of control—play a role, it also shows the difference institutional environments can make. The findings are particularly remarkable since the women focused on had family and educational backgrounds that generally make academic success less likely. Also noteworthy is that women experienced the environments of the two for-profit technical colleges, which are still predominantly male, as more supportive than the institutional climate of the community colleges, which have always had a high proportion of women students. The structures that the technical colleges originally established to serve (male) students with poor academic records have been adapted to assist women who are often juggling parental, work, and academic demands. Perhaps because these for-profit private institutions are more accountable for retention and job placement outcomes, it is in their interest to be encouraging to all those who enroll. Community colleges, on the other hand, face funding pressures that limit the amount of systematic support they can provide to their women students.

Notes

1.   U.S. Department of Education, National Center for Education Statistics (NCES), *Digest of Education Statistics*, 2001, Table 180, 214.

2. Anne Marie Borrego, "Study Tracks Growth of For-Profit Colleges," *Chronicle of Higher Education,* August 10, 2001, 44.

3. Richard N. Apling, "Proprietary Schools and Their Students," *Journal of Higher Education* 64 (1993): 379–416.

4. The two for-profit technical colleges discussed in this chapter are part of a sample from a larger study of two types of postsecondary institutions: community colleges and private occupational colleges. In both types of institutions, the author focused mainly on college credit programs leading to associate's and applied degrees. The research involved qualitative methods and a case-study format that included interviews combined with analyses of written materials, observations, and surveys in six community colleges and seven private vocational colleges in a large Midwestern city and surrounding suburbs. Four of the seven vocational colleges in the study are private for-profit, or proprietary, colleges. The other three are private nonprofit colleges that also offer one- and two-year degrees and have student populations similar to the proprietary schools, with a majority of low-income and racial minority students. Six community colleges in the same geographic region which offer programs comparable to those in the private colleges were also studied—a variety of business, health, computer, and technical occupational programs. The author conducted over 100 interviews of approximately one hour each with various administrators, administrative staff, program coordinators, deans, and departmental chairs. Interviews were semistructured, covering the same topics with respondents across different schools and program types. Approximately 80 community college students and 20 occupational college students were also interviewed. In addition, surveys were administered to over 4,300 students at the two types of colleges, which included questions about students' goals, background, attitudes, experiences, course-taking patterns, and perceptions. All interviews by Regina Deil-Amen, unless otherwise specified.

5. Bruce N. Chaloux, "State Oversight of the Proprietary Sector." *New Directions for Community Colleges* 91 (1995): 81–92.

6. T. Bailey, N. Badway, and P. Gumport, "For-Profit Higher Education and Community Colleges," National Center for Postsecondary Improvement, Stanford University, 2001, 11.

7. Apling; Bailey, Badway, and Gumport, 11.

8. Jon A. Hittman, "Changes in Mission, Governance, and Funding of Proprietary Postsecondary Institutions," *New Directions for Community Colleges* 91 (1995): 17–27; Craig A. Honick, "The Story behind Proprietary Schools in the United States," ibid., 27–39.

9. Bailey, Badway, and Gumport, 11.

10. Hittman, 17-27.

11. Bailey, Badway, and Gumport, 63.

12. William V. Morris, "Avoiding Community Colleges: Students Who Attend Proprietary National Schools," *Community College Journal of Research and Practice* 1 (1993): 21–28.

13. Bailey, Badway, and Gumport, 64.

14. Steven Brint and Jerome Karabel, *The Diverted Dream: Community Colleges and the Promise of Educational Opportunity in America, 1900–1985* (New York: Oxford Uni-

versity Press, 1989); Kevin J. Dougherty, *The Contradictory College: The Conflicting Origins, Impacts, and Cultures of the Community College* (Albany: State University of New York Press, 1994).

15. Dougherty; Bailey, Badway, and Gumport, 63; U.S. Department of Education, Fall Enrollment Survey, 1997, Table J, 20.

16. Brint and Karabel.

17. Bailey, Badway, and Gumport, 63; NCES, *Digest of Education Statistics*, 2001, chap. 3, Table 207.

18. Career development/general education faculty member, interview, Tech Institute Suburban Campus, February 22, 2000.

19. U.S. Department of Education, National Center for Education Statistics, Integrated Postsecondary Education Data System (IPEDS), 1995.

20. Director of external relations, interview, Tech Institute Urban Campus, May 30, 2002.

21. Figures are based on college catalog listings. Administrator percentages were confirmed in visits to the colleges.

22. Brint and Karabel.

23. The larger project also included health support and general, legal, and health secretarial programs. These students and programs are not included in this chapter.

24. Enrollment that includes students who are taking noncredit courses ranges from 7,900 to 14,500 each semester at the community colleges. The two private technical colleges offer only credit-level classes, whereas the community colleges offer both credit and noncredit. Noncredit includes courses in English as a second language and remedial courses preparing students to take high school equivalency examinations.

25. The term "helpless" is used in the psychological research literature. It is not the terminology preferred by this author.

26. Carol S. Dweck and Ellen L. Legget, "A Social-Cognitive Approach to Motivation and Personality," *Psychological Review* 95 (1988): 256–73.

27. Barbara Signer, T. Mark Beasley, and Elizabeth Bauer, "Interaction of Ethnicity, Mathematics Achievement Level, Socioeconomic Status, and Gender among High School Students' Mathematics Self-Concepts," *Journal of Education for Students Placed At-Risk* 2 (1997): 377–93.

28. For a study of the effects of family members, see Lola B. Smith, "The Socialization of Females with Regard to a Technology-Related Career: Recommendations for Change," *Meridian: A Middle School Computer Technologies Journal* 3 (2000). D. R. Entwisle and M. Webster, Jr., "Expectations in Mixed Racial Groups," *Sociology of Education* 47 (1974): 301–18, discuss the importance of teachers, and L. Jussim and J. Eccles, "Teacher Expectations: II. Construction and Reflection of Student Achievement," *Journal of Personality and Social Psychology* 63 (1992): 947–61, show how low teacher expectations have negative effects on female, low socioeconomic status, and minority students.

29. Pierre Bourdieu and Jean-Claude Passeron, *Reproduction in Education, Society, and Culture* (New York: Sage, 1977).

30. V. DiBenedetto, "El Paso Community College Women in Technology: End of the Year

Report, 1998–1999," El Paso Community College, 1999, ED 435 429; Bettina Lankard Brown, "Women and Minorities in High-Tech Careers," *ERIC Digest* 226 (2001).

31. Marcia C. Linn, "Science," in *Cognition and Instruction,* ed. Ronna Dillon and Robert Sternberg (San Diego: Academic Press, 1986), 187–93.

32. Sherry Turkle and Seymour Papert, "Epistemological Pluralism and the Revaluation of the Concrete," in *Constructionism,* ed. Idit Harel and Seymour Papert (Norwood, N.J.: Ablex, 1991).

33. Val Thurtle, Shaun Hammond, and Paul Jennings, "The Experience of Students in a Gender Minority in Courses at a College of Higher and Further Education," *Journal of Vocational Education and Training: The Vocational Aspect of Education* 50 (1998): 629–46.

34. Director of external relations interview, Technical Institute Urban Campus, May 30, 2002.

35. Student interview, ABC Tech Campus, April 29, 2002.

36. Student interview, ABC Tech campus, August 8, 2001.

37. Student interview, Tech Institute Suburban Campus, March 7, 2001.

38. DiBenedetto; Brown.

39. Student interview, ABC Tech, April 29, 2002.

40. Student interview, ABC Tech, August 8, 2001.

41. See n.4 above for a description of the survey questions.

42. The results of this regression analysis will be made available to any interested readers.

43. Student interview, ABC Tech, April 29, 2002; student interview, Tech Institute Suburban Campus, March 7, 2001.

44. Student interview, ABC Tech, April 29, 2002.

45. Ibid.

46. Student interview, Tech Institute, August 6, 2001.

47. Student interview, ABC Tech, April 29, 2002.

13

Conclusion

Coeducation and Gender Equal Education

Susan L. Poulson and Leslie Miller-Bernal

By the mid-twentieth century most American colleges and universities had long been coeducational. There were exceptions, however. Some of the nation's most prestigious institutions, located primarily along the eastern seaboard, were still single-sex. Colleges and universities such as Harvard, Yale, Dartmouth, Princeton, Williams, and Amherst continued to associate their high status with being all male. Catholic colleges and universities remained single-sex for different reasons—they were operated by single-sex religious orders whose conservative gender ideology favored separation of women and men. Some state universities, and a few private institutions, maintained a coordinate college system that segregated men from women. The case studies in *Going Coed* discuss some of the reasons why almost all these remaining men's colleges and universities decided to admit women in the late 1960s and 1970s. The case studies also show how women have struggled to become a normal and valued part of these formerly male institutions.

Factors Influencing the Transition to Coeducation

Financial, demographic, and cultural factors influenced many men's colleges to become coeducational in the 1970s, as Chapter 1 describes. The golden years of the 1960s, when the availability of federal money enabled many educational institutions to expand, had ended. Colleges and universities needed new sources of revenue. At the same time, the national proportion of women among undergraduates was increasing, and women tended to perform better academically than men. These two trends alone might have led men's colleges to admit women; in addition, however, the social movements of the 1960s stressed integration—of races and genders. Single-sex institutions began to be seen as old-fashioned or anachronistic, while coeducation seemed natural and progressive.

Almost all the colleges and universities discussed in this book were affected by these trends. The case studies have also revealed, however, how these common factors affected some institutions more than others. Moreover, different factors had a more critical impact on some colleges. The historically black institution Lincoln University, for example, found that its enrollment of academically superior men students declined beginning in the 1950s, as predominantly white institutions opened their doors to racial and ethnic minorities. Lincoln was reluctant to become coeducational and at first tried to overcome its enrollment and financial problems by developing an interracial and international student body. Ultimately the admission of women proved to be the most successful way of maintaining Lincoln's enrollments and its academic standards.

The greatest upsurge in coeducation occurred in the early 1970s, yet two universities discussed in *Going Coed* made the transition earlier. Lincoln University, as mentioned above, slowly became coeducational in the early 1960s. The University of Rochester, which had been coeducational for the first decade of the twentieth century and then established a coordinate unit for its women students, became coeducational again after World War II. The major impetus for coeducation the second time was that a new president perceived the coordinate system as inefficient and an impediment to his plan to make Rochester a large, centralized research institution.

The academic status hierarchy played a role in the order in which many all-male institutions became coeducational. Many colleges feared becoming coeducational given the historical link between academic status and an all-male student body. Once prestigious Princeton and Yale decided to admit women as undergraduates, in order not to lose the most highly qualified men who increasingly preferred coeducational institutions, other institutions followed. Not only did Princeton and Yale serve as models for other colleges, but they also served as competitive models for each other. Students and administrators at one campus were aware what was happening at the other campus and did not want to be left behind.

What is missing in this litany of reasons for adopting coeducation is a salient concern for the education of women. The majority of these institutions admitted women to preserve or enhance their status or to improve the educational climate for men. There was no initial discussion about equity for women or about admitting women to redress their subordinate role in society. As Douglass dean Marjory Foster argued before the Rutgers board of trustees, talk about coeducation at Rutgers seemed mostly about "the uses of women for the education of men."

Making the Coeducation Transition:
Who Took the Initiative?

In order for any institution to make a fundamental change, which becoming coeducational certainly is, some groups must be pushing for the change with sufficient force to overcome the inertia of tradition or organized opposition. Key internal groups favoring coeducation were generally administrators, faculty, and students; alumni and alumni representatives among trustees were the groups most likely to oppose it. Administrators often supported coeducation because it would improve finances; Georgetown and Boston College, for example, admitted women in order to generate revenue by expanding their student bodies. Faculty frequently saw the admission of women students as a means to improve academic standards. The Lehigh faculty believed that the admission of women would redress the imbalance in a curriculum that was heavily slanted toward science and engineering. Faculty at some institutions also saw coeducation as a way to extend tuition-free benefits to their daughters. In several institutions students took the initiative in pressing for coeducation. A petition for admitting women to Boston College generated 1,500 signatures; Yale and Princeton students organized coeducation weeks to demonstrate the benefits of having women as students.

In some colleges, however, men students opposed the introduction of women to their highly prized masculine culture. Dartmouth and the military academies are examples of institutions where women were seen as unsuitable for the type of rugged masculinity their institution promoted. Dartmouth's strong fraternities with their subculture of virility made women students seem inappropriate. VMI and West Point stressed physical rather than academic prowess, which put women at a disadvantage. Academic emphases also could make an institution seem masculine, as was true for Lehigh, which emphasized engineering, and the for-profit colleges, which had technical programs.

Alumni tended to be the group most opposed to changing "their" college or university. Emotional bonds to an alma mater tend to be particularly strong since they are forged in the years of early adulthood, when friends and collegial groups replace family as the primary arena for identity. Alumni feared the enormous change that women would bring to campus culture; it was the death of the institution as they had known it. When the alumni were strong and organized, they were sometimes able to exercise considerable influence over the transition to coeducation. The alumni, as well as opposition from Douglass College, forestalled coeducation at Rutgers for a year. Alumni pressure led several institutions to pledge that women would not reduce the number of admissions available to men; administrators planned instead either to expand their student body or to cap the number of women admitted. Yale, for example, initially intended to admit one woman for every three men, and Lehigh at first forecasted a permanent cap on women at 20 percent. On the other hand, where there was little endowment and relatively weak alumni, as at Georgetown, the alumni had almost no influence on the decision.

In some cases no internal group emerged that was strong enough, at least by itself, to lead an institution to coeducation. Not until the faculty threatened legal action did Rutgers agree to admit women. West Point did not become coeducational until the federal government passed a law in 1975 mandating that all of its military institutions admit women. Lawsuits and court decisions led to the admission of women at the University of Virginia and the Virginia Military Institute.

While coeducation tended to be seen as a progressive move, ironically the more conservative institutions could act more quickly to admit women. The best examples of this are Boston College and Georgetown, whose Catholic hierarchies did not see the need to consult with their constituencies once they decided it was in their best interests to become coeducational. One case in which coeducation was seen as less progressive than a coordinate system was Hamilton College in the late 1970s. Its coordinate college for women, Kirkland, was an innovative alternative to traditional Hamilton, so that when Hamilton took steps to absorb its financially poor "offspring," Kirkland women and their allies resisted fiercely.

Institutions' Preparation for and Reception of Women Students

As administrators planned for the admission of women, they did so with limited insight into the kinds of changes necessary for making women feel welcome in the classroom and on campus. They usually focused on physical necessities, such as housing and bathroom availability, often making stereotypical assumptions about women's preferences. Academic concerns rarely went beyond the redistribution of majors that women might bring. Beyond these efforts, however, most institutions did little to prepare the campus culture for women. It was as though women were expected to fit into the existing situation without disturbing the status quo.

A striking difference among the institutions described in *Going Coed* is the amount of resources colleges and universities had at their disposal when making the transition to coeducation. At one end of the spectrum was Yale, which estimated that it needed $30–55 million for new buildings, endowment for financial aid, and additional faculty. At the other end of the financial continuum was Lincoln University, which could not find sufficient money to build a dormitory for women and so had to postpone residential coeducation for years. Even when institutions had sufficient funds, however, they did not always see the need, at least at first, to spend money for hiring more women faculty and administrators or for supporting women's athletics.

Greater recognition of women's needs came about in various ways. The women's movement had an impact on colleges and universities several years after many of the institutions discussed in *Going Coed* admitted women as students. Not until the 1970s, for example, did the academic field of women's studies get organized. Federal legislation that has had a major impact on college women's experiences, in particular Title IX's effect on women's athletics, was likewise a development of the early 1970s. Young women's awareness of the newly named problem of "male chauvinism" or "sexism" meant that women students demanded fairer treatment. In many institutions they established women's centers to address issues important to them, such as eating disorders, date rape, and sexual harassment. Given the increase of minorities at most predominantly white institutions during the same time period as the upsurge of coeducation, at some campuses, minority women formed their own support groups. Likewise, gay students and lesbians frequently established clubs, later expanded to include bisexuals and transsexuals. Catholic universities, including Georgetown and Boston College, and historically black institutions like Lincoln University generally have been reluctant to establish support groups for gay and lesbian students, however.

Clearly the larger cultural environment changed dramatically with respect to women's issues between 1955, when the University of Rochester became coeducational, and 1997 when VMI was forced to admit women. Other institutions' experiences with integrating women successfully were available as models for the colleges and universities that became coeducational later in time. It is interesting to note, however, that institutions' reference points seemed to be limited to other institutions that administrators perceived to be similar to themselves—or perhaps the kinds of institutions they aspired to be. Princeton and Yale, for example, were each aware of what the other's experiences had been. Other liberal arts colleges and universities were more willing to establish academic fields like women's studies when Ivy League universities had this new discipline. Attempts to please constituencies also led to innovations; for-profit vocational colleges, for instance, became flexible, supportive institutions as they attempted to incorporate older women, many of whom had jobs and families.

Not surprisingly, the most difficult time for women students was during the earliest years of coeducation when their numbers were few and traditional stereotypes prevailed. Many women recall not being considered a serious student or receiving inappropriate sexual remarks or advances. At colleges and universities that had a strong self-image as masculine institutions, such as Lehigh and Dartmouth, the climate seemed particularly difficult. The earliest women admitted were often outstanding students who earned a disproportionate share of academic recognition and rewards, which made some men even more resentful. As the proportion of women increased and male students with memories of an all-male campus graduated, women students began to feel more normal and accepted. At West Point, administrative leadership encouraged such adjustment by making it clear that female cadets were a valued part of the community.

Even as the general campus climate improved, pockets of hostility and exclusion remained. Fraternities at many colleges, eating clubs at Princeton, and secret societies at Yale either fostered an uncomfortable atmosphere for women or excluded them altogether. Women at Princeton brought lawsuits against eating clubs and the university for supporting them until they opened to women. The Jefferson Literary Society at the University of Virginia excluded women until a potential lawsuit forced it open. At the military academies, male cadets experienced peer pressure not to support women publicly, and female cadets felt pressure not to group together to support each other.

Coeducation Today

The case studies of women's experiences in formerly men's colleges reveal some notable dynamics in American higher education. They remind us that education is a process that occurs in a particular time and place where prevailing notions about gender are taught in the classroom and transmitted through campus culture. Coeducation alone, without a transformation in consciousness, does not bring gender equity. The recent history of coeducation also demonstrates how important and powerful government influence is in promoting gender equity. Through lawsuits and legislation, the government mandated that several institutions open to women, including the military academies. Title IX helped redistribute athletic monies so that women's sports, which symbolize women's competitive abilities, both physical and mental, would flourish. More recently, government sexual harassment laws have strengthened a broad trend to delegitimize such behavior.

In assessing how far women have progressed, or how close the chilly climate is to being eliminated so that coeducation becomes gender-equal education, it is first helpful to consider the representation of women in different parts of institutions of higher education. Since 1979 female undergraduates have outnumbered male undergraduates nationally, with the imbalance being particularly great at historically black institutions like Lincoln. In some institutions with a scientific or technical bent, however, women are still in the minority. Women's proportion of the faculty has also increased in the past forty years. At liberal arts institutions, women make up about a third of the faculty; at institutions with a heavy emphasis on science, such as Lehigh and West Point, the percentage of women on the faculty is lower. At all institutions, women represent a smaller proportion of full professors than they do of assistant professors. Various institutions, including Hamilton and the University of Rochester, have raised the issue of why there is a higher turnover of women than men on the faculty, and the answer seems to be that women are still more likely than men to have child-rearing responsibilities that may conflict with full-time careers. A few institutions have established childcare centers and have instituted generous maternity leave policies in attempts to retain women on the faculty.

Women are still underrepresented at the highest levels of university administration and on boards of trustees. Yet, women presidents are becoming less rare; in the early twenty-first century, they make up about one-fifth of all university and college presidents. While it is true that women are more likely to be presidents of less prestigious institutions, such as community colleges, tribal colleges, women's colleges, and historically black colleges, some very prestigious coeducational institutions have or have had women as presidents, including Princeton, Duke, and Brown. Similarly, women's presence on boards of trustees has increased, and coeducational institutions have had women as chairs of their boards, but women are not close to a half of private coeducational institutions' boards.

In assessing institutions' chilly climate in terms of student leadership by gender and the symbolic ways that men's dominant status is communicated, the evidence is less clear cut. Those case studies that looked at student leadership of clubs generally found that today women are much more likely to lead clubs and have such important campus-wide positions as editor-in-chief of the student newspaper. Yet, other positions, particularly president of the student body, are still much more likely to be held by men than by women. Campus iconography has not changed nearly as much as has the gender composition of student bodies, and not surprisingly, given the slower rate at which new buildings appear, most buildings are still named after men. Histories of universities and colleges generally have not been substantially altered to give women's involvement in the institution much attention, as is evident from college and university websites.

What can universities do to enhance the education of women? It is clear that institutions vary widely in terms of the financial resources available to them to provide facilities, for example, for sports and women's centers. Yet by paying serious attention to gender and trying to make colleges and universities good places for women as well as for men, progress can be made in poor as well as wealthy institutions. Examples of particular ways that institutions of higher education can become more gender equal include striving to increase the representation of women at all levels. All searches for faculty and administrative positions, all appointments to special committees, should have equal representation of women and men. Recognizing that women students may need special encouragement to enter academic fields that have been traditionally male, such as engineering, institutions should strive to provide young women with role models. Hiring women faculty members or, where no new hires are possible, bringing in women as guest speakers in these areas helps break down the association of certain occupations with men. Student leadership by gender and faculty attention to gender in their courses are both issues that can be discussed, even while change cannot be mandated. Administrative leadership that makes it clear that gender is important to think about, whether in designing college websites, putting up photos of successful alumni and alumnae, naming rooms and buildings, or designing courses, should have both direct and indirect benefits for women.

A final question that might be asked about the consequences of the upsurge in coeducation is whether American higher education has been impoverished by the virtual disappearance of men's colleges and universities. Some commentators, including the late, famous sociologist David Riesman, argued that diversity among institutions is valuable in and of itself. Men's colleges are just as desirable as women's colleges, Riesman argued, as he defended all-male VMI. What this argument overlooks, however, is power. Men's colleges were historically the preserve of white, middle-class men; excluding women and minorities was a key way that such privilege was protected. Women's colleges and historically black colleges, on the other hand, have provided excluded groups with higher education when they had no or virtually no other options. Their existence today is one reminder that education where all groups feel equally supported and valued remains an ideal, closer to achievement than in the past, but still an ideal.

Contributors

Regina Deil-Amen is an assistant professor of education and sociology at Penn State University. She completed her Ph.D. at Northwestern University where she served as a research director for a study entitled "College to Careers" at Northwestern University's Institute for Policy Research—a mixed-methods case study of how community colleges and private postsecondary vocational colleges prepare students for sub-baccalaureate careers. Her research interests include mechanisms of educational stratification and inequality, the impact of community colleges on student aspirations and persistence, and the dynamics of race, ethnicity, and social class in educational settings.

Diane Diamond is a doctoral candidate in sociology at Stony Brook University and has taught at Stony Brook University and College of the Holy Cross. Her doctoral dissertation examines the admission of women to Virginia Military Institute and the United States Military Academy at West Point. Her research interests include gender integration and the attitudes and experiences of women and men in predominantly male institutions.

Mary Frances Donley Forcier is a Ph.D. candidate in history and policy at Carnegie Mellon University. She has served as a college, university, and independent-school administrator, as well as a corporate historian. Her dissertation focuses on the policy-making process at four institutions—both men's and women's colleges—as they considered coeducation in the post–World War II period.

Loretta P. Higgins received her Ed.D. from Boston College. She is the associate dean at Boston College's Connell School of Nursing. Her research and clinical areas are women's health and history. She is a contributing editor of *Dictionary of American Nursing Biography*. In addition to historical research, she is a member of a research team studying partner abuse during pregnancy. She has published articles including "Army Nurses in Wartime: Distinction and Pride," and has co-authored books on women's health.

Elizabeth L. Ihle earned her Ed.D. at the University of Tennessee-Knoxville in 1976 with an emphasis on the history of education. She has written about the history of African-American women's education and women's higher education in the South. She is professor of education and coordinator of secondary education at James Madison University in Harrisonburg, Va.

Michael S. Kimmel is professor of sociology at SUNY at Stony Brook. He began his college career at an all-male college, transferred to a formerly all-female college (Vassar), and was in its first coeducational graduating class. His books include *Changing Men* (1987), *Men Confront Pornography* (1990), *Men's Lives* (5th edition, 2000), *Against the Tide: Profeminist Men in the United States, 1776–1990* (1992), *The Politics of Manhood* (1996), *Manhood: A Cultural History* (1996), and *The Gendered Society* (2000). He was an expert witness for the U.S. Department of Justice in the VMI and Citadel litigation and testified in those trials. He edits *Men and Masculinities,* an interdisciplinary scholarly journal, is the spokesperson for the National Organization for Men against Sexism (NOMAS), and lectures extensively on campuses in the United States and abroad.

Christine M. Lundt earned her Ph.D. in the social foundations of education at the University at Buffalo in New York. Her current professional interests include community-based education for adults, especially women.

Leslie Miller-Bernal earned her Ph.D. in the sociology of development at Cornell University in 1979. She has previously published *Separate by Degree: Women Students' Experiences in Single-Sex and Coeducational Colleges* (2000) and articles comparing the experiences of women at coeducational and women's colleges. Since 1975 she has taught sociology at Wells College in Aurora, New York.

Susan Gunn Pevar earned her B.A. in anthropology from Bryn Mawr College and is working on an M.A. in history from West Chester University (Pa.). Since 2000 she has been the archivist assistant at Lincoln University of the Commonwealth of Pennsylvania.

Susan L. Poulson is a professor of history at the University of Scranton in northeastern Pennsylvania. She teaches women's history and recent U.S. history. Her publications address gender and higher education in the past fifty years. She and Leslie Miller-Bernal are currently studying how women's colleges have fared since the 1960s.

Marcia G. Synnott earned her Ph.D. at the University of Massachusetts, Amherst, and has taught at the University of South Carolina in Columbia for thirty years. Her teaching fields are the history of American women and twentieth-century U.S. history. She has previously published *The Half-Opened Door: Discrimination and Admissions at Harvard, Yale, and Princeton, 1900–1970* and chapters in other books on the desegregation of southern state universities.

Index

Page references in *italics* indicate tables.